# The Evolution of Communism

Our curiosity is naturally prompted to inquire by what means the Christian faith obtained so remarkable a victory over the established religions of the earth. To this inquiry an obvious but satisfactory answer may be returned; that it was owing to the convincing evidence of the doctrine itself, and to the ruling providence of its great Author. But as truth and reason seldom find so favourable a reception in the world, and as the wisdom of Providence frequently condescends to use the passions of the human heart, and the general circumstances of mankind, as instruments to execute its purpose, we may still be permitted, though with becoming submission, to ask, not indeed what were the first, but what were the secondary causes of the rapid growth of the Christian church?

Gibbon, *Decline and Fall*, XV

We, indeed, know our way and are seated in that historical train which at full speed takes us to our goal.

Plekhanov, *Socialism and the Political Struggle*, 1883

It goes without saying that the practical tasks and consequently the programmes of the socialists are bound to be more original and complicated in countries where capitalist production has not yet become dominant . . .

Plekhanov, *Programme of the Social-Democratic Emancipation of Labour Group*, 1884

We are living in a specially remarkable period. We find to our astonishment that progress has allied itself with barbarism.

Freud, *Moses and Monotheism*, 1939

# The Evolution of Communism

Adam Westoby

THE FREE PRESS
*A Division of Macmillan, Inc.*
NEW YORK

The Free Press
A Division of Macmillan, Inc.
866 Third Avenue, New York, N. Y. 10022

Collier Macmillan Canada, Inc.

First American Edition 1989

Printed in Great Britain

printing number
1 2 3 4 5 6 7 8 9 10

*Library of Congress Cataloging-in-Publication Data*

Westoby, Adam
  The evolution of communism
  "First published 1989 by Polity Press in association
with Basil Blackwell"–T.p. verso.
  Bibliography: p.
  Includes index.
  1. Communism—History—20th century.   2. Communist
parties—History—20th century.   I. Title.
HX40.W465   1989        335.43′09′04        89–11800
ISBN 0–02–934545–6

# Contents

# Acknowledgements

This book has been some time in gestation, and has caused me to incur numerous debts, of which I can mention only the most specific. David Held, for Polity Press, encouraged me throughout, bore patiently with my delays, and was ready with constructive criticism when I felt that I had ingested more than I could masticate. Leo Labedz gave selflessly of his time, energy and knowledge to comment in detail on the draft. Other friends and colleagues who read the manuscript, in whole or in part, and made improvements and suggestions include Robin Blick, Ben Cosin, Maria Hirsowicz, Ian McAlman, John Spencer, Bob Sutcliffe, Ken Weller and Tim Wohlforth. To Sam Cox I am indebted not only for penetrating comments, but for invaluable help with research. Annette Flynn and her colleagues of the Open University Library, and Pam Steele, were indefatigable in obtaining source materials. My grateful thanks go to all these, as well as to many others who have sharpened my interest in communism.

My greatest debt, however, is to my companion, Sabi Hasan, and our children, Ben and Sam. They have not only given me time to contemplate the computer screen, but have heightened my sense that political orders are to be changed as well as interpreted.

Adam Westoby
London

# Note on further reading

In order to reduce the number of references in the text, I have provided sources only for direct quotations and, occasionally, for factual details. However, since readers may find some suggestions for further reading helpful, I have included a few paragraphs on this at the end of each chapter. The items mentioned in them are almost all books, and all are in English. I have concentrated on works which provide a more thorough treatment of matters dealt with in the text, or their backgrounds or consequences, and have preferred those with good bibliographies or coverage of sources. For on-going events I have leaned towards recent writings. But I have not tried to give more than pointers to the large and amorphous interpretative literature, still less to provide a fragment of a bibliography on twentieth-century communism as a whole. The aim is merely to give useful starting points to pursue specific topics in greater depth.

# 1

## Introduction

The Introduction to a book of this sort should, I feel, do at least three things. It should outline the ground-plan on which the account is constructed. It should mention some of the main conceptions, signposting how the book attempts to address a topic of such size and complexity. And it should indicate, and if possible justify, respects in which the treatment or the choice of terminology are unconventional. This Introduction seeks to do these things, and in broadly that order (though with some unavoidable overlapping); it reflects my belief that the perils of simplification are more than compensated by the advantages of explicitness and candour.

### OUTLINE

Part I examines some of the phases and countries in which, during the twentieth century, non-ruling communist parties have evolved their most important characteristics. It begins, in chapter 2, with the genesis of Bolshevism among the editors of *Iskra* and in its watershed split with Menshevism at the 1903 Congress of Russian social democracy. This chapter highlights the essential innovation which Bolshevism represented within European socialism. Lenin's success in Russia in 1917 and the establishment of the Communist International (Comintern) in 1919 produced fundamentally different formative conditions for the second generation of communist parties – conditions in which Soviet stipulations and pressures played a crucial part. The early history of Comintern *could*, therefore, reasonably be summarized as a by-product of the problems and vicissitudes of the Soviet party. Instead, however, chapters 3 and 4 handle it more directly. They give an account of Comintern's role in the early 1920s, as seed-bed and forcing house of contrasting tactics, around the example of its most traumatic failure, Germany. Chapter 5 moves to Comintern's diverse efforts in Asia, where communism came to practical terms with anti-colonial nationalism and peasant revolution. The chapter describes the birth of the Chinese Communist Party's original and eventually successful strategy and, more briefly, the development of other Asian parties. One of the main things Part I aims to convey is how rich in experimentation and evolution the 1920s were, germinating many of the policies of later phases.

Part II considers from various angles the significance, and some of the contradictions, of communism as a global formation. Chapter 6 indicates the continuities between early Bolshevism's instrumental attitude to allies, and the 'egoism' of the Soviet and other ruling parties. One consequence of this 'egoism' is ruling parties' tendency to treat communists abroad as just part (and sometimes an expendable part) of larger political and strategic configurations. Such configurations may offer a range of opportunities to communist powers, including, for example, expansion by conquest. Chapter 7 focuses in more detail on the tactics of a specific advance of this sort, the Soviet-supported communist takeovers in Eastern Europe after the Second World War. Chapter 8 then broadens the account once more, making comparisons among some of the other very different routes through which communist rule has come about. In a number of cases (of which Cuba was the first) the organization which came to control the state was not communist, or opted for communism only *after* it had gained power. Such changes were not everywhere or wholly the result of dependence on larger communist powers; this chapter therefore discusses some advantages of communism, compared with other authoritarian forms of rule, for the controlling elites of underdeveloped states.

A plurality of communist states produces manifold possibilities for rivalry and schism amongst them. Chapter 9 reviews the international conse-quences (though little of the labyrinthine detail) of the Sino-Soviet split in the 1960s, and compares it briefly with others, such as Stalin's break with Tito. It also indicates some of the reasons why the Soviet Union has been so successful in remaining the world's main pole of communist loyalties. Chapter 10 looks at the problem from the other side, examining the internal reasons for the cumulative, but often limited, growth of autonomy among non-ruling parties – such as the emergence of 'Eurocommunism' in the 1960s.

The most distinctive *general* characteristic of communism (sometimes, it seems, the only one) is 'Leninism' – a fact evidenced by the acrimony which the shared but contested doctrinal framework of differing communisms can engender. Part III turns to the history of this essential dimension, within which all communists are obliged, at least publicly, to think, to phrase their initiatives, and to fight out their differences. Chapter 11 reverts to the Marxian origins of communism and its initial, Russian, modifications. It focuses on the arguments through which Marxists in historically 'unready' Russia sought to provide themselves with theoretical guidance and political hope, and discovered senses in which their country's 'backwardness' could be converted into an advantage. Chapter 12 then deals with some of Marxism's further adjustments once in power: Stalin's 'socialism in one country' versus Trotsky's theory of 'permanent revolution' and his critique of Soviet bureaucracy; Bukharin's gentler views, the ancestor of many subsequent 'reform' communisms; and Mao's criticisms and assaults upon the 'capitalist roaders' of the party bureaucracy. Chapter 13 turns to look at the persistent appeal of Marxism and communism in the developed West, especially among intellectual groups. It considers Leninism as (among other things) a crystallization of 'modernism' in politics, and it discusses the postwar popularity of Gramsci's views of 'hegemony', which seem to promise ways in which a communism loosely based among the educated strata can hope to prosper in social and cultural conditions very different from those with which Marx or Lenin were familiar.

Lastly, Part IV confronts some of the problems posed by 'actually existing socialism'. Chapter 14 situates communist states within the longer-term development of world society. It emphasizes their interdependence with the world market and the non-communist world, and the significance of their national processes of development taking place within a world process of innovation and economic growth. It considers some of their problems of adjustment, and indicates the rather narrow dimensions of the elites within which real power is concentrated. Chapter 15 gives an overview of the types of crisis that afflict communist rule, both those which arise from external opposition and those which stem from conflicts or moves for reform within the ruling party. It examines the wide range of resources and aptitudes ruling communism has been able to draw on to restabilize itself, and asks what hopes of change present and future crises of communist regimes may hold out for their subjects. Part IV also mentions some of the theoretical concepts and models which have been proposed to illuminate communist societies. But it does so selectively, rather than as a connected intellectual history of theories on the subject. In doing so it puts the main emphasis on those concepts which seek – as does this book as a whole – to bring communism in both its non-ruling and ruling metamorphoses within a common framework of understanding.

COMMUNISM'S MUTABILITY

As this summary shows, most of the book's matter is empirical – and sometimes just a skeletal rendering of events. Yet, of course, my presentation does explore some general ideas about communism. Rather than leave these scattered or implicit, it seems to me useful to indicate them here. There are, naturally, dangers to this. Even notions which *may* be generally applicable to communism need qualification in particular contexts; stripped of it, they can appear baldly approximate. Moreover, a book of this small scale and great selectivity can go only a little way towards *assessing* general conceptions about communism; mostly it illustrates, explores and suggests. But, if these dangers are kept in mind and allowance is made for them, I hope that the following paragraphs may help, when reading the substantive chapters, in thinking about communism as a unified phenomenon.

If I have explored one key concept it is that of communism as protean or mutable – protean but (indeed, thereby) distinctive. By this I mean that the quest for one, or a few, distinguishing characteristics of communism is somewhat futile. Proteus eluded capture by continually changing from one form into another. What distinguishes communism as a political, psychological, organizational and social phenomenon is the extraordinary diversity of its means of action, its political and organizational forms, and its bases of support. It uses these resources, in both combination and succession, while preserving a resilient continuity of purpose and (with rare exceptions) of organization. All communism's important *practical* features are marked by adaptability and diversity – its tactics, the national and local environments in which it operates, the human types it recruits, and the values and motives to which it appeals. The common ingredient is a formal one: Leninist theory and its organizational expression – the party. But this (as I argue in later chapters) has malleability at its heart, even though the apparent rigidity of its formulations can inflame the disputations to which different practical applications give rise.

What does Leninism's protean character mean in practical terms? As far as tactics are concerned a party may find itself engaged in activities as varied as peasant warfare, urban insurrection, bank robberies, political terrorism, electoral campaigns, legal cases, bureaucratic infiltration, entrism, action through front organizations, and state diplomacy. Communist parties have proved able to adapt, often very abruptly, between profoundly different political and social environments: from the enjoyment of full legal rights to total illegality and severe repression (and vice versa); from activity among militant urban workers and in highly sophisticated intellectual milieux, to organizing peasants in remote rural areas. Communism can draw in a comparable diversity of social categories and human types – not merely in those it appeals to, but in those it can muster into active service. The same party can incorporate individuals ranging from brilliant scientists and cosmopolitan intellectuals, through those with almost all forms of education and autodidacticism, to illiterates who have never left their village. It can mobilize bureaucrats and bohemians, free creative artists and resolute philistines, technicians and mystics, technocrats and environmentalists, feminists and stolid family men, monarchists and republicans, criminals and lawyers, pensioners and toddlers, land-hungry peasants and their landlords, workers and capitalists – all have a contribution to make to the cause.

The utopian – and therefore amorphous – character of communism's ideals assists this eclecticism. Part of its genius is to accomplish an effective division of political labour among many people, on the basis of goals which may be semantically shared but which are held, psychologically, as quite diverse. They enable communism to organize in one party (and sometimes in one cell) individuals ranging from the courageous resister against tyranny or the starry-eyed idealist, to the plodding bureaucrat or the jackboot ruffian. The key to effective organization, Lenin explained in 1902, consists 'in making use of *everything possible*, in "giving everyone something to do" ', while keeping command of the whole (Lenin, 1960–78, 6, p. 242).

Communism is equipped for an equally wide range of political alliances and stances. Leninism has shown itself well-adapted for cooperation with fascists and for organizing anti-fascist alliances, for pro- and anti-war agitation (sometimes in respect of the same war), for campaigns of strident internationalism, and for alliances with nationalists of virtually all hues, for joining hands with both generals and pacifists, as well as priests and prelates of almost every persuasion, for alliances both with and against socialist parties, for those which include 'bourgeois' parties (or leaders) and those which exclude them, as well as for unions based on the subtlest of distinctions between 'reactionaries' and 'progressives' among potential enemies and partners. Communism's tactical movements among this assortment of positions may be gradual and incremental, but they may also be distinctively rapid.

Both promiscuity and sudden change can be hazardous. But communism is distinguished by a capacity for resisting the infections of the former, and surviving the traumas of the latter. One of Leninism's central characteristics is its abhorrence of 'spontaneity' – any fundamental adaptation of goals or organization to the parochialism or fickleness of its supporters. This abstinence reinforces communism's ability to survive great and sudden changes of environment – perhaps with major losses and adjustments, but with a central core of members, with their loyalties and discipline intact.

The result of blanket political illegality – as in Europe in the Second World War, for example – is often a widespread extinction of political organizations. Those that rise again when legality returns may claim the names and the mantles of their predecessors, but there is frequently little organizational, or even political, continuity. In such periods communist parties stand out for their ability to adapt and survive, to grow under illegality, and to prepare for its collapse. Almost all the postwar European communist parties were continuous with the organizations which existed before the war. (The only exception was the Polish party, which was destroyed neither by Poles nor Germans, but was dissolved by Stalin in 1938

– along with the Communist Party of the Western Ukraine – most of the leaders being executed.) As important as organizational continuity was the fact that as the European Communist parties rapidly grew into mass organizations they remained of the same obedience as they had been when (as in some cases) their membership in their own countries numbered only a few dozen.

It is true that their political behaviour after the war varied greatly from country to country. But this turned relatively little on social and political environments, and far more on geography. The agreements reached between the great powers at the close of the war entailed different Soviet intentions for different countries, and consequently for their communist parties. Although Stalin dissolved the Comintern in 1943, this did nothing to diminish his centralized control over the national sections of the 'world party of communist revolution', and the 1940s vividly demonstrated this amid the heterogeneity of communist policies, both from country to country, and over time. The differences arose from variations of political decisions, rather than responses to the social environment, testifying to the most important dimension of communist parties' flexibility-cum-resilience – the ability to perform major, sometimes very rapid, but still relatively orderly switches of political direction at the call of the leadership.

Perhaps our examples of communist parties' resilience, through the Second World War, and through other great changes, suggest that we are exaggerating its *internal* causes? May not its main source lie in communism's uniquely international character? On this view the revival of national communist parties after the war would not differ essentially, but only in scale, from the re-founding of any other type of political party's organization in a town or neighbourhood where it had expired. I do not think the parallel is a close one. As I argue in later chapters, communism's intrinsic metabolism is more important than international discipline in explaining its strengths and adaptability. The Chinese Communist Party operated, from the time when it was driven from the cities after 1927, under only the loosest of Comintern direction, but it preserved (indeed in some respects developed) the Leninist principles of organization and action which it had internalized in its formative years – and it used them to the full when relations with the Soviet leadership came to an open breach after 1956. Tito's party in Yugoslavia crossed a similar watershed of emancipation through its control of partisan armies during the war, but it relied on its Leninism with redoubled vigour after it was excommunicated by Stalin in 1948.

Communism's quasi-military capacities have often been remarked upon. Selznick's (1952) sociological dissection of communist party organizations found that they had more in common with armies than other political parties, and communist leaders themselves, starting with Lenin, have been partial to military metaphors. In reality, however, parties' discipline is very variable, and even where it is strictest it never achieves the unanimity at which it ostensibly aims. Like all organizations communist parties contain difference and conflict, often exacerbated by the variety among their membership and the changeability of their policies. Communist principles of party organization and internal life may seek to muffle or conceal differences, but they never eradicate them.

## COMMUNISM IN POWER

So far I have spoken of communism's malleability, its protean character, mainly in the context of *non*-ruling parties. Is there a continuity between this, and communism's development as a *ruling* party? I think that there is. The case is considered more fully below (especially in chapters 14 and 15). But in order to sketch here why this is so, we may briefly contrast communism with the generality of politics and political processes.

In its attitude to politics communism lies at or near one end of a significant spectrum. Politics is considered by most people, and in most of its aspects, as a means rather than an end. By politics – through organization and agitation, election and representation, conflict, negotiation and compromise – groups can obtain the things, or some of the things, that they need or desire. Different groups need and desire different things, and have different political capacities; consequently they organize and act politically in different ways. The notion of representativeness – of both institutions and politicians – as reflecting the different needs and aspirations of different classes or groups is closely tied to the sense of politics as functional for getting other, non-political things – at its simplest as an instrument, or repertoire of instruments.

However, politics – in modern societies at least – also exists as a distinct and somewhat autonomous segment of social life. It becomes the subject of specialist activity, and develops institutions whose effective manipulation requires full-time attention and much experience. Within that segment the way to accomplish things is to acquire political power – mainly, though not exclusively, by gaining control of the machinery of the state, or parts of it. Much of that power, at least in the hands of specialist politicians, can be used for a variety of quite disparate purposes; it can be set to work in many directions. Moreover, power is not necessarily consumed when it is used; use often renews or even enlarges it. It is thus natural that there should exist, in modern professionalized politics, a tendency to pursue and accumulate power for its own sake, independently of social wishes which it might satisfy.

This nutshell account of politics and power is, of course, drastically abbreviated – and no doubt, from the standpoint of the theorist, more than a little naive. But it allows us to focus on one respect in which communism lies near an extreme: its marked ability, where the two conflict, to set the acquisition and retention of power, and especially state power, above satisfying the desires from which support springs. This is, moreover, a rather conscious capacity, being understood even by rank-and-file communists within a general theoretical framework. It lay at the root of of Leninism's original self-definition, in opposition to the 'spontaneous' and 'economist' appetites of militant workers. It also underlies its subsequent, and equally self-conscious, development of very different bases of support, methods and tactics.

If a party is only conditionally committed to the groups and bodies of opinion on which it rests, it will be well advised to reinforce itself, and secure its future, by cultivating other methods and stances, directed at other bases of support. It will also do well to structure its organization so as to confer autonomy and large powers on the leadership. It may be true that among the rank-and-file of communist parties sectional, expressive and emotional motives for membership are as important as they are in many others. But democratic centralism ensures they are less likely to make the party's policies into mere vehicles of their desires. In my account I have fallen in with the usual shorthand of writing that 'the Party' did this or that, when the actual decision is that of its leadership; the oversimplification involved is especially pronounced with communist parties.

When communism achieves state power, similar patterns of action assert themselves. But omnivorousness now seeks to become all-devouring. Communism's quicksilver nature, its readiness to penetrate many areas and crevices of society, which produces such wide variation among non-ruling parties, generates a definite similarity once state power is achieved. With control of the state it becomes possible to preserve and expand power by extinguishing political rivals. Moreover, communism is drawn to penetrate generally into society, so as to innoculate it, as far as possible, against extruding other sources of power and rival political currents, and to cauterize those that do arise. One fecund ground of countervailing power lies in economic relations and forms of property, and these aspects of communist overturns have strong political as well as economic motives; communism's reasons for nationalizing capitalist and peasant property have much in common with its motives for destroying independent trade unions. More generally, it is hostile to cumulations of interests, both to those which threaten to become poles of external resistance, and often to those which begin to coalesce as differentiations within the ruling party. Communism's spurning of limits in its quest for political power develops, when it comes to rule, into an urge to act generally against independent sources of power.

Everywhere, however, this impulse is to a greater or lesser degree frustrated. It is self-limiting, since even when the state is monopolized by one party, it remains dependent upon society, and the propensity to politics is so intimately connected to innumerable habits and wishes of social life that it can never be wholly eliminated. What ruling communist parties do aim at, in continuity with their non-ruling trajectories, and often successfully, is to make other formal political organizations, and much of informal politics, *illegitimate.*

But the extent to which they do this varies greatly. All communist regimes are obliged to seek some relation of symbiosis with society, balancing their dependence upon it against the vulnerability and suspicion which they feel in face of it. But the stances adopted may be very different, according to the host society and the history of the particular party. Polish communism has for many years resigned itself to coexistence with the Catholic Church, and to ruling through an officially atheist party most of whose members marry, baptize their babies, and confess, in church. At the other extreme Pol Pot's rule in Kampuchea during 1976–9 aimed at the forcible elimination not only of religion, but of money, and even of the family. What they have in common, though, is the party's desire itself to define the terms of its inter-penetrations with society, unfettered by rigid external constitutional bonds.

### ECONOMICS, REFORMS, CRISES

Communism's tendency to confine social life, and therefore sometimes to suffocate key functions on which it depends, has widespread consequences. Communism in power sets goals for the larger society, and particularly the economy, which are difficult to accomplish within the political and cultural limits which the party feels it prudent to enforce. One line of exit from the dilemma is official toleration of what is, more officially, proscribed: the proliferation of black and 'grey' markets. Another is to transfer part of the state's dependency to *other* societies. Thus even the most industrialized of communist economies have settled into a pattern of interchange with the developed West in which they seek to import (or otherwise appropriate) much of their advanced technology. Sometimes the dependency takes specifically political forms. According to the Chinese Communist Party's official criteria most of the time it has been in power, Hong Kong could only be considered a social and political cesspool. But it has also been an extraordinarily useful opening into the consumer and capital markets of the West. Chinese diplomacy has therefore been happy to keep it as a British colony; and when, in the international stockmarket crash of October 1987, the highly speculative Hong Kong stock exchange was threatened with general collapse (and pulling others in its wake), one of the main supports of the rescue operation was the central bank of communist China.

A second consequence of the communist party-state's intimacy with society (taken together with arrogance and privilege among the elite, and rigidity and waste in the economy) is that in the second half of the twentieth century communist states have become prime sites of political crisis and, often enough, of proletarian revolution. In part this is because, without private property in the major means of production, or a plurality of legal and competing organizations, communism lacks 'buffers' to insulate economic and social struggles from becoming political ones; the state's ubiquitousness makes it responsible for everything. It was natural for Romanian workers, when they were made redundant by their factories in Brasov in 1987, to march to the city Communist Party headquarters. It was equally natural for them to hold the party-state responsible for distribution as well as production. When the demonstrators saw that a reception for party bureaucrats at the headquarters was serving oranges – unknown in ordinary shops – they began spontaneously to graduate from economic to political struggle, burning pictures of President Ceausescu.

The incipience of anti-communist upheaval may often be detected by Lenin's central test for diagnosing revolutionary situations: the inability of the established order to continue ruling in the old way. This *may* arise from external resistance, but it may also stem from pressures for reform generated within the party. The Gorbachev programme of 'openness' and 'restructuring' is the latest, and potentially the most significant, of many similar efforts at economic reform and controlled liberalization which have been launched by ruling communist parties since the 1950s. The specific mixtures of motives vary, but they generally include economic slowdown, technical and organizational conservatism, and social stagnation. When these problems assert themselves within the ruling party as specific policies for reform, they almost always involve relaxation of control over intellectual life and administrative processes as ways of encouraging local effort and initiative. This is true of Gorbachev and his advisors, grappling with an economy based around heavy industry and centralized planning, whose officialdom have deeply entrenched interests and habits. They have already resisted previous efforts at reform, and form a colossal obstacle to the Soviet economy's ability to compete with the more advanced, 'post-industrial' Western nations.

Some degree of decentralization and relaxation of control, allowing autonomous interests to assert themselves, is an inescapable part of serious efforts to reinvigorate centrally planned economies. But the problem for the regime is that the brittle nature of communist rule – both the rule of the party over society, and that of the leadership over the party – means that once things begin to give, they can easily career out of control. Efforts at measured reform – as in Hungary in 1953–6, or Czechoslovakia in 1967–8 – can rapidly unroll beyond the grasp of party leaders, producing a situation where the communist monopoly of rule can be restored only by a larger exterior force. When, as with the Soviet Union, no such exterior force exists, dangers and inhibitions are all the greater. Yet there is nothing episodic or temporary about the pressures for reform. Communist states exist within an economically dynamic world society, and the pressures for reform arise from differences in the long-run comparative economic performance of competing, but unevenly developed, national political systems. They therefore insistently reassert themselves. Gorbachev's advent to power has already greatly altered the tone of world politics; by looking (especially in chapter 15) at previous efforts at self-reform by communist elites, and their limits, I try to throw some light on the prospects of his transforming Soviet and Eastern European societies.

Western politicians and states, and much journalism and other writing, are more attuned to divisions between communist regimes and within communist parties than to those between communist parties and the societies they rule. Large-scale movements, such as Solidarity in Poland, or nationalist protests in the Soviet Union, often take Western opinion by surprise. Western states are lethargic in encouraging those who speak up within communist societies for rights that are, on the whole, taken for granted in the developed west. The general effect is to produce a sort of optical illusion, making communist states seem more monolithic than they are; by way of correction I have tried to give due weight to the depth and complexity of divisions that exist, and sometimes erupt, in communist societies.

MISLEADING CONVENTIONS

One of the things which is implicit in the argument I have sketched above is that certain ideas, whose roots lie in communism's self-descriptions, but which run widely enough to approximate to conventions in discussion of it, can none the less be misleading. Since this book seeks as far as possible to eschew them, it may be useful to mention them, and the reasons why they should be set aside.

Partly because communism organizes itself in the form of *parties* it is conventional to regard it as a political phenomenon and to think of it within the framework (and, in academic contexts, the discipline) of politics. Yet this answers by default a question which should be posed explicitly: Is communism political or not? The answer is less obvious than might appear. Politics – at least in the modern terms of representation and party – entails permanent, legitimate competition and conflict, as well as negotiation and compromise. Parties struggle with each other, exerting pressures and directing thrusts which, if they were not held in check, could overwhelm their opponents. They normally *are* held in check, and a variety of rival political species is preserved, and this through two principal causes: (a) society itself is differentiated, and gives rise to a polity divided by sectional interests and loyalties; and (b) there are legal and ethical 'rules of the game' which restrict the means of combat it is permissible to use against political opponents.

But when a party does not feel itself bound by the checks and balances of normal political intercourse, when it makes the exigencies of competition a goal in itself, and evolves the will and capacity to destroy rivals as a central and not incidental characteristic, then it begins to be equipped not merely for competition, but for war. Communist success thus implies the extinction of politics in the party and representative sense (if not in the looser one of conflicts of interests and power). By an authentically dialectical process communism, in pushing political competition to its logical limit, is also anti-political.

Moreover, it is not necessarily limited to being *politically* anti-political. The communist party's rejection of external restraint means that it can even become 'socially' anti-political, turning on whole classes or nations that it judges reactionary. Suppression of open political competition and explicit political choices in the rest of society can never wholly eliminate resistance to the ruling party, but can only drive it into underground and surreptitious forms (and also, under certain circumstances, into the party). When that occurs, and if resistance is intense or for other reasons thought to be dangerous, it is a natural – if potentially very brutal – development for the party to begin to *infer* political opposition not from what people say or do, but from their social categories – 'bourgeois', 'landlord', 'kulak', etc.

My treatment cannot, of course, avoid discussing communism as part of political life, but I have tried to avoid the conventional habit of treating it as just one form of politics among others.


### LEFT AND RIGHT


A more specific convention is the habit of describing communism's internal differences, together with its place in the political world, in terms of 'left' and 'right', perpetuating the expressions first applied in Louis XVI's Estates-General at Versailles in 1789. Yet the geometry can confuse. Does it refer to policies, to methods, or to preferences among the party's potential non-communist allies? The different senses cohere poorly. It has generally been 'left' communist factions, distinguished by their greater appetite for street-fighting, who have been most enthusiastic in European communism's various flirtations with fascism. The 'right' in non-ruling communist parties has generally been the most attached to legality and democratic rights, to parliamentary and electoral activity, and the most keen on alliances with socialists and liberals. But many of the actual participants in factional divisions within a communist party will reject even these conventional descriptions. In accordance with standard Marxist theory, the 'left' is taken as the correct place to be, with the main opposition to oneself located furthest away, on the 'right', the area between being occupied by the 'centre' (though it is important also to leave conceptual space for erring on the other side: the 'ultra-left'). 'Left' and 'right', like other categories in communist usage ('progressive', for example) often primarily signify those who support the speaker versus those who do not.

With communism in power the terminology becomes even more perplexing. If cleavages emerge in the party leadership, for example, it is usual to speak of the faction most associated with central planning, nationalized property and the repression of opposition as the 'left', and of the advocates of market forces and political relaxation as the 'right'. Adding in foreign policies complicates matters still further. The domestic 'leftism' of Stalin's 'third period' (forced industrialization and 'liquidation of the kulaks') went with openings towards Hitler in Germany. Pol Pot's bloody attempt to transform Cambodian society, the epitome of 'leftism', was accompanied by a conventionally 'right-wing' external alignment. The left/right convention also helps underwrite the vague but persistent notion that the world's communist states are somehow collectively opposed by the anti-communist ones; in fact anti-communist official rhetoric is frequently combined with highly practical support for communist rulers, and this was so well before communist states themselves began to divide.

Communists themselves often seem to sense the inadequacy of the terminology. Mao, for example, frequently used formulae that ambiguously combine incompatibles – such as 'left in form and right in substance'. In my account I have sought to set the French parliamentary geometry aside (except where it unavoidably insinuates itself through the perceptions and self-descriptions of the actors). Its axioms are too elastic, and in any case no single dimension can serve as the axis of explanation.

## THE EVOLUTION OF COMMUNISMS?

By making the preceding points in such a summary fashion (and by titling the book *The Evolution of Communism*, in the singular) I may have given an impression of communism as more homogeneous and unified than it is. Yet any general treatment encounters two general questions, as simple to pose as they are difficult to answer:

Can the term 'communism' sensibly be used as though it referred to a single phenomenon? and

How firm a distinction is there between communism and other types of parties and movements?

Each of these questions offers immense scope for argument. Does the knowledge that they are 'communists' tell us anything substantial about people as diverse as an imprisoned black revolutionary in Johannesburg, a police informer in Bucharest, a church-going official of the party propaganda department in Warsaw, a production-line worker or teacher, a shop steward or trade union official, in Bologna or Birmingham? What do prominent communists who are as different as Zhdanov and Picasso, Beria and Gramsci, Pol Pot and Enrico Berlinguer have in common? Is there any sense in which today's Soviet or Chinese communist parties are similar organizations to the West's tinier Leninist sects – Maoists, Trotskyists, Bordigists, etc.? Can parties which started as communist gradually cease to be so – becoming, for example, social democratic?

Taking an historical, rather than a formal or taxonomic, approach to these issues helps avoid fruitless disputations. My choice of title points to the sense in which I have done this. I have circumscribed 'communism', in all its variety, by its common ancestry in Lenin's Bolshevik Party and the early Comintern. Within this definition I have concentrated on 'official' communism rather than the dissident forms that have split away from it. But within those limits I have paid as much attention to non-ruling parties as those which hold state power, and I have sought to highlight as much as possible of the variation to which the 'evolution' of communism has given rise. Such an approach, I feel, allows one to discuss different communisms' continuities and common features, together with their differences, without becoming mired in abstract arguments about whether or not 'communism' constitutes a single phenomenon.

My title also suggests an analogy. Evolutionary biologists classify higher organisms as *species* (defined, approximately, as populations of potentially interbreeding individuals), and study species as they have arisen historically, by processes of splitting or branching. One species can evolve into several, and these will often compete, 'hostility' coexisting with common origins and a largely common anatomy. Provided we bear its limits in mind the analogy with biological evolution can be helpful. It can draw our attention to the ways in which communism's mutability can act as an advantage, so that, from a common ancestor, very different types of communism can arise by mutation and adaptation to different circumstances. Yet the analogy also reminds us how deeply communist parties are conditioned by their histories, and how frequently their conflicts are the product of similarity as well as difference.

# PART I

Communism's formative phases

# 2

# Origins of Leninism

By communism we nowadays mean Leninism or its derivatives, other organized variants of Marxism being ineffectual or utopian curiosities. The formative phase of modern communism can be discerned with reasonable precision. Its characteristics emerge within the pointedly practical writings prepared by the Marxists who established *Iskra* (*Spark*) as the newspaper of Russian social democracy, between the launching of their newspaper in December 1900 and the split into Bolsheviks and Mensheviks at the Second Congress of the Russian Social Democratic Labour Party in the summer of 1903 – mainly, but by no means exclusively, in those prepared by the most energetic of the *Iskra* leaders, Vladimir Ilich Ulyanov, better known under his pseudonym, Lenin.

## PLEKHANOV'S MARXISM

The editors of *Iskra* were all intellectual Marxists who prided themselves upon their orthodoxy. The most immediate source of their ideas lay in the efforts by George Plekhanov in the 1880s, after his breach with the terrorists of 'People's Will', to apply Marxism to Russia and popularize it as a doctrine by which the radical intelligentsia could lead Russia's nascent industrial working class. Plekhanov held, following Marx, that eventual human emancipation, and the withering away of the state, turned upon the proletarian overthrow of capitalism, and that this general truth applied also to Russia. In tracing Russia's route towards communism Plekhanov inclined to economic determinism. Capitalist development would produce a growing but impoverished industrial workforce, whose experience of class struggle would nurture their class consciousness, and in due course provide fertile ground for the ideas and politics of the 'scientific socialists'. The needs of the Russian bourgeoisie would cause it to cast off Tsarist absolutism. But the ultimate beneficiary of political liberty would be Russian socialism, thereby set free to swell into a mass movement, based on an expanding working class.

On the whole Plekhanov followed Marx in seeing a mature capitalist economy and a large working class as preconditions for a successful socialist movement. It is true that his views also reflected the fact that he was attempting to set out a Marxist political programme for an under-developed country (he was, indeed, the first Marxist ever to do so; some of the problems involved are discussed more fully in chapter 11); but his main emphasis always lay on Russia's repeating the economic and social develop-ment of Western Europe. (Although later Plekhanov arrived at a more complex view of Russian history, as oscillating between European and Asiatic patterns of development; see Sawer, 1975.)

Historical confidence, however, was not the same thing as political efficacy. Plekhanov and his supporters, in exile, remained relatively isolated from the growth of worker militancy in the 1890s. Moreover Russia's industrial working class, though combative, was still only a small fraction of society. The political and intellectual influences upon workers were very mixed, and only in small part Marxist or even socialist. Indeed it was an exaggeration to speak of a workers' *movement*. What did exist were strikes and agitations against particular employers, plus more permanent, but much smaller, local circles of workers involved in political discussion and self-education, and sometimes also acting as the organizers of strikes. There was no national unity or leadership.

### ISKRA

*Iskra* was launched to change this situation. Though its ingredients were not original within pre-First World War socialism, the particular synthesis proved to have extraordinary powers of survival. Three elements are particularly important, and each of them is a distinctive innovation with respect to the Marxism of Marx: the use of centralized and disciplined organization; the recognition that in the war of political ideas all positions are 'ideological'; and the acceptance that industrial workers are not 'spontaneously' sympathetic to socialism.

It was the last which stemmed most directly from the Russians' experi-ence. The coalition formed to set up *Iskra* brought Lenin and Martov, returnees from exile in Siberia, into alliance with the veterans of Plekhanov's group, the Union of Social Democrats Abroad. They combined to defend an orthodoxy which felt threatened – by currents within Russian Marxism that reflected the unsatisfactory localism and immediacy of the struggles inside Russia. In particular, *Iskra*'s orthodoxy abhorred the creeping notion, fostered among some of the intelligentsia by the epidemic of bitter strikes during the 1890s, that industrial struggles would bring workers in the natural course of events to advance appropriate political aims – for both democratic reforms and socialism – when and as the time became right. As the main mouthpiece of this 'economism', the newspaper *Workers' Thought*, put it in a deftly heretical application of historical materialism: 'Politics always obediently follows economics and, in general, political chains are broken in passing' (Pipes, 1963, pp. 129–31).

### Against spontaneity

Not so, replied Lenin. His introductory editorial for *Iskra* resurrected earlier distinctions between intelligentsia-revolutionaries, propelled by abstractions, and the masses for whom, and with whose support, they were to act, and addressed itself rather evidently to the former rather than the latter. Without the ideological leadership of the social democrats the working-class movement 'inevitably becomes bourgeois'; what is most urgent is to 'combine' socialism with the militant workers' movement (Lenin, 1960–78, 4, pp. 368–9). As the conflict with 'economism' sharpened in the run-up to the Second Congress, Lenin expanded on this point in *What is to be Done?*, the pamphlet he prepared for the use of the 'agents' who distributed *Iskra* and spread its influence among the social democratic circles in Russia. (It was Ulyanov's use of 'N. Lenin' – one of his many pseudonyms – for *What is to be Done?* that made him well known to the groups inside Russia under that name.)

In all countries, Lenin asserted, scientific socialism arose 'altogether independently of the spontaneous growth of the working-class movement'; its source was the socialist intelligentsia. It followed that, in so far as the class struggle required the socialists also to engage in ideological war, an essential part of their fire must be directed towards the industrial working class itself – or at least at the reformist, partial, in a word 'bourgeois' attitudes to which it was spontaneously prone. This stance is one that communism has retained and extended as it has evolved to seek its support among other classes. Building communist movements based on peasants, for example, has not meant communism relinquishing its own outlook in favour of peasant attitudes and aspirations.

### Ideology

Lenin appropriated, and altered the meaning of, a crucial Marxist concept, 'ideology'. In the war of political ideas both – or all – sides were now seen as ideological. Marx had reserved the term 'ideology' for the outlooks of exploiting classes and their intellectual representatives, organically incapable of recognizing the historical necessities which doomed them. He was mainly referring to the intellectual productions of capitalist society; much of *Capital*, for example, is criticism of the ideological inversions of bourgeois political economy. It was true that it was the ideas of the ruling classes that predominated in society as a whole, but the working class had no need of such 'false' consciousness and could and should embrace 'science'.

For Lenin, however (and in all subsequent communist usage), this contrast is set aside. 'Ideology' is a neutral, and frequently a positive, term; it is up to social democratic ideology to succeed, and it can do so only in a struggle against all other ideologies. Not, of course, that *Iskra*'s editors relinquished the claim that their Marxism possessed scientific objectivity, but this was now explicitly linked to the advocacy of political, and even quasi-military, methods in the battle of ideas. Their emissaries were instructed in a standard form of capitulation to be sought from errant social democratic committees within Russia: a specific repudiation of past errors ('economism'), and acceptance of *Iskra*'s views, theoretical as well as tactical. Later, when Lenin's organization became the ruling party, this practical, combative understanding of ideology was to provide a natural justification for the use of pressure and coercion in intellectual life. It was not until after Stalin's death, in the 1950s, that some ruling communist parties began to come to grips with the problems they had created for themselves by using police methods to settle intellectual questions.

Harnessing organization to theory cohered naturally with a view of the working class as unreceptive to science. Conversely, rights of organizational control were better rested upon lasting verities than ephemeral majorities. 'On no account,' Martov cautioned *Iskra* supporters in St Petersburg in September 1902, during the skirmishing before the Second Congress, must they let matters 'be reduced to a question of majority rights, to a question of who has a right to the constitutional trademarks.' The 'economists' will argue thus, but 'You, on the other hand, must put the entire question on the basis of principle' (Frankel, 1969, p. 58).

The explicitness of the argument that socialism was a doctrine *for* but not *of* workers was more novel than its premises. It followed many earlier Russian (and other) socialist thinkers in seeing those with more education as the active element: from Lavrov's patient ethical enlightenment, through Tkachev's candidly elite Jacobinism, to Plekhanov's rendering of Marxism for Russia in the early 1880s, which saw the urban workers as a link or lever through which the intelligentsia revolutionaries could mobilize the much larger population of peasants. Similar ideas arose very widely in European socialism during the last two decades of the nineteenth century, reflecting principally the fact that, as industrial workers organized into strong unions and began to give large votes to socialist parliamentary parties, it became clear their most urgent concerns were a multitude of partial reforms, besides, or even instead of, root-and-branch transformation of the social order. *What is to be Done?* quoted the German socialist leader Karl Kautsky's 'profoundly true and important' words on the need for scientific socialist consciousness to be introduced into the proletariat 'from without', as against Edward Bernstein's 'revisionist' view of the movement as consisting in the accumulation of piecemeal gains.

On this point Lenin could have cited support from many others. The French socialist Jules Guesde claimed the backing of Marx and Paul Lafargue as he tried to turn his Parti Ouvrier into 'an openly and scientifically centralist' party with a single programme. 'For some time', he declared, 'the initiative must come from above, from those who "know more" '.

For similar reasons Guesde resisted local amendments to his national programme, or 'experimental' politics, lest they infiltrate reformist ideas; and he, like Lenin, was denounced as dictatorial, 'a Torquemada in pince-nez', by his 'possibilist' opponents. In Britain, H. H. Hyndman's equally didactic leadership of the Social Democratic Federation rested its socialism's claims on the authority of a small intellectual elite. (The Social Democratic Federation was also helpful to the Russian social democrats. Lenin edited *Iskra* from a desk in their offices for a year in 1902–3.) The Fabians, though they would have rejected *Iskra*'s revolutionism, were also in no doubt which class took most naturally to socialism. Shaw shared the scorn which Marx had expressed for English workers' conservatism; wage-earners, he declared in 1897, 'are far more conventional, prejudiced and "bourgeois" than the middle class' (Feuer, 1975, p. 119). (Fabianism, indeed, proved to have an enduring empathy with Leninism. Shaw, with his usual gusto, applauded the bloodletting of the Bolsheviks in power almost from the beginning (Dunn, 1984), and in the fullness of time, under his prompting, Sidney and Beatrice Webb embraced the view that Stalin's dictatorship in the 1930s *was* Fabianism; a communist party, they decided, was just what they needed, but had not thought of (Harrison, 1987, p. 75).)

## Organization

The *Iskra* leaders proposed to fuse doctrine and agency in organization. As they recast the tasks of scientific socialism and its representatives they also proposed, from the outset, reforged organizational weapons with which to attack them. Marxism had already devoted some theoretical energy to how the future socialist *society* should be organized. In comparison the question of how to organize the *parties* which would serve as vehicles to the future state was treated far more casually; even less was the first question seen as having much connection or continuity with the second.

Yet Russian circumstances, towards the turn of the century, presented a concatenation of factors impelling *her* Marxists to be innovative and original on these questions. The difficulties of illegality were compounded by a country – an empire – of vast internal differences and distances, and by the hostility of a state machine which, although archaic in its attitude to civil liberties, was technologically modern and sophisticated in its surveillance and pursuit of those who agitated for them. Indeed it was sometimes over-sophisticated: so keen were the political police, the Okhrana, on preserving their most valued agents in place that it was not unknown for Tsarism's senior officials to fall victim to bombs supplied by employees of the security services. Russian revolutionaries' natural interest in organizational means for operating successfully in illegality was heightened by their general proclivity for terrorism, and the consequent sharpening of relations with the police.

But efforts at organization ran up against awkward problems posed by its bases of support. Russia's industrial working class was small and young. In its large majority it was made up of new migrants from the countryside. But it already displayed the interest in partial gains as distinct from ultimate socialist goals that was troubling western Marxism. The peasantry remained an enigma – too vast to ignore but deaf to most of the efforts of political arousal directed at it. The principal revolutionary forces – the radical and semi-radical intelligentsia, fissiparous and temperamental – constituted a derisive challenge to the would-be organizer.

*Iskra* proposed centralized direction to tame the localism, variability, and consequent frictions among revolutionaries' activity. It was not a new problem. Three years earlier the rather 'economist' social democratic committee of Kiev, which took the initiative for the first Congress to found an all-Russian social democratic party (held at Minsk in 1898) was sensitive to the problem, and envisaged both the solution and at least one of its implications:

Once a central organization exists, it is possible to create immediately at all new points colony-committees. In this way one preserves the experience of old party workers. . . . In place of the parochial patriotism of particularists a party spirit [*partinost'*] is cultivated. This precludes the formation of an 'opposition'. (Wildman, 1967, p. 168)

In the event the short-lived national party which emerged from the Minsk congress adopted, under the pressure for autonomy of the large Jewish Bund, much looser organizational principles. But the reasons for centralism, and therefore the urge towards it, persisted, and *Iskra* justified its arrival as the 'scaffolding' upon which a new and stricter party edifice could be built. In Lenin's case, the opposition to 'ultra-democracy' had been strengthened and deepened by his reading of the Webbs' writings on trades unions (he and his wife translated their *History of Trade Unionism* in exile in Siberia in 1898–9). The experience of British trade unions provided him with powerful arguments against organizational 'primitivism', or leaving matters overmuch in the hands of the membership.

## The 1903 Congress

The editors of *Iskra* remained united up to the Second Congress of Russian social democrats, in the summer of 1903. But at the Congress they parted company, in the watershed split occasioned by Martov's amendment to the rules concerning party membership. But before the Congress split, it considered the eventual relation to be aimed at between party and state, and in doing so began to discover the implications that Lenin's organizational principles – then just beginning to divide the main body of delegates – might have for a future socialist order. The debate (after having weighed Trotsky's objections to proportional representation and the consequent multiplication of small parties) went on to elicit from Lenin's supporters the view that all democratic principles were relative. Thus Posadovsky, Trotsky's co-delegate from the Siberian social democratic organization, and a supporter of Lenin, explained:

There is not a single one among the principles of democracy which we ought not to subordinate *to the interests of our Party*. [Exclamations: 'Not inviolability of the person?'] No, not inviolability of the person! As a revolutionary party striving to achieve our ultimate aim, the social revolution, we must consider democratic principles exclusively from the standpoint of the most rapid achievement of that aim, from the standpoint of the interests of our Party.

Plekhanov endorsed the speaker: *salus revolutionis suprema lex*. This applied to parliaments in particular:

If, in an outburst of revolutionary enthusiasm, the people should elect a very good parliament – a sort of *Chambre Introuvable* – it would suit us to try and make that a *Long Parliament*; but if the elections turned out badly for us, we should have to try and disperse the resulting parliament not after two years but, if possible, after two weeks. (RSDLP, 1978, pp. 219–20)

Plekhanov's views on the usefulness of retaining the death penalty (which many delegates wanted abolished) were equally forthright; how else did they propose to deal with the Romanovs after the fall of the autocracy? It was such interventions that later caused Lenin's close lieutenant Zinoviev (in his quasi-official party history of 1923) to remind neophyte cadres that 'Plekhanov was at that time a Bolshevik in the best sense of the word: he was proud of his nickname "The Jacobin" ' (Zinoviev, 1973, pp. 94–5).

Some delegates hissed Plekhanov, and a representative of the Jewish Bund, seeing in his views on elections 'an imitation of bourgeois tactics', pointed out that to be logical they should strike the call for universal suffrage out of their programme. However, the delegates went on unanimously to adopt sweeping demands on civil and electoral rights. (What caused far more argument were the disputes over minority languages.)

In fact the exchanges at the Second Congress were only the end-result of the many months of discussion on a draft programme among the leading figures of the *Iskra* group. Having based themselves on two central ideas – (a) that the industrial working class was central to the struggle for socialism; and (b) that workers, unless under the firm tutelage of a social democratic organization, would fall back into 'bourgeois' ways – they inevitably had difficulty in reconciling the call for a democratic constitution, which was by that time accepted as fundamental by the mainstream of Russian revolutionary traditions, with the likelihood it would lead to the repulsive middle-class parliamentarism of Western Europe. (Similar tensions later led Parvus and Trotsky to develop their arguments that in Russia the working class was capable of leaping, in 'permanent revolution', over a capitalist phase of development.)

What even more taxed the proto-Bolsheviks of 1902–3 was the fear that the peasants would be erratic in the revolution against Tsarism and hostile to socialism. It was therefore necessary also to think in terms of 'the dictatorship of the proletariat'; if only peasant support were not so undependable, Lenin reflected, 'we could get on very well without a dictatorship'. But, with the majority of the population consisting of 'these unreliable and double-faced social elements' (as he considered them) it would be necessary to use force (Lenin, 1960–78, vol. 6, pp. 51, 53). Only Vera Zasulich commented, lightheartedly, on his intentions: 'Upon millions of people? Just you try it!' (Keep, 1963, p. 114).

Most of the protagonists felt it was specifically Russian conditions pushing them in the direction of coercive methods. They conceived dictatorship, if and when it proved necessary, as that of the Party; 'managerial' justifications for one-man rule were a later development. How far, then, did the split at the Second Congress represent *the* moment of inception of modern communism? It is certainly possible to cite opinions from participants which suggest that its impact upon them was to stimulate remarkable prescience. The 'egocentralism' of 'Maximilian Lenin', predicted Trotsky, would in due course lead 'to the Party organization substituting itself for the Party, the Central Committee substituting itself for the Party organization, and finally the dictator substituting himself for the Central Committee' (Trotsky, n.d. [1980], p. 77). Axelrod complained to Kautsky that Leninist centralism was but 'a simple copy or caricature of the bureaucratic-autocratic system of our Minister of the Interior' (Ascher, 1972, p. 211). The most percipient observer of the Second Congress was Vladimir Akimov, the 'economist' delegate who managed to worm his way through

*Iskra*'s careful campaign for the selection of favourable delegates from the Russian organizations. After the revolution, he warned, a government *à la* Plekhanov would feel most threatened by opposition movements among the working class itself. 'They will then be branded "not truly proletarian", "not conscious" and so on, and to them will be opposed the "enlightened despotism" of the revolutionary government' (Akimov, 1969, p. 139).

### EARLY BOLSHEVISM

Yet in reality things did not seem clear-cut. The rupture at the Congress took place over the principles and staffing of the organization, not its political programme, and Akimov remained an isolated outsider. Martov, though wounded by the breach with Lenin, his longstanding friend, could still parody the split with schoolboy levity. Bolshevik amateur cartoons of the time, with more affection than respect, pick up Vera Zasulich's nickname for Lenin, showing him as a tom-cat terrorizing verbose Menshevik mice (Getzler, 1967, pp. 87–95). And in the following years some individuals – Trotsky, for example – were to make almost a political profession as intermediary between the opponents.

Moreover projects or declarations for unification persisted until well after the February 1917 revolution. They reflected, principally, the attitudes among many rank-and-file party activists in Russia itself, impatient with the quarrellings of the emigré leaders, and more than willing to organize together in the years of police persecution. As late as the summer of 1917, when all left-wing parties, and especially the Bolsheviks, had grown meteorically since the fall of the Tsar, joint organizations of Bolshevik and Menshevik social democrats existed in many areas, and 31 per cent of the delegates to the Bolsheviks' Sixth Party Congress, in July 1917, had been Mensheviks before the First World War (Service, 1979, pp. 43, 49). It was against such a background that an All-Russian Congress of Bolsheviks in March 1917 had unanimously accepted Stalin's proposals aimed at reunification with the more anti-war Mensheviks, and mandated Stalin to pursue discussions with them (Slusser, 1987, pp. 46–8). However, Lenin's arrival in Petrograd, a few days later, put an end to such far-reaching projects.

Differences of emphasis, method and character were, thus, as important as the differences of principle which the polemicists so often invoked. Of the prominent intellectuals then involved in Russian social democracy only Plekhanov sided with Lenin after the Second Congress, and he abandoned him after a few months. Many years after he had become a Leninist, Trotsky still deplored the weight of 'committee men' in early Bolshevism: what Lenin did take with him out of the split was a number of seasoned organizational workers of lesser literary talent and – not exactly an organization, for he was soon in a minority in the bodies outside Russia – but the tempered determination to do in reality as he had pushed for within the *Iskra* grouping, and build up an effective network of full-time professional revolutionaries and local bodies inside Russia, all loyally attuned to the directing centre abroad (although, in 1904, this consisted of very few people). The problems of illegality and exile always threatened to condemn Russian revolutionaries driven abroad to remote ineffectuality; Lenin, however, fifteen years before he set about organizing the Comintern from Moscow, seized the nettle and went about creating, splitting and instructing local bodies from a distance to build up a purely Bolshevik (i.e. Leninist) network within Russia itself.

Even organizational principles, however, provide us with no absolute distinction between the factions. It was the Mensheviks, meeting at the crest of the revolutionary wave of 1905, who first adopted the phrase 'democratic centralism' as expressing their organizational principles, a month before a conference of Bolsheviks did the same thing. To be sure, the Mensheviks were more wedded to democracy, intending, in adopting the expression, merely to tighten the central direction of their work, while the Bolsheviks wished rather to make their centralism more successful, by emphasizing the 'democratic' in order to recruit more of those thrown into political activity by the revolution. Yet both still drew heavily on German social democracy as a model; the phrase itself originated there. When the Bolsheviks and Mensheviks uneasily reunified in 1906, the congress stipulated that all organizations of the party were to be constructed on the basis of 'democratic centralism'.

Lenin acquiesced in the 1906 reunification only because *de facto* fusions were taking place in many of the local committees, swollen by the revolution (during 1905–6 the total membership of all social democratic organizations within the Russian empire probably approached 150,000). At the time of reunification the Bolsheviks, placed in a narrow overall minority, also set up, as Zinoviev (1973, p. 143) recalled, 'their own internal, and for the Party, illegal, Central Committee' – the precursor of many subsequent Leninist exercises in 'entrism'. Its effective discipline (and the extreme reluctance of the Mensheviks to take steps against it) enabled it to tilt the balance of control back towards Lenin.

For most of the period from 1906 to 1917 the conditions under which social democratic organizations worked precluded either strict centralism or much democracy. Illegality and exile of leaders, and the delay and uncertainty of communications, made it impossible either to impose detailed rules on local party bodies or convene the sorts of assemblies that democracy would have required. Lenin's version of 'democratic centralism' focused on it as an inner-party organizational formula, interpreted in the phrase 'freedom of criticism plus unity in action' – members, and lower bodies, were free to debate decisions, but once they had been taken all must unite to carry them out. Lenin's vigorous application of the principle of unity gave him, during the years of recoil from 1907, two important advantages over his rivals. Bolshevism came, by degrees, to free itself of the longing to regroup the socialists, or even more the radical forces opposing Tsarism; the ideal of broad unity atrophied from a principle to an expendable tactic. And a close-knit and secretive organization proved effective at the 'expropriations' (usually armed robberies) through which the Bolshevik leaders got the funds to support agents and activities. In the years after 1906, Bolshevism further defined itself in battles against the 'liquidators' (i.e. those Mensheviks, led by A. N. Potresov, a co-founder of *Iskra*, who favoured giving up underground organization, and operating within the limits of parliamentary action set by Stolypin's government) and, scarcely less detested, the Menshevik leaders in emigration (Martov, Axelrod, Dan and, for a short time, Plekhanov) who countenanced them.

## BOLSHEVISM'S INTERNAL DISPUTES

It was, however, some years before Bolshevism became synonymous with Leninism. Lenin also found himself embattled internally, against those Bolsheviks who were eager for a showdown with the overcautious conduct of the social democratic deputies in the (much restricted) Third Duma: the 'recallists' and the 'ultimists'. The breach with the latter was also entwined with disputes over money, since their leading figure, Alexander Bogdanov, had control of the proceeds of a number of bank robberies, and with philosophy, since he was attempting to incorporate the neo-Kantian ideas of Ernst Mach into Marxism, 'God-building' for the popular religion of a future socialism. Bogdanov's Bolshevik 'left', fusing an enthusiasm for the shared 'myths' of working-class struggle, which they derived from Western European syndicalism, with a collectivist and relativist philosophy – with Bogdanov popularizing his ideas in ingenious science fiction – represented a challenge to Lenin's organizational precepts almost as serious as the earlier 'economism'.

An organizational reshuffle placed Zinoviev in charge of many of Bogdanov's funds, but Bogdanov and Lunacharsky's epistemological innovations required of Lenin an entire book, *Materialism and Empirio-Criticism* (1909), in which the history of philosophy was recast in party terms, as a running battle of ever more philosophical materialism. His opponents' enthusiasm for Mach drew Lenin's particular ire: 'Nothing in Marxism is subject to revision', he declared. 'There is only one answer to revisionism: smash its face in!' (Valentinov, 1968, pp. 184–5). Lenin's 'politicization of theory' subsumed even the most abstract ideas into the class struggle, in a text which set much of the style for later polemics. But centralization of control over the Bolshevik party was a process that took many more years, and was by no means complete by the 1917 revolution, or even by Lenin's death in 1924.

The breach with Bogdanov, however, though it deprived Lenin's Menshevik critics of some of their charges of 'extremism' against him, by the same token refuelled the pressures upon him to ally or collaborate with non-Bolsheviks – from the Mensheviks, who rejected the charges of 'liquidationism', from Plekhanov and his small following, who criticized both sides, from Trotsky and his, who tried to get them together, and even from 'Party Bolsheviks', whose wish for reunification had brought them to separate from Lenin. Thus, up until the outbreak of the European war – both when the popular influence of the socialists was at its lowest, in the revolutionary ebb of 1908–9, and when it had expanded again, as in the strike wave of 1912 – much of Lenin's energy, and that of Zinoviev and his other immediate collaborators, was taken up with holding the Bolshevik ranks together through interminable 'unity' manoeuvres. Literary collaboration with Plekhanov, Martov and Trotsky alternated with splits, the proclamation of a purely Bolshevik social democratic party (at the Prague Congress of 1912) and (following this, and much more visible to workers in Russia) the split between Bolshevik and Menshevik Duma deputies (organized by the former's leader, Roman Malinowski – a protégé of Lenin, but also an agent of the Okhrana).

Through the struggles and entanglements of Russian social democracy during 1905–17 – that is, in the period when it had demonstrated its ability to attract mass support – the Bolsheviks' centralism, though it was still in process of being shaped, conferred definite advantages upon them. Not only were Lenin's supporters more agile and obedient – and ethically uninhibited – in the manoeuvrings and disputes among the socialists, but vigorous direction and more plentiful funds provided them with a more professional organization stretching into Russia. In 1912–13, for example, they were able to run *Pravda* as a daily paper in St Petersburg, and during the war they propagated Lenin's policy of turning the imperialist war into a civil war with a unity and decisiveness that eluded the Mensheviks, with their pipe-dream of reunifying the Socialist International.

The construction of such a heavy-duty machine had, of course, its costs. Before it came within sight of power Bolshevism was, by and large, less congenial to the more thoughtful or able among the intellectuals; it tended to attract practical, but rather brutal, organizers like Stalin, or speechmakers like Zinoviev, as well as a certain number whose wish was for immediate or even violent action. Internally, its characteristics were of a peculiar sort – part political party, but merging into sect or coterie, part personal following, part conspiratorial network, with some of the talents of a criminal gang. The dominance, even dictatorship, of Lenin and the Bolshevik centre still left it very far, however, from the dead unanimity which later developed; that took over a decade after it came to power in 1917.

The early history of Bolshevik 'democratic centralism' is marked by a contradiction: it was advocated, and practised, as a solution to the specific difficulties of Russia. The difference of internal regime with, say, the German social democrats was a matter on which Lenin preferred not to be drawn. Yet the acuteness which 'the organizational question' took, and the venom which it engendered, could not but suggest that something with broader applicability than a small and vulnerable party, struggling with illegal conditions in Russia, was involved. It proved to be so: even when the Bolsheviks held power, and far from being police quarry were in control of the whole apparatus of internal security, 'democratic centralism' was not relaxed, but further centralized and reinforced. And when, to replace the 'bankrupt' leaders of the Second International, they launched a Third, they sought to construct its sections on the organizational template they had themselves evolved.

## BOLSHEVISM'S ENDURING CHARACTER

It would be possible to characterize Leninism, in its original form, by a number of characteristics which mark it off from other forms of socialism. But in retrospect it is possible to see that *one* of the qualitative changes which went into original Leninism was different in kind from others. The arguments among socialists about the prospects for their movement concerned the orthodoxy and efficacy of doctrine and ideas, the propensities of classes and other social groups, the present apathy of socialism's future beneficiaries, the peculiarities and difficulties of national circumstances, the problems of repression and illegality. Communism, at its inception, had something distinctive to say on all these matters. But its conclusions on each of them converged: in order to deal with these, and any other problems that may come up, what is essential is the right kind of party organization. The basic terrain of argument was thereby shifted – from debates which shuttled back and forth between present problems and ultimate goals, to arguments that revolved around the means, the general instrument or engine, which would permit the passage from the former to the latter.

It is in this sense, and not in any of the particular answers that it provided on methods of political work at that time, that Russian socialism engendered in Bolshevism a type of political machine that was to prove far more widely effective and (after it came to power in 1917) was so widely – and sometimes slavishly – imitated. Here is how Zinoviev (then head of the Comintern) described Lenin's invention in a popular account prepared in 1923:

> If we want to forge the working masses together and to merge the separate little fires flaring up here and there into one single big flame, then we need an exceptional, almost miraculous apparatus which is capable of realising all this. And for this it is no less necessary in turn that people really dedicated to the working class are brought together by us into one organization of professional revolutionaries; that is, people who would serve only the revolution and not concern themselves with anything else, and who in conditions of illegality and inconceivably rigorous situations would be capable of forming a very complex revolutionary system of co-operation with a precise division of labour, and mastering the art of easy and free manoeuvrability. (Zinoviev, 1973, p. 78)

This type of organization presupposed and required the shift in theory and day-to-day thinking which I have already mentioned: the separation of economic and political classes. In Bolshevism, Marxism maintained its claim that classes can be economically identified and possess historical interests which are defined, 'in the last instance', by their economic roles, and it retained the moral momentum which that view conferred. But it insulated this from its routine recognition of 'relative autonomy' when engaged in the buzzing confusion of daily politics. The advantages of such an outlook are more practical than explanatory, but – especially when linked to Lenin's novel type of organization – they are very real. Moreover, they are potentially applicable to other classes than the proletariat. If, as a matter of habit, the interests of classes and social groups come to be thought of as reflected in party-political purposes, rather than to be discovered in the thinking and conditions of those who comprise them, then the way is open for political syntheses which can claim to represent several, many, or even occasionally all, classes. Put thus, the point is rather abstract, and applies in some measure to many of the relationships between politics and the state, and civil society. But Leninism has grasped and pursued it with a particular clarity, which accounts for its sometimes perplexing combination of single-mindedness and political promiscuity.

Of course, the potential within the germ was not apparent all at once. Indeed, the very success of original Leninism contributed to the disasters which befell some of its descendants. Lenin put no less sense of party discipline into compiling the 'twenty-one points', which the Second Congress of Comintern adopted as the basis for sifting the political forces that should form the world communist movement, than he had into the organization of *Iskra* and, later, the Bolshevik faction. But the very precision of Comintern's supervision did much to weaken this second generation of communist parties. It made their relations with socialist and other parties of the left rigid and divisive (it often had less of this effect with their remoter relatives, such as nationalists – the intention was to select and split from within the traditional left). And the men who were selected as leaders of the new communist parties tended – though with many exceptions – to be or to become rule followers: organizational men trying to follow principles and operate organizational forms which had not grown up in their national societies. They were bound, moreover, as much by moment-to-moment instructions from Comintern as by principles gleaned from Bolshevism's history.

Leninism's successes since 1917 have generally required either the assistance of massive external force to bring the communist party to power or maintain it there (as in Eastern Europe), *or* a fundamental adaptation of methods – none the less real for often being concealed – to enable the communist party to succeed among the difficulties of its own national circumstances. Thus in China (and later in Indochina, Yugoslavia and Albania) persecution and survival in war taught the communist party to vary even those fundamentals – such as the central role of the working class – which they had as part of their Russian ideological inheritance. But different strategies and tactics, even a different social basis, proved compatible with Leninist principles of organization within the party.

Conversely, where parties fail to adapt independently, loyalty to the Soviet Union is no guarantee against extinction. Once Stalin – for reasons of Soviet foreign policy – had taken the decision to intervene in the Spanish Civil War, the Spanish Communist Party acted essentially as the extension of the Comintern, for which Spain was just one element of strategy; with Franco's victory the party's domestic organization was almost destroyed.

Too narrow a dependency can also jeopardize survival in power, as is evidenced by the series of near-disasters – averted only by Soviet intervention or the threat of it – which have beset ruling communist parties in Eastern Europe since the war. Their learning to rule has involved another important adaptation of Leninist centralism. Whereas before 1917 Bolsheviks did not – with very few exceptions – join the party or submit to its discipline for the sake of personal advantage, ruling communist parties have had to extend the principle of centralized control to give themselves, through a 'nomenklatura' or similar system, direct patronage over most of society's substantial controlling jobs. In doing so they have formed large strata (or, arguably, classes) benefiting from and loyal to the communist monopoly of rule.

Of course, these adaptations (and many others) have not sprung from trial and error alone; mixed with the improvisation there has been a great deal of deliberate learning, imitation and transfer of methods. One of the things that the evolution of modern communism reflects is the fact that world politics is now as much a symbiotic reality as world markets. Political methods, doctrines and slogans compete and prosper internationally.

Communism has lacked a formal controlling centre since 1943. But one of the things that most clearly registers its persistence as a world movement is the high level of mutual interest and transfer of political 'technologies' that continues between its national parts.

FURTHER READING

Venturi (1966) and Besançon (1981) treat of the intellectual antecedents of Leninism, and Wildman (1967) and Pipes (1963) of its background in the Russian workers' movement. Harding (1983a) is a useful collection of documents of Russian Marxism for the period 1879–1906. Frankel (1981) is an account of the Jewish Bund, at the turn of the century by far the largest labour movement organization in the Russian empire. The many worthwhile accounts of Lenin and the history of Bolshevism in his lifetime include Service (1985–), Ulam (1978), Shub (1966) and Harding (1983). Schapiro (1978) remains the standard overall history of the Soviet Communist Party. There is a recent English translation of the proceedings of the 1903 Congress (RSDLP, 1978). As far as personal reminiscences of Lenin go, Valentinov's (1968) are more informative than those of Lenin's wife, Krupskaya (1975).

Other major figures are the subject of biographies or special studies: Baron (1963) on Plekhanov; Ascher (1972) on Axelrod; Getzler (1967) on Martov; Deutscher (1979, 1979a, 1979b), Howe (1978) and Knei-Paz (1979) on Trotsky; Tucker (1973), Deutscher (1970) and Ulam (1973) on Stalin; Williams (1986) on Bogdanov's opposition to Lenin. To set their thinking against its background one cannot improve on Kolakowski's (1982) three comprehensive but extremely lucid volumes on the development of theoretical Marxism.

# 3

# Comintern: splitting the masses from the leaders

This chapter, together with chapters 4 and 5, mainly discuss the formative years of the second generation of communist parties, set up in the years following the Russian revolution. To a considerable extent they were organized in imitation of Bolshevism, through the Bolsheviks' new international body, the Communist (or Third) International – the Comintern.

The summer of 1914 found Lenin pondering how to elude the proposals – instructions would be too strong a term – to reunify the Russian social democrats which had been put to the Bolsheviks by the Second International. The outbreak of the First World War released him from the dilemma, and the latter part of the war found him in a position to organize a Third International to replace the Second. Many European socialist leaders favoured the Second International's undemanding, 'postbox' internationalism. But it had proved quite ineffectual at preventing the First World War, and virtually disintegrated on the outbreak of hostilities. Lenin set out to replace it by a sort of Bolshevism writ large, reviving the laudable centralism of Marx's First International. The parties which issued from the Bolshevik leaders' efforts to put their apparently simple ambition into practice within the complex, new and dangerous political configurations thrown up by the close of the war formed the second generation of communist parties, and the basis of the modern world communist movement.

Whatever its disarray as between its national sections the European labour movement grew very considerably between the beginning and the end of the war. Membership of socialist and labour parties increased everywhere, often more than doubling, while trade union strength grew even more, in many cases tripling. This new support accrued to leaders who had, in the majority of cases, supported their own governments' war efforts; but at the same time it expressed the suffering and consequent radicalization caused by the war. Very few of the rank-and-file of the European labour movement aspired to *imitate* the Bolsheviks, but a much larger number felt a general sympathy for the revolution in Russia. Thus even in Britain, for example, Labour Party and trade union bodies were prominent in the campaigns to defend the infant Soviet state, and in the Polish–Soviet war crisis of August 1920 the TUC threatened strike action if Lloyd George supported Poland militarily. However, the Communist Party that was formed in the same month was minuscule.

The communists were compelled to learn fast among new intricacies. The difficulties of putting together a new international socialist confederation intersected with those of protecting, then attempting to secure, the Soviet republic. The expectation that the premature Russian overturn would be rescued by European socialist revolution was repeatedly disappointed; with each setback the new Soviet leaders were pushed into fresh zig-zags of policy, into theoretical improvisation to explain the problems that beset them, and into exploring more diverse forms of action and alliance. The sluggishness of revolution in Europe led them to consider, for the first time, whether Soviet military force might not be required to supplement – or even to lead – the efforts of foreign communists; the same disappointments brought them to encourage novel and sometimes startling forms of political alliance by their junior communist parties. During the period 1917–23 many subsequent elements of Soviet international policy and communist politics were rehearsed, at least in germ. They are explored in this and the following chapter.

### PERIODS, PHASES, TURNS

Just as communism's political alterations can only very approximately be described within the geometry of left and right, so divisions into periods are of little more help. It became conventional for communist (and some other) historiography to speak in terms of three primary 'periods' after 1917, followed by echoes or imitations of them: a revolutionary 'first period', merging from 1922–3 into a non-revolutionary 'second period' with greater stress on 'united front' tactics; and a 'third period' of renewed class struggle and revolutionary efforts from 1928. The popular front phase (1935–8/9) is then considered as a modification of the 'united front', the radicalism of 1939–41 and 1947–53 by analogy with the 'third period', and so on.

However, even the 'first period', 1917 to approximately 1923, contains fundamental variations – in the situations facing the young communist parties, in the internal conditions of the Soviet state and its international position, and in the rivalries and groupings of the Soviet leaders. In response to these changes Comintern leaders devised responses even more flexible and varied than those pioneered by the Russian party. In the first five years of Soviet power we encounter the prototypes of tactics and methods that have lasted far longer.

The main turning points were events bearing on the survival and security of the Soviet state. In outline, they were as follows:

- In the immediate aftermath of October 1917 the overwhelming problem was peace, or at least a breathing space, with Germany. The Treaty of Brest-Litovsk, in March 1918, secured this, at the cost of swallowing Bolshevik opposition to annexationist settlements and some Russian national pride.

- The unexpected collapse of Germany in the autumn of 1918 (followed by the failure of the German revolutionary movement in early 1919) created a quite new situation, in which the main threat to Soviet power was that of 'White' Russian forces and their backers among the Entente nations. The Comintern, formed in March 1919, was unable to propel the revolutions of that year in Central Europe to success, and served, during the first year of its life, mainly as a conduit for Bolshevik propaganda, aimed at overcoming their isolation by fomenting opposition on their enemies' home territory.

- However, by the beginning of 1920, the successes of the Bolsheviks' armies against the 'White' generals Denikin and Kolchak, and the reluctance of the Western Powers to become more than indirectly involved in the Russian civil war, brought a favourable lull, in which Soviet diplomatic initiatives aimed at breaching their economic isolation began to bear fruit.

- This period in turn, though, was ended by the Polish–Soviet war of the spring and summer of 1920. Its first phase, which raised the prospect of Red Army conquest extending communist power westward, coincided with the high point of Comintern's success among the mass socialist parties of Western Europe. But then, following Pilsudski's triumphant defence of Warsaw, Soviet power appeared newly vulnerable.

- The Bolsheviks took advantage of the restabilization of international relations following the Polish war to reinforce their position. March 1921 brought linked policies of economic relaxation (the replacement of 'war communism' by the New Economic Policy) and political repression – the crushing of the Kronstadt uprising and the ban on factions within the ruling party adopted by its Tenth Congress. The first months of 1921 also brought international accommodation, expressed in a series of treaty arrangements, of which the most important was the Anglo-Soviet trade agreement in March.

- By the treaty of Rapallo, in April 1922, the Soviet state frustrated the Western Powers' hopes of reducing her to dependency. By rebuilding her relations with Germany she returned to the company of European powers, and improved her prospects of economic and military recuperation.

- But increasing pressure from France over reparations payments led, in January 1923, to Poincaré's occupation of the Ruhr, opening a protracted political crisis in Germany. This culminated in the German communists' attempt at revolution (which was planned by the Soviet leaders, but which proved abortive) and in Hitler's attempted *putsch* in Bavaria.

During this period the Russian party, together with its juniors, were riven by divisions, both among their leaderships, and, to a lesser and diminishingly visible extent, their memberships. If, in giving accounts of events, I concentrate on the figures and policies who at the given moment had won out in internal party disputes, this should not be taken to imply that those disputes were not of consequence. While one can detect in the early years of the Comintern many of the processes that were to lead to the regimented unanimity of party life under Stalin, they were far from complete.


THE IMPORTANCE OF GERMANY

Many accounts of international communism start with its victory and early consolidation in Russia. However, the main focus in this and the following chapter is on the country in which it suffered its most important, repeated, and eventually conclusive defeats – Germany. This offers, in many respects, a better axis round which to organize a sketch of the problems that shaped Comintern's parties in *their* formative years. Geographically, politically and psychologically Germany stood at the centre of events. The Soviet rulers were accustomed to think of themselves as graduates of German Marxism, even if their teachers had forgotten what they once taught. Germany appeared to be the site for the classic Marxist proletarian revolution, the first night for which the October revolution had been but the dress rehearsal. It was to the German working class that they principally looked to rescue Soviet Russia, seeking now to decipher German struggles in terms not of 1848, but of their own February revolution, Kornilov coup, July days, and October victory.

As a result of defeat in the war, German society was subjected to an acute and protracted crisis and its technically modern economy to an inexorable and eventually catastrophic inflation. As a result political loyalties were thrown into turmoil, and a large minority of workers – employed as well as unemployed – gave a ready ear to revolutionary appeals. German politics became a European testbed for the innovations of both the left and – more successfully – the right. And enduring through the failures of the German revolution, the German state itself, though reduced by Versailles, could be perceived by the Bolsheviks as threat, bulwark or ally in the relations between them and the Western Powers. The weakness of the Russian and German states gave both of them an interest in reasserting a European balance of power against Versailles.

During the war and military rule it was the revolutionary wing of the German Social Democratic Party (SPD), led by Rosa Luxemburg and given a lone voice 'through the window of parliament' by Karl Liebknecht, which offered the most energetic internal resistance. Luxemburg's sympathy for Leninism went with distaste for its organizational methods; it was, as she pointed out, the centralism of their party caucus which disciplined the Socialist deputies, Liebknecht included, to vote unanimously for war credits in the Reichstag on 4 August 1914 and 'made it possible for a handful of parliamentarians to command this organism of four million people to about-face within twenty-four hours' (Angress, 1963, p. 11). Luxemburg exaggerated the effects of party discipline relative to the German patriotism and reformist caution of the party membership. But the sense that political discipline was a weapon that could be pointed in various directions was one that deeply conditioned the early history of German communism.

Even the most radical sections of German social democracy never adopted Lenin's drastic policy of 'revolutionary defeatism' – welcoming the defeat of one's own side. But the deaths, hardship and militarization brought by the war itself produced, by January 1917, a basic split in the SPD, placing Luxemburg's 'Spartacists' temporarily under the same roof as the pacifism of Kautsky and Bernstein, in the Independent Social Democratic Party (USPD) – a body averse, from the outset, to strong organization or powerful executive organs. The embryo of German communism thus approached the revolutionary crisis of November 1918 by healing, not deepening, the rift with the 'theoreticians of the swamp' – as Luxemburg excoriated Kautsky and his argument that the Second International was an essentially peacetime organization, that could not be expected to be effective in war (Salvadori, 1979, p. 186). Nor had the Germans anything resembling the Bolshevik's cohesive and long-standing party machine. When Trotsky, temporarily encouraged by the wave of anti-war strikes in Germany in January 1918, sought to spin out the negotiations at Brest-Litovsk with 'revolutionary phrase-making', the fact was that the leadership of the German revolutionary movement remained pitiably slender. Paradoxically the Bolsheviks, who set such great store by their own party organization for having achieved the Russian revolution, still sometimes looked direct to the spontaneity of the Western European working class to rescue it. And even when, at the end of 1918, the Spartacists split from the USPD to join with Karl Radek's Left Radicals and form a German Communist Party (the KPD (Spartacusbund)), the relationship of its central committee to local organizations was that of guidance, not command – poor equipment for a party already engaged in street battles.

It was not just internal organizational factors, though, which led the Spartacists to disaster in the uprising of January 1919. They looked to the workers' council movement as an alternative to parliamentary restabilization and as promising a German sequel to the Russian soviets. But the National Congress of Councils voted by a majority of eight to one in favour of elections to a national assembly, thereby nailing in place the first and most basic plank of the Weimar Republic. The majority of the workers' representatives were content with the fall of the Hohenzollerns and the political revolution it brought, and had no stomach for social revolution. The Communist Party leaders were tilted into a *putsch* they could neither lead nor control, with nothing like the nine months allowed the Bolsheviks to gestate their support in the soviets, and, even more important, with large, intact armed forces opposed to them. During their last days, in January 1919, Luxemburg and Liebknecht were attempting to lead a revolutionary uprising while sleeping in a different place each night, on the run from police who shortly caught and lynched them.

### THE FORMATION OF THE COMINTERN

The murders of Luxemburg and Liebknecht (and, shortly afterwards, Leo Jogiches, Luxemburg's companion and an earlier thorn in the Bolsheviks' side in their dealings with Kautsky) made the establishment of the Comintern, at its first congress in March 1919, a good deal easier. Luxemburg, when she lived, had resisted Radek's urgings to split from the USPD and form a communist party as premature and not reflecting mass support; shortly before she died she advised Hugo Eberlein, who in the event was the sole German Communist Party delegate at the congress, that the declaration of a new International should be postponed, for the same reasons. This was also the view of the surviving Communist Party leaders.

When he arrived in Moscow for the Congress – a gathering summoned in haste, as a response to a conference at Berne to re-form the Second International – Eberlein restated these objections: 'Real Communist parties exist in only a few countries, and most of these were created only in the last few weeks.' All of Western Europe was missing; the delegates from America and the Balkans did not represent their organizations. But why, Zinoviev retorted for the Russians, should the formation of a new International be postponed? 'You have a victorious revolution; that is more than a formal launching. In Germany you have a party that is striding towards power and that in a few months will form a proletarian government. And we are supposed to hesitate?' (Riddell, 1987, pp. 169–71). His words were underlined by reports of the upheavals in Central Europe, and Eberlein was persuaded to abstain, and accept a place of honour for his party on the Executive Committee of the new International. It did briefly seem from Moscow (as Zinoviev, now the Comintern's first president, put it on May Day 1919) that 'The movement is advancing so dizzyingly fast that one can say with certainty in a year's time we will already begin to forget there was a struggle for communism in Europe' (Degras, 1956–65, I, p. 51).

Yet Bela Kun's Hungarian Soviet Republic, and the Munich Soviet government, were soon beaten, and in Germany the Communist Party had almost no strength in the council movement and spent most of 1919 virtually outlawed. Paul Levi, the cultivated but uncharismatic intellectual who replaced Jogiches as 'first among equals' in its (still highly collective) leadership, attempted to put its ship in order, first by dealing with the 'ultra-left' and sometimes hooligan elements attracted by the party's involvement in violent struggles. The effect was a split away by the 'left', in August 1919, to form the Communist Workers Party (KAPD), reducing the KPD to a total membership of perhaps 50,000.

Politically, Levi achieved a significant shift of the Communist Party relative to the approach of its founding congress: agreement to participate in parliamentary elections and in the SPD-dominated trade unions. But it was an uncertain adjustment, and made on the defensive.

### COMMUNISM AND NATIONALISM

The breach with the KAPD also raised a recurring issue for communism in Germany and elsewhere, the tendency towards what was known as 'national bolshevism'. On one plane, this was the German form of a more general problem that faced (and faces) communists in many countries, especially underdeveloped and colonial ones – how, and how far, to make common cause with nationalists, especially the more radical among them. In Germany revolutionary nationalism arose in the context of an economically developed nation oppressed by military defeat, and its most successful strands, in terms of gathering mass support, merged to form National Socialism. But Germany was only one of many countries in which Soviet leaders and native communists experimented with overtures to nationalism. In the early 1920s they explored similar possibilities among the nationalists of China, Asia and the Middle East, and in 1925 Trotsky was urging the revolutionary significance of British national resentment against the usurping imperialist power of the United States. Such 'national Bolshevism' also made headway within the Soviet state, as the Bolshevik leaders summoned Russian nationalism to their aid. Subsequently, the appeal to nationalist emotions has become a commonplace of both ruling and non-ruling parties.

In Germany the Communist Party shared with almost the whole nation resentment at the peace terms imposed by the victorious powers, and the wish for a 'revision' of Versailles. Early Weimar governments however, and in particular the social democratic leaders, were bound to its acceptance. But on the far right, particularly among the officers and *Freikorps* detachments cast loose by the great reduction of the German army under the treaty's military provisions (forces who lent much of the support for national socialism), the call for 'revolutionary war' to restore Germany's frontiers was widely popular. Might not an alliance be possible? The Hamburg KPD leaders who split away to form the KAPD, Heinrich Laufenberg and Fritz Wolffheim, thought so, though their early efforts at unity in action with *Freikorps* groups brought few results (Angress, 1963, pp. 41–2).

Equally significant were certain emerging strands of Soviet policy (though at this stage there was little *direct* Comintern interference in the German party). During most of 1919 the inventive Karl Radek (kept in comfortable confinement in Berlin after the January fighting, and elected in his absence as the secretary of Comintern) was the main Soviet figure in Germany. Through his 'political salon' came figures from right across the political spectrum, making the contacts and flying the kites which two years later fertilized Soviet–German rapprochement and produced the treaty of Rapallo.

Radek drew from direct familiarity with the situation a much more cautious view of the imminence of German revolution than Bolsheviks in Moscow, and was thus already open to explorations for other alliances. When he returned to Russia in 1920 he became one of the earliest advocates of a protracted 'peaceful coexistence' with capitalist states. While Radek was in Berlin he also found ways to send counsel to the leaders of the German party, and it is perhaps significant that he (like Lenin) disapproved of Levi's readiness for a split with Laufenberg and Wolffheim, whose willingness to join with the nationalist right went hand in hand with traditionally 'leftist' preferences for armed action, and against participation in parliamentary elections or joining with social democrats in the trade unions.

The German party thus entered its next – and again unsought – battle, the so-called Kapp *putsch*, still with a hankering for the extremism of the minority. In March 1920 a section of the army command, led by officers who shared Ludendorff's absolute opposition to the Versailles settlement, attempted a coup in Berlin; it was the first appearance in action of the swastika, which some units took as their emblem. Though Ebert's SPD-led government was forced briefly to flee Berlin, the coup was immediately contained, and shortly routed, by the large support for the general strike called by the trade union leaders.

The communist leadership, disoriented, and with Levi in gaol, wavered catastrophically. Initially they opposed the strike, called for the overthrow of the government ('a threadbare mask for the dictatorship of the bourgeoisie') – though remembering also to call for the defeat of the putschists – and made propaganda gestures towards raising a 'Red Army'. But as communist workers joined the strike, and with the *putsch* about to collapse, the leadership shifted, to declare that they would be a 'loyal opposition' to the socialist government (Lazitch and Drachkovitch, 1972, I, p. 247). The only serious fighting took place after the coup's collapse, in the Ruhr, where a 'Red Army of the Ruhr' did spring up. It was, however, put down by the main army command, which had cautiously stood aside from the *putsch* and now, rejoining forces with the government as its rescuer, took its place as the main power behind the scenes of Weimar politics. The Communist Party's conduct was not simply 'leftist'; at the Second Comintern Congress in August a syndicalist delegate was able to make the telling point that: 'Those who defend parliamentarism here are those gentlemen who tried to call off the general strike during the Kapp week in Germany' (Communist International, 1977, vol. 2, p. 37).

The initial reaction of the Soviet leadership, however, was equally inept. *Izvestia* urged German workers not to 'raise a finger' in response to the general strike call. 'To the working class both the constitutional government and a dictatorship by the generals are only different political forms of economic autocracy by the bourgeoisie.' For German workers military dictatorship would be (as White generals had been for Russians) a 'hard, bloody but efficacious' school, bringing communist victory nearer. *Pravda* added that the putschists had conspired in advance with Ebert's government, while Radek commented that the rule of rightist officers opposed to Versailles would obviously bring the Soviet state 'an enormous improvement in her international position' (Ascher, 1966–7, pp. 428–9).

This last factor came to have a new, more permanent significance in the first part of 1920. As the civil war turned in the Bolsheviks' favour, but the European revolution failed to eventuate, the prospect stretched much further into the future that the first workers' state would need to coexist for some time within a more-or-less settled system of states, many of them potentially hostile. The resumption of external exchanges, aimed principally at ending economic isolation, was therefore combined with an alertness to any opportunities that might offer the Soviet republic a safer position within the European state system.

Such a possibility soon arose, during the Soviet–Polish war of 1920, and the Soviet leaders' responses when presented with it rehearsed many future events. The Entente powers had sponsored Polish nationalism in interposing a Polish state between Russia and Germany, and hostile to both. The new Poland involved sizeable subtraction from Germany, and it was detested as the keystone of the victory settlement. Any threat to Poland was therefore enthusiastically welcomed in Germany. After the German armies interposed between Russia and Poland withdrew in February 1919, frontier skirmishes between Polish and Red Army forces escalated, in April 1920, into an offensive by Pilsudski's armies, which penetrated deep into the Ukraine. But, by capturing Kiev, the Poles overreached themselves; from June the Red Armies regained the initiative and began a long offensive until they converged on Warsaw in early August, while the second Congress of Comintern was in session. Pilsudski's Poland suddenly appeared highly vulnerable. If it, or part of it, could be federated to the Soviet Union, or placed under a pro-Bolshevik government, would not that represent an enormous gain for Soviet security? The Red Armies' success raised the question (as Zinoviev, in an excess of directness, was later to put it) of 'whether a victorious workers' republic could carry socialism into other countries at the point of bayonets' (Ascher, 1966–7). This prospect combined with a cooling of hopes in the European revolution (though they were by no means yet extinct) to produce three momentous new developments in Soviet international policy.

The first was a more-or-less plain willingness to conquer and sovietize other nations from the outside. As Soviet forces penetrated into eastern Poland, Tukhachevsky's orders of the day dropped all reference to Polish self-determination, and proclaimed far wider ambitions. 'To the West!' was the battle-cry: 'Over the corpse of White Poland shines the road to worldwide conflagration. On our bayonets we shall bring happiness and peace to toiling humanity!' (Davies, 1972, p. 145).

The second was the expendability of foreign parties. The Polish Communist Party had been formed in December 1918. From the beginning it stood for Poland's absorption into the Soviet Socialist Republic – in the tradition of the anti-nationalist wing of Polish socialism associated with Rosa Luxemburg. By early 1919 it had considerable support in industrial areas, but the surge of Polish nationalism during the war largely destroyed it behind Pilsudski's lines, so that its only effective portion was travelling on the heels of the Red Army. In a striking preview of Stalin's similar action in 1938, it was then wound up as an independent party and in its place was formed the Polish Bureau of the *Russian* Communist Party. The new agency (formed on the opening day of the Comintern's Second Congress) was chaired by the first head of the Cheka, the Polish nobleman Felix Dzerzhinsky – a long-standing critic of Lenin's arguments for self-determination for the peoples of the Russian empire. Dzerzhinsky promptly ordered all Poles among his Chekists transferred to the Polish front under his direction. His very appointment, as well as such methods, testified to the slender support for Soviet forces – despite a colossal propaganda effort – once they were on Polish soil.

The third element of Soviet policy was more surreptitious. As Poland wobbled, so did the whole Versailles settlement. The two main beneficiaries of its disintegration would be German nationalism and Soviet Russia. Might it not be possible to contemplate their combination? During the summer of 1920 a number of covert 'feelers' were extended from Trotsky's entourage, exploring the possibilities for joint military action to dismember Poland and restore Germany's eastern frontier of 1914; the rump of the Polish state would then have been annexed or attached to Russia. The main target of these approaches was General Hans von Seeckt, now head of the Reichswehr and a major influence on foreign policy – the most senior of those many German officers who, while having no intention of tolerating Bolshevism at home, looked to an alliance with Russia to free Germany from the consequences of defeat in 1918. (Seeckt subsequently acted as military adviser to Chiang Kai-shek, devising the 'encirclement' campaign that finally destroyed the south China soviets and forced Chinese communism on its Long March.) However, before Soviet overtures to Seeckt could produce any substantial results, Pilsudski had rallied his forces and, in the Poles' much-prayed-for 'Miracle on the Vistula', routed the Red Armies outside Warsaw; the ensuing armistice and treaty stabilized Poland's frontiers until August 1939.

But such a strategy also required wider political forces within Germany, and this gave rise to the fourth prong of Soviet policy: joint action of the communists with militant nationalism – prototype of the sort of 'front' that was later to be so widely employed in underdeveloped and colonial countries. Lenin produced a justification for this in the notion that the Versailles treaty had made the Germans into a colonial people – and the Soviet republic was the only force capable of combating colonialism. Thus (as he reflected a few months afterwards), 'this situation has led to a political mix up in Germany: the German Black Hundreds sympathise with the Russian Bolsheviks in the same way as the Spartacus League does. This can well be understood because it derives from economic causes, and it is the basis of the entire economic situation and of our foreign policy' (Lenin, 1960–78, 31, p. 475). There was, in fact, a good measure of support for the Red Army from nationalists and *Freikorps* officers in Upper Silesia and other areas of German population within the Polish frontiers during August 1920, though how far this was coordinated is unclear.

Little or nothing was visible at the time of these more audacious schemes. The new thrust of policy was covert, and was in any case aborted by military defeat. Since, in addition, leaders may be divided on eventual goals while agreeing on concrete steps, it is difficult to put precise limits to the strategy of 'revolution by conquest' which began to germinate in the window of opportunity opened up by their military successes. The approaches and contacts which had been made during the Polish war did, however, very shortly bear fruit. The Soviet representative Kopp, through his contacts in Berlin, became the intermediary in arranging for Germany's clandestine manufacture and testing of weaponry in Russia (thus escaping the military provisions of Versailles), in return for Reichswehr officers giving training to the Red Army. This secret military collaboration, beginning in 1921, in turn paved the way for Russia's diplomatic 'breakout' and agreement with Germany at Rapallo in April 1922.

The Polish war illustrates a further point of great long-term significance: the continuum that connects the transformation of societies by armed force from within – revolution – to their transformation by armed force from outside – conquest. Somewhat as, when people join in society, it proves impossible for the political theorist to draw any absolute distinction between needs and desires, so, for a Soviet state embroiled in dangerous international relations, survival merged easily into expansion. The desperate struggles of the civil wars naturally produced, once the danger had passed, an appetite for moves which could enhance future safety – and the most obvious of these was to secure additional, preferably communist-ruled, territories on Russia's borders. This goal – if not the means – coincided with the purposes of the international communist movement, and foreign communists readily embraced it. Zinoviev described how the delegates to the Second Comintern Congress gathered eagerly each morning before the map showing the advance of the Red Armies into Poland:

It was a sort of symbol: the best representatives of the international proletariat with breathless interest, with palpitating heart, followed every advance of our armies, and all perfectly realised that, if the military aim set by our army was achieved, it would mean an immense acceleration of the international proletarian revolution. (Carr, 1977, III, p. 192)

However, after the short-lived euphoria, the Soviet leaders also recognized the deradicalizing effects of Russian bayonets. By the time they reached Warsaw, reflected Lenin, our troops were exhausted, 'whereas the Polish troops, supported by a wave of patriotism in Warsaw, and with a feeling [sic] that they were now on their own soil' rallied to defeat them (Lenin,

1960–78, 31, p. 302). Tukhachevsky regretted that 'class reinforcement' (by which he meant recruitment to his revolutionary armies from territory they had already conquered) had proved a failure in Poland.

## THE SECOND COMINTERN CONGRESS

The triumph of Soviet arms determined the mood of the Second Congress of Comintern, in July–August 1920, the high-point in that organization's self-confidence. Up to that time the German party, it is true, had in a sense represented Bolshevism's influence in Germany, but its relations with the Third International were essentially bilateral ones in which it was treated as a junior equal of the Russian party. The Second Congress, however, set about ordering relations between the International and its national sections (or would-be sections) in a more authoritative manner. The time was ripe for this. A large number of parties and groupings had established relations with Comintern since the First Congress, and the problems which now absorbed it were not immediately those of defending the Soviet republic but of extending the world revolution. The large socialist parties of Italy and France were represented. From Germany the Communist Party KPD representatives were accompanied by 'consultative' delegates from the KAPD (who had split from them) and the USPD (from whose 'left' the KPD had earlier split); this was a source of some chagrin to Levi, heading the KPD delegation, who felt that the Russians in Comintern were arranging remarriages with inadequate affinity or consultation. The robust embryos of communist organizations attended from many other countries, while Britain and the US each contributed several small competing sects.

The general problem which the Congress confronted was one of leaders and masses. There undeniably existed, in the Western European socialist movements, widespread radical, arguably revolutionary, aspirations, together with a considerable reservoir of sympathy for the Bolshevik revolution. However the leaders of these movements tended to be reformist politicians explicitly hostile to Bolshevism, or 'centrists', whose attitude towards Bolshevism was only ambiguously sympathetic, and whose approach to revolution was at best indecisive. The mass of the members, deeply attached to their organizations, remained under the sway of such leaders. How to detach the former from the latter?

The Bolsheviks were not so naive as to believe what their utterances sometimes suggested: that the European workers lagged behind them *purely* through the machinations of the 'social traitors' or 'centrists'; they sought also a broader sociological explanation. The doctrine which Lenin advanced had similarities with the account he had earlier given of the ubiquitous 'economism' that caused *Iskra*, and later the Bolsheviks, to evolve their particular approach to politics: workers naturally inclined, left to their own devices, to concentrate on, and organize for, more immediate bread-and-butter demands, and on the basis of trade union outlooks; *political* consciousness had to be brought, even injected, into them from the outside, by trained social democratic agitators. However, in Western Europe the dilemma recurred on a higher plane. Many workers *were* politically organized and, in a real if stereotyped sense, 'conscious'; they had, after all, accomplished the central political goal of many Russian revolutionaries, a parliament and general suffrage. The trouble was that their politics were not, or were only partly, revolutionary; even workers highly sympathetic to Soviet Russia often remained attached to the institutions of the 'democratic counter-revolution' (as the Comintern termed, in particular, the recovery of the German republic under the Weimar coalition) and to the modest but tangible benefits it promised them.

A convenient explanation for this, however, lay already to hand in the official theoretical corpus. Engels, developing a remark of Marx, had already explained how 'a privileged minority' of England's working class had come to share in capitalism's prosperity. Lenin developed this idea further. In *Imperialism, the Highest Stage of Capitalism* (1916) he connected the corruption of a part of the working class out of the 'super-profits' of imperialism with the development of revisionism and reformism among the leaders of European social democracy, and, specifically, their shameful support for their 'own' bourgeoisies in the war. Thus evolved the Leninist theory of the *labour aristocracy*.* A portion of the workers' movement was 'bought' by capitalism, and acted as its ideological agency within the broader working class – though it was often unclear whether it was merely political leaders who were so bought, or whether the concept referred to the larger strata of skilled, better-paid workers who formed the basis of reformist socialism. Where Lenin's original doctrine treated all workers as intrinsically 'bourgeois', but merely in their political *limitations*, Leninists now saw a decadent bourgeois society prolonging its life by disabling from within the political life and organizations of the proletariat.

Such a theory helped Comintern respond to some of the main difficulties it faced. It held that mass support for communism was out there in Western Europe, waiting to be used; the evidence lay in the fact that large parties attended upon Comintern, reflecting the pressure of a radical membership upon pliant leaders. This potential support needed only to be freed of its attachment to the 'social traitors'. But for this deft surgery was needed – the

* Elements of the theory emerged earlier. For example, in 1907 Lenin explained how 'The British bourgeoisie, for example, derives more profit from the many millions of the population of India and other colonies than from the British workers. In certain countries this provides the material and economic basis for infecting the proletariat with colonial chauvinism. Of course, this may be only a temporary phenomenon . . .' (Lenin, 1960–78, 13, p. 77).

large parties, and particularly those where 'centrists' held sway in the leadership, were to be split down ideologically appropriate lines of fissure, yielding communist parties of both mass proportions and proper revolutionary determination, and hence effective in the expected upheavals. Lenin accordingly presented the Second Congress with a list of nineteen conditions to be applied to all parties wishing to be members of Comintern. Provocatively, the conditions were to apply not only to those who now sought admission (such as the USPD) but also to those large parties, such as the Italian Socialist Party, which had already affiliated, but without expecting to be subjected to serious discipline. Lenin's conditions required *communist* parties, *inter alia*: to call themselves that; to 'methodically remove reformists and centrists from every responsible post in the labour movement'; to form an underground apparatus; to operate on the basis of democratic centralism; and to obey the directives of Comintern.

In the spirit of the new sectarianism speakers at the Second Congress vied with each other to distance themselves from undesirable allies. While Zinoviev drew a theoretical distinction between the right wing of the European labour movement ('the dog Noske'), and the centre (personified in 'the renegade Kautsky'), it was the latter who presented the greatest difficulties to advantageous separations, and who drew the most venom. At the beginning of discussion two further conditions were proposed by the Italian 'left' communist Amadeo Bordiga (and accepted by the other Comintern leaders), the second of which provided a copper-bottomed guarantee of splits: party members who opposed the conditions were themselves to be expelled.

## APPLYING THE TWENTY-ONE CONDITIONS

The 'twenty-one conditions' thus assembled, the delegates departed armed (or, as some felt, saddled) with them to put their national parties to the test. In codifying Comintern's character as Bolshevism writ large, the Second Congress also re-echoed the 1903 debate on conditions of party membership, but as a higher twist of the spiral. It was now not individuals, but parties commanding millions of votes, who were required to show really professional revolutionary credentials. Since parties were not indivisible, but heterogeneous aggregates, they would generally have to split to qualify. The lines of division emanating from the Second Congress thus extended the enmities between Bolshevism and Menshevism internationally – as did the methods, for Comintern inherited in full measure Bolshevism's approach to ideological struggle as warfare, not debate.

The first major application of the 'twenty-one conditions' was to the German Independent Socialist Party (USPD), culminating at its congress at

Halle in October 1920. The campaign in Germany was also the most successful for Comintern's leaders, since it took place at a time when Soviet military successes and predictions of revolution still dominated the climate; coming later, the congresses, and then splits, in the French, and even more the Italian, socialist parties gave them less cause for self-congratulation.

However it was not a question of simply presenting the 'twenty-one conditions' to the Halle congress. The USPD's four delegates to Comintern had been split two:two on joining, but political alignments within the party – or any other large socialist party – by no means fell neatly into the 'left', 'centre' and 'right' categories of Comintern, and it therefore became a matter of fine judgement – on which the German communist leaders were closely consulted – precisely where the line should be drawn. As Levi (who, with Radek, pulled many of the behind-the-scenes wires for the congress) explained, it was a question of admitting some of the more left 'centrists', and not others. The fact that the result of the crucial vote was determined, through the selection of delegates, before the congress met, did nothing to diminish the display of rhetoric. Zinoviev, who attended as the Comintern's chief official spokesman, was opposed, from the USDP, by Rudolf Hilferding – supported by Martov, newly released from Russia. Zinoviev outdid himself in a four-hour peroration in imperfect but fluent German, taking as his premise that the Western European bourgeoisie was seated on a powderkeg, insulated only by 'social treachery':

The situation is this. The working class is already strong enough to knock over the bourgeoisie by, say, tomorrow morning – if we all stand together and firmly support communism. If the workers are still slaves, the only reason is that we have not shaken off the accursed legacy of that foul ideology within our own ranks . . . (Wolfe, 1981, p. 169)

A clear majority of delegates – 236 to 150 – voted for the Comintern, and there was an immediate split. But the rank-and-file membership proved more attached to the political 'centre' – and the USPD's trade union connections – than the delegates, and the party's voters even more so. Of the USPD's 900,000 members, less than a third joined the Communist Party at the December unification congress, and in elections in February 1921 the two parties divided the far left vote almost exactly equally. Even with these qualifications to its success, however, the German party was now enlarged from about 80,000 to about 350,000 members, and was well on the way to being a mass organization; only the Russian Communist Party, with almost 750,000 members, was larger. None the less, by far the largest vote – and the main trade union links – remained with the SPD, and by autumn 1922 the USPD minority had merged back into the SPD to produce a party of about 1,300,000.

Elsewhere, the splitting strategy produced mixed, and often rather unsuccessful, results. In France, as a victor nation, the Socialist Party underwent no substantial split in the war, though pacifist and radical currents developed an increasing hostility towards *l'union sacrée*. A central preoccupation for the Russian leaders during 1920 was how to separate the revolutionary wheat from the centrist chaff among the varied figures of French socialism who made their pilgrimage towards Moscow. The main pair eventually selected were the experienced and flexible academic and parliamentarian, Marcel Cachin, an apprentice of Guesde, and the young schoolteacher Louis Frossard. The main dilemma was the large centrist grouping, which favoured dialogue with Comintern, but also supported steps to reconstruct the Second International, and was inconveniently led by Jean Longuet, Karl Marx's grandson. The centre's support was, however, gradually eroded, and Longuet himself was isolated, with the result that at the Tours congress, at the end of 1920, two-thirds of the votes went for acceptance of the twenty-one conditions, leaving Leon Blum's straight-forwardly anti-Bolshevik current in a very small minority. The price of this success, however, was that the renamed Communist Party contained a very high proportion of members whose conversion to Comintern and its principles was recent and uncertain; it remained firmly rooted in French socialist tradition, and gave Comintern problems from the moment of its birth. The situation engendered a native pleasantry about the twenty-second condition: that the preceding twenty-one were optional.

The Italian Communist Party was, at its birth, the most sectarian of all. When the Socialist Party met in Livorno's Goldoni Theatre, in January 1921, to review its membership of Comintern in the light of the Second Congress, the expectation that Soviet military triumphs could ignite Europe had long passed. So too had the strikes and factory occupations which gripped northern Italy in the summer of 1920, though Lenin and the Russian leaders of Comintern continued to declare the country ripe for revolution, held back only by the lack of a united and determined communist party. The Italian Socialist Party, which had been affiliated to Comintern since March 1919, was a coalition of currents, with the *Ordine Nuovo* grouping in Turin, favoured by the Comintern leaders, in a small minority.

The Russian leaders thus posed the make-or-break issue, on the basis of the twenty-one points, as whether or not the preponderant 'left' grouping, headed by the able but liberal-minded Comintern Executive member Giacinto Serrati, would expel the reformist minority of Turati, the main culprit (in the Comintern's view) holding back the Italian proletariat from socialist revolution. Serrati was unwilling to accept such an amputation, nor did the Italian revolution seem as imminent to him in Milan as it did from Moscow. This sealed Moscow's view of him; when Longuet reported Serrati's doubts to Zinoviev in October 1920, the response was: 'Then

Serrati is a traitor too' (Lazitch and Drachkovitch, 1972, I, p. 451). Connection with him was, accordingly, also to be severed, and Lenin's unofficial Russian agents within the PSI worked vigorously to prepare the ground. As Tranquilli, the communist youth leader who opened the Livorno congress with 'fraternal' greetings declared, they were there 'to burn the effigy of unity' (Spriano, 1967, p. 107).

However, matters were handled on the spot, and the ukase against Serrati was delivered, by two second-string and somewhat inept Comintern emissaries nominated by Zinoviev, the Bulgarian Khristo Kabakchiev and the subsequent chief of communist Hungary, Matyas Rakosi, neither of whom spoke Italian. The former delivered, verbatim, a speech of twenty-six typed pages entirely devoted to attacking Serrati. Zinoviev later deplored the resulting *commedia del partito*: the congress 'was transformed literally into a circus. When Kabakchiev spoke, they shouted "Long live the Pope!" Someone released a dove, and there were unheard-of displays of chauvinism. Then everyone blamed Kabakchiev' (Spriano, 1967, p. 111). Of the chief figures of Italian communism, Bordiga made himself the most prominent instrument of the Comintern line; Gramsci spoke little, and Togliatti was not at Livorno. In the result the communists collected only a third of the delegates' votes (and this proved to reflect even less in terms of grass-roots support). Defiant, they marched out, singing the *Internationale*, to Livorno's other theatre, where they formed a new communist party. The split – which was later deepened by the communists' refusal to accept Comintern's shift to 'united front' tactics with the socialists in early 1922 – did not begin to be healed until the autumn of 1922, after Mussolini's coup. Radek's judgement at the time was that the Livorno 'cleavage' had 'greatly worsened the prospects for revolution. . . . Our having a Communist party in Italy is an illusion' (Lazitch and Drachkovitch, 1972, I, p. 459).

OTHER PARTIES

The fiasco at Livorno also sowed the seeds of Paul Levi's subsequent disgrace in the German party. Levi, an unofficial but naturally influential visitor at Livorno, had attempted to mediate, and even to stiffen Serrati against the Comintern representatives. Irate, Rakosi and Kabakchiev paused in Berlin on their return journey from Livorno and obtained a vote censuring Levi from the German party leadership. Rakosi's opinion was that the German party had 'become far too big', and, like the Italian, required improvement by purging (Carr, 1977, III, pp. 334, 387). Levi's deposition began the German party's slide into the 'theory of the offensive', culminating in the disastrous 'action' of March 1921.

But matters were not always so difficult as in Italy. In Kabakchiev's native (and traditionally pro-Russian) Bulgaria the more radical majority of the large Social Democratic Party (the 'Narrow' faction) converted itself, shortly after the First Comintern Congress, into the Bulgarian Communist Party. It was overwhelmingly larger than the residual social democratic organization; its main rival was the powerful Peasant Party, which commanded a parliamentary majority. However, the Bulgarian communists were deeply conditioned by their pre-war history as 'Narrow' socialists under Dimiter Blagoev, with his longstanding and somewhat doctrinaire opposition to 'petit bourgeois' contaminations of socialism, and they proved unable to devise effective tactics towards the Agrarians.

The other mass communist party – exceeded in size only by the German – which took shape in Europe after the war was in Czechoslovakia, where support for Comintern grew steadily within the well-established social democratic movements, especially in the Czech lands. But communism initially developed as separate national organizations – Czech, German and Slovak – and only in 1921 were these able to report a timetable for fusion to Comintern. Certain other sizeable socialist parties had only a fleeting relationship with Comintern: the nonconformist Norwegian Labour Party declined at first to change its name or properly to subordinate itself to the Comintern Executive, and in late 1923 departed altogether.

Elsewhere the picture was one of much smaller bodies flailing (or nibbling) ineffectually at larger social democratic parties. The British Communist Party was at last assembled from a number of small groupings in August 1920 (it was later joined by a minority faction from the Independent Labour Party). It had no immediate hope of splitting the Labour Party, and therefore sought to join it. But its application for affiliation was overwhelmingly rebuffed at the 1921 Brighton conference, and ever since then communist activity inside the Labour Party has been covert. In the United States no large political party of the labour movement existed, and the founding convention for a US Communist Party, in Chicago in September 1919, attracted mainly sects and nationally or linguistically particularist organizations. Its outcome was two communist parties, headed, respectively, by the young intellectual John Reed and the Italian immigrant Louis Fraina. It took some years before Comintern was able successfully to regulate at a distance the byzantine internal affairs of communism in the largest capitalist nation.

## CHOOSING COMMUNIST LEADERS

The international strategy of party splitting and assembling launched in 1920 was justified mainly through a distinction between members and their reformist or vacillating leaders. But leaders proved agile and the separation was difficult to make in practice; and because of the nature of political machines Comintern was frequently obliged to engage with the socialist parties on which it had set its sights by allying with, or employing, leaders whose records and credentials were less than ideal. The main litmus test was still officially considered to be a socialist's stance towards the war. Yet Antonio Gramsci, the brains of the *Ordine Nuovo* group in Turin, and later leader of the Italian Communist Party, had enthused over Mussolini's belligerent nationalism early in the war. The record of Walter Stoecker, the USPD delegate to Comintern in 1920, who became co-chairman of the German Communist Party in early 1921, on Levi's fall, was that of a definite 'social chauvinist'.

Marcel Cachin, who proved the more dependable of the two French delegates who returned from the Second Comintern Congress to win their Socialist Party for communism, should certainly have been rejected outright if his attitude to the war had been a serious criterion. He began the war as a vociferous 'social patriot', and travelled to Russia in March 1917 in a delegation of socialists (which included Plekhanov) sent by the Allied governments to reinvigorate the Russian war effort (Sukhanov, 1984, pp. 260–3). He was responsible for channelling French government money to finance Mussolini's nationalist-socialist *Il Popolo d'Italia* and its campaign for Italian intervention on the side of the Entente. Though he adapted somewhat to anti-war sentiment, as late as 1918 he still remained fervently anti-Bolshevik, in indignation at the advantages to Germany of the Treaty of Brest-Litovsk. Service with Comintern, however, finally stabilized Cachin's loyalties, and he remained an adhesively loyal leader of the French Communist Party from its formation to his death in 1958.

The general problem was that subordination of local 'sections' to a remote 'world party' tended to alienate or weaken the more independent-minded national leaders, leaving a heavier reliance on pliable men of the machine, epitomized by such as Cachin. When a French socialist meets such men as the Russian leaders, he informed his comrades in 1920, 'He has lessons to take; he has none to give' (Mortimer, 1984, p. 60). In addition, in mid and late 1920 the Soviet state appeared to be riding a successful wave, and to have a real possibility of carrying Bolshevism into Europe. Consequently the support gathered for Comintern also included many seasoned political appetites excited by the prospect of power.

FURTHER READING

Schorske (1983) is an excellent account of German social democracy in the years up to 1917. Angress (1963) treats German communism up to the defeat of 1923, and Fowkes (1984), in less detail, up to Hitler's victory in 1933. Riddell (1986), one of a series of volumes of documents on the Communist International in Lenin's lifetime, covers the 1918–19 German revolution. Volume 3 of Carr's *The Bolshevik Revolution* (1977) (which spans 1917–23) discusses the German Communist Party in some detail. Nettl (1966) is still the best biography of Rosa Luxemburg; Tuck (1988) is a biography of Radek.

Treatments of the formation and early years of a number of other communist parties are in: Wohl (1966) on France; Cammett (1967) and Clark (1977) on Italy; Kendall (1969) and Dewar (1976) on Britain; Banac (1983) on Eastern Europe; and Draper (1966) and Howe and Coser (1958) on the United States. Several of the essays in Wolfe (1981) are also relevant.

The civil war in Russia is treated in Mawdsley (1987), and the Polish–Soviet war of 1920 in Davies (1972). Degras's (1956–65) three-volume selection of documents, with commentary, covers the lifetime of Comintern (1919–43); Adler (1983) and Trotsky (1973) cover the earlier years. Ridell (1987) deals with the First Congress (1919), while the proceedings of the Second Congress (1920) are translated (Communist International, 1977). Debo (1979) is an account of Soviet foreign policy in 1918–19.

# 4

## United fronts

Within a short time of the Second Congress, from early 1921, the world communist movement – for such it was now beginning to be – embarked on a cautious and uneven, but none the less fundamental, political turn: towards 'united fronts'. The frictions and contradictions of this shift are very visible in Germany, and highlight the difficulties of trying to understand the evolution of Comintern's politics within the geometry of 'left' and 'right'. Within the Russian Communist Party disagreements and factional divisions were undergoing a complex process of realignment, as the Russian leaders adjusted to the expectation that they would remain in power, but isolated by the delay of the European revolution. Even as, in 1920–1, they laboured to impose their Bolshevik discipline on the newborn sections of Comintern, that same discipline was being fractured and undermined in the highest reaches of the Russian party. Yet as often as not, this paradoxical situation merely intensified the vigour with which Comintern demanded obedience of its non-Russian sections.

### SOVIET RETRENCHMENT

The underlying causes of the great political 'turn' of 1921 lay in the situation of the Soviet state. The defeat of the Red Army outside Warsaw in August 1920, followed by its long retreat, signalled the end of the civil wars; by the Treaty of Riga the Soviet republic accepted unambitious Polish frontiers and put the prospect of carrying the revolution westwards with bayonets into cold storage. Radical and revolutionary foment in Europe waned. Within Russia the economic and political stresses of 'war communism' converged in a crisis. In February–March 1921 strikes spread through Petrograd, and the soviet of the Kronstadt naval fortress (previously a citadel of revolutionary fervour) openly defied the Bolshevik monopoly of power. Trotsky took personal charge of the suppression and slaughter of the Kronstadt 'rebels', but the general situation required a retreat. At the Tenth Russian Party Congress the Bolshevik leaders tightened their political monopoly, but introduced a comprehensive change of economic course, with widespread reintroduction of markets – the 'New Economic Policy'. They also opted for an altered diplomatic perspective – cultivating stable relations with those foreign powers who could be persuaded to countenance 'peaceful coexistence'. To the political and military importance of doing this was added the now very urgent necessity of trade and industrial equipment from abroad to repair Russia's war-torn economy – a task central to the thinking behind NEP.

Counsels divided. As with Brest-Litovsk the advocates of a more sedate realism found their proposed adjustments running into a 'left-wing' resistance which had no difficulty in appealing to the revolutionary absolutism in Bolshevism's history. This was exacerbated by the fact that communism outside Russia had attracted many whose principal enthusiasm was for revolution, and who despised parliamentary representation and all the practices of political life, with its trimming and combinations. Thus, for example, a KAPD pamphlet of 1920 castigated the German Communist Party not only for its parliamentarism but simply for being 'a political party'. In fact, a significant fraction of Comintern's foreign support before 1921 came from revolutionaries who were more anarchist or syndicalist than Marxist. The zenith of the 'left' current in Comintern came in 1920, when it achieved, through the Comintern offices in Amsterdam and Vienna, a degree of international linkage, and it remained a considerable pressure in 1921.

Matters were complicated also by the fact that the instruments of Soviet policy were still developing the division of labour necessary for an essentially two-pronged approach. The Soviet Ministry of Foreign affairs, headed, after Trotsky's brief tenure, by the career diplomat-turned-communist Boris Chicherin, took as its business the nurturance of sober, and if possible constructive, relations with foreign states, while Comintern, under the inflammatory Zinoviev, existed to overthrow the governments with which Chicherin's neophyte diplomats were seeking to negotiate. This obviously generated dilemmas, to which the separation of state diplomacy from the Comintern in terms of organizations and personnel, and Chicherin's diplomatic denials that the exhortations of Comintern were congruent with the attitude of the Soviet state, offered but formal and implausible solutions. Yet, although the enemies of communism were often not confused, its own leaders sometimes could be – and this, added to the political and tactical differences among leading communists, made it quite possible for Comintern and its national sections to get their wires crossed.

## THE 'MARCH ACTION'

This appears to have been what befell the German Communist Party in the spring of 1921. At the beginning of the year Paul Levi, prompted by Radek and attempting to head off the pressure on him from the left of the German party, caused the party press to publish an 'Open Letter' to the German left. This reiterated the communist goal of the dictatorship of the proletariat, but more concretely it proposed joint action on the wretched economic position of the workers, and the formation of joint defence organizations. Levi's initiative foreshadowed the later united front tactics, but he made the mistake of being right too soon. Moreover the Open Letter was rejected by the rest of the German left, from the SPD, which refused all dealings with the KPD, to the KAPD which denounced it as opportunism, and it weakened Levi's position *vis-à-vis* the left in his own party leadership, which shortly afterwards removed him for his role at the Italian Socialist Party congress. The new German party leadership thus remained committed to a go-it-alone stance, and was inclined to seek early opportunities for action.

Into this situation, at the beginning of March, arrived a clandestine trio of Comintern emissaries, instructed by Zinoviev, but apparently without consultation with the other leaders of the Russian party. It was led by Bela Kun, the sanguinary chief of the short-lived Hungarian soviet republic of 1919, and, since his flight from Budapest, a roving Comintern agent. Bela Kun immediately engaged in discussions, amounting to briefings, with members of the German Communist Party's central committee, the gist of which was that they should make an early bid for power, and that if a suitable occasion did not present itself soon, then one should be created. These urgings combined with the local growth – and somewhat amateurish preparations – of illegal armed units of the party, formed in accordance with the policies laid down at the Second Comintern Congress, but, owing to the necessary opacities of clandestine activity, often not known to, and not under the close control of, the national leadership.

The police and military authorities, in turn, were aware in general terms of these armed units, and of the party leadership's discussion of a revolutionary attempt, and were themselves actively preparing for a trial of strength. They thus – probably unintentionally – triggered the party's own preparations, and did so before they were ripe. On 16 March, after bombs had been discovered and clashes had taken place between police and miners in communist strongholds, the government announced the occupation of the area round Halle. In reply the party's national leadership issued a call to insurrection. Fighting erupted in several areas but was contained within a week; the party's attempt, at that point, to call a general strike was an almost complete failure, which resulted only in many communist workers losing their jobs. Only in central Germany did the rising present the government with a severe test, and there much of the actual fighting was led by non-communist freelance revolutionaries, such as the colourful Max Hoelz. For the German party and thus for the communist movement as a whole the 'March action' was a very substantial defeat – though this was only reluctantly recognized by the party leaders. The episode lost the party almost half its members within a few months, and carved lasting and acrimonious divisions into its leadership. Levi, aghast at what had happened, published his outspoken criticisms, and was expelled.

Yet even as the *putsch* was being prepared, so was its repudiation. In November 1920 Lenin had explained that the restabilized international situation following the Polish war had given the Soviet state 'the right to our fundamental international existence in the network of capitalist states'; at the same time he began to signal a shift away from international revolution (Lenin, 1960–78, 31, pp. 408–15). The retrenchment which the Russian leaders were carrying out on both domestic and international fronts took clear form in March 1921, when the Kronstadt revolt was followed by the NEP and the quest for much broader economic relations with the West. On the diplomatic front treaties with Poland, Persia and Afghanistan in February were followed in March by agreements with Turkey and Britain; by the last of these the Soviet government undertook, in return for trading rights, to abstain from all direct or indirect propaganda against British imperialism. World revolution was coming to be seen, as Trotsky had it, in terms not of weeks or months, but years.

Comintern absorbed the implications of this at its Third Congress, held in Moscow in June–July 1921, and delivered an ambiguous reprimand to the Germans. The Russian leaders (who, having argued their differences in the 'caucus' of the Politburo beforehand, now all adhered to the line proposed by Lenin) faced the delicate task of confirming the German party's expulsion of Levi, while adopting his policies and many of his criticisms of the March 'action'. This was accomplished by careful stage-management. Bela Kun was kept out of the limelight, and no one mentioned his promptings to the German party leaders. First Levi's expulsion was upheld (for he had, indeed, offended against democratic centralism). Only then, in a separate debate, were Levi's supporters, led by the sixty-three-year-old Klara Zetkin, offered consolation. The German party's action was officially explained as a defensive response to government provocation, but this led straight into a recital of criticisms of the German party. They 'failed to emphasise clearly the defensive character of the struggle', and thus allowed its enemies to represent it as a *putsch* (Adler, 1983, p. 290). Trotsky summed up for the prosecution: attempting to put the 'philosophy of the offensive' into practice was 'the greatest political crime'. 'We must say that this attempt was completely unsuccessful in this sense – that were it repeated it might actually ruin this splendid party' (Trotsky, 1973, pp. 328–9).


TOWARDS UNITED FRONTS

Comintern's repudiation of the 'March action' was ambiguous in a broader sense. It was both tactical and local, in the sense that the German leadership was pilloried with choosing the wrong moment to react offensively, and then doing so ineptly, but also strategic and international: it marked a turn back from splitting with 'centrist' leaders to a renewed attempt at contact with the – very sizeable – rank and file who still followed them. As such it was premised on the European revolution's being in recoil; the seizure of power was no longer an early prospect. The tasks were therefore those of day-by-day broadening and strengthening of support. Most communist parties were supported only by a minority of workers; the Congress thus launched the general slogan 'To the Masses!', precursor of the 'united front' tactics, based on formal proposals for cooperation with the social democratic parties, which were adopted at the end of 1921.

It was not to be expected that such a 'turn' would go unresisted in parties which, within the last year, had been formed or fundamentally reshaped according to very different principles. The German, Italian and Austrian delegations combined to propose amendments to the Executive resolution. They were contained by redrafting, but more worryingly the censured 'left' majority of the German party leadership was pursuing contacts with members of Shliapnikov's 'Workers' Opposition' within the Russian party. The 'turn', none the less, cohered better with the new requirements of Soviet foreign policy. The effort to break out of diplomatic and economic isolation would be reinforced more effectively if the native communist party, the natural spearhead of domestic pressure for good relations with the Soviet state, were engaged in broad alliances within the accepted political spectrum. The consultative delegates from the KAPD (shortly afterwards to be expelled from Comintern) warily approached the problem by suggesting that treaties with Russia might strengthen capitalist states. Should there not be a greater and more formal separation of Comintern from the Soviet state machine to prevent such conflicts of interest? The idea was pooh-poohed by Radek and Bukharin, and the response of the Executive was, naturally enough, to tighten up international centralization. None the less, the reorientation towards the 'united front' imposed very large strains on Comintern's main parties. In addition to protracted problems with the 'left' in the German Communist Party leadership, the Executive faced the flat refusal of the Italian party, under Bordiga, to accept united front tactics towards the socialists, and extreme reluctance to put them into practice from the French and Spanish parties. Having selected the constituents of the new parties by a blanket application of the 'twenty-one conditions' and through a process which produced many new enmities besides those it built on, it was not surprising that Comintern now found many of the new recruits ill-disposed to overtures towards yesterday's 'social traitors'. The prestige and administrative grip of the Russian leaders ensured that this first of the world communist movement's great 'turns' was executed, but at the cost of further purges, reducing the capacity for independent action among the leaders of the non-ruling communist parties, and increasing the disarray among their rank-and-file members.

In the German party the effect of the Third Comintern Congress was to create a resilient constellation of 'left' opposition groupings, while the approved party leadership moved, at least in its visible tactics, to the 'right', pioneering the type of 'united front' initiatives which Comintern officially set forth in December 1921: alliances on economic demands, against political assassinations by the right, and in favour of 'workers' governments' in those German states where the parliamentary arithmetic made it possible. It was in this phase, particularly, that the German Communist Party became the laboratory of Comintern's organizational and political experiments throughout Western Europe.

The proper limits of unity in the united front required, indeed, careful experimentation. Lenin had already explained, in the context of urging British 'left' communists to support the Labour Party at the ballot box, that this should be done 'in the same way as the rope supports a hanged man' (Lenin, 1960–78, 31, p. 88). Zinoviev elaborated on the 'united front from below' as an international tactic: a common struggle may mean 'that on occasions we shall have to sit at one table with the traitorous leaders'. But there must be no question of either electoral combination or, even worse, organizational union. 'Every one of us would rather have his hand cut off than to underwrite a union with the greatest traitors of the working class, who are now our enemies and the last prop of the bourgeoisie. This is by no means a united front' (Angress, 1963, p. 227). Such distaste did not, however, preclude building 'underground' cells of secret communist supporters within socialist and labour organizations – a tactic which has continued in widespread use.

Lenin's and Zinoviev's formulations placed the leaders of other communist parties in an awkward position, since proposals for joint action which genuinely met the socialist leaders part-way – and these were the only type with a chance of being accepted – risked subsequently incurring Moscow's wrath for 'opportunism', or worse. Thus the German party's conduct in the political agreement 'for the protection of the republic', which they made with the USPD and SPD after the assassination of Foreign

Minister Walther Rathenau by a right-wing nationalist (the culmination of hundreds of acts of violence by the far right since 1919) led to their almost immediate 'expulsion' by their partners, and did much to facilitate the reunification of the USPD with the SPD, in September 1922. Perhaps the least unsuccessful of the communists' efforts at united front tactics in Germany was their support for socialist governments in Thuringia and Saxony. The awkward manoeuvre of drawing allies – and equally important, large numbers of their supporters – into common action, while retaining the political initiative and the ability to resume the offensive, was one which communist parties needed much trial and error to master.

RAPALLO

German communists, in particular, were also disoriented by the surprise announcement of the Russian–German treaty, begun secretly in Berlin and signed and announced a fortnight later, during the Genoa economic conference of April 1922, at nearby Rapallo. At Genoa the Western Powers had sought in effect to form an economic consortium to benefit from the agriculture and raw materials of an impoverished Russia, while denying her the political status or guarantees a major power would expect. She could exit from this predicament only by accord with her fellow victim of Versailles, Germany; and a favourable agreement demanded the proper management of German wishes and fears in several fora, most importantly the army command, under Seeckt, and the 'easterners' of Rathenau's Foreign Ministry. This was mainly the task of Radek, behind the scenes, who prepared the ground for Chicherin's subtle speech-making at Genoa and the subsequent coming together of the Soviet and German delegations at Rapallo.

Although the German communists had always pressed for alliance with Russia, the Rapallo treaty took them by surprise, to the extent that their press remained almost mute on it for six weeks. The agreement reinserted Soviet Russia into the European balance of power, but it evidently had almost nothing to do with the communists' pressures or manoeuvres within domestic politics, and the social democrats were the major party opposing the treaty. It placed the German communists in the uneasy position of enthusiasts for a treaty reached at the initiative – and presumably, therefore, to the advantage – of German conservative and big business interests. Internationally, Rapallo was presented very differently by Soviet leaders according to the circumstances and the organ involved. The Central Committee of the Russian party greeted it soberly and commended it as a precedent for future inter-state agreements. Comintern treated it within the parameters of revolutionary optimism. The treaty was 'of enormous historical importance'; it was true that it had to be signed with 'the present bourgeois-menshevik government', but this was 'a temporary thing', and soon 'Germany will become a Soviet republic.' Within Germany, the pact was a ready target for criticism from socialists; Arthur Crispien, who had been one of the USPD delegates to the Second Comintern Congress, denounced it as an alliance with the bourgeoisie, 'the 4 August 1914 of the Third International'. For the German Communist Party, Thalheimer urged the German workers to build on Rapallo with 'further steps in the direction of *Anschluss* with Soviet Russia' (Degras 1956–65, I, pp. 343, 347). Radek, assessing his handiwork more realistically, reflected on the inverse, if heretical, proposition: the Entente's 'policy of strangling Germany implied in fact the destruction of Russia as a great power'. But they had been outmanoeuvred, 'for, no matter how Russia is governed, it is always to her interest that Germany should exist . . .' (Carr, 1977, III, p. 380).

At the time of the Genoa conference Radek, then a regular commuter between Moscow and Berlin, also began to revive the 'national Bolshevism' of 1919, together with theoretical observations to justify it. The Western Powers, headed by France, intended to make Russia an 'agricultural colony', while Germany became their 'industrial colony' (Degrass, 1956–65, I, p. 343). The natural corollary of a German–Soviet treaty against this threat would be common action by German patriots and German communists against the 'imperialism' of Versailles, and (according to Ruth Fischer) Radek urged such a combination at this time, in the shape of a 'national front' of all classes. This facet of Comintern policy, however, with its whiff of the policies which were to help Hitler to power from 1929, became much more prominent during the Ruhr crisis of 1923.

### THE RUHR CRISIS

In January 1923 Poincaré's government sent troops into the Ruhr to enforce German reparations. In Germany the effect was greatly to raise the temperature of nationalist sentiment, and, within a few months, to accelerate inflation out of control. The German party found it difficult to project effective and consistent policies, and was in effect groping around. Hostility to the occupation was universal, but what of the Cuno government's policy of 'passive resistance' in the Ruhr, which enjoyed much popular sympathy? Generally speaking, the line of communist propaganda was to attack the government's response as inadequate, even treasonable; but this raised the further problem: inadequate against what yardstick? The one most obviously to hand was nationalist indignation against the French and against the social democrats, as advocates of compliance with Versailles. The radical right was now a force to be reckoned with, both in the north and in Hitler's movement in Bavaria.

There thus developed German communism's brief but revealing 'extension' of united front tactics towards the extreme right, launched by Radek's 'Schlageter speech' at the Executive Committee of Comintern in June 1923. Without explicitly qualifying the communists' hostility to the ultra-nationalist leaders (just as the united front towards the socialists sought to maintain just such a hostility *vis-à-vis* the leaders) Radek now used the occasion of the execution of a young German nationalist, Albert Schlageter, by the French occupation forces in the Ruhr, to propose a bid for 'the nationalist petty bourgeois masses', and 'those German Fascisti, who honestly thought to serve the German people' (Radek, 1923, pp. 460–1). Extreme nationalism was a revolutionary act, as in the colonies.

Radek's initiative – which certainly had the support of Zinoviev and the other Comintern leaders – was taken up vigorously by the German party and led it into a brief but energetic campaign of attempted rapprochement 'from below' with the ultra-nationalist and fascist right, appealing to a similar 'social' radicalism. Communists organized joint meetings with Nazis, and their efforts did not stop short of appeals to the 'class' anti-Semitism of their intended converts ('You are against the stock market jobbers?' Ruth Fischer asked an enthusiastic audience of Berlin students. 'Fine. Trample the Jewish capitalists down, hang them from the lampposts' (Angress, 1963, pp. 340).) Parallel campaigns were directed at officers, professionals and intellectuals, and civil servants – all groups whose economic situation was being devastated, from May onwards, by the collapse in the value of the mark.

The Germans thus acted in line with Lenin's injunction against hoping for a 'pure' revolution; effective revolutionary movements, he argued during the war, would have to embrace 'all and sundry oppressed and discontented elements', with all 'their prejudices, their reactionary fantasies' (Lenin, 1960–78, 22, p. 356). The communists' joint activities with Nazis, however, were brought to an end by the Nazi leadership, who found it an embarrassment, and who pointed out that the communists ('led by Radek-Sobelsohn and whatever the other Jews were called') stood for international, not national, socialism (Carr, 1969, p. 191). Moreover, this interlude of 'national Bolshevism', however, occurred within the strategic framework of the united front and its generally anti-fascist stance. The extension of the united front to the far right was most popular with the 'left' of the German party, offering them the chance of linking with Lenin's 'socially explosive material', readier for revolutionary action than staid social democratic workers.

The communists registered modest gains during the foment of 1923. Their actions, however, were to be shaped more by international than internal events. During 1923 the Bolshevik leaders were cautiously manoeuvring for position, with Lenin off the scene through illness, but none of them knowing when he might return. Day-to-day authority was concentrated in the 'triumvirate': Zinoviev, Kamenev, and Stalin, as their cautious junior, together forming a defensive 'bloc' against their critic and potential rival Trotsky. The Soviet government had been been shaken in May by an aggressive diplomatic 'ultimatum' from Curzon, the British Foreign Secretary. In conjunction with French action in the Ruhr, and the suspicion of French preparations for military support to Poland, the situation raised the renewed spectre of military threats or intervention. Chicherin was instructed to bow to the British complaints and on the central one – that of anti-British activity in Asia contrary to the 1921 agreement – a new and more comprehensive form of prohibition was negotiated. The episode thus passed, but left the Soviet leaders with a renewed sense of international insecurity.

Events in Bulgaria added to this. In June the elected government of Stambolisky, the Peasant Union leader, was overthrown by a military coup. Despite the new Comintern line of united front, and the fact that the large Bulgarian Communist Party was in principle in favour of a 'workers' and peasants' government', the Bulgarian party stood aside, as had the German party at the beginning of the Kapp *putsch*. (It was now under the leadership of Kabakchiev, the splitter of the Italian Socialist Party at Livorno.) Subsequent attempts at united action with peasant leaders against the military regime only led to the party being decimated and driven completely underground.

## The 'German October'

In Germany itself the political situation was fundamentally changed in August, when strikes of bank-note printers, superadded to inflation, finally toppled the Cuno government. Cuno was replaced by the industrialist Gustav Stresemann, leading a coalition which excluded only the extremes of right and left, and which promptly embarked on a twin-pronged (and ultimately successful) policy of financial stabilization, and of placating France and its reparations claims. The change filled the Soviet leaders with a mixture of alarm and excitement. Alarm, because they foresaw the Stresemann government's attitude towards France putting both Rapallo and their secret military collaboration with Germany at risk; and excitement, because its position appeared to them weak, and vulnerable to the mounting political clashes within Germany and the Rhineland.

The Russian leaders accordingly broke off their vacations and converged on Moscow for an emergency Politburo meeting on 23 August. In July they had collectively counselled the German communists to be wary of mass demonstrations. But now they debated when and how to launch the German insurrection. Trotsky, the theorist of 'permanent revolution', whereby revolution in Germany would rescue Russia – but perhaps now moved as much by the sense that success in Germany would do much to transform the situation in the Russian party – was the most enthusiastic advocate of action. Zinoviev concurred in general terms, but proposed a perspective of months rather than weeks. Only Stalin expressed scepticism, and that mutedly. Trotsky's persuasions, as organizer of the Russian October, carried the day, and a committee of five (all Russians) was put in charge of detailed arrangements. These included Krestinsky, the Soviet ambassador in Berlin, who was to channel the large sums required for the attempt, Radek, acting as the main link-man to the German party leadership, and Unszlicht, previously Dzerzhinsky's deputy in the Cheka, in charge of both military preparations and of organizing the suppression of resistance after the take-over had succeeded (Bajanov, 1930, pp. 195–7). It only remained to set a date and instruct the German Communist Party.

This was done when Heinrich Brandler, the stolid German party leader upon whom insurrection was being wished, visited Moscow in September. Brandler's objections overcome, he prudently asked if Trotsky could not come incognito to Germany to mastermind proceedings. Trotsky was more than willing, but his rivals thought it safer to keep him back; an alternative team, under Radek, was thus assembled, and hurried preparations were made to provide the German communists with money, arms and military and intelligence training. The *political* strategy, however, rested on wishful thinking and was symptomatic of German communism's internal divisions, containing elements to gain it the support of both the right, represented by Brandler, and the left. The communists were to develop their 'united front' with social democratic leaders and enter the governments in the central states of Saxony and Thuringia, where electoral arithmetic had made this a possibility; but communist ministers were to use their positions to get access to arms and neutralize the police, and at a chosen moment coordinated uprisings across the country were to be backed by a general strike.

Trotsky's sense of history favoured the anniversary of his storming of the Winter Palace, but Brandler baulked at setting a precise date in Moscow, and too far in advance; he was, reluctantly, allowed to set the exact time-table on his return. Soviet internal and diplomatic policy was retuned in the expectation of an imminent 'workers' state' in Germany, with massive propaganda and appeals for collections for the German workers' movement, and large quantities of grain stockpiled in western Russia for urgent shipment to a revolutionary Germany. The fact that the Soviet republic was territorially separated from Germany by Poland raised a number of problems – might Poland attack, or seek to seize territory from, a Germany in turmoil? Could Russia send aid to Germany through Poland? Speeches by Trotsky, as Red Army leader, sought to neutralize Poland with warnings that she could be either 'bridge or barrier' (Trotsky, 1979–81, 5, pp. 191ff), and it was secretly suggested to the Polish government that, in return for recognition of a communist Germany, they should receive East Prussia (Carr, 1969, p. 227).

It seems, in retrospect, almost incredible that plans could have been laid from a distance with such diligent optimism. In the event the 'German October' was precipitated prematurely (by the central government's military occupation of Saxony) and then misfired, due to the refusal of the social democratic and trade union leaders to support the communists' general strike call. Only in Hamburg, through faulty communications, did the communists go so far as to launch an uprising, and this isolated attempt, after brief but bloody fighting, was easily suppressed. A few days later Stresemann's government was faced by an even stiffer challenge when the foment of armed nationalism in Bavaria came to a head in Munich in Hitler's 'beerhall *putsch*', but this, too, the authorities successfully put down. Had the German party not shot its bolt it might have been able to strike at a later date, but – although this did not immediately sink in – the defeat was irretrievable.

The post-mortems and recriminations on the German débâcle immediately became entangled with the sharpening antagonisms in the top leadership of the Russian party, one result of which was that no participant was able to take an objective view of the outcome. In October Trotsky voiced – in parallel with the similar criticisms of the so-called 'Declaration of the Forty-Six' – his complaints about bureaucracy in the party. Lenin had been incapacitated since 1922; in January 1924 his death brought about a gear shift in the battle for the succession. At this stage the struggle within the Russian party was almost entirely concerned with domestic issues – if we exclude Georgia and the question of nationalities within the Russian empire. But one important outcome of the struggles becoming more visible was that foreign party leaders – who were most directly affected by the conduct of Comintern – began to feel tempted to get involved in them; and by the same token Russian leaders kept in mind the support to be expected from foreign parties. This pattern of interaction, produced essentially by the partial breakdown of 'democratic centralism' in the Russian party under the strains it was faced with, and the consequent failure of its chief leaders to act as a convincing 'caucus', went through transmogrifications over some years, subjecting foreign communist party leaderships to a complex and protracted process of 'sifting' connected with the crises of the Russian party. This was completed only with the elimination of Trotsky's supporters within Comintern parties. Thereafter no similar situation recurred until the period after Stalin's death in 1953 when, for a short time, leaders of the ruling parties in Eastern Europe and some Western communist leaders became aware they were dealing with a divided Politburo in Moscow.

At the beginning of these Russian inner-party struggles, however, none of the principals was ready to blame the others for the German defeat. Though

Stalin could with justice have blamed Trotsky's impatience, he could not do so without also accusing Zinoviev, the voice of Comintern's forward and 'left' policy. At this time, in any case, Stalin was still constructing his hold on the party bureaucracy, and avoided the limelight in debate, especially on international questions. The German post-mortem, therefore, intersected with Russian party conflicts mainly in the form of a search for lesser scapegoats by the ruling triumvirate, Zinoviev, Kamenev and Stalin. Brandler, in immediate charge of the failure, was an obvious candidate, and to him was added Radek, an associate of and convenient surrogate for Trotsky. Trotsky agreed that the German leadership was to blame for failing truly to shift from propaganda to action, and thus missing a unique opportunity. Stalin maintained a prudent reserve. Zinoviev had Comintern condemn both Radek and Brandler for 'right-wing opportunism'; the latter was replaced in the leadership of the German party by Ruth Fischer and the 'left', who promptly embarked on a purge of their critics.

The conditions that faced German communists from 1919 onwards were not untypical, but they faced them in an extreme form. Defeat in war produced severe economic and social crises, and a heightened and frustrated nationalism. A large reformist social democratic and trade union movement, its leaders experienced in combating their revolutionary critics, acted as a key buttress of the parliamentary order. Soviet support for German communism entangled and conflicted with Soviet reasons of state. In their attempts to gather and organize the forces for revolution, the communists frequently found themselves competing with the revolutionary nationalists. This gave the communism of the Weimar Republic a distinctive 'edge' – of hostility and resentment towards their larger rivals in the labour movement, and of ambivalence towards the nationalist ultra-right. The reshuffle of the German communist leadership to put the 'left' in control reflected a larger frustration: in the immediate aftermath of the October 1923 defeat Zinoviev, speaking for Comintern and the German communist leadership, declared that 'the leaders of German Social Democracy have become fascist through and through' (Fowkes, 1984, p. 114). This standpoint, branding the social democrats rather than the Nazis as the main enemy, became the basis of policy in the 'third period', from 1929 to 1934. It was a recipe for division in the labour movement that did much to help Nazism to power in 1933, and encouraged the significant flow of German communists to the ascendant Nazis.

Comintern's overall conclusions on the German defeat of 1923 contained almost as much wishful thinking as its original scheme for insurrection. They left the essential premise of Comintern's plans – that Germany was passing through a phase of revolutionary opportunity similar to Russia in late 1917 – unquestioned. Yet the differences were fundamental. The Stresemann government, though it was under great strain, had reached nothing like the stage of paralysis, of 'being unable to govern in the old way', that Kerensky's had. In particular the army – a professional rather than conscript force – remained almost untouched by revolutionary agitation and ready to intervene energetically in domestic politics. The communist-encouraged movement of factory councils had nothing like the scope of the Russian soviets in late 1917; there was no real 'dual power'. And, above all, the temper of most of the urban working class – which was a much larger section of society in Germany than in Russia – was not attuned to revolution, and many remained loyal to the Social Democratic Party within the governing coalition. 'It is not true, comrades', pleaded Radek to his critics, 'that the leadership did not want to fight, and that the masses are everywhere raging. It did not happen like that.' Or, as Brandler later observed in his own defence, there had been no 'labour aristocracy' in Russia (Carr, 1969, pp. 237, 245).

That the influence of the 'labour aristocracy', or even the spontaneous political proclivities of the mass of Western European workers, might be fundamental factors against a repetition of the Russian revolution, were not suggestions that could then be uttered in Comintern. Its leaders were still psychologically far from accepting that Western proletariats might not be inclined to support violent assaults on the state, and it required a 'Puck', such as Radek, even to point to the fact that the conjuncture was unfavourable. But more mutely and gradually the failure of the German revolution of 1923 had a profound effect on the Russian communist leaders. They felt themselves cast back on their own resources; socialism, for the time being, would have to survive in one large and backward country. No one yet doubted that it could in due course be rescued, but the balance of expectation began slowly to shift; if the Western European workers' movements proved incapable of repeating the October revolution on other soil, perhaps socialism's future lay in diplomacy or conquest?

FURTHER READING

Many of the items mentioned as further reading for chapter 3 are also relevant for this chapter. In addition, Carr's *The Interregnum* (1969) extends his account through 1923, while D'Agostino (1988) contains an interesting and unconventional account of the political struggles among Soviet leaders round the succession to Lenin.

# 5

# Asian communism

The First Congress of Comintern, held when the Soviet republic was almost entirely isolated by civil war in 1919, was attended by few non-Russian delegates with meaningful credentials from movements in their own countries, and it paid scant attention to the problems of communism in Asia. The Second Congress, however, in the summer of 1920, was different. Its much more substantial attendance included representatives from several embryonic but vigorous communist movements in colonial and backward countries, and the Congress as a whole did not at all share the attitude of Serrati, leader of the Italian Socialist Party delegation, who considered the revolution in the metropolitan countries *so* decisive that he was impatient with the arguments over if, and how far, communists of the colonial world should collaborate with 'bourgeois' or 'petit bourgeois' nationalist movements.

## LENIN AND M. N. ROY

This question was taken up as part of a lengthy debate on 'the national and colonial question', round the alternative theses of Lenin and the young Indian communist, M. N. Roy. Lenin, on the whole, favoured a flexible attitude, and allowed that there were circumstances where it would be right for communists in a backward country to allow the 'bourgeois nationalists' to take the lead in a combined movement. Roy rejected the idea of thus subordinating the communist movement, and only reluctantly conceded that it could be useful to cooperate with 'bourgeois nationalist revolutionary elements' (Carrere d'Encausse and Schram, 1969, p. 162).

Part of the grounds of their differences emerged in the discussion of the role of peasants and how it would be possible to mobilize them. Roy, resting his case on the argument that in much of Asia there already existed a working class which – although not large – was highly class-conscious, conceived of soviets as being composed of workers with, and leading, peasants. Lenin, however, was prepared to contemplate a wholly peasant-based soviet movement: 'The idea of Soviet organization is a simple one and is applicable, not only to proletarian, but also to peasant feudal and semi-feudal relations.' Communist parties must, he urged, immediately begin work in this direction in all parts of the world, 'even the most remote nations' (Lenin, 1960–78, 31, pp. 243–4).

The divergences – which were composed, but by no means obliterated, by some redrafting and by the Congress's ambiguous acceptance of *both* sets of theses – reflected more than differences of assessment within the Asian countries themselves. Roy came to the Congress convinced of the central importance of the Asian revolution to the future of world communism. In part his reasoning was purely economic: European capitalism was able to buy off its labour aristocracy with super-profits from its colonies. 'The European working class will not succeed in overthrowing the capitalist order until this source has been definitely cut off' (Carrere d'Encausse and Schram, 1969, p. 160).

Lenin, while he had admitted the *political* significance of national struggles earlier and more fully than many of his comrades, was also the custodian of a still-vulnerable revolution in Russia, and had to consider how the Comintern's policy for Asian and colonial communism could help protect the Soviet state. Discussion of how far the communists of backward countries should collaborate with, or even accept the leadership of, radical nationalist forces, skirted round the problem that relations between them could easily become – especially where the communists were energetic in pushing the social demands of the urban workers and rural poor – sharply antagonistic. The problem was recognized, and resulted in a drafting decision to incline towards Roy and speak only of collaboration with *revolutionary* nationalism. But it was too substantial to yield to drafting alone.

## THE NEAR EAST

In practice, it was Lenin's theses, implying considerably more elastic limits to political action and collaboration, which were accepted. The high point of nationalist militancy came a few weeks after the Second Comintern Congress, at the Baku 'Congress of Toilers of the East', which gathered large delegations of nationalist and religious, rather than communist, leaders from the Soviet borderlands and the Middle East. 'Zinoviev's circus' – as it was contemptuously termed by Roy, who refused to attend – was indeed an exercise in demagogy. The Congress heard loudly applauded calls for the stricter seclusion of women, and witnessed sword-brandishing mullahs leaping on their seats to applaud Russian atheists' calls to 'holy war' against British imperialism (Baku Congress, 1977, pp. 36–7).

Yet conflict was plainly likely in a number of countries between radical nationalism and their nascent communist movements. One of the first in which it came to a head was Turkey, which furnished an early and dramatic example of the sacrifice of native communists to Soviet reasons of state. The Soviet Union looked to an alliance with the military-nationalist regime of Mustafa Kemal (Ataturk) against the Entente powers. Initially, Kemal's diplomatic statements seemed to bear out Soviet enthusiasm for him, but his domestic policies and political stance precluded any real likelihood of an alliance with the small forces of Turkish communism; indeed Kemal was sufficiently concerned that their radical agrarian agitation could bring pressure upon him that at one stage he sponsored a 'Green' communist movement to outflank them in parts of the countryside. Conversely, his openness to peaceful and friendly relations with his Soviet neighbours was not extended to their protégés.

The small organization that formed the 'seed' of Soviet-sponsored Turkish communism was led by the lawyer and sociologist Mustafa Subhi (a protégé of Stalin, in particular, among the Bolshevik leaders) and operated from Bolshevik-controlled territory during 1918–20. Subhi's policies, reflecting the contradictions of Soviet policy, alternated awkwardly between efforts to organize an independent military force from among Turkish war prisoners, and calls for a united front with the Kemalists. In January 1921, as leader of the Turkish Communist Party, reorganized after the Baku Congress, Subhi returned to Turkey. To the relief, if not with the connivance, of Ataturk he and fourteen of his companions were seized and murdered at Trabzon, the victims being taken out in a boat into the Black Sea and thrown overboard to drown.

Yet the Soviet response was exceedingly muted. Discreet inquiries into the killings were not allowed, for example, to obstruct the visit of a Turkish delegation to Moscow to sign a Turkish–Soviet friendship treaty in March (Harris, 1967, pp. 91ff). A few months later an Ankara court sentenced communists to long prison sentences, but at the Comintern's Third Congress, in July 1921, the Turkish delegate continued to express loyal support for Ataturk. There was further persecution of Turkish communists in 1922, as, with the defeat of Greece, the Turkish government felt less need of Russian support. But, at the Fourth Comintern Congress in November 1922, Radek was still admonishing his Turkish comrades that 'you still have a long road to travel in the company of the bourgeois revolutionaries' (Lazitch and Drachkovitch, 1972, II, p. 562).

A similar dilemma was posed in Persia, where the radical separatist movement of Kuchik Khan established itself in control of Gilan, the country's northernmost province, during the First World War. During 1920 it was joined by the newly-formed Persian Communist Party. These combined forces were supported by Red Army units in neighbouring Soviet Azerbaijan, and attempted (unsuccessfully) to march on Teheran; simultaneously, however, Soviet diplomacy sought to mollify the Teheran government. A military coup by supporters of Riza Khan in 1921 forced a choice. Soviet policy favoured a strong state and army, both as an obstacle to continued British interference in the area, and as the best vehicles of modernization; the natural diplomatic corollary was the comprehensive Persian–Soviet friendship treaty which was signed in February. Yet, initially, local Soviet commanders also supported Kuchik's pre-emptive attempt during the summer to march on Teheran. The diplomats appealed to Moscow, and Soviet troops were shortly withdrawn from Gilan, leaving Kuchik and his supporters to their fate at the hands of the government forces which shortly afterwards reconquered the area.

However, cultivating anti-communist regimes on the Soviet borders, which had as one object the formation of a satisfactory buffer against British or British-inspired encroachment, also ran in parallel with the protracted negotiations for an Anglo-Soviet trade treaty. This was finally signed in March 1921, on the same day as the Turkish treaty and shortly after the launch of the NEP. Its provisions, however, went far beyond a trade agreement. The Soviet government undertook to refrain from any propaganda outside its own borders against the British empire, and particularly against British interests in Asia (while the British reciprocally undertook not to inflame the peoples of the former Russian empire against their new rulers). There is evidence that the widespread Russian efforts at inflaming anti-British sentiment during 1920, which climaxed in the Baku congress, were essentially a tactical device aimed at putting pressure on the British. As Trotsky wrote to Chicherin (then in charge of Soviet foreign affairs) in June 1920, a Soviet revolution in the Near East would be 'a most important item of diplomatic exchange with England'; everything should be done 'to underline our readiness to do a deal with England regarding the East' (Trotsky, 1971, 2, p. 509). After the Anglo-Soviet agreement, the propaganda bodies and training schools set up following the Baku congress were abruptly curtailed, to the distress of Asian communists.

The agreement with Britain, of course, could scarcely prevent efforts at subversion by either party, but only cause them to be more 'unofficial' and surreptitious; on the Soviet side the treaty reinforced the emphasis already given to the distinction between the Soviet *state*, and other bodies, including the Comintern, which were represented as being independent of it. But the importance of the treaty, both to the Soviet state's economic reconstruction and to its larger diplomatic strategy of peaceful international relations, was very great. Thus when, in 1923, the British threatened to denounce it for alleged Soviet abuses, Chicherin was quick to give ground, and the Soviet government consented to an enlarged political abstinence – 'not to support with funds or in any other form persons or bodies or agencies or institutions whose aim is to spread discontent or to foment rebellion in any part of the British Empire' (Carr, 1969, p. 180). Yet if undertakings of this sort – and more generally, the Soviet state's wider establishment of diplomatic relations – required more discreet channels for transmitting funds and political guidance, they did little to weaken the determining influence which the Soviet leaders, both directly and through their control of Comintern, had on the efforts of communists in the underdeveloped nations.

They were, however, often perplexed and divided on what guidance to give, and they lacked any settled theoretical framework within which to devise and justify policy; there was, consequently, much improvisation. Roy, the one participant in the debate at the Second Comintern Congress who did predict that the most decisive next advances of world communism would be made in Asia, was heard civilly but with implied disbelief; for many years most communists continued to look towards the West. Although Roy's prediction was to prove, in an abstract sense, accurate, the arguments by which he reached it were less so. More to the point they had the smack of heresy, in some ways reminiscent of the idea of permanent revolution. Basic to Roy's view was a pessimism about revolution in the industrialized countries. It is true that a similar pessimism, stemming from the delay in revolution in the West, was beginning to affect Russian leaders of Comintern in 1920–1, and implicitly underlay their adjustments of policy, but perhaps for that reason they rejected the more strenuously Roy's explicit articulation of such a view. Roy held that it would be necessary for colonial revolution to undermine the economies of the imperialist world before the resulting hardship could break the working classes of the metropolitan countries from their conservatism and complacency. (On this matter Roy received some support: Tom Quelch, a delegate from the British Socialist Party at the Second Comintern Congress, averred that most British workers would regard support for a rebellion in India as treason.) Within the colonial countries Roy saw the communists' support as coming from the working classes, not the peasants. Though small, these young proletariats possessed exceptional revolutionary capacities, and were able to take the political lead of the whole of society. Like Parvus and Trotsky before him, with their theory of permanent revolution, Roy rearranged the order, and thereby the causation and relative importance, of some of the key components in a received Marxist historical scenario.

It was natural, therefore, that much of the debate should revolve on the roles and potentials of various more or less 'bourgeois' nationalist forces. Yet the contribution of Lenin's which was to prove most prescient was his casual (and heretical, though in view of its authorship this was overlooked) suggestion of the possibility of a communist movement with no mass social basis in the towns, but only among the peasants.

## THE FAR EAST AND CHINA

The country where this first came about, though, was not Roy's India (where the Communist Party, formed in 1925, neither led peasant struggles on a sufficient scale, nor made itself central to the struggle against British rule) but China. And it was only after Lenin's death, and after suffering traumatic defeat in 1927 in pursuit of Lenin's own stategy of alliance with revolutionary nationalism, that Chinese communism finally, though never admitting as much, began to emancipate itself from Soviet guidance and from Comintern, and to build a viable and resilient, but purely peasant-based movement.

The Soviet Union's main political efforts in the Far East were initially directed towards Japan, whose large industrial working class made her appear ripest for revolution. A 'Congress of Toilers of the Far East' was held in Moscow in January 1922 – a sequel to the Baku gathering. It was attended by members of several revolutionary grouplets among the Japanese intelligentsia, and the most promising among them were provided with guidance and funds, and returned to found a Communist Party in Tokyo in July. It remained, however, both illegal and rather small; only under the postwar US occupation did it begin to flourish, reaching about 100,000 members in 1947.

The Chinese delegates to the 1922 Moscow Congress included representatives of two political groupings which were at that time distinct. Most were supporters or associates of the Chinese Communist Party. Founded in Shanghai in July 1921, of small groups from China's major cities, by early 1922 it was still a small organization of intellectuals, though beginning to develop a larger youth movement. But there was also a delegate from Sun Yat-sen's far larger revolutionary nationalist party, the Kuomintang, a powerful force in south China, and one with which Soviet foreign policy was already beginning to project closer ties.

Relations with the internationally recognized government in Peking were in any case complicated – by the fact that in reality it controlled only a small fragment in the north, much of China being the domain of local warlords, or lacking any state authority, and by the frictions resulting from Soviet installation of a dependent government in Outer Mongolia in the summer of 1921. Soviet support of Kuomintang – towards which Sun Yat-sen, failing in his efforts to get support from the Western Powers, was well disposed – thus seemed to offer a faster and more probable route towards close Soviet–Chinese relations, as well as a possible way forward for Chinese communists.

Sun, however, seeking to retain control over a single political force, rejected an alliance of the two organizations, proposing instead that communists enter the Kuomintang as individual members. Accordingly, in August 1922, the Dutch Comintern agent Maring (Sneevliet) directed the

CCP leaders – against their considerable opposition – to enter this 'united front from within'. Maring was an appropriate figure to convey such instructions, having already organized a similar policy of dual membership of communists in the religious-nationalist Sarakat Islam movement in Indonesia.

The other axis of the alliance was direct Soviet endorsement and aid for the Kuomintang, and was sealed when a senior Soviet diplomat met Sun Yat-sen in Shanghai in January 1923. Adolf Joffe (a close associate of Trotsky, who had led in the initial negotiations with Germany at Brest-Litovsk, and had subsequently acted as diplomatic representative-cum-insurrectionary quartermaster in Berlin during the October 1918 revolution) was on this occasion bent on gradualness. Sun and Joffe's joint manifesto agreed that China lacked conditions for 'Communism or even the Soviet system', and that the tasks of the moment were those of national unification and independence.

It was for this that Soviet aid was given. The building of the Kuomintang as a fighting organization before 1927 was in large part due to the efforts of the communists within it and Soviet advisors, both military and political, attached to its organs. In the summer of 1923, Sun Yat-sen sent one of his most able young lieutenants, Chiang Kai-shek, on a lengthy visit to Russia to obtain arms and study Soviet military methods. On his return Chiang became director of a mixed Soviet–Chinese team of military instructors at the new officer training school with which Soviet aid had equipped the Kuomintang, the Whampoa Military Academy, near Sun's now-secured seat of government in Canton. Chinese communist intellectuals provided much of the *political* training at Whampoa, which also served as nursery to some of their own cadres; Chou En-lai became deputy head of political instruction when he returned from France in 1924, and Lin Piao was an early graduate.

A former Chicago teacher, Michael Borodin, replacing Maring as chief Soviet representative in China in October 1923, took in hand the reorganization of the Kuomintang along Leninist lines, under Sun Yat-sen's benevolent gaze. Borodin headed the committee (which also included Li Ta-chao, one of the founders of the Chinese Communist Party, and Mao Tse-tung) which drafted the new Kuomintang constitution adopted by its Congress in February 1924. It provided for a much clearer hierarchy of organizational levels, and a concentration of political direction in a Central Executive Committee and Political Council, the latter controlled by radicals. The Kuomintang's organization had to serve not only the functions of a party but, in the territories of south China which it controlled, those of a state as well. Communists were very strongly represented among the staff of the Kuomintang's functional bureaux, especially those concerned with party organization, labour and propaganda. They were complemented by

Borodin's Soviet advisory staff who, by 1926, numbered several hundred, including the young Ho Chi Minh, who sent a number of neophyte Vietnamese communists to be trained at the Whampoa Military Academy. The very large influence which the communists quickly obtained within the Kuomintang was out of all proportion to their numbers; as late as its Fourth National Congress, in January 1925, the CCP was claiming a membership of only 950. Yet this small total included most of the men who were to be the party's senior leaders throughout the period up to the 1960s; and for many of them their baptism into political command was as functionaries of the Kuomintang.

CHINESE COMMUNISM'S BREAK WITH THE KUOMINTANG

In just over a year, starting in May 1925, the CCP was transformed into a mass party. Its leadership of the May Thirtieth Movement, starting in textile strikes in Shanghai, and spreading to embrace a year-long strike and boycott against foreign concessions in Canton and Hong Kong, brought it a membership of about 30,000 by July 1926. The growth of labour struggles, however (combined with Sun Yat-sen's unexpected illness and death in March 1925, and the formation of an organized anti-communist fraction in the upper echelons of the Kuomintang in November), only sharpened the frictions of the 'bloc within' the Kuomintang. Chiang Kai-shek, now acting as military commander increasingly independently of the Kuomintang political leadership, staged a limited coup in Canton in March 1926, and pressured the Kuomintang leadership to accept substantial limitations on communist activity within its organizations. Communists remained well entrenched and welcome within the Kuomintang government in Wuhan, but as the nationalists' consolidated their military conquest of the south, and Chiang Kai-shek launched his 'Northern Expedition' during 1926, a *de facto* division within the Kuomintang developed, with Chiang becoming his own political master over the armies he commanded.

The situation represented an obvious danger for the communists, and different sections of the Party, during 1926 and early 1927, urged a variety of solutions or precautions: should they expand to the maximum their organization within the Kuomintang, and seek to take it over? Should they withdraw from the 'united front from within', and either break the alliance or continue it as a bloc 'from without'. Or should they rein in their own more radical policies to preserve influence within the Kuomintang? Should they seek to remove Chiang, or by political combinations within the Kuomintang to tie his hands from moving against them? Basic to the dilemma was the fact that their influence in the Kuomintang's *military* command was nowhere near as strong as it was in the political and administrative offices. The party leadership, under Ch'en Tu-hsiu, favoured shifting to a 'bloc without' strategy. But Comintern vetoed this: they were to remain within the Kuomintang, and to give no provocation. In March 1927 communists entered the Wuhan government as ministers. And in April, a week before Chiang launched an onslaught against the communists and trades unions in Shanghai, Stalin was proclaiming that Chiang and the Kuomintang would be 'utilised to the end, squeezed like a lemon, and then flung away' (Trotsky, 1966, p. 390).

The reverse occurred. As Chiang's armies approached Shanghai, in March 1927, he paused, allowing the leaders of the strike which the communists launched in his support to be decapitated. Once in command of the city he prepared carefully, and on 12 April he struck, disarming communist pickets at key points, then undertaking a general massacre of active members of the labour movement. This gave the cue for a general turn within the Kuomintang against the communists. Yet the CCP leadership, regrouping in the south, attempted to remain obedient to the instructions which still flowed from Moscow to preserve the united front at all costs. The Chinese Commission of the Executive Committee of Comintern met urgently in May, on reports of spreading repression of communists, and Stalin, Bukharin and Togliatti demanded that the Chinese communists try to preserve their position within the Kuomintang by restraining 'peasant excesses'. 'If we do not curb the agrarian movement', declared Stalin, 'we will lose our left allies, and it will have become impossible to win a majority in the Kuomintang. . . . By curbing it, we will enlarge our influence in it, and when we have become more powerful, we will go beyond our present allies.' 'We possess sufficient authority over the Chinese masses', he added, 'to make them accept our decision' (North and Eudin, 1963, pp. 90–1). As late as the end of June Bukharin was reaffirming the alliance, asserting in its favour that relations with the Nationalists were no worse than those with Mussolini! (Harrison, 1972, p. 113). (A surprising fact is that the refusal to separate from the Kuomintang was still being used as an object-lesson in the Comintern school at Ufa in the Soviet Union at the end of 1942, drilling students in the dangers of 'sectarianism' in preparation for communist action at the end of the war in Europe. The official instructor summed up the lesson of China in 1927: 'the first defection from an existing united front should be made by the other party and not by ourselves' (Leonhard, 1979, p. 212).)

The breach was forced by the other side, but only in mid-July did Comintern finally allow the Communist Party to break with the Wuhan government. This, it declared, was 'becoming counter-revolutionary', but it none the less ordered communists to remain (clandestinely!) within the Kuomintang. The Party's General Secretary, Ch'en Tu-hsiu, resigned and went into hiding, and in almost the same moment the top Kuomintang leaders in Wuhan, applying the Leninist decisiveness in which they had been trained, launched a general purge of communists, and despatched Borodin and his Russian fellow 'advisers' back to Moscow. As repression spread, the Communist Party was reduced to a fragment – between April and November 1927 membership was cut from 58,000 to perhaps 10,000. Its belated turns to insurrection ended in disaster. A series of local uprisings in Hupeh and Hunan (the Autumn Harvest Uprisings) and in Nanking and the south proved abortive, and a final attempt at revolution in Canton, in December, failed to attract any mass support whatsoever, and collapsed in a bloodbath.

### RETREAT FROM THE CITIES

However in the next few months the remnants of these unsuccessful struggles succeeded in assembling themselves in control of small territories and population, mainly in the remote Chingkang mountains on the borders of Hunan and Kiangsi provinces. Mao Tse-tung was one of the political cadres who survived (he was rescued by a force of about 1000 men, retreating from skirmishes with Kuomintang troops in Hunan) and eventually linked up with other armed groups, including one led by Chu Teh, the future leader of the Red Army. It was thus in an archipelago of 'soviet' rural areas in inland central and south China, during 1928–34, and then in the heroic series of retreats and regroupments in 1934–6 that become known as the 'Long March', that Chinese communism evolved the strategies that were to carry it to victory, and conducted the factional battles through which Mao placed himself in its leadership. By 1931 the resilience of the Red Armies in the base areas, coupled with persecution in the cities, had shifted the party's centre of mass to the inland rural soviets. Comintern guidance – and information – became spasmodic; in 1930 an obituary of Mao appeared in the Soviet press, stating that he had died of tuberculosis.

Chief among the Chinese communists' innovations was a political-military strategy aimed at arousing the poor peasantry, the large majority of the population. Though some local communist leaders had already been active in mass peasant associations – notably, and first, P'eng P'ai in coastal districts of Kwangtung province – communist agrarian policy until mid-1927 was inhibited by the 'bloc within' the Kuomintang, whose leaders opposed any general land redistribution and sought to win rural support by protecting the property of landlords and landowning peasants (including many with very small holdings) who gave support to the nationalists. They sought to limit reform to a 25 per cent reduction in rents, relegating Sun Yat-sen's policy of 'Land to the tiller' to the remote future. In a land where half or more of most peasants' crop was eaten up by rents and usury, and perhaps 70 per cent of peasant families lived under the continual threat of hunger through being landless or having too small plots and being too heavily indebted to feed themselves, Comintern policies kept the communists shackled to a profoundly conservative policy, preservers rather than destroyers of the misery that engulfed hundreds of millions of rural Chinese. No wonder, therefore, that the July 1926 Central Committee Plenum lamented that 'The peasant movement has developed the disease of left deviation everywhere. Either the slogans are extreme or action is excessively Left-inclined' (Wilbur and Howe, 1956, p. 277), or that Mao's 'Report on an investigation of the peasant movement in Hunan' was moved to endorse the disease: 'If you are a person of firm revolutionary ideology and visit the countryside, you will experience a satisfaction never felt before; tens of thousands of slaves – the peasants – are overthrowing their man-eating enemy' (for the Report see Brandt, Schwartz and Fairbank, 1973, pp. 80–9).

Mao's Report, which subsequently became so famous as a milestone document of Chinese communism, arose out of his work as a peasant organizer and teacher of organizers within the Kuomintang, and was first printed in a Kuomintang journal. It none the less reflected the control the communists wielded over much peasant work, and expressed a communist point of view. As such it incorporated a significant omission: the leading role in the Chinese revolution ('seven points out of ten') was ascribed to the 'hundreds of millions of peasants [who] will rise in Central, South and North China, with the fury of a hurricane; no power, however strong, can restrain them.' In contrast, the usual Marxist affirmations of the leading role of the urban working class were entirely lacking. This seminal document, in implicitly turning its back on the proletariat and the cities, departed from the standpoints of all the disputants in the battles that were then under way in the Russian party. And it was wholly inconsistent with the Comintern's advice, still being transmitted as late as Stalin's telegram at the end of May 1927: not to allow confiscation of Nationalists' land, and to 'check the peasants' overzealous action with the power of Party Headquarters' (Ch'en, 1967, p. 121), in order to preserve the entente with the Wuhan government.

But Mao's perspective of peasant revolution, like Lenin's earlier proposal of purely peasant soviets, lacked one further ingredient that was to prove crucial: their military protection. The communists' rural uprisings in the autumn of 1927 were all suppressed relatively easily by Kuomintang troops. The problem which the communists painfully and pragmatically faced up to in the mountains of Kiangsi in 1927–8 was how to devise combined military-political strategies through which an army could nourish itself from the peasantry, and in turn protect the area on which it was based.

Protection did not necessarily mean static defence; for many years the

Red Army conducted guerrilla war over large areas. Nor was there any fixity in the policies of 'class struggle' in the countryside which were applied to win the support of the rural population. Its framework was formed by a triple economic division of peasants into 'rich', 'middle' and 'poor'. In general land was to be taken from the 'rich' peasants (those who employed others) and landlords, and given to the landless and 'poor' peasants (those who had no land or too little to feed themselves, and were obliged to seek wage-labour). The 'middle' peasants were to be left as they were. But 'rich', 'middle' and 'poor' were practical and political rather than descriptively economic categories, and their definition and application varied greatly according to locality, social conditions and political conjuncture. In impoverished areas, in the aftermath of the 1927 catastrophes, policies of exemplary 'burning and killing' against 'evil gentry' and 'bullies' were general. In contrast, during the Second United Front with the Kuomintang after the outbreak of open war with Japan in 1937, agrarian policy was often limited to rent reductions. The aim at this stage was not deep-going social revolution, but to create micro-political conditions where the villages would willingly provide taxes, supplies and some soldiers for the communist armies. This was done by sometimes more and sometimes less redistribution, but equally important by reducing the insecurity and indignities of most peasants' lives. One long-term result of this was to face the communist state, after 1949, with hundreds of millions of small peasant claims and expectations, standing as a vast barrier to collectivization of the land.

## COMMUNIST NATIONALISM

The Second United Front saw a vast and rapid growth of communist power. Party membership grew from 20,000 in 1936, after the attritions of the Long March, to 800,000 by 1940. Nationalism was a powerful factor in much of the recruitment, especially behind the Japanese lines. The communists' nationalism of this period was, however, quite different from that of the First United Front before 1927. Mao and most of his fellow leaders might be willing to bend to Comintern pressure in particular matters – as in the 'Sian incident' of December 1936, when they agreed to the release of Chiang Kai-shek after he had been arrested by nationalist forces sympathetic to the communists. And Mao, at least, was quite willing to countenance formulations for the renewed united front which would subordinate the communists to the nationalist government (with which the Soviet Union signed a non-agression pact in August 1937). But they had no intention of allowing Comintern urgings to lead them back into subordinacy to the Kuomintang. On the contrary, their aim was now to capture nationalism for their own use, to use it to weld together and expand their mass movements, and to exploit it to the full in their political 'peaceful competition' with Chiang Kai-shek. In fact, as early as February 1932, in a purely propaganda gesture from their Kuomintang-surrounded Kiangsi soviets, the Party had declared war on Japan, and from 1935 onwards the need for a new national united front to resist Japan became a theme of party propaganda – but on the basis of demands aimed at counterposing popular, communist-inspired resistance to the restricted nationalism of the Kuomintang government. In their creation of a popular peasant nationalism the Chinese communist leaders were remarkably successful, powerfully aided, from 1937, by the policies and habits of the Japanese occupation forces, which reinforced existing exploitation and oppression in the countryside, and thus fostered nationalism in the minds of millions of peasant families who had previously been innocent of all ideological conceptions.

PEASANT COMMUNISM

Its peasant basis reshaped the CCP's methods. The leadership's general line had to be put into action, in the villages, by peasant cadres with rudimentary education and usually no prior socialist or even political traditions, speaking to poor peasants the large majority of whom were illiterate. Definitions thus had to be simple; as Chang Kuo-t'ao summarized communist propaganda: 'A Communist Party is a political party of the poor. A proletarian is one who is so poor that he has nothing. Every poor man will be distributed a piece of land, and this is Communism' (Harrison, 1972, p. 146). Mao came to impose his personal style, in the enunciation of campaigns as a small list of simple 'points' (the 'four principles', the 'three antis', and so on). This simplicity, combining vagueness (with its potential for flexibility) with an assertive dogmatism, became the hallmark of Maoist campaigns down to the Cultural Revolution. (After Mao's death it was turned against him, when in 1979 Deng Xiaoping launched a modest drive of his own against the 'two whatevers': that whatever Mao said must not be changed, and whatever Mao did not say must not be done.) Applied to the countryside in the 1930s and 1940s, however, such communist slogans imposed on the Red Armies what no warlord had ever required of his troops – a rough decency towards the poorer peasants. This often went alongside extreme brutality towards their immediate exploiters; Mao himself conceded that three-quarters of a million people were 'executed' in the land redistribution of the early 1950s (the land of those killed being distributed), and other estimates are much higher. Together, these elicited the support that carried the communists to victory.

The new strategic doctrine was expressed in the party's make-up. At the zenith of its urban growth, in early 1927, half the members were factory workers, only 5 per cent were peasants, and a mere 2 per cent were soldiers. By 1930 95 per cent of a claimed membership of 120,000 was in the inland 'soviet' areas, and 70 per cent were peasants. Moreover the army and the party overlapped to a very high degree: at the beginning of 1934, before the Long March, 45 per cent of Red Army soldiers were members of the Party or its youth wing (Harrison, 1972, pp. 64, 70, 201). The change to a peasant basis was a lasting one; as late as 1956, when it had controlled the whole of mainland China for seven years, the party's reported membership still consisted of 69 per cent peasants and only 14 per cent workers (Lewis, 1966, p. 108).

Thus from the period of the Kiangsi soviets the CCP ceased to be an urban-based party. It did not have, before it turned to the conquest of the mainland in the spring of 1949, any substantial orientation towards the cities. The crucial instrument of strategy was land policy. When after 1947 Mao decided to open the floodgates against the Kuomintang he did so by reverting to a policy of 'land to the tiller', inciting the poorer peasants. But even as the communist armies swept Chiang southward they discouraged strike movements in the cities. In 1948 they sent New Year cards ahead to capitalists in the cities they still had to conquer, reassuring them that communist rule would bring prosperity. The underlying motive was the party's extreme shortage of cadres with the education or experience to administer urban industry or commerce. Even property-owners who had fled to the Kuomintang areas were urged to return, their concerns being returned to them if they did (Pepper, 1978, pp. 368-9).

However the great change in the CCP after 1927 cannot be described simply in terms of exchanging one social basis of support for another. In retreating from the cities to the countryside it left behind an environment that was nascently political for one that was profoundly pre-political. Correspondingly the nature of party organization had to change, becoming fused into military organization and also acting, within the areas it controlled, as a form of rudimentary state authority. Peasant support flowed to the CCP not on the basis of a political struggle between *parties*, but because the communist party-army was able to substitute itself for the old and ramshackle state power which supported the privileged in the countryside. In an undeclared fashion the CCP substituted for the arguments on communist strategy in terms of political competition and struggle a fundamentally different approach: aiming at state power via a protracted civil war. And in this it defeated the Kuomintang by using policies of social reinforcement to which its opponents could not respond without jeopardizing their *own* basis of support among the propertied strata. However, although the Communist Party deliberately reshaped itself to seek and win the loyalty of the peasant, it never became dependent upon it, nor did the poor peasant make his presence much felt within the middle and upper reaches of the party organization, which were staffed mainly by refugee individuals from the urban middle classes and the more prosperous rural strata. In a word, the CCP did not become a peasant party, and the clearest evidence lay in the fact that within a few years of achieving state power it turned against its former basis of support and, overriding peasant resistance, began to carry out sweeping collectivization of land into 'cooperatives'.

In one sense, Mao converted Lenin's attitude to the proletariat and applied it to the peasantry, creating a party founded on peasant support but also on the premise that the peasant, no more than the worker, was spontaneously capable of political direction and organization, and that these tasks would fall to professional revolutionaries, their efforts organized through and within the party machine. But with this difference: that the party's route to power lay through an essentially unpolitical terrain, in which the party accumulated and extended its power *militarily*, as itself the state-in-embryo in quite practical terms. Thus it was possible for processes of internal bureaucratization and the elimination of political competition to precede by many years the formal capture of state power; bureaucratic settlement and the enlargement of revolutionary strategy went hand in hand. Mao created an 'anti-counter-revolutionary committee' in 1930 and put it to violent use against his party critics in the rural base areas. Later, an important element of the party 'rectification' purges of 1942–4 in the Yenan bases was a drive against those who criticized the ' "big shots" who act as a race apart and get more than is reasonable to eat or drink' – sentiments voiced by some of the party's literary supporters, such as Wang Shih-wei (Benton, 1975). From this phase stems the quintessentially Maoist demand that art and the intelligentsia be directly subordinate to politics. The rewriting of party history to the detriment of Mao's adversaries, in the 1945 'Resolution on some questions in the history of our party', and the writing of 'Mao Tse-tung thought' into the party statutes were both natural corollaries – though the latter did not inhibit Chou En-lai from telling General Marshall in 1946 that the CCP sought democracy for China on 'the American model', with 'free enterprises, a favourable intellectual climate, and the development of personality' (Fejto, 1973, p. 17).

Such ruses were a natural part – like the remaking and breaking of alliances with the Kuomintang – of a strategy of protracted war pursued among numerous potential allies, suppliers and opponents. They were unlikely to be damaging provided the communists preserved the independence of their military forces – as they jealously did, even at the height of the renewed united front with Chiang Kai-shek during the Japanese war. Chiang, for his part, had an equally clear perception of what the communists intended to do with their armies in the long term, and opposed all American efforts to supply them independently or treat them as equal partners. American, and Soviet, efforts in the latter part of the Second

World War to arrange the future of China on the basis of some form of political or territorial power-sharing between the CCP and Kuomintang all ran aground on what the chief adversaries perceived more clearly than anyone else: the fundamental irreconcilability of the two state powers.

INDOCHINA

Other communist parties which pursued an independent, peasant-based military route to power have had to resort to similar combinations: eclectic political alliances on the international plane, together with rather ruthless elimination of their domestic political competitors. This has been particularly true of Indochinese communism. Before the war Indochinese communists were neither the strongest nor the most radical of the opponents of French colonialism. When France's Popular Front government allowed forms of elections in the colonies, the Indochinese Communist Party won only limited support in the towns. In part this was due to their role in the rebellion and soviet movement in Nghe An and Ha Tinh provinces, repressed by the French in 1931. In elections to the Saigon city council in 1939 official communist candidates gathered only one per cent of the votes, the majority going to Trotskyists and militant nationalists.

The war, however, drove the Communist Party into the villages, and, operating across the Chinese frontier into northern Vietnam, by early 1945 it had gained control of six rural provinces and a much wider patchwork of guerrilla strength. This rural strategy was not yet a settled one, but it became the basis of the thirty-year struggle for control of Vietnam. On the collapse of Japan, in August 1945, Ho Chi Minh with his guerrilla forces, trained and armed with American help, stepped into control of the north and proclaimed the Democratic Republic of Vietnam at Hanoi, using phraseology drawn from the American Declaration of Independence. But simultaneously the Vietminh agreed to the entry of British and French troops in the south. It was here that their rivals – militant nationalists, religious sects and Trotskyists – were strongest, and the Vietminh undertook a campaign of arrests and killing which, in a few months, eliminated many of their potential critics among radical or revolutionary currents. In November 1945, with an eye to projecting a less-than-revolutionary image internationally, Ho 'dissolved' the Indochinese Communist Party, replacing it with an institute 'for those desirous of continuing their Marxist studies'. In the north the communists, organized through the Vietminh, sought to bolster their position by enforcing a high turnout in the elections to their National Assembly in the north in 1946 – by only stamping the ration cards of those who voted. With famine in the north (two million northerners are estimated to have died of starvation in this period) and held at bay only by Burmese

rice, which was being distributed through government channels, declining
to vote would for many have been equivalent to suicide.

This combination of internal despotism with the ability to wage revolutionary war is illustrated by the transition from guerrilla warfare against
the French during 1946–54 into consolidation through land reform and
party 'rectification'. In the siege of Dien Bien Phu in 1954 Giap's Vietminh
forces overcame the cream of the French army because they were socially
part of the countryside, while General Navarre's troops found themselves
surrounded and isolated. Peasants provided the Vietminh with both front-
line fighters, and those who supplied and supported the armed men, and the
villages gave them food, information and shelter. Yet peasant support for
the Vietminh, which destroyed the French, by no means led into easy land
reform. In the first place the application of political categories, which made
matters easier for 'patriotic' landlords, led to an invasion of the rural party
cadre by landlords and 'rich' peasants. Land reform thus had to be combined with grassroots party purges, as a result of which the landlord and
rich peasant party membership fell during 1953–6 from over 60 per cent to
nothing, while poor peasant membership rose from less than 4 per cent to
50–60 per cent – about their proportion in the rural population itself. These
figures, it is true, may exaggerate the true shifts somewhat, and conceal
some individuals' managing to switch categories. But the ability to preside
over changes of such magnitude testifies to the resilience and independence
of the top party leadership. It was, however, shaken, and it was further
threatened by the peasant revolts against land reform that erupted in North
Vietnam in the autumn of 1956. Later in the same year Giap led a 'rectification of errors' campaign to restabilize the party organization, in which
the drive against the richer social strata was reversed and an effort was
made to recruit more educated and administratively competent individuals
back into the party.

The formative processes of the peasant-based communist movements of
Asia produced a different breed of party. They relied less, and in some
phases hardly at all, upon backing in the towns, but the basis of support
which they dared not lose came from militarily-organized peasants in the
countryside, ranging from embryo guerrilla squads to large regular armies.
This was true of Mao's conquest of China, and largely true throughout
Vietnamese communism's war, from December 1946, when Ho accepted
Giap's advice to abandon Hanoi in face of the French and retreat back to
'resistance' in the northern countryside, right through the latter stages of
the war for the south in the 1960s and 1970s. It was also true of the parallel
movements elsewhere in the Indochinese peninsula – both in Laos, where
the Pathet Lao were essentially a satellite organization of Vietnamese communism, and especially in Kampuchea, where the Khmer Rouge developed
an extreme antipathy towards the urban population.

The Vietcong's largest urban offensive in the last phase of the war, the Tet (New Year) operation of February 1968 in over a hundred towns of South Vietnam, brought no lasting territorial gains, secured no significant urban areas, and involved sending virtual suicide detachments to seize symbolic points which could not be held. But it was unexpectedly effective in undermining the will to escalate in Washington, ousting General Westmoreland and determining President Johnson not to run for a second term. This *political* success arose, in turn, from widespread military control in rural South Vietnam, whence troops in disguise could be infiltrated into the towns – a control of the countryside nourished, by this time, by regular supplies and troops down the 'Ho Chi Minh trail' from the north. The Tet offensive also allowed a brief but murderous period of terror against pro-government individuals and 'tyrants' in Hue and those other centres which communist forces did succeed in holding for a few days. But what it did *not* do was elicit any significant movements of support in those towns.

The result – as American commanders responded by bombing some contested areas flat – was the further political traumatization of South Vietnam. During March–April 1975, as the South collapsed, huge numbers of the urban population fled southwards in panic, recalling the Tet killings. Saigon fell as a silent city, except for the crowds gathered at the US embassy hoping to escape in the last helicopters. The soldiers who took Saigon were for the most part regulars of the North Vietnamese army, young men from the villages, handling up-to-date Soviet weapons but often unable to read a watch.

## THE PHILIPPINES

The other country in which a successful peasant-based communist movement has evolved is the Philippines. This followed the Sino-Soviet split, but was only partly the product of direct Chinese influence. Rather, the Chinese communists' larger experience was repeated: a substantial defeat led to rethinking and the devising of genuinely original strategies to attack particular national circumstances. This also involved an organizational break.

During the war the Philippine Communist Party (PKP) mobilized very substantial guerrilla resistance, mainly in Central Luzon, to the Japanese occupation – the 'Huk' movement, which also encouraged peasants to occupy the land of landlords who had fled. After the war this agrarian movement – though formally disbanded by the Communist Party – in fact continued, in response to renewed oppression by landowners. This applied pressure on the party leadership to continue armed struggle, in order to protect the peasant appropriations now being challenged by returned landowners, who were backed by government troops. By 1950, propelled by peasant desperation and affected by the general 'leftism' of the Cominform period, the party was preparing for insurrection, but having severed its relations with other potential allies. At this point President Quirino was able to call on US help and, with the aid of American counter-insurgency officers, inflict a series of defeats on the Huk forces. By 1954 both the party (now under the leadership of Jesus Lava, who favoured returning to a parliamentary strategy) and its mass organizations were decimated, and it was forced into a low-profile propaganda existence, from which it never recovered. Indeed in 1974 the PKP Politburo met President Marcos and his military chiefs, undertaking to hand over any remaining weapons and to collaborate loyally with the government.

However in the mid-1960s a mixture of forces combined to *replace* the moribund PKP. These included opposition nationalist currents, radical students, some peasant and labour organizations, a Philippine chapter of the Bertrand Russell Peace Foundation, together with still-active remnants of the Huk, and PKP members who aspired to recommence mass work. In December 1968 a new Communist Party of the Philippines (CPP) was 're-established' under the leadership of a young, quasi-Maoist poet expelled from the PKP, Jose Maria Sison, and shortly afterwards armed groups in the countryside were reconstituted as the 'New People's Army' (NPA).

The CPP formally rejected the passivity of the PKP and its 'revisionist Lava clique'* since 1957, and adopted a number of formulations of 'Mao Tse-tung thought'. In its first few years it received modest material support from China. Its NPA initially adopted the Chinese communist strategy of the Yenan period – of securing large base areas, later to 'surround the cities from the countryside'. But early setbacks led to rethinking, and in the mid-1970s the CPP developed its own novel strategy. Its military component had more in common with communist tactics in South Vietnam than in China: small mobile units, conducting surprise attacks or assassinations of unpopular government officials, then retreat into the countryside. The immediate object is not the conquest of territory but building up support and sympathy among the rural population. These tactics have been further modified to allow for the archipelago geography and ethnolinguistic variety of the Philippines – 7000 islands containing over 70 distinct languages (the lingua franca being English, a result of the United States' having supplanted Spain as the colonial power at the beginning of the twentieth century). Each local guerrilla command is therefore also trained and equipped to act as a political leadership, and given a great deal of leeway to experiment with

* The PKP was led, at different times, by *three* Lava brothers. Vincente Lava was general secretary for the first part of the war. In 1944 he was replaced by Pedro Castro, but in 1945 Castro, who favoured parliamentary methods, was in turn replaced by Vincente's younger brother Jose, an advocate of armed peasant struggle. Jose was arrested in 1950, at the zenith of post-war 'leftism', and was replaced by the third brother, Jesus (see Rosenberg, 1984).

local tactics; the NPA has some military presence in each of the Philippines 74 provinces.

The other, equally important plank of strategy, however, is largely parliamentarist: an umbrella 'front' organization, the National Democratic Front, linking the CPP to the increasing number of groups that took up stances in opposition to the Marcos government, including radical tendencies within the Philippines' important Catholic clergy, and to numerous local organizations among the urban workers and poor.

Moreover, the international affiliations of the CPP soon shifted. In the late 1970s, as part of building its bridges with pro-American regimes throughout southeast Asia, China cut off its assistance to the CPP and NPA, and began to support the maintenance of US military bases in the Philippines. Before long, the CPP was collaborating with the old PKP (which had always remained obediently pro-Soviet), and in 1980 the two parties merged their trade union organizations. There is also some evidence of the CPP getting Soviet financial support to replace their lost Chinese income (Rosenberger, 1985, pp. 136–7).

When Marcos was ousted in the revolution following the 1986 elections, and Corazon Aquino installed, the prospects for both the CPP's guerrilla warfare and its urban agitation improved appreciably. The Aquino government is relatively ineffective in repressing its revolutionary opponents, having a hostile relationship with the military establishment, which is itself factionally divided; its countenancing of 'vigilante' assassination squads against political opponents merely expresses the unreliability of the state's machinery. In addition, Aquino has done little to respond to the economic plight of the growing number of landless peasants or the urban poor. Thus, although a number of senior CPP figures were captured by government forces early in 1988, its decentralized organization, and the deep social needs to which its policies are coupled, meant that Philippines communism was very far from having been decapitated.

INDIA

The history of Indian communism also contains deep divisions over peasant policies, but it has never led to lasting rural armed struggles. Moreover, under the British Raj its subordinacy to Soviet requirements severely undermined its nationalist claims; after the Soviet Union entered the Second World War the party aligned itself with the British war effort, shelving its demands for independence and refusing to support Congress's 'Quit India' agitation. Nor did it have a decided policy during the partition of British India. However, in 1948 it shifted to a more radical policy of urban strikes and rural risings. Sections of the party in rural Hyderabad went further, advancing a programme of peasant struggle along the lines of Mao's 'New Democracy', and placed themselves at the head of a movement that at one stage controlled several thousand villages.

The party's *general* shift towards a 'left' line at this time was prompted by the switch of Soviet policy expressed in the formation of Cominform, with Tito being held up as a model to Indian communists. But this phase was relatively short, and the Hyderabad communists' attempt to adapt Maoism to rural India was repudiated by the party leadership, under B. T. Ranadive, at the same time as it was being suppressed by government troops. It is interesting that Ranadive's denunciations included an explicit attack upon Mao – a clue which underlines the significance of the hostile silence which *Pravda* maintained on the Chinese communists' sweep southwards to victory during 1949.

From 1951–2 the Indian Communist Party readapted, resuming electoral competition, and developing – and separating – along lines shaped very much by regional and state conditions. In 1957 electoral success, based on effective organization of the poor and landless, allowed the Communist Party in the southwestern state of Kerala, led by E. M. S. Namboodiripad, to form a ministry – the first elected communist government ever to take power. Kerala communism, with its electoral successes and openness to coalitions, has sometimes been compared to 'Eurocommunism'. It first took office, however, in conditions of considerable tension and violence, with its leaders, under pressure from Nehru and the central government, warning of the danger of civil war. But communist strength in India has remained concentrated in relatively few regions, of which the most important are Kerala and West Bengal, and it has not represented a serious threat to the national government.


INDONESIA


After their open split in 1960–2, the Chinese and Soviet parties contended explicitly for the loyalty of Asian parties. The largest of these by far was Aidit's Indonesian Communist Party (PKI). Its fate illustrates – negatively – how vital it is for peasant-based communism to wield its own armed force, and to succeed in 'capturing' nationalism for itself, rather than relying on symbiosis with other nationalist forces (and also, incidentally, how little the Sino-Soviet split was concerned with communism's actual strategic principles). At the height of its strength in the early 1960s, before it was destroyed by General Suharto's military coup in 1965, the Indonesian party was the world's third largest communist party, claiming a membership of 3.5 million, larger than most ruling parties, and smaller only than the Chinese and Soviet parties. It was, moreover, based on mass peasant support, in a country whose land crisis was (and is) one of the most severe in the world; in parts of eastern Java peasants could be found cultivating plots as small as *one metre* square.

The Indonesian communist leaders took the Chinese side in the Sino-Soviet dispute; indeed it was Aidit who in 1963 first put forward the global communist strategy of encircling the world's cities by the world's country-side, later taken up by the Chinese leadership against Soviet 'revisionism'. However the Indonesian party was wedded essentially rather than contingently to collaboration with Sukarno's nationalism. This had not always been so. The communists – in line with Stalin's benign attitudes to the colonies of his allies – greeted Sukarno's declaration of national independence in 1945 with suspicion. Though they later took places in his republican government, they turned, and in 1948 supported an attempt to overthrow it, declaring a rival government at Madiun. But from 1951, when Aidit, with Soviet sponsorship, assumed the leadership, the PKI embarked on a new trajectory, based on the Maoist doctrine of assembling a 'bloc of four classes'. This implied that at the present stage of the 'anti-imperialist revolution' Sukarno and the national bourgeoisie (represented by the National Party) had an essential role and should not be antagonized. (Collaboration with the other main nationalist party of the 1950s, the Masjumi, was ruled out by its determined Moslem anti-communism. Sukarno, however, espoused a more vaguely religious nationalism, and was satisfied with the communists' generalized assent to belief in one god.)

Sukarno, as head of state, attempted unsuccessfully to ride above parties. Buffeted from numerous directions, he came to rely heavily on the communists, who grew rapidly in the 1950s to become the largest party, with by far the most cohesive organization. They trailed cautiously behind his more radical domestic policies (the nationalization of Dutch property in 1957, and land redistribution in 1959), but gave full support to his foreign and territorial policies, culminating in his vigorous construction of a Chinese–Indonesian axis in 1964–5. Expansion, of course, brought the PKI a multiplication of enemies, but its leaders seem to have regarded their intimate relationship with Sukarno as adequate protection.

International conditions, however, were changing dangerously. In particular, the Soviet Union and the United States both felt similarly offended by Sukarno and the PKI's support of Chinese ambitions. Soviet diplomats made it increasingly apparent (so the American ambassador in Jakarta reported) 'that it was clearly not in the Soviet interests to see Indonesia wind up a communist state dominated by China – which, interestingly, made Soviet desires very much coincident with our own', and urged that the US should not cut back on aid to Indonesia lest China fill the gap (Jones, 1971, pp. 337–8).

The component of Indonesian politics which it was natural for both powers to look to was the officer corps of the armed forces, an economic as well as military caste, largely independent of the civil state, tied closely into the propertied classes and reaping fortunes in graft from their positions as managers of state enterprises. But, unlike the officers of many under-developed states, they commanded a large and efficient war machine, first tempered in action against the Dutch and British in 1945–6. US influence among officers was always strong, independently of the shifts in Sukarno's policies; up to 1965 4000 Indonesian officers were trained in the US. The Soviet Union also began to seek support in similar quarters as its relations with Sukarno and the PKI deteriorated in the early 1960s. During a visit to Jakarta in June 1964, Mikoyan, the Soviet deputy premier, continually pressed the theme of the Indonesian forces' dependence on generous Soviet military supplies. Through Adam Malik (a former Indonesian ambassador in Moscow) the Soviet Union sponsored and financed the small Murba party and, through it, the army's 'trade union' front (a bitter rival of the PKI-controlled trade union federation); both organizations reciprocated with public praise for Soviet policy.

But it was the US who was the main beneficiary of the coup which – after earlier alarms and attempts – finally came in October 1965. The PKI's own organization – though hugely impressive in membership statistics – proved to be made of paper when force came into play: essentially a vast edifice of parliamentary, trade union, rural and welfare structures, wielding vast patronage and influence, but backed by virtually no armed force whatso-ever. Its cultivation of some middle-ranking officers and their conspiracy against the Army general staff served merely to provide senior commanders with grounds for action against it. The PKI thus fell a helpless victim to Suharto's careful preparations, and was destroyed during the following months in the greatest massacre of communists ever to have occurred out-side the Soviet Union. Hundreds of thousands of communists and their supporters were killed; for months canals in east and central Java were clogged by the bodies thrown into them at night.

Before the coup the Chinese leadership strained every sinew to secure the PKI's support against the Soviet Union, but all in the cause of reinforcing their own alliance with Sukarno. At no point did they put pressure on its leaders to alter their strategy and adopt the revolutionary and guerrilla methods which Chinese propaganda was busy proclaiming against 'Krushchevite peaceful coexistence' (though this was precisely what they blamed Aidit for, posthumously). There was a keener irony: there were few more striking precedents for the disaster which Suharto visited on the PKI than the decimation of the Chinese Communist Party at the hands of Chiang Kai-shek in 1927. But Chinese diplomacy – which had also included efforts to win supporters among senior Indonesian officers – dictated that this was not a parallel to be mentioned.

Experience thus delivered mixed judgement on the disputes between Roy and Lenin at the Second Congress of Comintern on the prospects for Asia. Roy was proved right in his expectation that communism in the East would provide the next wave of independent communist successes. The reasons for this owed not a little to his other expectation – that the colonial countries could provide support to determined revolutionary leaderships, while the working classes of the metropolitan countries were too much attached to reformist and liberal politicians. But Roy's perspective that it would be the small but militant urban working class to provide the spearhead of colonial socialist revolution went quite unrealized (except in the official self-descriptions of the communist parties). It was Lenin's almost casual suggestion of a soviet or communist movement based entirely on peasants that pointed the way forward – even though peasant communism actually adopted soviet forms only in relatively brief phases. And the reasons why that was so had much to do with the main question over which Roy, Lenin and the Comintern delegates of 1920 had argued and worried: whether or not to collaborate with 'bourgeois' nationalism. To that there proved no unambiguous answer: every successful communist trajectory has involved collaboration, assimilation, sometimes fusion, at other times violent antagonism with nationalists, with success depending on astute judgement of the combinations and timing of the turns.

FURTHER READING

Carrere d'Encausse and Schram's general selection, *Marxism and Asia* (1969), includes useful extracts on the early years of Asian communism. Eudin and North (1957) is a useful documentary history of Soviet policy in Asia up to 1927. Haithcox (1971) covers M. N. Roy's career up to 1939; Roy (1987) is a selection of his works, 1917–22. Harris (1967) treats the early years of Turkish communism. Zabih (1966) and Halliday (1980) have accounts of the Gilan soviet movement of 1920–1. There is an English translation of the proceedings of the 1920 Baku Congress (1977). Ullman (1961–73), vol. 3, deals with the Anglo-Soviet agreement of 1921.

Histories of Japanese communism include Beckman and Okubo Genji (1969) (up to 1945), and Scalapino (1967) and Langer (1972) (mainly on the post-war period). The best general history of Chinese communism's route to power is Harrison (1972); Guillermas (1972) and Bianco (1971) also cover the party's history up to 1949, and Brandt, Schwartz and Fairbank (1973) is a selection of party documents over the same period. Chesneaux (1968) deals with communist activity in the urban working class during 1919–27, Isaacs (1961) considers political aspects of the Chinese Communist Party's early years and its 1927 defeat, and Schwartz (1958) discusses the rise of Mao. Feigon (1983) is a biography of the founder and early leader of the party, Ch'en Tu-hsiu. Lotveit (1979) describes the Kiangsi soviet bases, Wilson (1971) the Long March, and Johnson (1963) and Selden (1971) the Communist Party's subsequent expansion from Yenan. Pepper (1978) recounts the final years of its duel with Chiang Kai-shek, 1945–9.

Turner (1975) and Pike (1978) are general studies of Vietnamese communism. Huynh (1982) covers its early history, 1925–45. The Second World War and the war with France are described in Sachs (1960) and Hammer (1966), the Geneva settlement in Randle (1969), the war with the US in Smith (1983) and Turley (1986), and the years since the fall of South Vietnam in 1975 in Nguyen (1983). Lacouture (1968), though dated, is a good biography of Ho Chi Minh. Kiernan (1985) is a history of Kampuchean communism to 1975, and Vickery (1984) an account of the Pol Pot regime and its demise. Brown and Zasloff (1986) is a history of Laotian communism – essentially an offshoot of the larger Vietnamese party – from its beginnings in the 1930s to 1985.

Kerkvliet (1977) gives an account of the Huk movement of the 1940s and 1950s in the Philippines. Rosenberg (1984) is a summary history of communist organizations in the Philippines, and Porter (1987) reviews their condition and prospects after the fall of Marcos. On Indian communism see Overstreet and Windmiller (1959) and Sharma (1984); Nossiter (1982) describes communism's success in Kerala. McVey (1965) treats the origins of Indonesian communism; later periods are covered in Mintz (1960), Van der Kroef (1965) and Mortimer (1974). Controversies about the 1965 coup are summarized in Westoby (1981), chapter 10. Van der Kroef (1980) gives an overview of communism across southeast Asia.

# PART II

## Communism spreads and divides

# 6

# Means and ends in communist politics

'The entire history of Bolshevism, both before and after the October Revolution', Lenin reminded the purists within Comintern in 1921, 'is jam-packed with instances of manoeuvering, temporizing and compromising with other parties (including bourgeois parties)!' Stalin expressed himself more robustly when, at the close of the war, he urged Tito to accept King Peter of Yugoslavia back: 'You don't have to take him back forever. Just temporarily, and then at the right moment – a knife in the back!' (Djilas, 1977, p. 407).

## STRATEGIES AND MANOEUVRES

Is there a characteristically communist approach to political strategy? The notion of strategy makes sense only in the context of a distinction between immediate and more remote goals, and its corollary, the notion that policies and alliances pursued in the present will, in future, be exchanged for others. If we can identify a distinctively communist stance on strategy understood in such terms it lies in the attitude towards the rights and objectives of the communist party within its passing patterns of support and alliance. As Lenin, in 1920, described his manoeuvres against the Mensheviks, both before and after October 1917, he used only those changes of tack and compromises which 'assisted, boosted and consolidated the Bolsheviks at the expense of the Mensheviks' (Lenin, 1960–78, 31, p. 75). He should have added that this principle of action applied generally, to the wide range of allies and collaborators with which communism has from time to time sought relations. As we saw in chapter 2, it receives a general justification in Leninist political sociology: parties and factions represent hostile classes; and rival parties which may claim to represent the working classes do not really do so, since their leaders' true loyalties lie elsewhere, their members following them only through a false consciousness of their own interests.

The principle continues to apply when state power is at stake, and political action becomes a matter not only of contention but command. Then communism's instinct is to press to the limit its own party interests *vis-à-vis* those of both rivals and allies (all of whom are potential rivals), a process which pushes towards the one-party state. It pushes, also, beyond politics into economics. To eliminate political rivals permanently one must also – all the more if one is guided by Marxism – seek to plough over the economic soil from which they spring: hence, for example, communism's general strategy in power of nationalizing large-scale private property. Once reached, however, the limit of the one-party state implies the extinction of political strategy in the earlier sense. The negotiations, renegotiations and uncertainties of alliances apply only when one's allies (and others) have themselves some freedom to manoeuvre, to join or separate, to grow, even possibly to overwhelm one. If these possibilities are removed then political strategy, too, becomes absorbed into the ruling party – and by that fact transmuted into something different: not the visible contest of rival organizations and policies, in which the management of one's record and image is of central importance, but the hand-to-mouth struggles of undeclared factions, all concealing themselves within a larger official unity. Moreover, as the party tries to bring numerous additional forms of economic and social control directly within its own organizational machinery, it necessarily creates further internal differences and rivalries corresponding to the functions it absorbs. Thus, for example, a frequent source of internal friction in ruling communist parties is that between ideological and economic organs, the latter chafing against the rigidities stipulated by the former. By crushing the permitted play of political rivalry, communism can never destroy it, but only absorb it and become, so to speak, internally infected by it. Communist state power, apparently monolithic, fractures and dissolves upon closer inspection; politics, in that sense, survives even its own abolition. Moreover, after state power is obtained, explicit politics resurrects itself on the international plane, and the party must make its way among the enmities and alliances of state-to-state and state-to-party relations.

The urge to command the whole political stage is not, of course, unique to communist parties. Politics as such (in its modern, party, sense) carries within itself the dialectic of war and coexistence, conducted within rules which for the time being constitute the political game, but at the same time modifying and threatening them. Communism merely lies near one end of the spectrum as far as the self-consciousness and single-mindedness of its purposes, and the methods with which it pursues them, are concerned. But just as political variety and pluralism enervate its monopolies of power, so its style within competitive politics often reveals a highly expedient adherence to alliances.

## ALLIANCES AND ANTAGONISMS

How has this spirit worked out in practice? Its origins lie in the problems of managing relations with other political organizations. At the inception of the *Iskra* group in 1900-1 the 'orthodox' social democrats who led it tackled the problem of ensuring their identity and 'hegemony' within an alliance with former Marxists who were on their way to becoming leaders of Russian liberalism. They considered men such as Peter Struve (the author of Russian social democracy's agreed programme for its first congress, in 1898, but now cultivating liberal circles) definitely set upon a political course hostile to themselves. But at the same time they were potentially very useful, being well placed to provide *Iskra* with valuable information and money, and amenable to an amicable division of labour between the illegal, revolutionary social democrats and a legally circumscribed liberalism.

The *Iskra* leaders' tactics within this original 'united front' were thrashed out collectively. Martov was from the outset unenthusiastic about the alliance, and Plekhanov the most hostile of all. Yet it was Plekhanov who laid the basis for agreement with his proposal that Struve – who readily agreed – renounce his personal affiliation to social democracy. Lenin, once it became clear to him that Struve aimed eventually at an independent liberal party, characterized him privately as 'a politician in the worst sense of the word, an old fox, and a brazen huckster' (Lenin, 1960-78, 4, p. 380). But he willingly acquiesced in the secret 'coalition' negotiated by Plekhanov. In the event the agreement was shortlived, through events beyond the control of either party. But it was one whose scope both sides later found embarrassing, and concealed, since it provided not only for a political alliance for an indefinite period, but for Struve and his prosperous backers to subsidize *Iskra* and the illegal social democratic networks.

On one level the episode merely illustrates the general difficulty most political currents experience in entering into advantageous practical collaboration while avoiding restrictive or damaging political entanglements. The *Iskra* leaders approached negotiations with a peculiarly clear-cut sense of expediency, which carried over into the Bolshevik tradition. But they also highlighted a doctrinal problem, specific to a party claiming to be based in the working-class movement and to be equipped with a scientific political sociology – that of drawing distinctions between the 'socialist' and the 'bourgeois', among both parties and politicians. If Struve was, at the time of these negotiations, only partly and incipiently a political liberal, it was because he remained in part a socialist – but a socialist who had taken the side of Bernstein in the 'revisionist' controversy. The revisionists' view of political strategy – summarized in Bernstein's aphorism 'The movement is everything, the final goal nothing' – naturally predisposed them to take a benign view of alliances with those with whom they differed, provided that the parties had immediate goals in common. In fact, redepicting Marxian socialism as the evolutionary outgrowth of 'socializing' tendencies within capitalism, Bernstein saw it as wholly contained in the piecemeal growth of mass organizations and the accumulation of reforms and political power which they could win; separate or in abstraction from these, talk of ultimate goals was unreal.

That 'revisionism' offended against orthodoxy was by no means its only sin. In more practical terms it undercut the efforts the *Iskra* leaders had been making to organize a scientific socialism for Russia, and to define it as something quite distinct from – if allied to – both the economic and trade union strivings of industrial workers, and their more generalized aspirations for political liberation. From their point of view Bernstein's aphorism should be reversed: socialism, the goal, was everything; movements were of value only in so far as they could help towards it.

The 'orthodox' Russian Marxists drew a further distinction, charging in their polemics against revisionism that it was an anti-socialist current insinuating itself into the socialist movement. This was years before the Leninist doctrine of the labour aristocracy and of socialist organizations being in the grip of 'bourgeois' leaders, yet the germ of that distinction was contained in Plekhanov's demand that Struve personally renounce his previous adherence to social democracy. The theoretical separation between the progressive body of an ally and its reactionary leaders was to become an essential element of the Leninist strategic approach to alliances.

The opposed standpoints of goal and movement carried, of course, different ethical and epistemological implications, as well as merely tactical and political ones. Marxist orthodoxy placed socialism's essential purposes into the future. But the future, after all, does not yet exist, and cannot directly subordinate the present to itself. In order to assert itself in the here-and-now, therefore, it must be *represented*, and not just as hope or goal, but tangibly – and it was this requirement which, with increasing explicitness, underlay the gropings towards the proper form of a party during the 1890s.

The 'orthodox' Russian Marxists, of course, did not doubt that socialism was in the general, essential, most truly real, interests of Russian workers – or, for that matter, of Russian society as a whole. After all, when the whole European working class was still in its infancy, Marx and Engels' *Communist Manifesto* had defined the communists, in contradistinction to the workers' movement of which they formed a part, as being those who recognized the general goals of the class struggle. Their self-justifications and their ethics, therefore, tended to be concerned more with the future than the immediate, more with goals than means. Leninism, in its developed form, came to be self-consciously hostile to morality as a restraint on political action in a way that previous socialisms – including, for all his thunderings against 'bourgeois' morality, Marx's – never were. Yet values – or the emancipation from them – followed from facts: if socialism was to make progress where spontaneous conditions and desires for it were feeble and the constellation of other political forces inauspicious it must, of necessity, be prepared to treat the wishes and beliefs of supporters and allies as means, and not as limits.

This characteristic emerged clearly – and was criticized as such – in the *Iskra* group at the Second Congress. The *Iskra* programme for peasants, for example, quite deliberately promised land which, once in power, it never intended to deliver – the operative question was how to arouse peasant revolt and undercut the social democrats' rivals, the social revolutionaries. Subsequently political 'Machiavellianism' and morality – one of Bernstein's other departures from Marx was to seek an explicitly ethical basis for socialism in Kant – became a fundamental recurrent issue, argued in many different contexts between Mensheviks and Bolsheviks, socialists and communists.

### RUSSIA

The peculiarities of the Russian revolution as it actually occurred added a further dimension, cognitive rather than moral. Those Marxists who were predicting, from the turn of the century, that socialist revolution would first succeed in Russia, could be understood by their contemporaries as saying something paradoxical and surprising, but by no means unbelievable. And, if it were granted that this might occur, then it would be natural that the Russian revolution should act as a spur, and in that sense give a lead, to revolutionary movements in Europe. But if at the beginning of the twentieth century a Russian Marxist had foretold that, following the success of revolution in Russia, socialist political leadership in the rest of Europe – indeed, in the whole world – should fall to a single, centralized 'world party of socialist revolution', all of whose key leaders would be Russian, which should lay down the strategy and even tactics to be followed in other countries, the idea would have been dismissed as laughable and surreal. Yet this is precisely what happened with Comintern, partly because the very success of Bolshevik organizational methods encouraged their extension onto the international arena, and partly because most of the political support on which the Bolsheviks were able to count in other countries was weak and easily assumed a dependent or sycophantic relationship with them. The first cause, naturally enough, encouraged the second; the centralized, militarized discipline with which the Bolsheviks acted against opposition within Russia – including all varieties of socialist opposition – tended to repel support for them among socialists abroad.

While, therefore, we may detect in the pre-1917 history of socialism, and particularly Bolshevism, a number of seeds that flourished vigorously in communism's later evolution, we must also remind ourselves that history, being cumulative, is incapable of repeating itself and sets a limit to all parallels. Communism after 1917 is conditioned by a state, and a political mentor, which was absent before then. Later other states, and rival mentors, arose, but none has come near to displacing the influence of the Soviet state.

Nor was all such influence in any sense rational. The coming to pass of what would have seemed a fantasy before the First World War – a Russian-dominated and led organization aspiring to be the, single, global socialist party – meant that Comintern policy evolved from a basis of limited experience and slanted perception. Russian dominance has by no means been simply a matter of the considered injection of Soviet-decided goals and interests, via other communist parties, into domestic politics. Other crucial components were those often underestimated factors – dogma, ignorance and self-delusion. They led the Comintern, in its early years, to see revolutionary opportunities in Italy, Germany, Britain and China where any sober observer could have told them they did not exist, and not infrequently to order political manoeuvres or combinations quite contrary to the advice of the local communists who were required to execute them. The consequent political zig-zags arose – as their authors sometimes later conceded – from wishful thinking and mirages of revolution.

Conversely, however, the leadership of the Soviet Communist Party has attempted to come to terms with, and compensate for, its own lack of omni-competence. This process contains several elements, which have developed unevenly. There has been an effort to rely on broader, fuller, more empirical sources of information, giving a more realistic, less cut-and-dried, picture. This has necessarily entailed shelving, at least in private, many of the Marxist categories in which policies are couched, and assessing events far more empirically. And correspondingly the evaluation of situations, and the evolution of policy options, have come to allow for more possibilities, to seek to keep more options open, and to reduce risk in a more systematic and rational way. The policy horizon has lengthened greatly, with all the conservatism that entails.

### POLICY TOWARDS GERMANY

Consider, for example, the development of the Soviet approach to Germany, always seen as the keystone of their European policy. Until 1923 the Soviet leaders looked, primarily and publicly, to communist-led revolution, but also more covertly explored agreements with the German military and right.

It was as though they realized that reliance on the German Communist Party alone was a fragile plank on which to build, and sought already to hedge their bets. In a somewhat different form this stance resurfaced in the early 1930s, with its expectation that 'After Hitler, us.'

By the late 1930s the German left was annihilated. Stalin shifted to a policy of equal or greater reliance on Hitler, trusting in the 1939 pact up to the eve of Germany's attack on Russia, despite the warnings from other governments and his own intelligence sources about Hitler's 'Barbarossa' plan of attack. In the late 1930s he decimated the Red Army's senior officer corps, much of it on 'information' conveniently provided by the German intelligence services. Few steps were taken to relocate industry and supplies, even though after 1939 German forces were deployed along much of the Soviet frontier. As a result much of Russia's industry was overrun in the first weeks of the German advance in 1941. In the early period of the Nazi–Soviet pact Stalin even contemplated its forming the basis of a more grandiose political settlement. In occupied Belgium and Norway communists sought to act as the local political administration under the Nazis. In The Netherlands the communist press reappeared legally, and in France the Communist Party applied to the German occupation authorities to resume legal publication of *L'Humanité*, explaining that it would agitate for a French–Soviet treaty as counterpart of the German–Soviet treaty, the two pacts being twin pillars of a lasting European peace (Mortimer, 1984, p. 295).

Nowadays – their distrust having been deepened by the breach with Tito and later by the Sino-Soviet schism – the Soviet leadership would not dream of placing such reliance on one substantial power which they could not control. One of the main risks they cannot reduce or balance is that popular opposition or revolt in Eastern Europe will erode their control over the other Warsaw Pact states. One of their fears of a reunified Germany, therefore, is that the political freedoms that would unavoidably be built into it would have an eventually disastrous liberalizing effect elsewhere in Eastern Europe, and that in abandoning the East German government and party they would seriously undermine the internal and external stability of other client and satellite regimes. The corollary to the Soviet Union's pre-war role as sponsor and leader of other communist parties is the expectation that it will act as their protector once they are come to power. That is the significance of Krushchev and Malenkov's posthumous accusation against Beria – that in the aftermath of Stalin's death he sought to legalize the Social Democratic Party in East Germany and open the door to German reunification.

Post-war Soviet policy towards Germany, reconciled to the fact that the division and contrast of the two states prevents the growth of any strong communist party in West Germany, is founded on preventing reunification.

At the same time it seeks to cultivate the more amenable sectors of West German politics with the prospect of an eventually reunified nation, plus the threat that Germany would be the main battlefield in any European war. This double theme – varied, naturally, according to time and audience – has the further advantage of complementing Soviet military policy, in particular the maintenance of conventional forces able to overwhelm Western Europe in a few days.

Policy thus looks to a range of points of support, each of which taken separately would be weak or unreliable. This is the basis, in normal times, of Soviet political action in all the major West European states, including those with sizeable communist parties. Indeed, the existence of a large communist party can, from this point of view, even be seen to carry a disadvantage, since it tends to attract, and thus concentrate and weaken, pro- or philo-Soviet sentiments and currents which would be more effective if dispersed.

SOVIET 'EGOISM'

The progress which the Soviet party leadership have made in acting in a better-informed, more cautious and sophisticated way within world politics, and its consequences for the strategies of local communist parties, are something conceptually quite distinct – if often difficult to separate in practice – from the other aspect of Russian-centredness in the evolution of communist strategy: the entrenchment and growth of the *interests* of the Soviet state. Secular changes in understanding the global political environment have developed in parallel with changes in goals and priorities. Both, in interaction, through the influence exerted by the Soviet party, have been major factors in the evolution of other communists' strategies and fates – even to the point of their being treated as expendable pawns in larger gambits.

One view of the changes in goals rests on a distinction between original Bolshevism and Soviet interests, and may be summarized as follows: in the immediate aftermath of 1917 the Soviet leadership drew no fundamental distinction between Russian and international revolution, the former being but the opening movement, and essential catalyst, of the latter. Moreover, they did not conceive that, in the long run, the Soviet state could survive without socialist allies. The sway the Russian revolutionists exercised stemmed from the great prestige of their own revolution, and the sense that their talents and experience equipped them to lead the international movement.

With time, however (this view holds) internal social developments brought changed political pressures. The Soviet Union did survive, but remained isolated; Comintern's other parties all disappointed it. Under great stress, it turned to resolve its own problems with a strong, authoritarian and increasingly egotistical party-state bureaucracy. Positions of control at the lower and middle levels were gradually permeated by those with more selfish motives – members of the educated classes of the pre-revolutionary regime, and those who saw in an administrative or political career a route to self-advancement. Beneath them stood the enormous peasantry, whose horizons stretched little beyond the village. Much of the urban working class, and virtually all its most class-conscious members, were killed or dispersed in the civil wars. In due course such dispositions began to have an effect even in the leadership of the Bolshevik party, where they greatly encouraged the growth of nationalist and ad hoc expedients in international policy. Office politics writ large, so to speak, together with the apathy of the majority, sapped the early idealism of Comintern.

This view, or crucial elements of it, have a long lineage, starting from the early criticisms of 'left' communists, both in Russia and abroad, and their echoes among social democrats. It was taken up by Trotsky and his followers in the mid-1920s, as they discovered in Stalin the personification of conservatism at home and opportunism in Comintern (see chapter 12). It has found favour with historians who have wanted to treat Comintern's evolution with sympathetic realism – Isaac Deutscher and E. H. Carr are well-known examples. And, most recently, it has become popular with 'Eurocommunists', in quest of a theory to explain the defects which they so long forbore to criticize. It has the advantage of offering a 'sociological' framework of explanation, and at the same time allows an encouraging separation between an original, fallible and perhaps naive, but idealistic, communism, and its later corruption by external forces beyond its control – for example, between the Comintern while Lenin directed it, and its use under Stalin. It can also rather easily be extended to explain communist state-to-state relations, and the frictions, cynicism and national 'egoisms' that characterize them.

However, it fits the facts only with difficulty. As we saw (in chapters 3–5) the survival and safety of the Soviet state asserted itself as an imperative right from the beginning, facing the Bolshevik leaders with choices between their interests and the pursuit of revolution abroad. The divisions among them over the Brest-Litovsk negotiations showed the reality, and the difficulty, of such choices, eroding their abstract doctrine that the cause of global revolution was indivisible. Lenin was the first, albeit silently and pragmatically, to ditch it, and initially he had an uphill struggle to take his colleagues with him. The leader who had had no problems rallying his party in July 1917 in face of government revelations that their propaganda was being subsidized by the German general staff, had the greatest of difficulty, in January 1918, in prevailing over the 'revolutionary phrasemakers' in his

Central Committee who wanted to continue the war in the hope that this, in combination with propaganda for peace, would accelerate the German revolution. To count on the German revolution, Lenin warned Bukharin and his supporters on the central committee, was to set a hypothesis against a fact. In Germany the revolutionary movement had not yet started, but 'here it already has a newborn, lusty child and if we do not make it clear now that we agree to a peace, then we will perish. It is important for us to hold out until the general socialist revolution and this can only be achieved when we have concluded peace' (RSDLP, 1977, p. 178).

The reluctance to risk the Soviet republic on mere possibilities was sharpened by the sense that revolutionary prospects elsewhere had indifferent leaders. Trotsky, who agreed to support Lenin's 'capitulation' at Brest-Litovsk if his own tactic of 'Neither war nor peace' failed, knew, behind his revolutionary oratory, that Europe's reformist socialist leaders were succeeding in containing support for the Russian revolution. And in October, as social unrest began to disintegrate Germany, Lenin put his finger on the central problem: 'Europe's greatest misfortune and danger is that it has *no* revolutionary party' (Lenin, 1960–78, 28, p. 113).

The process, therefore, by which international revolution remained a theoretical premise of Soviet policy but was less and less a practical one, began early. While much effort and money went into creating other communist parties, it was very seldom that Soviet leaders forwent diplomatic or political moves that promised real advantage to the Soviet state merely because they might disrupt the efforts of foreign communists. On the contrary, the latter were generally expected to adhere to and justify all Soviet policies. Their training in the art of sudden tactical adaptations was therefore different from the Bolsheviks' in one crucial regard; from the outset it was conditioned by Russian before domestic exigencies. Many nascent communist groups found both their political fates and their lives tossed around among much larger considerations. The national egoism of the Soviet party (and other subsequent ruling parties) is evident so early that it may be regarded as an original characteristic.

### INTERNATIONALISM AND CONQUEST

A variant of the trade-off between the interests of the Soviet state and other communist parties hinges on territorial expansion. The propaganda of communist states has very frequently cited their security needs as reasons for expanding their borders or interfering with their neighbours (and it would be wrong to discount all such arguments as pure apologetics), but an ancillary reason given is often that of giving aid to revolutionary or 'progressive' domestic forces. The balance of motives varies greatly. But their combination means it is often impossible to draw any hard-and-fast demarcation between expansion of a communist state – or of a buffer-zone of client regimes on its periphery – and helping communist movements to power which would be too weak to win it in their own right. The aid given may greatly outweigh the support that its recipients are able to mobilize on their own account; in Leninism's view the objective interests of nations, like those of working classes, are not to be equated with the spontaneous wishes of the individuals composing them.

At one extreme it is a case of expansion into areas where communism enjoys no prior support whatsoever. The Chinese annexation of Tibet, for example, involved the absorption of a people and culture with no socialist – or even secular – tradition whatsoever. The same process of assimilation applied to many of the Asian and Turkomen peoples of the Russian empire whom the Bolsheviks reconquered in 1920–2, with the difference that most of these had previously also been under Russian administration. Not that the communist movements of all the Soviet borderlands were negligible. Both they, and their affinity for nationalism (under the influence of Lenin's doctrine of self-determination), were significant factors in undermining the Provisional Government and in combating the White Armies, generally hostile to any dismantling of the Russian empire. Subsequently communist nationalism, especially that of the Georgians, was one of the factors that had to be overcome when, in 1923–4, the makeshift array of bilateral treaties linking their Soviet republics to the Russian Soviet state was replaced by a federated 'Union of Soviet Socialist Republics'.

The expansionism of the Soviet Union is partly continuous with the much longer tendency to military extension of the Russian state – a tendency whose roots in the internal characteristics of Russian society, and its lack of natural external frontiers, has been much debated by historians. Certainly it has won Russian communism, in its expansionist moments, some extraordinary allies. At the height of the 1920 Soviet advance into Poland, Trotsky, as Red Army commander, received the support of General Alexei Brusilov, the Tsar's last commander-in-chief, who was given space in *Pravda* to urge former officers to sink their differences with Bolshevism and rally to the colours against the traditional Polish enemy. In 1939 Stalin's annexations of eastern Poland and the Baltic states received approval in turn from the exiled Trotsky (though his own name was by that time a synonym for 'white' and 'fascist' in the Soviet Union). And in 1945 the genuine leader of Russian fascism, Konstantin Rodzaevsky, then a refugee in North China, recognized Stalin as an ally, pursuing Russia's historic territorial goals of 'gathering in the Muscovite lands' in Eastern Europe. Stalinism, he declared, 'is our Russian Fascism cleansed of extremes, illusions and errors' (Stephan, 1978, p. 338).

FURTHER READING

Struve's early career is sympathetically recounted in the first of the two volumes of Pipes' biography (1970). The repercussions of Bernstein's 'revisionism' in Russia, and 'economism', are discussed in Frankel (1969). Ulam (1974) outlines the development of Soviet foreign policy, while Pipes (1974) deals with the formation of the Soviet Union from the early soviet republics.

# 7

# The takeovers in Eastern Europe

As early as February 1945, with the Red Armies occupying Hungary and most of Poland, it was Goebbels who warned of the 'iron curtain' which would bisect Europe if the agreements reached at Yalta were imposed on the peoples of the continent (Bramsted, 1965, p. 336). In fact, much less territory in Eastern Europe was assimilated to the Soviet state (eastern Poland, part of East Prussia, Ruthenia, subtracted from Czechoslovakia, and Moldavia, taken from Romania), than was eventually brought under communist rule and Soviet domination. Stalin's precautionary annexations suggest that he had only provisional plans for the much larger areas occupied by his armies. And the variety and changeability of the Eastern European communist parties' policies – all, except the Yugoslav and Albanian, under close Soviet direction – suggest some measure of 'openness' to Soviet policy towards the area at the close of the war. In Romania, for example, the monarchy was retained until December 1947, and almost everywhere there was an attempt to cultivate relations with other political parties and forces, even to the point of the communists deliberately taking a back seat. Communists, Ulbricht instructed his assistants in eastern Germany in 1945, should not be mayors but deputies; the principal public position should either be occupied by a social democrat or by a figure from the 'bourgeois' parties, depending on the district. And at the beginning of 1946 the future of Czechoslovakia, where both American and Soviet troops had been withdrawn from what was, after all, a much-wronged allied state, might on the face of it have been expected to be not dissimilar to that of France, another country with parliamentary traditions and a strong, but minority, Communist Party.

CONTROLLING THE MEANS OF COERCION

Such appearances, however, diverged from the substance, which it was frequently their function to conceal. The question facing Stalin's emissaries in Eastern Europe in 1944–45 was how could a small – and in some cases microscopic – communist cadre hold and wield the essentials of state power without relying on a large occupation force? Only one precedent was to be found in the previous history of Soviet foreign policy, and that in a country very different from most of Eastern Europe – Outer Mongolia in the 1920s. All other previous expansions took the form of assimilation to the Soviet Union, and involved extensions of the existing state and party structures. It is true that the experience of Outer Mongolia formed a 'case study' in Comintern schools in the 1930s (Hammond, 1975, p. 110), but that society – largely nomadic, with an urban 'proletariat' numbering a few dozen, and in all essentials pre-political – offered very limited guidance for Eastern Europe.

In the result national strategies all combined certain basic common elements, though with different relative weights according to circumstances. In the first place came control over the means of organized force (a strategy principle rehearsed by the small Spanish Communist Party, at the behest of the Comintern, during the civil war of 1936–9). Poland, which had the most substantial anti-Nazi resistance movement, and where almost one fifth of the population perished during the war, was in principle an ally, but was in many respects treated as a conquered enemy. One of the first acts of the proto-government (the Committee of National Liberation) which Gomulka formed in July 1944 was to license the Soviet authorities' full control over civilian security in the rear of the Soviet armies. In practice this meant a free hand for the NKVD, who installed administrators obedient to themselves down to the smallest localities, and shot and imprisoned members of the resistance. In the summer of 1944 the Nazi extermination camp at Maidanek, near Lublin, was brought back into use to imprison members of the Home Army (Davies, 1977, p. 43). During this period the Polish security services, under communist leadership and close Soviet control, were built up rapidly. None the less widespread armed resistance developed, in which communists and anti-communists fought each other, and which lasted in some areas until 1947 – even while (at least until the elections of January 1947) residues of cooperation continued between the political leaders in Warsaw. The outcome, however, was a foregone conclusion, since after the destruction of the Home Army in the Warsaw rising of August–October 1944 (while the Russian armies waited to the east of the Vistula), and the Nazis' subsequent razing of the capital, there existed no forces capable of challenging Stalin's protégés. Indeed, when Soviet forces entered Warsaw in January 1945, it contained not one living person.

In Czechoslovakia, in whose government communists weighed much less heavily at the outset, they none the less controlled the police from the beginning, through the affable Minister of the Interior, Vaclav Nosek. Full unionization of the police force, coupled with control over the trade union organizations, allowed the communists to use the police in a thoroughly partisan manner, appointing communist senior officers and using the police services to gather information on other parties. This was a continuing cause of friction, and communist manipulation of police appointments was the occasion of the disastrously misjudged resignation of twelve ministers in February 1948, which precipitated a political crisis and led to the communist takeover. The armed forces were similarly under powerful communist sway through the Minister of Defence, General Svoboda.

The other Eastern European countries occupied by the Red Army were subject to Allied Control Commissions in which the Western Allies consented to play essentially cosmetic parts. Communists or those acting on their behalf could thus be placed in charge of key police services. In Hungary the first crisis of the initial four-party coalition occurred in the summer of 1945, when the social democrats attempted to assert a say over the political police under the Interior Minister (Ferenc Erdei, nominally a member of the National Peasants' Party, but in reality a communist). Their attempt was defeated, and in the autumn Imre Nagy, an open communist returnee from Moscow, took over as Interior Minister. By that time he commanded a sizeable political police force in Budapest, based in the former headquarters of the fascist Arrow Cross Party. In the summer of 1946 the government of the Smallholder Party premier, Ferenc Nagy, found itself impotent to reorganize the police, and the Smallholder Party was itself soon the target of an investigation by the military security services (also communist-controlled). In addition to the power given them by control of the police the communists also employed Hungary's anti-Semitism as a means of pressure: at least two pogroms, disguised as anti-capitalist outbreaks, occurred during 1946 (Nagy, 1948, pp. 245–8).

In Bulgaria, which had a much larger communist partisan movement, communists laid hold of local police functions after their 'Fatherland Front' came to power in the coup of September 1944, and consolidated them under its communist Minister of the Interior, Yugov. This control was then used for a general terror in the first months of 1945: 100 high officials of the former regime were executed in February, and thousands of lesser figures died in a campaign of vengeance against those who had persecuted the partisans. In Romania the Red Army helped local communists to estab-lish control in many areas, and kept a very large force in the country

(600,000–900,000) men until 1946). With the advent of the pro-Soviet government of Dr Groza in March 1945, this power was consolidated by the communist Interior Minister Teohari Georgescu.

### TRANSFERS OF POPULATIONS

Thus, even if a formal account of elections and coalition reshufflings in much of Eastern Europe after the collapse of German power might give an impression of political normalcy, this was belied by communist control of state force. It was also belied by the forcible transfers of populations, most of them carried out with great brutality, but provoking little or no protest from the Western Allies. The Potsdam agreement provided for the transfer to Germany of Germans in Poland, Czechoslovakia and Hungary. Some of them had moved there as part of Nazi colonizing policies, but the families of many had lived there for hundreds of years. Notions of justice for which the war had ostensibly been fought went out of the window, and the horror that greeted the revelations of the Nazi strategy of extermination served to fuel, among both political leaders and peoples, the view that Germans should be treated as collectively guilty. The largest number of victims came from German lands at the frontiers of the new Poland. The Polish state was displaced 150 miles to the west, absorbing German lands to balance the subtractions to the east, where Stalin retained most of what he had grabbed in concert with Hitler in 1939. As the Red Army conquered East Prussia, in February 1945, the troops were set loose against the largely German civilian population, effecting, by death, flight or deportation to labour camps, a general clearance. In addition, the majority of the population of Pomerania and Silesia were evicted and shipped to within the reduced frontiers of Germany. 'No single German remained', Stalin declared with satisfaction at Potsdam, in the area to be given to Poland (Thomas, 1986, p. 321). Their places and land were taken by Polish settlers, millions of whom were brought from the territory annexed by the Soviet Union. This gave the communist leader Gomulka, as minister for the 'recovered territories', enormous powers of patronage. Later, in the spring of 1947, around 200,000 Ukrainians were forcibly resettled from their homelands on the south-eastern border of Poland to the western territories; General Jaruzelski, as a young officer, took part in this military deportation, 'Operation Vistula'. In all, around seven million persons were driven from Poland and Russia's new territories.

To this was added the Czech government's deportation of Germans from the Sudetenland of Czechoslovakia. Over two million people were driven into the American and Soviet occupation zones of Germany in the winter of

1945–6, with no notice, and allowed to take with them no more than they could carry. In Brno, for example, 25,000 Germans were given a quarter of an hour to gather their belongings; many died in the resulting hardship and starvation (in addition to the numerous murders of Germans in Czechoslovakia at the close of the war). The equally long-standing Hungarian minority in Czechoslovakia also suffered mass, though less violent, persecution, and ethnic Germans from the Balkans (most of whom came of families long settled there) were deported to Germany in large numbers. Smaller (but still very large) numbers of other national minorities were deported or otherwise persecuted.

Germans deported *to* Germany were perhaps fortunate in comparison with soldiers who became prisoners of the Soviet Union, and others (Poles and Ukrainians, as well as Germans) who were shipped to Soviet labour camps. Many returned only ten years later, or never. The Western leaders at Potsdam agreed that the Allied Powers might detain such prisoners at their discretion, and the Hague Convention was specifically held not to apply to them. But the same happened in states which were, theoretically, sovereign: most able-bodied adults of the German minority in Romania, for example, disappeared to Siberia in 1944–5. Equally unfortunate were Soviet citizens who had been brought to German-occupied territory during the war, as prisoners of war or forced labourers; the Western Allies cooperated with the Soviet authorities in shipping them eastwards, frequently at gunpoint.

To what was inflicted on people was added the impact of Soviet occupation on property: both casual looting by soldiers and larger-scale expropriations under the formula of reparations. In a programme overseen by Malenkov the Soviet-occupied zone of Germany was combed for industrial plant and material. The same thing happened, on a lesser scale, in Hungary and the Balkans, and in the formerly German territories now attached to Poland: one of the Red Army's more bizarre accomplishments was to carry off the entire electrification equipment of the Upper Silesian railway system. Much of the equipment taken, of course, could not be used: the added economic disruption caused to East and Central Europe was very far from being balanced by improved Soviet economic recovery.


BUILDING COMMUNIST STRENGTH


These conditions, superadded to the experience of the war, left much of the population psychologically and morally traumatized. In considering political developments we must bear in mind that in the choices of many people simple safety and survival overshadowed political opinion. This was a major factor in the very rapid expansion of the communist parties after the war. The most spectacular was the Hungarian party, which had barely a dozen members in contact with each other in the underground in 1942, but a membership of 500,000 by the end of 1945 (Molnar, 1978, pp. 39, 43). Other parties managed similar feats of expansion. According to Romanian communist leader Ana Pauker, her party had a membership of 1000 at the time of the coup by which the country switched sides in August 1944; by the spring of 1946 the membership was about 400,000. More telling than the numbers were the origins of some of the new recruits: in both Hungary and Romania organized groups of fascists (Arrow Cross and Iron Guard) exchanged their former affiliations for Communist Party cards. Polish communists were slightly more numerous during the war, but still a very small part of the resistance to Hitler; their 'People's Guard' accounted for at most 10,000 of resistance forces which totalled over 400,000 in 1943, and the party itself was far smaller (Davies, 1986, 2, p. 466). By 1948, however, after much reorganization and absorption, it had a membership of one million.

In addition to the growth of opportunistic membership, the communists were able to place or find many agents and collaborators in other parties. To read the indictments in the purges after the break with Tito in 1948, one would think that the communists themselves had been the main victims of infiltration by agents after the war. In reality, though, Leninist organization protected them, even during their periods of most swift and eclectic recruitment, while in return they themselves practised what they denounced with gusto and success. The founding of the Cominform, in September 1947, offered, among other things, the opportunity for a confidential international review of experience in this field. Thus Gheorgiu-Dej, for the Romanian party, reported that of the 340 deputies elected in the recent elections, 180 were communists, although officially there were no more than 70. And Revai, for the Hungarian communists, described their control of the National Peasant Party as follows: 'It acts under our guidance. The secretary is a Communist; one of the two ministers representing it in the government is a Communist. Fifteen of its thirty-two deputies are Communists; eight are sympathisers' (Reale, 1966, p. 255).

Such methods could provide very useful allies – some temporary, some long-lasting – and could also be used to reinforce the growth of the Communist Party itself. It provided them, too, with a substantial advantage in derailing, eroding or capturing rivals. As in the early 1920s an important part of building the communist parties consisted of splitting factions away from other parties, particularly the social democratic parties, or building up rivals to them, sometimes under the same name. It was the ostensibly socialist prime minister of Poland, Jozef Cyranciewicz, who organized a merger with the communists to form the Polish United Workers Party. The consolidation of one-party rule took a qualified *form*, however, with retention of two distinct but obedient minor parties, the Democratic Movement, and the counterfeit Peasant Movement, which had been formed when the original of that name rebuffed the communists' proposals for unity within the 'democratic bloc' of 1944. In Poland it seems to have been Stalin, who feared that introducing communism to the country was 'like putting a saddle on a cow', who pressed for the tactics of splitting rivals in order to control a formally independent rump. There were even attempts, using the pre-war fascist Boleslaw Piasecki, to split away a national secession from that more experienced centralist hierarchy, the Catholic Church, and to set up rivals, such as the Pax organization, to the Church's cultural and welfare bodies (Blit, 1965, pp. 223ff).

In Germany the leader of the Social Democratic Party (SPD) in Berlin, Otto Grotewohl, played a similar role to Cyranciewicz in the merger of the Soviet zone SPD with the Communist Party to form the Socialist Unity Party (SED). The leaders who first reformed the SPD, in June 1945, immediately after the collapse of Nazism, had favoured unity with the communists; at that time it was Ulbricht who declined. But six months later the SPD's more radical social programme and the wholesale seizure of factories by Soviet soldiers was causing it to grow rapidly, at the expense of the Communist Party. It was the communists who now demanded fusion, and opposition to it among the SPD rank-and-file rallied behind the demand that fusion should only go ahead if approved by a general vote of SPD members. Except in West Berlin, where the communists could not prevent a referendum of SPD members on the merger (and 82 per cent voted against) this campaign was crushed and the joint leaderships' decision pushed through. The West German social democrats later estimated that 20,000 party members were disciplined, imprisoned (some being sent back to the previously Nazi prisons from which they had so recently emerged) or in a few cases even killed during the 'unity campaign' of December 1945 to April 1946. The communists took over the human, as well as the physical, equipment of Nazism. In the autumn of 1946 the SED began a policy of admitting 'little Nazis'; and in 1948, to outflank their other feeble but authentic rivals, the communists created, as they had in Poland, tame versions of liberal and peasants' parties. The former body, the National Democratic Party of Germany, attracted officers and former Nazis, being led by an ex-Nazi, Professor Heilmann (McAuley, 1977, pp. 65, 69). 'De-nazification' was even more selective than in the Western zones. This was in any case pre-figured in the patriotic and militarist tone of the 'National Committee for a Free Germany', set up in Moscow after the war had begun to turn in the Soviet Union's favour in 1943, which Stalin briefly contemplated using as the embryo of a future German government.

## CONTESTS WITH OTHER PARTIES

That the backing of armed forces was an essential premise of the communists' ability to manipulate the social democrats is suggested by the contrasting case of Austria, where Allied military occupation (outside Vienna) was joint, not zonal, giving the Soviet Union preponderance but not control. Here Stalin caused general surprise by selecting the 75-year-old and rather nationalist socialist veteran Karl Renner as President. The Russian leader – who did not consult the Austrian communists – doubtless calculated that Renner's past would so compromise him as to make him easy to use. Lenin had made 'the Renners' a generic term of abuse and this 'servile lackey of German imperialism' (as Lenin (1960–78, 23, p. 267) described him) had, indeed, come out publicly for Austria's annexation to Germany in Hitler's plebiscite of 1938. 'What, is that old traitor still alive?' Stalin is reported to have said. 'He is exactly the man we need' (Thomas, 1986, p. 352).

In fact, however, the client outmanoeuvred his patron. Initially deferential, Renner none the less insisted on early elections. These were duly held, in November 1945, and he was rewarded by the communists receiving, to their great surprise and chagrin, less than 5 per cent of the vote. Though they had succeeded in placing their men strategically in the police services, in Austria these remained under the supervision of Allied occupation authorities which were genuinely joint, and could not so easily be used as means of partisan pressure. Although the communists launched strikes in 1947 and 1950, they were unable to do more than dent the moderate democracy which Renner installed. It was the Austrian elections of November 1945 which alerted the German communist leaders to the likelihood that they would be outstripped by the social democrats, and determined them on their campaign for forcible unity.

Similar lessons were drawn in the rest of Eastern Europe. In Hungary the social democrats, whose leadership mainly favoured collaboration with the communists, were a less important target than the Smallholders' Party, which won 57 per cent of the votes in the relatively free elections of November 1945. Zoltan Tildy, the Smallholders' leader, was likened in the contemporary jest to a man who has won a lion in a lottery and dared not take it home, and their success made them the prime object of what Rakosi later defined as 'salami' tactics. First communist demonstrations put pressure on the Smallholders' leadership to disown their anti-communist right, then, from the end of 1946, that leadership itself came under fire, for allegedly conspiring against the state and the allied (i.e. Soviet) occupation authorities. By financing opposition factions and splits within the Smallholders' Party the communists tamed and reduced it. They forced the

Smallholder prime minister, Ferenc Nagy, to resign while he was in Switzerland in the summer of 1947, holding his infant son hostage to compel him to comply (Nagy, 1948, pp. 420–6). The lesson was reinforced by the banning and arrest of some of the Smallholder leaders who had split away with communist encouragement. Only then was it the turn of the social democrats. At the initiative of the Soviet ambassador and under the protection of the political police, a meeting of the 'left wing' of the Social Democratic Party, in February 1948, called for fusion with the Communist Party, and by June this had been pushed through.

In Czechoslovakia President Beneš's action in banning the two largest pre-war political parties, the Agrarians and the Catholic People's Party in Slovakia, gave the communists a great advantage from the outset. Social democracy was no great obstacle for the country's powerful post-war Communist Party. The prime minister of the 1945 coalition government, and leader of the socialist left-wing, Zdenek Fierlinger, had spent years in Moscow and was Stalin's loyal collaborator. Because the socialist leaders, taken as a whole, represented useful allies and camouflage rather than any pressing threat, their absorption into the Communist Party took place only in June 1948, after the communists' 'legal' takeover in February. Rather less than half of the total socialist membership of over 350,000 was absorbed into the Communist Party. And in the months after the February overturn communist-controlled 'action committees' purged other rival political organizations.

Romania was the country where communist power was hammered out of the most diverse political materials. In February 1945, immediately after the Yalta conference, Vyshinsky, then a Soviet deputy foreign minister, flew to Bucharest and demanded that the monarch, King Michael, dismiss his prime minister, the vigorously anti-communist General Radescu, and appoint instead the communist who posed as head of the minuscule 'Ploughman's Front', Dr Petru Groza. The demand was underscored by violent communist demonstrations and by the fact that the Romanian armed forces had been ordered away from the capital. Being under Russian command they had mostly been sent to the front, while Romania was garrisoned with Soviet troops. Under protest, and unable to get any Western support, the King complied with Vyshinsky's demand. In the resulting coalition seventeen communists occupied all the important ministries. They were joined by such figures as Father Burducea, an anti-Semitic former member of the Iron Guard, now Minister of Religion, Mihai Ralea, a collaborator with the Nazis, now Minister of Culture, and the socialist Stefan Voitec who, as Minister of Education, set about an energetic purge of teachers, and Bolshevization of the school system. The Social Democratic Party – which before the war had been much larger than the communists – now faced a two-pronged campaign of splitting and infiltration, and by March 1946 the pro-communists commanded a majority. In October 1947, just after the establishment of Cominform, the two parties were formally fused.

## ECONOMIC TRANSFORMATIONS

Patterns of economic transformation also developed unevenly across Eastern Europe, overlapping with the development of communist political control, and aiming to reinforce it. The earliest sweeping nationalizations and land redistributions were in Czechoslovakia and Poland, and were motivated by the need to remove workers from enterprises they had occupied as Germany collapsed, and to evict peasants from land where they were laying claim to estates. In Poland Gomulka even launched (from May 1945, when the war in Europe was safely over) a campaign for the 'reprivatization' of industry, removing occupied factories from the hands of workers' committees, and sentencing socialist workers caught organizing strikes to long gaol sentences (Reynolds, 1978, pp. 520–3).

But the main drive, which eventually went a good way towards transforming Eastern European economies into near replicas of the Soviet Union's, followed the United States' sweeping offer of capital aid for European reconstruction, unveiled in the Marshall Plan in June 1947. The Soviet response wavered: despite a hostile initial reaction in *Pravda*, Molotov, the Soviet Foreign Minister, and a large delegation joined the Paris conference for preliminary discussions. Eastern European governments' reactions were even more uncertain: Poland and Czechoslovakia first reacted favourably, and only later withdrew. (The Polish and Romanian governments first learned of their refusals from *Radio Moscow.*) Soviet policy seems to have hardened only as it became clear that the American offer was conditional on lowering the trade and investment barriers that divided Europe. With Eastern Europe's trade already moving back towards its pre-war attachment to Western Europe, and towards larger exchanges with the US, acceptance would have made it vastly more difficult to consolidate communist monopolies of power in the Eastern states. In this case, economics followed politics.

### FURTHER READING

There are a number of general studies of Eastern Europe which cover the period from the war through the communist transformations. For example, Carrere d'Encausse (1987), Staar (1982), Brzezinski (1967), Seton-Watson (1956) and Gluckstein (1952). Mastny (1979) analyses Russia's wartime diplomacy, 1941–5, Thomas (1986) has chapters on Eastern Europe during 1945–6, while Fejto (1974) deals mainly with events after Stalin's death in 1953. Useful essays in individual countries are in the collections edited by Betts (1950) and McCauley (1977).

Studies concentrating on the post-war period in particular countries include Zinner (1963), Bloomfield (1979) and Kaplan (1987) on Czechoslovakia, Staar (1975) on Poland, and Sandford (1983) on eastern Germany. The histories of Eastern Europe's national communist parties, mostly up to fairly recent years, may be studied in the following books: Suda (1980) for Czechoslovakia, de Weydenthal (1978) and Dziewanowski (1976) for Poland, Molnar (1978) and Kovrig (1979) for Hungary, McCauley (1979) for East Germany, King (1980) for Romania, Oren (1971 and 1973) and Bell (1986) for Bulgaria, Prifti (1978) for Albania since 1944, and Wilson (1980) for Yugoslavia.

# 8

# Differing routes to communist power

Communist routes to power differ more than their results. The Bolsheviks' 'October revolution' – an insurrectionary coup based in an urban revolutionary movement – has had no close sequel. A number of other parties have come to power under their own steam, but on different bases, principally (as in China and Indochina) peasant or rural armies in nationalist civil wars. In yet other cases (as in most of Eastern Europe; see chapter 7) quite weak communist parties were installed in power in their own countries by exterior force. Some organizations (such as Castro's movement in Cuba, and several movements among military personnel in Africa) were not communist – indeed, in some cases quite anti-communist – when they came to power, but opted for communism after they controlled the state. In other cases (such as the Sandinistas in Nicaragua) a movement has come to power which contains a significant admixture of Leninism, but which is quite separate from and opposed to the national communist party. This chapter contrasts and briefly compares some of these different routes to communist rule, and their results.

DIVIDING NATIONS

The existence of a major communist state has always been a factor in the conduct and expectations of non-ruling communist movements. But the Second World War, followed by Stalin's social conversion of Eastern Europe, established the Soviet Union as a world power, whose conflicts or collaboration with other powers could determine events across the globe. Thus its readiness to employ military force and political pressures to convert other lands into political and social likenesses of itself came to be – as it was not before the war – an essential ingredient in the strategy and calculations of many non-ruling parties.

But the war also destroyed many existing states, and one result was that

even nations which *had* a robust and integrated national communist movement were peremptorily divided in the course of dealings between communist and Western powers. Decisions taken in and between Moscow,
Peking and Washington have split up countries as diverse as Germany,
Korea and Vietnam, diplomatic surgery bisecting the evolution of both the
communist party and society as a whole. The contrast is perhaps greatest
between East and West Germany. In the less industrialized – and, in terms
of political history, more conservative – section of the country the
communist party was built up, from a nucleus of communist refugees from
Hitler, brought in from the Soviet Union, into a whole apparatus of rule,
while communism in West Germany, which contained the heartlands of the
labour movement and communism before 1933, has never grown beyond a
sect.

As with Germany, such divisions are generally begun during periods of
cordiality between the great states. The victorious powers decided on the
partition of Korea into spheres of influence at Yalta, and put this into effect
on the collapse of the Japanese occupation of the country in August–
September 1945. In October of that year the communist press hailed the
return of 'two great leaders' of the Korean nation: Stalin's nominee, the
hitherto virtually unknown Kim Il-Sung, and Dr Syngman Rhee, the admirer
of Chiang Kai-shek who was Truman's selection as ruler of the south (and
who was soon to be heard, during the Korean war, as one of the world's
loudest advocates of nuclear war against communist China). After the
Korean war, in 1953–4, the partition of the country was reconfirmed by
the powers (and sealed by the purge and execution of Kim's opponents in
the leadership of the Korean Communist Party, who wanted a more active
line against the South).

In Vietnam, in 1945, the powerful communist guerrilla movement led by
Ho Chi Minh acquiesced in the arrangements for their country agreed at
Potsdam (see chapter 5). The whole of Indochina was to be restored to
France, but, temporarily, Kuomintang forces were to occupy the north and
British ones the south. Following the Japanese surrender, the Vietminh
were faced with large demonstrations for independence in Saigon. To force
compliance with the British troops who were then landing to retake Indochina for France, the Vietnamese communists arrested and killed a number
of their more nationalist critics. They found themselves, however, almost
immediately in conflict with the British occupation authorities, who were
shortly followed by the returning French. For many months the Vietnamese
communists negotiated with Paris, apparently hoping that with communists
in the cabinet French colonialism would have changed its character. But by
late 1946 they were faced with full-scale war. At the Geneva conference of
1954, they were forced by Soviet and Chinese pressure to accept a dividing
line well to the north of what military realities indicated. In the 1960s,

however, the North Vietnamese leaders' ability to sponsor guerrilla war against Diem and his successors, and eventually to send units of their regular armed forces into the south, depended upon the knowledge that both the Soviet Union and China held the United States' capacity to use force within limits.

CUBA

External protection does not necessarily depend on geographical contiguity. Cuba was the first to demonstrate that the state power of the most powerful communist state bloc had developed, in effect, a global reach. But Kennedy's aborted invasion at the Bay of Pigs was followed by Krushchev's humiliating retreat in the 1962 missile crisis. The Soviet Union attempted to compensate for its inferiority in nuclear warheads and inter-*continental* means of delivering them by installing *intermediate* range missiles in Cuba – a move by which the United States government also felt threatened with a first strike against their nuclear bases. Kennedy reacted by throwing a naval 'quarantine' around the island, to exclude the Soviet ships bringing further missiles. During the October 1962 crisis the military uses and political character – and hence, in the longer term, the social nature – of Cuba were negotiated direct between the great powers, without reference to Havana. Indeed it appears that at the height of the crisis the Castro regime felt that there was such a severe threat of their being traded back to the US that they seized Soviet surface-to-air missile bases, to be able to defend themselves alone. In the outcome, a deal was struck: Soviet strategic weaponry was withdrawn, but the US acknowledged Cuba as a Soviet protectorate. (Moreover, the deal proved durable between Krushchev and Kennedy's successors. In 1970, when the Soviet Union began to build a base for missile-carrying submarines at Cienfuegos Bay in Cuba, Nixon cited the 1962 agreements and extracted a withdrawal of the vessels.)

The political formation over which Soviet protection had been extended, however, Castro and Guevara's 26 July Movement, was in 1962 very far from being either communist or willing to coexist easily with the Cuban Communist Party. It was, moreover placed in a state of incensed alert by the knowledge that its safety had become a bargaining-counter in global Soviet dealings with the US. The Cuban Communist Party itself had a history as one of the more substantial Latin American parties, characterized by an almost total obedience to Moscow and, as a consequence, by a mottled history of political associations. It supported Fulgencio Batista's dictatorship from 1938 to 1944, having two cabinet seats from 1942 on, and it stood almost completely aside from the efforts of Castro's movement before it toppled Batista's second dictatorship in late 1958.

On the other hand, Castro assumed power with command of only about

1500 armed men, and with a tiny, politically unseasoned, team of leaders, and thus stood acutely in need of an administrative apparatus. The eventual fusion of the two organizations produced inevitable frictions. In terms of internal control these were resolved in Castro's favour, with the expulsion of Annibal Escalante in 1962, followed by a major purge of former Communist Party members. But in external matters Cuba aligned with the Soviet Union, although the situation was only finally sealed by Castro's endorsement (after momentary hesitation) for the Soviet invasion of Czechoslovakia in 1968. Internally the ruling party, and the state and 'people's' bodies through which it exercised control, came to resemble other ruling communist parties, not only in name but in methods and organization.

In this case, therefore, military-political protection brought not only political but social assimilation. Cuba, moreover, has continued to play a particular role on the Soviet Union's behalf since 1968 – sending, for instance, weapons and troops to the support of movements favoured by the Soviet Union in Africa, where direct Soviet intervention, or Soviet aid alone, might have been politically inept, but at the same time conducting a superficially independent foreign policy in many matters and playing an energetic part among the 'non-aligned' states. Cuba's small size and close proximity to the United States served, paradoxically, to deepen its dependency upon the Soviet Union, as it became clear to the ruling group that, in the long term, no third way would be viable.

GRENADA

The continuing importance of Soviet protection is illustrated, negatively, by the revolution of 1979–83 in Grenada, whose population of less than 100,000 could aspire to statehood only by virtue of living on an island. The organization which overthrew the gangster regime of Eric Gairy in March 1979 may have had some assistance from Cuba but was only in small part Leninist: the New Jewel Movement assumed power as an affiliate of the Second (Socialist) International, with a leadership, personified by Maurice Bishop, that was far more populist than democratic centralist. But it came to lean on Cuba and the Soviet bloc for economic, military and political aid.

The Soviet Union, for its part, built up support cautiously, concentrating on militarizing the regime and drawing it into the Soviet political orbit. (One reason that Gairy was overthrown so easily was that he maintained an army of just 65 men; in contrast, when United States forces invaded in October 1983 they claimed to have found arms and equipment for 10,000 soldiers – one-tenth of the total population.) The Soviet Union, averring to the Grenadian leaders that they wished to avoid provoking the US, conducted political intercourse principally on a party-to-party rather than state-to-state basis, providing (and paying for the Cuban provision of) political training, a new party headquarters, and other facilities. Internally, the regime was tightened up, including crackdowns on such 'anti-socialists' as Rastafarians, while internationally the New Jewel Movement was affiliated to the World Peace Council and a variety of other Soviet, Cuban and Libyan political fronts, and the island's tourist facilities became the scene of Cuban-sponsored 'anti-imperialist' and 'non-aligned' meetings.

None the less Bishop and his immediate supporters in the Politburo (as the New Jewel Movement's leading body was retitled) favoured keeping the option of a middle way open. Thus, as late as June 1983, Bishop visited the US with representatives of Grenada's remaining private sector, and, in secret conversations with US officials, explored conditions for reopening diplomatic relations. Against Bishop, Soviet officials appear to have given covert encouragement to a more orthodoxly Leninist faction in the Politburo, led by Bernard Coard and supported by the Soviet-trained officers heading the army and internal security services. It was this grouping that, in October 1983, carried the Politburo against Bishop, then ousted and arrested him. When large crowds gathered in his support, they were dispersed by troops (with considerable bloodshed) and Bishop and his associates summarily shot. The coup against Bishop, however, left the new regime peculiarly vulnerable, and when the Reagan administration, acting on intelligence that proved accurate, very shortly invaded the island, it was able to claim a rapid victory and a modest political success. Neither Cuba nor the Soviet Union had at that time the military or political means to raise the cost of US action to unacceptable levels.

### THE HORN OF AFRICA

In the Red Sea and northeast Africa (one of several areas where Cuban troops have played an important role on the Soviet Union's behalf) Soviet strategy has been more complex and outcomes less clear-cut. A central strategic objective has been to win allies or clients who can provide access to territory from which military forces could control the Red Sea or its entrance to the Indian Ocean. But this and other goals of policy have had to be pursued with several states and along a variety of political channels.

In North Yemen, for example, ever since the royal family was overthrown by Nasserist officers in 1962, the Soviet Union has sought to cultivate the beneficiaries of a succession of coups and assassinations. However, these policies have required delicate balancing with Soviet support to a series of rival Marxist factions in South Yemen, where the National Liberation Front gained power in 1967. And, from 1972, the Soviet Union has given discreet backing to South Yemen and South Yemen-backed guerrilla forces in the intermittent hostilities between the two states. Thus military leaders in Sanaa, the capital of North Yemen, have been periodically enraged to discover that their Soviet-supplied bomber aircraft, attacking guerrilla positions in the south, were being shot down by up-to-date Soviet anti-aircraft weapons. Within South Yemen itself, since the ascendancy of the communists over the Nasserists in 1969, Soviet policy has had to deal with Marxists – their differences exacerbated by tribal animosities – violently replacing each other. Salem Robea Ali was deposed and executed in 1978, a palace coup took place in 1980, factional rivalries in the Party leadership came to the brink of fighting in 1985, and in January 1986 they erupted in a bloody two-week civil war. In this last conflict Moscow sought unsuccessfully to mediate, but finished up backing the ousters of its previous protégé, Ali Nasser Mohammed.

On the other side of the Red Sea Sudan became the recipient of a great deal of Soviet aid after General Nimeiri seized power in 1969, and incorporated several supporters of the country's relatively strong communist movement in his government. The situation also allowed a much larger scale of supply to the secessionist rebels – at that time also supported by the Soviet bloc – in Eritrea, Ethiopia's most northerly province, with a long Red Sea shoreline. However, the honeymoon with Nimeiri was soon over. In the spring of 1971 he sought to bring the trade unions – a main base of the powerful and growing Communist Party – under tighter control, and in July a communist attempt to seize power almost unseated him. However, Nimeiri retained power, executed a number of his communist opponents, and became one of the most pro-Western heads of state in Africa until being toppled by strikes and urban unrest in 1985.

The Soviet Union also sought to build up behind-scenes influence in Egypt, in tandem with its diplomatic alignment with Nasser in the late 1950s and 1960s. It encouraged the refounding of the Egyptian Communist Party in 1958 (though it did not protest when Nasser interned most of its leading members). In 1965 the Communist Party dissolved itself and thereafter made vigorous efforts to develop an organized faction within the sole legal party, the Arab Socialist Union. But Nasser's unexpected death in 1970 brought this tactic to nought. Nasser's successor as head of state, Anwar al-Sadat, remained pro-Soviet in foreign policy until after Egypt's defeat by Israel in the October 1973 war, but moved earlier to secure his domestic position, arresting Ali Sabri, chairman of the Arab Socialist Union, and outlawing the 'socialist vanguard' network within it in mid-1971.

In Ethiopia, however, a Soviet-supported military regime was able to put down deeper roots and effect an important social transformation. When, in September 1974, unrest in Addis Ababa deposed Haile Selassie, the 81-year-old emperor, and allowed an *ad hoc* grouping of officers (the Provisional Military Administrative Committee, or Derg) to seize power, the situation offered novel opportunities for Soviet policy. But, to take advantage of them, it had to make abrupt adjustments to its policies elsewhere in the region. First, it put a halt to the aid previously given by pro-Soviet states to the secessionist rebellion in Eritrea; this had included the training of Eritrean guerrillas in Cuba, and supplies of weapons from Eastern Europe. The Eritrean movement was a contributory factor in the fall of Haile Selassie, but one towards which the Derg, consolidated by a purge in which all its liberal elements were executed in late 1974, was equally hostile. In abandoning Eritrea the Soviet Union relinquished the prospect of a sovereign but dependent state giving it military bases on the west shores of the Red Sea in favour of the chance of the more substantial gain of Ethiopia as a whole.

But yet further changes of sides were necessary. Moscow had been a substantial provider of armaments to the (profoundly anti-communist) Somali government since the mid-1960s, and after the army chief, Siad Barre, seized power in 1969 supplies were stepped up. The accumulation of Soviet weaponry nourished Siad Barre's ambitions. First, in 1976, he converted his military junta into the central committee of a new Revolutionary Socialist Party and announced his confidence in the inevitable triumph of scientific socialism. Then, less prudently, he sought to take advantage of the political turmoil in his much larger Ethiopian neighbour and, in July 1977, launched an attack to claim the Ogaden, a large territory populated by ethnically Somali nomads on the inland border between the two states.

The Soviet Union cannot have been unaware of Somali preparations for full-scale war. But they had also been seeking, particularly since Carter's election as United States President in November 1976, to wean Ethiopia from dependence on US arms supplies, and to invest in military assistance and political influence there themselves. The war forced them to choose (though they sought to ride both horses as long as possible), and they opted to rescue Ethiopia, where Colonel Mengistu had emerged as clear leader of the Derg. A large airlift of weapons, support personnel and Cuban soldiers to Ethiopia (some of them transported there direct after being expelled from Somalia) turned the tide against the initial Somali successes, and by early 1978 Somali efforts were reduced to guerrilla warfare in the Ogaden. Siad Barre's regime, so rudely ditched by Moscow, then reoriented to rely on Chinese, US and Italian aid. It was not, however, required to reconsider either its recently acquired Marxism or the more than 99.9 per cent of votes it claimed in the 1979 general elections.

### Ethiopian military communism

The Soviet decision to make support of the Derg the main thrust of their quest for allies in the Horn also required an adjustment of political tactics within Ethiopia. Hitherto the Soviet and other communist parties (such as the Italian) had offered encouragement to a variety of Marxist currents, many of them associated with the rapidly grown and loosely organized Ethiopian People's Revolutionary Party (EPRP), which at its zenith had a membership of perhaps 30,000, and had also encouraged a variety of political bodies established by factions within the military. But after Colonel Mengistu Mariam achieved the chairmanship of the Derg (by assassinating his chief rivals in a palace shoot-out in February 1977), he exerted himself to eliminate opposition, and the Somali war was accompanied by a general terror against political rivals, most of whom were Marxists of one description or another. By early 1978 all potential opposition was either dead or in hiding.

This left, however, the problem of political organization, particularly acute in face of the radical land reform and other economic reorganizations on which the Derg embarked soon after the 1974 'revolution'. The forms of parliamentary government had been ditched in 1974. Yet Mengistu and his associates long resisted Soviet pressure to establish a Leninist party; only in September 1984, to mark the tenth anniversary of the deposition of Haile Selassie, did they announce their own vanguard party, the Workers' Party of Ethiopia. Although the military rulers deployed a ubiquitous Marxism-Leninism of slogans and images, national administration continued to be government by decree, through an array of ministries and *ad hoc* government agencies, directed by a still *provisional* military government. The institutions of a civilian state were not inaugurated until September 1987, and even then in a form which gave Mengistu all the leading positions – state president, president of the state council, and secretary-general of the party, as well as commander-in-chief.

Economic and administrative transformation remains partial. Much of the middle and lower levels of administration are in the hands of civil servants from before the overthrow of Haile Selassie, and a substantial class of middlemen and merchants survives. Ethiopia was hit by a series of droughts and famines, especially in 1984–6; an important factor aggravating the food crisis was the mutual interference between state bureaucrats and merchants involved in purchasing and distributing foodstuffs. In political terms the military regime – though reluctant to act through a national party – *has* sought to establish something approaching an ideological monopoly for their domesticated version of Marxism-Leninism; it remains, however, limited to politics and to the rather narrow politicized stratum. Thus both Christian and Muslim church leaders are given freedom and encouragement, and Mengistu's wife, for example, participates ceremonially in the principal annual Christian pilgrimage.

The Derg's reluctance to pass control through a party organization was part of a wider resistance to becoming over-dependent on the Soviet Union.

In contrast to Cuba, the Ethiopian regime, threatened by less direct and substantial external pressures, has so far been able to preserve more autonomy. In fact, a number of key policies pursued by Mengistu and his supporters since 1975 – political purges and terror, economic collectivization, and an international stance turning sharply away from the US and the West – have resulted more from concrete domestic problems and the intrinsic inclinations of these groups of officers than Soviet pressures; Soviet policy has merely sought to consolidate these with closer political and organizational ties. But the Somali war, and even Ethiopia's intractable separatist problems (of which Eritrea is only the most important), are not such threats as to push Mengistu into a 'satellite' relationship. And, since the major threats are internal or local, with little likelihood of military intervention by a Western power, the Soviet Union can, in the nature of things, offer less direct protection than it does to, say, Cuba.

## LENINISM'S COMPARATIVE ADVANTAGES

The cases of Cuba, Grenada and northeast Africa illustrate a more general point. In most of the communist states outside Europe and Asia the key organizations *at the stage where they achieved power* have not been communist – or, frequently, even parties – but more usually forms of radical and anti-western, often military, *nationalism*. This is true in Africa – Benin and Congo-Brazzaville, the anti-colonial movements in Portuguese territories (Angola, Mozambique and Guinea-Bissau), and Zimbabwe – as it is in Nicaragua or elsewhere in Central America, or, for example, in South Yemen. Such movements generally contain currents and elements that, given a combination of propitious opportunities and pressures, and the availability or promise of support and protection from established communist powers, *can* evolve a more-or-less wholly communist approach to administration of the state and – by winning or if necessary fracturing the parent organization – impose it on society as a whole. And the hostility of Western states, sometimes carried to the point of attempts to undermine or overthrow them by force, have helped push them along such a path.

Third World nationalists or officers who become communist do not, of course, do so spontaneously or as an original creation, but rather by importing and adopting organizational equipment and methods that they have seen in efficacious use elsewhere. Accelerated development through imitation, that is to say, applies as much to politics as to economics. Britain in the nineteenth century acted as the nursery of the industrial methods and economic forms that other nations required to follow her on the path of economic development. It was in part the traumas of being a 'late developer' that produced, in Russia, Lenin's original type of political machine. Leninist party-state organization then presented itself – as it was from the earliest years presented by the Comintern, and is now rather differently promoted by the more powerful communist regimes – as a promisingly effective set of political devices for the laggards in an unevenly developed world.

Is the Leninist party, however, *qualitatively* different from the other forms of political combat and state organization that arise under such conditions? In nations where poverty and local, subsistence production are general, where the world market invades not to nourish but to strangle indigenous economic activities, where native wealth is feeble, and concentrated in few hands which have only a remote connection with production, it is natural that the acquisition and use of state power comes to have an extraordinary potency for the rather small stratum that is potentially political. In certain cases the variants of Marxism-Leninism that have been adopted in underdeveloped countries do not aspire strongly to transform society, and have many resemblances to other types of elite authoritarianism in the Third World.

### BENIN AND CONGO-BRAZZAVILLE

Yet, Leninist political forms have definite appeals for elite groups. They provide an effective and intellectually plausible framework for the suppression of political rivals. And they can provide at least as rich prospects and pickings for the individuals in control as other forms of dictatorship. One can, consequently, point to cases where it is more the form than the substance of the Leninist party which has been transferred, and in which the impact on society has been relatively superficial. Benin, for example (the small former French colony of Dahomey), underwent almost ten years of political turmoil before its present ruler, Matthieu Kerekou, came to power by a military coup in 1972. By 1974, as president, Kerekou declared that Benin would become a socialist society and transformed his military council into a Marxist-Leninist party, the Benin People's Revolutionary Party. As a political organization, however, it remains decidedly top-heavy: guided by a Central Committee of forty-five, its total membership is only a few hundred, and its daily newspaper has a circulation of little more than 1000. The former French colony of Congo-Brazzaville has evolved somewhat similarly. An army seizure of power in 1968 was followed by the formation of a 'Leninist' ruling party. Though this is a body which has never exceeded 2000 members, and has several times been reduced almost to nothing by purges, it has provided the formal – and lasting – political framework for military rule, succession by assassination and coup, and spectacular corruption (Decalo, 1985).

Rather than a political party taking over and monopolizing power in the state, in Benin and the Congo something resembling the opposite process has occurred: an un- (or pre-) political grouping succeeded in seizing control of the rudimentary state apparatus within a society where social interests had only begun to crystallize out from local and ethnic or clan loyalties; they then sought to adopt a political form, but one which would exclude party politics, with all its dangers of becoming a battlefield of ethnic and regional interests. Thus political equipment ostensibly designed for the most advanced class of a mature industrial society is 'exported' for use in holding together the state where civil society has only begun to form. Even Leninist forms of organization prove subject to deep internal fracturing along ethnic, regional and clique lines, and persist only because the new ideology is joined to the levers of military command. That they are adopted principally in response to internal problems is suggested, for example, by their persistence through Kerekou's ideological and foreign policy shifts in Benin. In recognition of large sums of money from Libya Kerekou had himself officially converted to Islam in the presence of Colonel Gaddafi; from 1983, however, he mended his political fences with France, even switching sides to support France against Libya over Chad. Throughout their political alterations, both Benin and the Congo's principal economic linkages have remained with France.

## NICARAGUA

Nicaragua's Sandinista National Liberation Front (FSLN) is also equipped with an eclectic Leninism. The FSLN has been the dominant political organization governing Nicaragua since the civil war which overthrew Anastasio Somoza in 1979 – no military coup, but an armed movement with a popular and very broad basis of support. The FSLN was formed and began guerrilla struggle in 1960, a few months after Castro's victory. It was thus shaped after Castro's 26 July Movement before it gained power as well as by the Leninist currents within it; the chief model for Sandinista *'militantes'*, after Augusto Sandino, is still Che Guevara. Its early methods of struggle, however, had more in common with those of Chinese than Cuban communists – a slow, trial-and-error cultivation of peasant sympathy in remote rural areas, eventually winning sizeable zones from Somoza's National Guard. But urban support was more important than it was in China, with large-scale movements of opposition and insurrection developing in the towns and barrios in the later stages. Sandinista methods of fund-raising for arms in the 1970s included, for example: 'teams of three [who would] board city buses. One would keep watch, the second would make a pitch for aid for the *companeros* fighting Somoza, and the third would collect donations. The three would then jump from the bus between stops to elude police'

(Booth, 1985, p. 149). The scale of popular opposition to the dictatorship allowed them to make hundreds of such forays a month.

Although Carlos Fonseca and other early leaders of the FSLN had backgrounds in the communist movement, and tried to structure it along broadly Leninist lines, it split into three quite distinct factions in 1975, which only fully reunited in early 1979 when it was clear they had immediate possibilities to lead in Somoza's overthrow. Indeed, one of the main turningpoints of the war, Eden Pastora's capture of the deputies of Somoza's 'parliament' in the National Palace in August 1978, was the initiative of one faction, the Ortega brothers' *'terceristas'*.

By leading an armed struggle to the end against Somoza, the FSLN were able to install their own choice of revolutionary junta, without the representatives of the old regime which the Carter administration sought to negotiate. Among the forces arrayed against Somoza the pro-Moscow Communist Party (the Nicaraguan Socialist Party) was and has remained a distinct and very small organization; the significant Soviet bloc political links are with the FSLN. Since 1979 the FSLN's relations with the United States have become increasingly hostile. As it has developed closer economic and political ties with the Soviet bloc, it has shed many of its non-Leninist supporters and allies, and has unified its leadership and composed many of their earlier factional divisions. Yet the Sandinistas' treatment of internal opposition has been selective, and fluctuates (partly, of course, with a view to countering Washington's hostility and splitting public opinion in the United States). The FSLN itself is a relatively small organization of 24,000 (out of a total population of three million). It has come to protect its position by selective repression and a large internal security force, backed by neighbourhood and mass organizations controlled by the FSLN. But independent and critical radio stations and one newspaper exist (*La Prensa*, prominent in the struggle against Somoza), the opposition deputies elected in the 1984 elections are active, and there are independent trade union organizations. The impulse towards a one-party regime is certainly present, but the situation is very different from, say, that in Eastern Europe after the outbreak of the Cold War; external conditions converge to protect countervailing forces.

Another important factor has been the intertwining of the FSLN's evolution with political divisions within the Catholic Church, opposing a 'People's Church' to the Vatican-supported hierarchy, and sustaining the Sandinistas' popular support. In 1986 Daniel Ortega's FSLN government included three priests (though under censure by the Vatican), depended for much of its economic advice on radical Jesuits, and received an important part of its grass-roots support through the efforts of parish clergy. Franciscan priests in Managua have inserted an addition in the Mass, chanting: 'Between the faith and the revolution'; to which the congregation make response: 'No hay contradicion!' Rather generally in Latin America, and in a number of other countries where popular Catholicism is entrenched, such as the Philippines, the appalling conditions of the poor have elicited revolutionary tendencies and theological reinterpretations among the priesthood – tendencies with which local variants of Leninism are generally willing to collaborate. In fact, the Sandinistas' attitude to religion can be highly ecumenical; in early 1988 Jimmy Swaggart, the anti-communist TV evangelist from the US Bible belt, brought his road show to conduct vast rallies in Managua.

From their very different directions, Sandinista rule in Nicaragua, and Leninist military juntas such as those in Benin and Congo-Brazzaville, indicate how greatly Leninist ideology can vary doctrinally, and still be a serviceable instrument of rule. Its different variants, however, are very differently buttressed. The Sandinistas mix it with numerous other, and opposed ingredients. Their continued ability to rule, in the face of considerable, United States-supported, military opposition, and while still extending a fluctuating toleration to oppositionists and critics within the country, turns far more on the fact that they came to power on a mass and intensely popular movement against Somoza's dictatorship, than on their Leninism. In Benin and the Congo rule runs through military organizations, and, in the longer term, rests on patronage in and through the state bureaucracy, neither of them much affected by the rulers' official Leninism.

The African examples and those of Cuba and Nicaragua also remind us that, in the 'evolution' of communism, the Leninism of ruling organizations need not be a consequence of direct descent. In adopting Leninism the ruling group may be imitating a model it considers efficacious, or acting in a way that its international position makes convenient (or some mixture of those motives). In either case, the sources and character of the ruling Leninism may have very little to do with the traditions of other native communist movements and it may (as for example in Ethiopia) be very hostile to them. Just as Leninism has evolved so as to be able to draw support from a wide variety of social bases, it can also be adapted for the use of a very wide variety of ruling elites. (Indeed, of political groupings more generally, as the variety of, and warfare between, rival western Leninisms demonstrates.)

### TRUJILLO: ORGANIZATION WITHOUT IDEOLOGY

Perhaps, then, one could conceive of a state which took advantage of Leninism's *organizational* methods, while discarding its ideology altogether? On the face of it some actual regimes, such as the thirty-year despotism (1930–61) of the extreme anti-communist Rafael Trujillo in the

Dominican Republic, appear to approximate to this type. Yet without the distinctive contribution which Leninism can make to their ideology of rule, such regimes lack an important ingredient, as a closer look at Trujillo's dictatorship suggests.

Few regimes have been more closely tied to US economic and political interests. Before coming to power Trujillo served his apprenticeship as pimp, company spy, gangster, then policeman. The state, once he controlled it, was run for the benefit of himself and his extended illegitimate family. Yet at various times he resorted to many Leninist-style devices: a single party, the Partido Dominicano, which all state employees were compelled to join, paying dues of one tenth of their salary; punctilliously regular elections in which Trujillo routinely obtained the votes of over 99 per cent (and sometimes over 100 per cent) of the electors; a general surveillance of the population through identity cards, which had to be carried at all times, and served (since they had to be stamped at the polling station at elections) as a means of encouraging a high level of political participation; control through a variety of rival security services, providing Trujillo with additional safeguards against alternative foci of power (but quite unrestrained against arrested citizens, and just as violent against crimes of opinion as those of action); regular and subtly unpredictable reassignments and purges of subordinates worthy of a Stalin or Mao; a thoroughgoing attention to political indoctrination in the education system; together with a 'cult of personality', whose sartorial extravagance would have placed any communist equivalent in the shade, and which stretched to the appointment of Trujillo's three-year-old son as a colonel in the national army.

With all this, what could Leninism have added? Not enough, certainly, to compensate Trujillo for the affront it would have given his American and Vatican supporters and the sacrifice of the ready-made body of doctrine provided by traditional Catholicism as the state religion. Yet, if Trujillo was no communist, he was not beyond flirting with communism, and in his last months, when the Kennedy administration was attempting to get rid of him for the sake of OAS unity against Castro, he even legalized the Communist Party, promised land reform, and allowed some of Castro's speeches to be broadcast. But his assassination, in June 1961, showed the fragility of authoritarianism minus 'modern' ideas and values – there was no question of a party-organized succession and his system survived him by less than a week. The key weakness lay in the fact that political monopoly was unsupported by a comprehensive secular ideology to hold the ruling party together, and in terms of which its bureaucracies could express practical problems of rule. Party and state administration were not really unintegrated, the requirement of party membership for public employment being merely one of Trujillo's many methods for milking the state. There was no system of ideas suitable to incorporate radical currents, only the *ad hoc* co-optation of opponents; and no system of ideas adapted for controlling and justifying economic arrangements, or mobilizing people round collective aspirations to economic development.

The principle of the one-party state or the 'leading role of the party', and its extinction of competitive politics, is one that communism shares with other political species, including fascism and a variety of nationalisms. In the hands of others, it is a principle by which communism can find itself both tempted and threatened. An example is Iraq, where the relatively small but influential Iraqi Communist Party, which had already suffered harsh repression at the hands of both the monarchy and nationalism, none the less entered Saddam Hussein's 'National Progressive Front' in 1972, under an agreement which stipulated the 'leading role' of the Ba'ath party within the Front. But in 1978–9, when Saddam Hussein was shifting his international allegiance away from the Soviet Union and back towards the West, and consequently resumed violent repression of the communists, it was this very stipulation that he invoked to execute communists for organizing their cells in the army. The sharpness of their dilemma can be judged from the fact that communist ministers remained in the government even when the regime's killings of party members – both judicial and undeclared – had been going on for many months.

### FURTHER READING

The divisions of Germany and Vietnam are covered in readings given above. Histories of Korean communism are Scalapino and Chong-sik Lee (1972) and Lee (1978). Stone (1969), Simmons (1975) and MacDonald (1987) are concerned with the Korean war.

Basic books on Cuba are Thomas (1971) for the historical background, and Dominguez (1978) for Castro's rule. Goldenberg (1970) is an historical sketch of the Cuban Communist Party up to 1959. Abel (1969) is a detailed account of the 1962 missiles crisis. Grenada's period under the New Jewel Movement is described in Valenta (1984) and Thorndike (1985).

Kostiner (1984) describes the struggle for South Yemen. Warburg (1978) contains a case study of the Sudanese Communist Party. The 1974 Ethiopian revolution is described in Ottaway and Ottaway (1978) and the roles of the Soviet Union and the US are discussed in Korn (1986). The recent history of Somalia is in Laitan and Somatar (1987). Szajkowski (1981, vol. 1) contains accounts by Decalo of Benin and the Congo.

Booth (1985) gives a sympathetic account of the revolution in Nicaragua, while Leighton (1985) stresses the FSLN's linkages with communist states. Hodges (1986) outlines the Sandinistas' intellectual roots. Enzenberger (1976) and Wiarda (1968) examine Trujillo's dictatorship in the Dominican Republic, while Galindez Suarez (1973) is an account by one of Trujillo's assassinated critics. Batatu (1978) contains a survey of Iraqi communism.

# 9

## Soviet hegemony

The initial effect of further communist states being formed has generally been to enlarge the Soviet Union's international stature. But plurality contains the potential for separation, and the existence of divisions among a *number* of substantial communist powers has altered and complicated the patterns of patronage and loyalty among the smaller communist states and non-ruling parties. What is perhaps surprising is the clear predominance the Soviet Union has maintained. Despite the frequency with which it has seemed to treat the political success – and even the existence – of other communist movements as expendable, the Soviet Union continues to be far more effective in exercising a global influence through its associated parties and states than any other communist power.

At no point, even at the height of his sponsorship of guerrilla struggles in Latin America in the 1960s – in some measure an effort at 'go-it-alone' pressure and self-defence against the US – has Castro upset Moscow's overall 'hegemony'. This was not a matter of small size and dependency alone. Tito represented no very serious challenge either. After his break with Stalin in 1948, he attempted to generate currents and organizations in his support, particularly within Western European communism and socialism. In some places this caused a flurry; for example, in 1949 the small Norwegian party expelled its general secretary, Peder Furubotn (the rather courageous leader of communist activity in the wartime resistance after 1941), and eight other central committee members as 'Titoites and Trotskyites'. (The accusation appears to have been unfounded; Furubotn continued loyally to praise Stalin, and took to drink.) In general, the assaults on 'Titoism' during the 1948–52 purges vastly exaggerated the extent of organized support for it.

THE SINO-SOVIET SPLIT

Given China's far greater weight relative to Yugoslavia or Cuba, the Sino-Soviet split might have been expected to produce a different outcome. But the result was again highly asymmetrical. 'Maoist' eddies or currents were generated in many Western, and even more powerfully in Asian, communist parties. But these represented as much dissatisfaction with Krushchev's diplomacy and his ebulliently heretical approach to some of communism's sacred cows. Hostility between China and the Soviet Union, moreover, unlike the Stalin–Tito breach, developed hesitantly and uneasily, each side trying to load the onus on the other, and pleading their own devotion to the unity of the international communist movement. The situation, therefore, while it produced some turmoil almost everywhere, was not one conducive to large-scale, clear-cut transfers of allegiances, and tended therefore to preserve the status quo of predominantly pro-Soviet loyalties.

THE DIVISION OF INDIAN COMMUNISM

Indian communism was one of the important non-ruling movements to experience a significant split (as distinct from the loss of small splinters). It was one that only in part reflected the differences over guerrilla and revolutionary struggle, then being advocated by Maoists. There were natural pressures upon Indian (as well as many other Third World) communists to take Chinese rather than Russian experience as their model. The Indian Communist Party had already been divided over the question of peasant revolution in the Hyderabad movement of 1948–9 (see chapter 5). Chinese success with a peasant-based communism continued to have an obvious appeal, and the initial exchanges between China and the Soviet Union after 1956 elicited a significant pro-Chinese current within the Communist Party of India (CPI). No less a figure than Mikhail Suslov attended the CPI Congress in 1961, to support the more pro-Soviet 'right', but also to counsel against splits.

What eventually did bring the party to a rupture were the Sino-Indian hostilities in Tibet and Ladakh, culminating in the frontier war of October 1962, and the consequent sharpening of Sino-Soviet hostility, with Krushchev continuing arms supplies to India while the border clashes were under way. The 'rightist' majority of the Communist Party leadership united behind the Nehru government against China, and shortly afterwards the government arrested about 1000 CPI 'leftists' (using, it was asserted, lists supplied by the party leadership). The pro-Soviet faction was headed by S. A. Dange who, it later emerged, had once been an informer to the British colonial police; perhaps for this reason he was particularly responsive to Moscow's instructions. Dange's leadership then used the opportunity provided by their critics' detention to reorganize party bodies and push through suitable resolutions. After further manoeuvres the 'left' formed their own party, the Communist Party of India – Marxist (CPM) in 1964.

In fact, the expressions 'right' and 'left' (used above for convenience) are very poor descriptions. But neither did the split correspond neatly to the Sino-Soviet differences of the time. It is true that the CPI, having shed its 'left', took a course fairly resolutely congruent with Soviet foreign policy; it moved to closer collaboration with Congress, and was the only significant opposition grouping to support Indira Gandhi's 'emergency' rule in 1975-7.

But within the CPM the Maoists were in a minority, and in any case split away in 1969, subsequently to disintegrate into terrorist groups. A prominent figure in the CPM's leadership was E. M. S. Namboodiripad, the venerable architect of parliamentary communism in Kerala, and the new party established its position by routing the CPI in the 1965 elections there. (This was despite the government's detention of 800 of its members during the election campaign; of forty 'left' communists elected, twenty-nine were in prison.) Subsequently, the CPM's electoral strength has enabled it to form state governments in West Bengal and Tripura. As early as 1966 it resumed informal contacts with Moscow, and showed itself ready for *ad hoc* cooperation with a chastened CPI. By the 1980s the CPM was supporting the Soviet Union on major international issues.

In Indonesia there was no split, and the immediate outcome was more clear-cut. The Chinese were successful in securing the allegiance of the vast Indonesian Communist Party, but the advantages of this to them were shortly brought almost to nought, when it was destroyed in the coup of October 1965 – in important part because it gave too great an importance to political collaboration with China's prospective allies for its own safety. In the Philippines Maoism elicited the rebirth of revolutionary peasant communism, in the formation of the Communist Party of the Philippines, based on a guerrilla strategy. But this party, like the Indochinese, evolved its own nationally original strategy, and was never simply a Chinese dependant. (See chapter 5 on Indonesia and the Philippines.)

Outside Asia the Chinese harvest was puny. Tiny groups were provided with political franchises and funds in many countries, but seldom did they make many inroads, either upon national politics or upon the parent (and preponderantly pro-Soviet) communist parties. With the eclipse of Mao's reputation in China, most of them expired. Their prospects were never brilliant, and were further darkened, even in the heyday of international Maoism produced by the Cultural Revolution, by the Chinese leadership's propensity to pursue warm relations with foreign leaders given to the most energetic anti-communism. As Mao told a surprised Nixon in 1972, 'I like rightists. I am comparatively happy when these people on the right come to power' (Nixon, 1979, p. 562).

### COMMUNIST STATES: CUBA, ALBANIA, ROMANIA

As far as communist *states* went, the situation was similar. Chinese efforts to entice Cuba to their side were unsuccessful; they could offer neither as much economic support nor, much more to the point, anything like such plausible protection against the United States. Even while Castro was busy encouraging guerrilla struggle in Latin America, at the time of his maximum frictions with the Soviet Union, he generally limited himself to oblique criticism of Moscow. But Mao, he robustly announced in 1966, was 'senile, barbarous, and no longer competent to stay in office', and China was worse than an absolute monarchy (Thomas, 1971, pp. 1477–8). Vietnam, while its war with the US lasted, contrived to maintain tolerable relations with China by keeping a certain distance from the Soviet Union. After South Vietnam collapsed in 1975, however, relations between China and Vietnam rapidly worsened. Peking became the sponsor, against Hanoi, of Pol Pot's bloody and brief rule of Kampuchea, with the friction culminating in China's invasion of Vietnam's northern frontier areas in January 1979.

The only real satellite-cum-supporter which adhered to China for any period of time was Enver Hoxha's Albania. Initially, Hoxha reported favourably on the Twentieth CPSU Congress, telling his own party congress in May 1956 that Stalin's 'cult of personality' was 'foreign and obnoxious to the spirit of Marxism-Leninism' (BICO, 1975, p. 8). But he was pushed in the direction of China when Krushchev sponsored a coup attempt by his rivals, and became China's mouthpiece in the surrogate polemics through which the Sino-Soviet dispute emerged: China attacking Yugoslavia and 'Titoites', which were well understood to include Krushchev, and the Soviet Union responding against Albania. The Albanians, feeling themselves under real threat from Yugoslavia after Belgrade's rapprochement with Moscow, could be exceedingly blunt. Stalin had made just two mistakes, Mehmet Shehu (the Albanian Prime Minister) told Mikoyan: 'First he died too early; and second he failed to liquidate the entire present Soviet leadership' (Steele, 1974, p. 101). After the Sino-*Albanian* schism in 1978 Albania herself sought to maintain small organizations in Western Europe, but these never grew beyond microscopic size.

The Sino-Soviet dispute was also important in cutting adrift another close Soviet satellite, Romania. Starting in the early 1960s under Gheorghiu-Dej, leader of the Romanian party from the war until his death in 1965, the process continued under his successor, Ceausescu. Romania first began to assert its independence in resistance to Soviet plans to strengthen Comecon and make it the agency of greater specialization within the 'international socialist division of labour'. The Romanian leadership rightly feared that such plans (which were actively promoted by the Poles and East Germans) would entrench its status as an exporter of agricultural products and importer of manufactures, and torpedo, in particular, its ambitions for a large-scale steel industry. Encouraged by China, the Romanians successfully opposed all ideas of a Comecon planning body which might override national sovereignty, and began to diversify her trade patterns; by the late 1960s almost half her trade was with Western Europe. To reinforce her position, she adopted an obstinate neutrality in the Sino-Soviet dispute, and began to extricate herself from the military arrangements of the Warsaw Pact. As with Albania, though, disengagement from Soviet hegemony was in no way connected to internal reform; the Ceausescu regime has always been one of the most autocratic and nepotistic in Eastern Europe, the rulers extending their control by a web of family appointments to senior positions. (For an outline of the Ceausescu family tree, see de Flers, 1984.)

No other communist power, thus, emerged or looked likely to emerge with anything remotely resembling the attraction and influence of the Soviet Union over *organized* communist parties in other lands. This 'hegemony' has survived the dissolution of the Comintern and the Cominform, and the difficulties of the various *ad hoc* Soviet-sponsored international conferences of communist parties since then. Perhaps more remarkable, it has endured despite powerful external factors flowing the other way: the growth of 'Eurocommunism' and the wider spread of autonomy on the part of communist parties, ruling and not; and also an important, if less formal and organized factor: the erosion of much of the admiration which the Soviet Union earlier enjoyed, and its transfer to other states with fresher credentials. Since the war the Soviet Union has been elbowed aside as a political Mecca by, successively, Yugoslavia, China, Cuba, Vietnam, Mozambique, and, most recently, Nicaragua. But, helped by its growth as a world power, it has still retained its preponderant influence over non-ruling communist parties, as well as drawing into its increasingly eclectic orbit many non-communist organizations and parties. The world-wide basis of support for the Soviet state has grown much more diffuse and complex, and a smaller proportion of it rests on moral idealism, but it has not diminished.

## The International Department of the CPSU

Soviet pre-eminence in this rests not only on the economic and military strengths that have made it the world's second power, but also on its development of rather sophisticated machinery and techniques for seeding and reaping political advantages. When the Comintern was dissolved in

1943, a new organ, the International Department of the CPSU Central Committee, was formed to handle relations with and control over foreign communists. Headed by Boris Ponomarev, it was staffed largely from Comintern officials, both Russians, and the senior foreign communists who had taken refuge in the Soviet Union during the war: such figures as Thorez, Togliatti, Dimitrov, Rakosi and Erno Gero. The dissolution of Comintern also involved the transfer of many of its intelligence-gathering functions and staff to the intelligence services proper, the NKVD and GRU (for an outline of the history of Soviet intelligence organizations see p. 250). Ditching the formally representative framework of Comintern thus allowed a certain streamlining of functions; at the same time it required that the lines of detailed Soviet control over individual parties and their organs be more surreptitious and less public. The International Department was thus, from the beginning, an important body.

However, it only assumed its modern form after the dissolution of the Cominform in 1956, when relations with the existing *ruling* communist parties were split away as another agency. Then, in the following years Krushchev's more active policy towards Third World countries brought an expansion of the International Department's tasks, to handling relations with a large number of non-communist organizations, national revolutionary or liberation movements, etc. For these purposes a public and 'representative' body giving general political guidance and enunciating shared programmes and goals in the manner of Comintern would not have been viable; more frequently it has been a question of rather slight political unity, but *ad hoc* and temporary collaboration against shared opponents, best discreetly arranged by officials.

The International Department has thus developed as a powerful body in Soviet international policy-making, having a substantial role in interpreting information gathered by the intelligence services and making independent recommendations to the Politburo on a par with the Ministry of Foreign Affairs. It has day-to-day supervision – generally through Soviet deputy chairmen – of the various Soviet international front organizations (World Peace Council, World Federation of Trade Unions, International Union of Students, etc.), each of which acts as an 'umbrella' over affiliated bodies in many countries, together with numerous bilateral 'friendship' or 'cultural' organizations. At the same time it manages relations with overseas parties and movements, covering both material support and political influence or direction. The former may range from arms supplies and training for guerrilla movements to financial subsidies for 'fraternal' parties – for example, by purchasing their publications in bulk at favourable prices, or by arranging profitable trade with the Soviet bloc for companies controlled by local parties. As far as political direction is concerned, the growth of autonomy among communist parties, together with the multiplication of close Soviet relations with many non-communist but substantially dependent organizations, has further blurred the distinction between influence and control. Moreover, many matters on which the Soviet Union wishes to enlist the efforts of friendly forces internationally do not involve any conflict, or reluctance on their part; it is simply a matter of clear, timely and coordinated briefings, and, where necessary, persuasion. The International Department's responsibilities have expanded with the diversification of the Soviet Union's external political support, and its machinery has grown apace. Since the late 1960s, for example, it has organized units of its own officers abroad as diplomats in Soviet missions, on a basis similar to, but separate from, the intelligence services' longstanding use of diplomatic immunity. Since 1986 it has been headed by Anatoly Dobrynin, for many years the Soviet ambassador in Washington.

The increasing subtlety and discreetness of political intervention reflects not just the accumulation of experience, but the almost universal growth of independence among communist parties. If perorations by Soviet representatives aimed at splitting and creating whole parties (such as those of Zinoviev and his assistants after the Second Congress of Comintern; see pp. 48–50) would now be counterproductive in the extreme, so would the sorts of private harangues to which senior Italian and French communists were subjected by Djilas and Zhdanov at the founding meeting of Cominform (Reale, 1966, pp. 263–7), or even Krushchev's highhandedness. The confluence of causes which have required communist great powers to treat even quite small communist parties as independent and sovereign organizations are examined in the next chapter.

FURTHER READING

Tito's breach with Stalin is the subject of Ulam (1952) and Vucinich (1983); it also forms a major theme of Claudin (1975). Griffith (1964) is a useful volume on the initial Sino-Soviet split; two volumes by Gittings (1964, 1968) cover the years 1956–67. Kitrinos (1984) describes the history and role of the CPSU's International Department; his account is supplemented and updated by Spaulding (1987).

# 10

# Bases of independence among communist parties

The post-war break-up of the international communist movement has been partly federative. The forces loosening communists from their former attachment to the Soviet leadership have been, in part, the attractions exerted by other parties or groupings. But perturbations due to ruptures between communist states take effect only through a more fundamental factor in communism's evolution – the growth of intrinsic independence among communist parties themselves.

The major post-war international crises of Soviet 'hegemony' offer vivid 'windows' on the degree of development of independence among non-ruling parties. The period after Stalin's death in 1953 generated much questioning, and the invasion of Hungary in 1956 produced a haemorrhage of membership and support away from communist parties internationally, but no major party failed to adhere to Moscow's line (and seldom with more than small factions dissenting in their leaderships). In 1968, however, the invasion of Czechoslovakia produced outright condemnation from a number of parties, and critical comment from most. And reaction to the invasion of Afghanistan and the military crackdown against Solidarity in Poland was even more adverse.

The change had little to do with *formal* political arrangements; communists were perhaps surprised, but communist linkages to Moscow were scarcely at all disturbed, by the dissolution of the Comintern in 1943, nor, for that matter, by the equally unceremonious end of Cominform in April 1956, a peace offering (together with the dismissal of Stalin's Foreign Minister, Molotov) to smooth the way for Tito's trip to an apologetic Moscow. The Sino-Soviet split did certainly produce a marked loosening of ties, which went far wider than direct support for China. But the importance of the loosening lay not just in itself, but in allowing other forces to act.

## MILITARY BASES OF INDEPENDENCE

The intrinsic roots of independence among non-ruling parties – including some very small organizations – are not altogether dissimilar from the developments that have led communist states into friction with, or splits from, their *confrères*: entrenchment of the interests, and a growing national 'egoism', on the part of a maturing party apparatus. But this developed earliest into a strong form of independence where two conditions were present: first, a party controlling substantial territory and population, and with military means at its disposal such that its administrative functions became general in scope and made it the *de facto* state power; and, second, a sufficiently secure indigenous selection of leading cadres that they came to feel themselves answerable first to their own party machine, and only thereafter to international communism, or Moscow. The Chinese Communist Party, starting from its rural bases in south China in the late 1920s, followed by the Yugoslav and Albanian parties during the Second World War, were the first for which these conditions ripened, and their later histories exhibit tenacious, independent nationalisms. Moreover from the first of the Kuomintang 'encirclement' campaigns in 1930 the Chinese party had sufficient difficulties of communication with the Soviet Union that lines of guidance necessarily became attenuated, whatever either side wished.

### A CONTRAST: YUGOSLAVIA AND GREECE

In the case of Yugoslavia the diplomacy of 1940–1 provided the communists with a series of sharp lessons in the virtues of independence, and left lasting anti-Russian residues in popular memory. In March 1941 the Yugoslav government, after lengthy efforts to remain neutral, acceded under increasing German pressure to the Tripartite Pact (of Germany, Italy and Japan), but was immediately faced with large, hostile demonstrations, and shortly overthrown in a military coup. Its successor failed to get any promise of military or political support from the Soviet Union, and succeeded only in signing (on 5 April) a treaty of 'friendship and non-aggression' with it. This was followed, the next day, by the German invasion, and within a month the Soviet Union had withdrawn recognition from the Yugoslav government-in-exile. In fact, Hitler's haste to settle matters in the Balkans flowed from his plans to attack Russia in the summer of 1941 – on which both Yugoslav government intelligence agents and Yugoslav communists delivered a number of prior warnings to Moscow. But only after the German attack on the Soviet Union, in June, did the Soviet government restore recognition to the royalist government, and endorse armed struggle against the occupying forces.

More generally, in both the Balkans and China war changed the character of the most important decisions to be made; the first priority became effective military command and struggle, and neither broad strategic plans nor, even less, tactical dispositions, could be made effectively by distant political leaders. Most of all, war greatly speeded up the turnover, casualty and promotion rates of the party cadres. New young people were continually being thrust into positions of command, and war conditions naturally exerted a very strong pressure to select them not in accordance with remote political pronouncements but on the basis of concrete and immediate effectiveness. Conversely, their loyalty to their native party leadership was cemented by the fact that they depended on it not merely for their careers, but often for their lives; of the 12,000 members of the Yugoslav communist party in 1941, just one quarter survived the war.

Not that the link with the Soviet Union and its policies ceased to be of importance, but now it came into direct conflict with the imperatives of survival. In the early part of the war Tito repeatedly protested to Dimitrov (the Comintern official responsible for the Balkans) at Moscow's favourable radio coverage of his rival nationalist forces, the Chetniks, and he several times had to reject, as dangerous to their military efforts, proposals from Moscow that the partisans drop the forms of organization and discipline of their 'Proletarian Brigades' in favour of a more all-embracing 'national' front.

In neighbouring Greece, however, external factors brought about a very different result. During the later part of the war, the Greek Communist Party headed a guerrilla army comparable with Tito's in Yugoslavia. By late 1943 their People's Liberation Army (ELAS) controlled about two-thirds of rural Greece and claimed a membership of one-sixth of the total population. As the British officer C. M. Woodhouse described it, much of its work

was of an administrative nature, on the border-line between military and civil affairs; some of it was dangerously close to legislation . . . EAM/ELAS set the pace in the creation of something that governments of Greece had neglected: an organized state in the Greek mountains. (Woodhouse, 1948, p. 147)

The popular partisan movement was overwhelmingly hostile to the return of the pre-war monarchy, and in April 1944 there was a mutiny against the monarchy in the Greek army in Egypt. This was suppressed by British troops, who despatched 20,000 Greeks to prisoner-of-war camps. None the less Stalin agreed at his October 1944 Moscow meeting with Churchill to allot Greece '90 per cent' to the British sphere of influence, unlike Yugoslavia, where British influence was to be only '50 per cent'. Churchill was determined to restore the Greek monarchy as a buttress of British power in the eastern Mediterranean, and British troops under General Scobie landed in Athens as the Germans retreated north. Fighting immediately broke out, pitting ELAS units against British forces (and various of the right-wing irregulars tacitly countenanced by them, such as Grivas' 'X-Organization'), but the Greek communists continued to hope for a share in a coalition government, and in February 1945 agreed to dissolve ELAS. This, however, merely led to months of underground strife and, in 1946, to an open civil war, which ended only with the defeat of the communist partisans in 1949.

The two most important differences with Yugoslavia lay in Greece's different place in the division of Europe agreed between Stalin and Churchill (in their 'percentages' agreement), and in the closer – though still not complete – subordination of the Greek communist leaders to Stalin. Although the extent of communist control over territory and population during the war was broadly comparable in the two countries, it was only Tito who felt independent enough to ignore Stalin's advice and assert the reality of his proto-state by declaring a republic in 1943. Where the Greek communists acquiesced in a proposed coalition, and agreed to disarm in face of British and monarchist troops, Tito's forces, at the close of the war, were engaged in the extermination of many of the internal forces hostile to them – not only Chetnik irregulars, but whole populations viewed as collaborationist (atrocities in which the British political administration in lower Austria collaborated by forcibly returning Croatian and Chetnik refugees to the Yugoslav communists). Tito even held at arm's length the forces he could have been expected to regard as most friendly; when his government gave Soviet troops permission to enter Yugoslavia in September 1944 it was on the explicit condition that civil administration stayed in the hands of the partisans. It is true that the February 1945 agreement to disarm was forced on the Greek party only with difficulty. It necessitated large purges, and Aris Velouchiotis, one of its leading guerrilla commanders and the man responsible for a sanguinary 'cleansing' of the Peloponnese of collaborators in 1944, but who refused to accept the agreement, was shortly afterwards killed. The resistance to disarming was natural, since the immediate result was to lay communists and ELAS members open to the violence of the royalist regime and the armed right-wing bands which it encouraged.

None the less, the explanation that the eventual defeat of the Greek communists was just a delayed consequence of Stalin's agreement that Greece should be allocated to the Western sphere of influence may be too simple. Stalin *did* give cautious support to the Greek communists in the earlier stages of the civil war, only withdrawing it at the beginning of 1948. During 1946 and part of 1947 the communist guerrillas in the north were getting sizeable supplies from Yugoslavia and Bulgaria, apparently with Soviet knowledge and approval. In late 1947 they made strenuous efforts to capture a northern town suitable to serve as the capital of a provisional government. And in January 1948, Georgi Dimitrov, head of the Bulgarian party, made a surprise proposal in Bucharest for a grand federation of *all* the Eastern European states (except Germany), *plus* Greece – a scheme which had been under negotiation, principally between the Bulgarians and the Yugoslavs, for some time.

*Pravda*, however, repudiated the idea of any such federation (Stalin presumably doubted his ability to keep a federal state comparable in size with the Soviet Union as an obedient satellite) and the Bulgarians and Yugoslavs were summoned to Moscow for correction. They were also told: 'The uprising in Greece must be stopped, and as quickly as possible' (Djilas, 1969, p. 141). Then, in June 1948, Yugoslavia was abruptly expelled from the Cominform and blockaded by the other Eastern European states. Forced to turn to the West for aid, Tito acceded to their demand that he seal the frontier against the Greek communists.

The details of these developments remain obscure, as do their connections with rivalries in the Soviet leadership below Stalin, which surfaced in Malenkov's purge of Zdhanov's supporters after the latter's death in August 1948 (Zdhanov being the figure most associated with Tito and his radical stance in the Cominform). Within the Greek Communist Party, at that time struggling for its existence, a vast purge of 'Titoites' was launched after the Cominform split. General Markos, the popular commander of the 'Democratic Army' and head of the communists' rival 'government' in the north, who refused to condemn Tito, was removed in August 1948 and replaced by party chief Nicos Zachariades, who, allegedly, attempted to have his predecessor murdered (Eudes, 1972, pp. 329–32). In the summer of 1949 the last strongholds of the 'Democratic Army' were overrun, and the communist leaders fled into exile.

### THE AUTONOMY OF NON-RULING PARTIES

Possession of independent state or military power is not a necessary condition for a communist party to emancipate itself from the Soviet Union. More recently many non-ruling parties have begun to act independently, including communist parties in illegality and exile. In 1968 a large section of the illegal Greek Party's membership within the country (Greece was then under military dictatorship), supported by exiles in Romania and Czechoslovakia, split away in reaction against the Soviet invasion of Czechoslovakia, and formed the 'Communist Party of the Interior'.

What accumulation of factors has encouraged non-ruling parties' independence? A clash between a party's national political interests, and Soviet purposes, was long settled in favour of the latter. Soviet policy at the close of the war imposed severe stresses on a number of communist parties, but few of them failed to comply with Soviet requirements. One early and partial exception – whose elliptical character proves the general rule operating at the time – was the Communist Party of Burma, which split in 1946. An opposition faction, behind Thakin Soe, denounced the majority of the leadership, under Thakin Than Tun, for 'Browderism' – i.e. dissolving the Communist Party, as Earl Browder, leader of the US communists was charged with having attempted at the time of Comintern's dissolution in 1943.

The background to this exotic ideological import was the role of the Burmese party in the later stages of the war. Immersing itself in an 'Anti-Fascist People's Freedom League', together with the Socialist Party and pro-British army officers, it ensured that the advancing British forces were able to collect up weapons in the hands of anti-Japanese resisters, and ensure that independence went to a pro-British administration. The accusation of 'Browderism' was by way of being a protest on behalf of Burmese nationalism – it sought, in effect, to use a code-word endorsed by Moscow to denounce conformity with the settlement between the Western Powers and the Soviet Union.

Similar pressures produced eddies and rank-and-file protests, sometimes short-lived oppositions, in many other parties as, in many cases with revolutionary situations simmering around them, they none the less complied with the spheres-of-influence undertakings Moscow had given as the war drew towards an Allied victory. This was true in many of the colonies due for return to the European powers; Stalin, more than the liberal Roosevelt, was prepared to shelve his objections to continued rule over colonies for the sake of strategic and political gains through larger agreements, and local communists were accordingly obliged to swallow their traditional support for nationalism against the colonial power. Sometimes this situation set the colonial communists against their metropolitan comrades (and implicitly, therefore, against Moscow). In the Dutch East Indies, for example, the declaration of independence by Sukarno in August 1945 was ignored by Radio Moscow and denounced as a 'fascist provocation' and 'Japanese time-bomb' by Dutch communists. The Indonesian Communist Party, potentially a strong force, was thoroughly confused and played little part in the 'August revolution'. But the Dutch Communist Party (and some prominent Indonesian communists closely connected with it) stalwartly favoured the re-establishment of colonial rule; and the Dutch government naturally gave such figures help in returning from exile in Holland.

WESTERN EUROPEAN COMMUNISM

In most of Western Europe the retreat of the German armies during 1944–5 placed communists – prominent in many of the resistance movements after the German attack on the Soviet Union in 1941 – in positions of considerable strength, with the backing of sizeable armed force. In all cases, however, the political leaders – mostly returnees from Moscow – instructed peaceful collaboration in broad coalition governments, and an end to revolutionary agitation or industrial militancy. The French communist leader, Thorez, returned to Paris in November 1944, Stalin having obtained from de Gaulle an amnesty from his legal conviction as a deserter in 1939. (Thorez followed his own advice to party members at the outbreak of war and joined the colours to fight Nazism; only when, at the end of September, it became clear that Soviet instructions were to oppose the French war effort as 'imperialist' did he desert his unit and flee to Moscow.) At the close of the war Thorez and the leadership of the PCF joined de Gaulle's government as enthusiasts. They supported the repression of nationalism in Algeria and the French colonies, and opposed all strikes at home. Those who criticized the ultra-patriotic party line of 1944–6 were at best 'sectarian', at worst 'disruptive elements, trouble-makers, agents of the enemy, Hitlero-Trotskyites, who usually hide behind left-wing phrases' (Claudin, 1975, p. 332). There proved, for a time, to be no contradiction between the most extreme loyalty to Stalin and full support to the capitalist order at home.

In general, resistance to the post-war settlement in Western Europe was restricted to rumblings and occasional outbreaks at the base, from industrial militants and local resistance leaders. It required many years longer, and much further internal development, before the leaderships and main organizations of Western communist parties began openly to exhibit any independent critical spirit towards Moscow (as distinct from equivocation in the Sino-Soviet dispute); and only in the 1960s did a number of Western European parties begin to move along this track in an open and concerted way.

The turning point was the 1956 crises. Although 1956 did not cause the defection of any party leadership, it reduced the Soviet party's ability to impose its will. The first trial of strength, in 1958, involved Axel Larsen, leader of the small Danish party. Larsen favoured greater and more public independence from the Soviet Union, in the interests of improving his party's electoral performance. Moscow also suspected him of being sympathetic to Tito, who was, in 1958, again estranged from Krushchev. Soviet emissaries, intervening in the leadership of the Danish party, succeeded in unseating Larsen. However, he took many of the rank and file with him to form a new party, the Socialist People's Party, considerably larger than the remains of the official Communist Party.

In other countries, the first stirrings of party leaders towards independence were more Stalinist than 'Eurocommunist'. It was the sense of having their regard for Stalin thrown back in their face by Krushchev that provoked an active split away from Moscow, by Paul de Groot's relatively small Dutch party. De Groot used time-honoured methods to protect his position against Krushchev's interference, banning party members from travelling to the East or meeting Soviet diplomats. And in 1961 Thorez presumed to bargain quite impudently with Krushchev: the French party would support Moscow against Peking, provided Krushchev would approve Thorez' removal of 'Krushchevites' from his own leadership.

When Western European parties did embark on 'Eurocommunism' they were widely considered to be undergoing not a process of autonomous radicalization, but one of re-absorption into their national polities, dissolving the distinctive party forms crystallized out by the efforts of Cominform in the 1920s, and moving towards becoming, perhaps, a novel type of social democratic party. Longer developments do not bear out this view (or at least do so only in part). Eurocommunism is a political species which, while attenuating its relations with the Soviet Union, and basing its strategy and responses far more on domestic politics, often retains much that is Leninist in its internal metabolism.

### THE POPULAR FRONTS

If we except the explicit criticism of the Soviet Union, there was little in the *policies* of 'Eurocommunism' that had not been rehearsed in earlier years. The tactic of advantageous alliances with social democratic parties was launched in 1921 with Comintern's switch to the 'united front'. In this phase it was often understood as the 'united front from below' – unity with the rank-and-file social democrats, axiomatically identified with its 'left', and against its leadership. The *popular* (or anti-fascist) front, pioneered in France and Spain from 1935, was a more full-hearted unity, directed to the leaders of other parties and embracing also 'bourgeois' formations, such as the Radicals. It also carried a real commitment to restraining class struggle in the interests of the alliance. While the French communists explained in 1936 that a 'true' popular front would signify soviets and the dictatorship of the proletariat, when a wave of spontaneous strikes and factory occupations broke out in June of that year, the party strove to bring them to a speedy end. In Spain the communists acted, during the civil war, as the most violent opponents of attempts to carry out social revolution and the revolutionary currents which advocated it.

The popular front remained, none the less, a tactic, and under Moscow's close control: in 1936 Thorez wanted to accept portfolios in Blum's cabinet, but was prohibited by Comintern. The Spanish Communist Party, under similar instructions, did not enter Largo Caballero's ministry until September 1936, after the insurrection of the generals had tilted the country into civil war. Nor were all the proposed alliances of the Popular Front period necessarily anti-fascist. In the autumn of 1935 Togliatti was urging Italian communists to concentrate on unity with those fascists who were opposed to the Ethiopian war, rather than with the socialists, and a PCI manifesto of August 1936 roundly declared that 'we Communists take as our own the Fascist Programme of 1919' (i.e. Mussolini's original, radical and egalitarian, platform). In September the party declared that the fascist unions should be considered authentic workers' unions (Urban, 1986, pp. 127–30). The difference with France and Spain was that in Italy the party was illegal and had no prospect of agreement with the political leadership of fascism; what was proposed was a front 'from below', as in the 1920s.

The popular front brought the European communist parties, wherever they remained legal, a vast growth of membership and support, and allies from improbable parts of the political spectrum. The strength of the French party, for example, cut by two-thirds by the sectarianism of the 'third period' – to 28,000 in 1932 – rose to 280,000 by 1936, and even higher by 1938. Partly for this reason Eurocommunists have been inclined to point back to the Popular Front – relatively brief interval though it is in the life-span of twentieth-century communism – as a sort of golden age, and to indulge in a certain amount of hagiography around the figure of Georgi Dimitrov, who happened to be chosen to announce the switch of policy at the Seventh Comintern Congress in 1935.

Yet the popular front in no way betokened any 'organic' response to domestic politics. Both French and Spanish communists have retrospectively claimed that its origins lay in their private intercessions with Comintern about the disastrous results of the 'class against class' line of the 'third period'. It may well be that they complained of their problems to Moscow, but there was no question, at that stage, of the policies they were to follow being determined by themselves, or even of any compromise on the matter. The European communist parties had been thoroughly 'Bolshevized' for almost a decade – in part this was Moscow's response to the resistance and occasional rebellion from 'leftists' which it encountered in the early 1920s when getting the united front accepted. And the European communist parties were to prove their obedience to the hilt in 1939 when (with exceptions – as in Britain – that amounted to no more than hesitations) they turned their backs on their erstwhile anti-fascist allies to support the Stalin–Hitler pact. Nor was the next period of national unity – from the German attack on the Soviet Union to the early post-war years – any different in this respect; it was almost with relish, for example, that the French Communist Party resumed its role as 'leftist' opposition and fomenter of strikes after being thrown out of the government in 1947, with Thorez, demonstrating a lively continuity of vituperation, comparing François Mitterrand, then a minister, to Goering.

EUROCOMMUNISM

What was new in the 1960s thus lay less in the policies than in their motives, and in the changed longer-term political horizons of which they formed part. Party leaders and large portions of the party apparatuses became ready for a shift in strategic planning which would avoid their being mechanically tied to the coat-tails of each shift of Soviet policy – with all the embarrassing accusations and political damage that entailed – and better attuned to local possibilities. Already in the spring of 1956, in the aftermath of Krushchev's 'secret speech', Togliatti began to speak of the 'systematic degeneration' of the Soviet state, and to urge 'polycentrism'. It was only a brief harbinger, however, and in November the PCI fell into line over Hungary, expelling the more outspoken critics of the Soviet intervention. The French CP was more audibly unanimous over Hungary, but more hostile to 'Krushchevism' behind the scenes. But the rise of the 'new left', culminating in an international wave of student demonstrations and even insurrections in 1968, added further pressures for more flexible, inclusive strategies. The Italian Communist Party was one of the earliest to adapt to the mood of the 'Vietnam generation', with Togliatti's successor, Luigi Longo, seeking a 'new bloc' with the youth movement after meeting with student groups in April 1968. The French communist leaders, faced in May with student revolution in Paris (which shortly triggered a general strike), took a more hostile attitude, joining the government in denouncing the ultra-left, while ineffectually trying to manipulate themselves into a position to influence the students. Louis Aragon, mounting a soap-box in support of the communist student organization, was heckled by Cohn-Bendit's group: 'Vive le GPU!' But after the invasion of Czechoslovakia in August, the French communists also recognized the need for a more supple policy.

The shift to 'Eurocommunism' could not have come about had it not recommended itself to the main core of the party *machines*, that is, to the paid officials and activist members who ran the parties, communists with a much higher commitment than the 'penumbra' of ordinary members, with their higher rate of turnover and more casual involvement. If 'Euro-communism' had been the outcome of a process of absorption of Leninist party machines by their surrounding parliamentary, pluralist political ethos, one would have expected a struggle between membership currents and the highly seasoned party machines. But this was not how it occurred; it was, in virtually all cases, an internal adaptation by the apparatus. Thus, in the Italian Communist Party, 'Eurocommunism' had been established for many years before the movement for 'transparency' associated with Pietro Ingrao got under way. This explains one of the principal apparent para-doxes of Eurocommunism: communist parties don the outer integument of parliamentary democracy, while preserving Leninist practices in their internal life.

## Italy

The apparatuses were not, of course, all made of exactly the same cloth, and some parts took more readily to a degree of authentic independence than others. The process of 'Bolshevization' of the Italian party in the 1920s was not so thoroughgoing as elsewhere, since the party was already being driven underground and abroad by Mussolini. A number of leaders opposed the Hitler–Stalin pact, for example, and Umberto Terracini was expelled for this by his fellow communist inmates in prison, being reinstated by Togliatti only in 1945. The organization which rose again after 1943 – though its strategic policies remained dominated by relatively small circles of intellectuals – grew rapidly to be the largest communist party in Europe, and was from the outset a central factor of post-war Italian life. In its period of most explosive growth, from the closing stages of the war in Italy, in the spring of 1945, to the end of that year, it expanded itself essentially as an electoral machine rather than a cadre party; in 8–9 months it quadrupled in size, to over 1,750,000 in December 1945. Political screening was dropped and branches were encouraged to recruit regardless of religious faith or philosophical conviction. Recruitment was so eclectic that the party absorbed a good number of former fascists; and it always allowed itself ample latitude for *ad hoc* dealings, on both local and parliamentary planes, with Christian Democrats and others, and sought 'hegemony' and influence, rather than direct control, within cultural and intellectual circles (see chapter 13).

Such a large and innovative organization as Togliatti's 'partito nuovo' could not be led by simple-minded application of precepts of democratic centralism learned in Comintern; it required – and, in return, underpinned – a great deal of independence on the part of the leadership. There were, therefore, early harbingers of the later resistance to Moscow. Togliatti, probably sensing that he was in for criticism, absented himself from the founding meeting of Cominform in 1947 and advised Thorez to do likewise;

Luigi Longo, Togliatti's deputy, who attended instead, replied with dignity to the charges heaped on him (unlike the French representative, Jacques Duclos, who grovelled). Later, in 1951, recuperating in Moscow from a road accident, Togliatti flatly rejected Stalin's repeated requests that he become head of Cominform, based in Prague or Moscow.

### Spain

The Spanish case is particularly interesting. 'Eurocommunism' developed first and furthest in the Spanish Communist Party (PCE), but it became deeply afflicted by factionalism and Soviet interference, and has been far less successful than in Italy. Though its background was very different from Italy or France, illegality under the Franco regime did produce some of the same motives as arose from leading large established parties in Italy and France – especially the wish for an end to doctrines or international alignments which stood in the way of flexible negotiation and broad alliances, or, with the return of legality, could lose votes.

Santiago Carrillo, the moving spirit of Spanish 'Eurocommunism', came to the Communist Party in 1936 as leader of the socialist youth movement and organizer of its merger with the communists. Head of the communist youth movement during the civil war, he spent very little of his ensuing period of exile in Russia, and most of it in France. He became a critic of the authoritarianism and sectarianism of the exile party, with its astonishing internal purges and even assassinations in the 1940s and early 1950s. Krushchev's secret speech saved Carrillo from expulsion in 1956 (together with his friend Fernando Claudin, subsequently in 1964 to be expelled by Carrillo himself, essentially for becoming an advocate of 'Eurocommunist' positions too soon). Gradually Carrillo's strategies of reconciliation and cooperation with other anti-Francoist forces, to overcome the communists' 'exile within exile', prospered within the party leadership abroad, and brought him to formal leadership by 1960. From 1966 the PCE was beginning its qualified criticisms of police methods in the Soviet bloc, and starting to fudge or contradict, particularly in speeches and pamphlets, its traditional positions on the dictatorship of the proletariat, the vanguard role of the Leninist party, etc. But from 1969 onwards, as a result of its round condemnation of the Soviet invasion of Czechoslovakia, the PCE leadership faced the first of many pro-Soviet rivals, headed by the civil war veteran Enrique Lister.

Moreover, the PCE proved inept at profiting from the decay of the Franco regime and the shift to legality. (Franco died, after protracted illness, in November 1975, and Adolfo Suarez, appointed prime minister by King Juan Carlos in July 1976, curtailed police activity against the communists by the autumn of that year.) The Achilles' heel of the quintessentially 'Eurocommunist' Carrillo leadership was its inability to compete with

Spain's reviving Socialist Party (PSOE). Carrillo combined a 'leftist' perspective of a national strike to force the 'rupture' of the Franco regime, with perceptibly 'rightist' choices among allies. The PCE's initial anti-Franco front, formed when the dictator was taken ill in July 1974, amounted to little more than the communists, the large, communist-controlled workers, commissions, and some minor political groups headed by former Francoists, Carlists and Socialists. The leadership displayed a more marked hostility to the Socialist Party than to Suarez's political coalition of the centre (the UCD).

Formal changes, too, were ill-managed in ways that belied the party's claims to democratic credentials. In the spring of 1977 (*before* the party was officially legalized) the Central Committee decided, with no prior discussion, on the deeply symbolic step of recognizing the monarchy and its flag; thereafter anyone who displayed the flag of the Spanish republic at communist events was 'removed' by the party's security forces. When, with almost equal suddenness, the leadership proposed to the April 1978 party congress that the party drop its description of itself as 'Leninist' from its programme, the decision had to be pushed through organizationally; as an Executive Committee member put it: 'It is Leninist to drop Leninism' (Mujal-Leon, 1986, p. 6). Part of the opposition stemmed from strongly pro-Soviet currents, some among whom, having maintained their attitudes through forty years of clandestinity, were not inclined to cloak them now; the rest came from a much smaller opposite wing, thoroughgoing reformers who were disturbed at the French Communist Party's unanimous vote to drop Leninism, and wanted more comprehensive debate to establish the matter.

This pincer of pressures, acting on the contradictions of Carrillo's Euro-communism, coupled with internal drives for national and regional autonomy, and exacerbated by the inability to rival the Socialist Party electorally, started the tortuous process of decline and fragmentation which the PCE experienced over the next decade. In the event, Spanish communism's zenith – perhaps 200,000 members, but a disappointing 9.2 per cent of the votes in the general election – came in 1977, the year it was legalized. The 1982 elections, in which the communists received just 3.8 per cent of the vote, caused Carrillo to resign as secretary-general, and opened a further ferocious faction fight between his supporters and those of his successor, Gerardo Iglesias. The differences of policy involved – essentially, that the *'gerardistas'* were more favourable to cooperating with the socialists and 'social movements' than the *'carrillistas'* – did not explain the venom involved, which had more to do with personal rivalries in a declining party machine; one letter in the party press likened Central Committee meetings to 'a pack of dogs fighting over meat' (Mujal-Leon, 1986, p. 18).

To this was added, in January 1984, the fusion of most of the pro-Soviet groups outside the party to form the Communist Party of the Peoples of Spain (PCPE), an organization large enough to form a rival, and enjoying a measure of formal recognition (as well as clandestine funding) from the Soviet Union. In the spring of 1985 the *'carrillistas'* were ousted from the PCE, and before the end of the year both sides were engaged in negotiations with the PCPE; by that time, however, all three bodies were marginal to Spanish electoral politics.

The decline of Spanish 'Eurocommunism' was made all the more galling by the success of communism in neighbouring Portugal, where it had an even longer history of illegality, from 1926 until the military revolution of April 1974. The Portuguese Communist Party came briefly under the influence of the Spanish party's domestic orientation in the late 1950s, but from 1960, when Alvaro Cunhal escaped from prison and resumed its leadership, it dropped such 'broad front' policies and never wavered in its support of the Soviet Union; from the late 1960s its exiled leadership served as an important mouthpiece for Soviet bloc criticisms of 'Eurocommunism'. It had a membership of 3000 or less before the overthrow of Caetano in 1974, but expanded very rapidly thereafter, especially among the rural labourers of the large holdings in the south of the country. Though it was ousted from the government in 1976, it continued to grow, and became, as a proportion of the population, the second strongest communist party in Western Europe, second only to the Italian.

While a common feature of Eurocommunism was an orientation towards longer-term governmental and electoral alliances with other 'democratic' parties, the nature of communist inner-party democracy itself changed appreciably less: the Political Committee (or equivalent body) retained wide powers over internal life and parliamentary and local government representatives, and remained to a large extent self-renewing. There never developed the sort of entrenched symbiotic coexistence of 'wings' characteristic of social democratic parties. And, conversely, the various 'left'-communist groupings which – especially after the disappointment of the revolutionary hopes of the late 1960s – have made their 'entrist' homes in the bosoms of social democratic parties, have seldom attempted entrism within the communist parties themselves. The internal regime makes it very difficult to get a toe-hold, and even where they do succeed in infiltrating the leadership of bodies regarded by the communist party as theirs – as did Trotskyists in the French union of students in the 1960s – they are liable, when detected, to be thrown out with very little ceremony.

### Britain

Political divisions in the British Communist Party – exacerbated by the steady decline of its press and electoral achievements – moved towards a head in 1984–5. The organizational combativeness of both sides, once battle for the leading bodies had been joined, meant that matters moved briskly towards a division – in this case, the expulsion of leading opponents of 'Eurocommunist' adaptations of policy, including some, such as Ken Gill, with very senior positions in the trade union movement. The more traditionally Leninist current, however, fought back and succeeded in capturing the party's daily newspaper, the *Morning Star* (which had been actually but not technically a party publication). Arguments between the two sides on the justice or otherwise of the expulsions, and the *Morning Star*'s right to criticize the party, were conducted within the framework of Leninist organizational principles.

One point that this particular split in the British party illustrated (there have been several other lesser splits) was that neither side considered strength to be measured principally by counts of members at particular moments, still less by votes among the electorate (the British first-past-the-post system discriminates particularly strongly against small parties by virtually making all votes for them wasted votes). The *Morning Star* current recognized that its strength lay in control of the paper (to which Soviet and Eastern European subsidies through bulk purchase continued) and in the informal networks built up over many years in the Labour Party and trades unions, through numerous cooperative 'peace', 'democratic', etc. organizations. In a manner that, in some respects, resembled the work of a Communist Party deprived of the right to legal existence – but not otherwise repressed – the *Morning Star* proved able to continue operating a political machine with scarcely any visible organization or membership.

The Communist Party leadership, despite being as remote as ever from any parliamentary presence, put its main emphasis on an anti-Thatcher broad front to embrace communists, Labour, Social Democrats and very possibly dissident Conservatives – but aimed at parliamentary success more than exploiting trade union power. The fact that the communists were not likely to contribute to a possible anti-Thatcher electoral majority did not inhibit them from staking their claims as its theorists, sponsors and hopeful beneficiaries. In that role they found that a critical tone towards Soviet history is essential in rehabilitating Marxism within the political spectrum. Yet on either side of the split in British communism the power of the machine was to be measured by its leverage within other machines, and, this being so, the retention of essentially Leninist methods of internal organization conferred a comparative advantage which neither side wished to relinquish.

Another point which the case of British communism illustrates is the considerable eclecticism practised by the Soviet Union in bestowing its 'franchise', indicative of its wish to preserve as many linkages and points of support as possible. When a previous faction was expelled from the

Communist Party and formed the New Communist Party in 1977, the Soviet Union gave it partial but unambiguous support, while reserving primary backing for the main Communist Party. With the 1985 split the Soviet Union continued its large purchases of the *Morning Star*, and sent speakers to its political events, while still not withdrawing primary recognition from the majority Communist Party. At the same time it continued, as it had for some years, to give occasional crumbs of endorsement to the 100 per cent pro-Soviet grouplets on the perimeter of the party, as well as to a publication of similar complexion run by communists within the Labour Party.

To the larger non-ruling communist parties such irritants could have appeared a provocation, and in Italy or France, for example, the Soviet Union has on the whole avoided giving gross offence of this sort by undiscriminating support of rivals to the main communist party. In Italy, for example, even after the sharp polemics arising from the Soviet invasion of Afghanistan and Jaruzelski's coup in Poland, the Soviet Union limited itself to discreetly financing a small journal (*Interstampa*) and cementing its influence over the pro-communist daily *Paese Sera*. But smaller parties, like the British, have had to live with the fact that they are only one – and perhaps not even the most important – domestic point of support of Soviet policy, and that the loyalty so painfully tempered over many years could prove an embarrassment to its object. As long ago as the Twentieth Congress of CPSU, in 1956, it was being whispered in the corridors, behind the back of the unfortunate Harry Pollitt, that the Soviet leadership was seriously considering dissolving the British Communist Party and encouraging in its stead a broader Bevanist, left-wing within the Labour Party (Vidali, 1984, p. 63).

## Other Eurocommunist variants

The factors leading a range of non-ruling communist parties to assert their independence of Moscow contained several common ingredients, but were very far from being identical; still less did they develop in the same relative strengths or at the same pace. The French Communist Party's 'Eurocommunist' phase, for example, was effectively brought to an end in 1980 by Marchais's public support for the Soviet occupation of Afghanistan. This was a blow to its electoral performance, which has since declined further, losing votes both to the resurgent Socialist Party and to Le Pen's xenophobic National Front. The party's shrinking vote, and its failure to adapt to the decline of smokestack industry and the increasing importance of white-collar and middle-class occupations, has given rise to a series of internal criticisms and splits and – perhaps most wounding of all – to attacks on it for 'conservatism' by the Soviet press under Gorbachev.

The Dutch party, whose Stalinism earlier defied Krushchev's revisionist breeze from Moscow (see p. 147), went furthest in the 1980s – but with little better electoral results. During the 1970s its manual worker membership declined drastically, but total membership rose, mainly through an influx of students and social workers. This change in social composition was an important factor in enabling the central committee majority to rebuff an attempted 'coup' by the veteran party leader, Paul de Groot, in 1977, attempting to return the organization to a more traditional and pro-Moscow line. De Groot's failure opened the way to an offensive by feminists (as late as 1980 the party was still paying less to its female cadres than their male colleagues), and a congress in 1984 adopted a new programme based jointly on feminism and Marxism, and abandoned both democratic centralism and proletarian internationalism. A critical watershed for the Dutch party's international orientation was the banning of the Solidarity movement in Poland, towards which it had taken a position of emphatic support. The Dutch party is the one which has come nearest to 'mutating' into an authentically social democratic organization, though it has rejected proposals to merge with other left-wing parties.

The large Japanese Communist Party is a rather different case from the Western European parties. It began its 'Eurocommunist' evolution earlier, and in reaction against Chinese tutelage. Its post-war leader, Sanjo Nosaka, returned to Japan from the Chinese Communist Party headquarters at Yenan in 1946 and (with full Soviet agreement) devoted himself to making his party 'lovable' to the 'progressive bourgeoisie' – meaning principally the US occupation authorities. The Cold War brought this stance under great pressure, but Nosaka's majority on the leadership survived both repression by the occupation authorities and a blistering public attack from the Cominform in 1950. In 1964 the Japanese party took China's side in the Sino-Soviet dispute, expelling a vigorous pro-Soviet minority (which formed an independent party). But in 1967 the main Communist Party shifted to an independent position and expelled its Maoist leaders, and by 1976 it had relinquished the dictatorship of the proletariat and 'Marxism-Leninism' from its programme, replacing them with expressions of respect for political pluralism, human rights, freedom of speech, and individual property. Recently it has come to be held up as something of a model by Western European 'Eurocommunist' leaders.

'Eurocommunism' came to a head in several different countries in the same period, and formed a movement with some internal cohesion. This was not just a matter of national, insular processes coinciding, but of the great desirability of mutual support and protection for the leadership of any non-ruling Communist Party contemplating a visibly independent course, and persisting in it in face of Moscow's opposition. And conversely, the need for the loose but vigorous alliance that broke the ice of public obedience to the Soviet Union goes far to explain how parties with very different histories, goals and attitudes could come to group themselves under a common banner. To an important degree the common programme of Euro-communism has proved an abstract or even negative one: asserting the right to dissent from and criticize the countries of 'actually existing socialism' when, and to the extent that, this appears domestically advantageous in terms of national politics or inner-party balances. That such a right should have had to take such an assertive form is merely an index of the parties' earlier subservience.

SOVIET REACTIONS

Soviet and Eastern European reactions to Eurocommunism have been – as I indicated above in connection with the British Communist Party – many layered. The same is true more generally of Soviet reactions to the much greater autonomy and 'federalism' within world communism. It is, therefore, futile to seek any single pronouncement or theme reflecting an 'authentic' response: reactions address a variety of audiences, external and internal, and must allow for combinations of pressure and continued allegiance, on diverse parties and currents within them, as well as for the uncertainties of the future. Brezhnev's often quoted remark to the Czecho-slovak leaders (flown to Moscow as prisoners after the 1968 invasion) – that Berlinguer and other leaders of Western European communism were 'going to sound off – but so what? . . . For fifty years now they have not mattered one way or the other' (Urban, 1979, p. 132) – expresses only part of the Soviet stance. Certainly Soviet leaders were not going to allow the 'normal-ization' of Czechoslovakia to be deflected in any important ways by Euro-communist criticisms, but they were far from holding the Western European parties at nought, and they persisted in efforts to preserve useful relations with them, while applying pressure and engaging in polemics against that in them of which they disapproved.

The formal results of their efforts to retain central – if looser-rein – management of much of the world communist movements over the next years, however, were unimpressive. The conference of sixty-seven com-munist parties, which finally assembled – after sixteen preparatory meetings – in East Berlin in June 1976, achieved unanimity in its declaration only at the cost of vacuity. There was no mention of 'proletarian internationalism', the conventional expression for Soviet leadership, and the oft-repeated major premise of Brezhnev's doctrine, after the occupation of Czecho-slovakia, of the limited sovereignty of socialist states; no clear condemnation of 'anti-Sovietism'; nor any pronunciamento on the vexed question of 'democratic centralism'.

In fact, the first party to drop the expression was the impeccably pro-Soviet Portuguese party at its Congress in the autumn of 1975, when it was in quest of a governing alliance with the officers of the Armed Forces Movement (MFA). Party leader Alvaro Cunhal explained that the phrase 'would not facilitate understanding of the party's policies', but added that 'the present life in the socialist countries' remained their model (MacLeod, 1984, p. 35). The following year the phrase was officially erased from the statutes of the French party. (In 1977 the new Soviet Constitution responded by extending the 'dictatorship of the proletariat' from the ruling principle of *party* to that of *state* organization.)

Speakers at the East Berlin conference all took the opportunity to proclaim their own point of view, Carrillo being the most outspoken of the Westerners. 'For years', he declared, 'Moscow was our Rome. We spoke of the great October Socialist revolution as if it were our Christmas. That was the period of our infancy. Today we have grown up. We Communists do not have a leading centre, no international discipline which can be imposed upon us' (Mujal-Leon, 1983, p. 122). All delegates, once back home, sought to fill the unanimous document with their own content and present the resulting mélange as a victory for their standpoint.

On a doctrinal level Soviet theorists sought to establish a degree of insulation between Soviet and Eastern European realities, and Western parties' actual and implied criticisms of them, by developing a distinction between alternative *roads* to socialism (an allowable possibility, and one already enunciated, after all, in Stalin's day), and deviations from the sole and correct model of scientific socialist *state*, which were not to be tolerated. The distinction had the merit of permitting agreements to differ with Western European parties over current policy and statements, while drawing them into an endorsement of the Soviet as against the Chinese example (the isolation of which had been one purpose of the East Berlin conference). Yet alongside this potentially measured approach Czech commentators, in particular, were allowed licence for much stronger attacks; they owed their position, after all, to the fact that Eurocommunist protests had been ignored by Soviet policy in Czechoslovakia. Thus Vasik Bilak declared for the Czech leadership in 1977 that 'Eurocommunism' was a term which no true communist would accept; it was a product of imperialism and 'tantamount to treason' (Brown and Schopflin, 1979, p. 263). But it was well understood that such statements were intended essentially for domestic consumption, a signal that Czech dissidents could not expect to be indulged because Eurocommunists interceded for them. And, read like that, it was not a substantial breach of the agreement to differ.

Eudes (1972) describes the civil war in Greece. Kousoulas (1976) is a history of Greek communism.

Sources on Indonesian communism are given in the further reading to chapter 5 (p. 92). On Burmese communism during and after the war, see Thomson (1960) and Badgley (1974).

Overall histories of the French Communist Party include Tiersky (1974), Mortimer (1984) and Adereth (1984). Rieber (1962) covers the period 1941–7; Kriegel (1972) dissects the party's internal social life.

Sassoon (1981) is a fairly sympathetic account of the Italian party's politics from the war, while Urban (1986) concentrates on its relations with Moscow. Alba (1983) is a history of the Spanish party; Semprun (1980) is a former leader's stream-of-consciousness recollections of it during the Franco era; and Mujal-Leon (1983, 1986) recounts its emergence into legality, and subsequent decline and fragmentation.

Dewar (1976) covers the history of the British Communist Party up to the Second World War, and Pelling (1958) through the 1956 crisis. There is as yet no full and sober study of its 1983–4 split, but Callaghan (1988) gives a brief account, and Mitchell (1984) is polemical but well informed. Samuel (1985–6), a former member, provides colourful reminiscences around the event.

Filo della Torre, Mortimer and Storey (1979), Middlemas (1980) and Kindersley (1982) discuss 'Eurocommunism' among the parties of Western Europe, while Narkiewicz (1987) is a bibliography of the scattered literature on 'Eurocommunism'. The essays in Waller and Fennema (1988) provide accounts of Western European parties since approximately 1968. McInnes (1975) is a sociological and organizational dissection of the Western European parties since the war, while Graham and Preston (1987) have edited a volume of essays on the Popular Front.

# PART III

---

# Ideas, theories and doctrines

# 11

## The Marxism of the unready

Nineteenth-century Marxism envisaged that it would be in economically mature capitalist societies, with large industrial proletariats, that the communists would be best placed for political victory. Yet no autonomous communist movement has so far come to power in a highly industrialized capitalist state. The most industrialized European countries in which it has succeeded are Germany and Czechoslovakia. But in both of these it gained power only under Soviet protection, and in East Germany the leadership of a new party had to be flown in from Moscow. In Russia, where native communism first succeeded, industrial development was very far from mature, and industrial workers were only one, and not the most important, base of Bolshevik strength. Later communist parties which forged independent successes departed even further from the classical Marxist perspective.

The preference for the industrialized, 'civilized' societies of Europe and the United States, and the presumption that socialism would arise there first, carrying the torch on a path where others would later follow, were attitudes shared by many varieties of socialists and Marxists before the First World War. They imposed severe rigidities of outlook and practice, and before Russian Marxism could emancipate itself from these in its political action, it had to question in its fundamentals the Eurocentric theory it had adopted.

### EUROCENTRIC SOCIALISM

Before the First World War socialism shared much of the self-confidence of propertied society in Western Europe, its sense that it stood at the forefront of human achievement and that it pointed the way forward for less advanced societies. Socialist thinking and organization were the fruits of the highest development of capitalist civilization; the starting point, if they were in due course to be transmitted more widely, lay at home. There were few inhibitions about imposing progress, and in due course socialism, upon peoples who were still distant from accomplishing them under their own steam.

Such attitudes found directly political reflections. In Britain, where the socialists were divided by the Boer War, most of the leading Fabians – jolted from their preoccupation with domestic affairs – decided they were on the side of imperialism (though eschewing the vulgarities of jingoism). Shaw, compositing their views, declared that 'the notion that a nation has a right to do what it pleases with its own territory' is no more tenable 'from the International Socialist point of view – that is from the point of view of the twentieth century' – than the idea that a landlord has unrestricted rights with his estate. Moreover, since 'the value of a State to the world lies in the quality of its civilization', it followed that 'The State which obstructs international civilization will have to go, be it big or little. Thus huge China and little Monaco may share the same fate, little Switzerland and the vast United States the same fortune' (*Fabianism and the Empire* (1900), quoted in McBriar, 1966, pp. 125–8).

In the case of the Webbs (as with many other socialists of the time) this sense of the superiority of European civilization flowed, through Darwinism, into a form of socialist racialism. The different social and moral potentialities of human races were formed by evolution and could not be altered in the short term. The Chinese, Beatrice Webb found when touring the Far East at the time of the 1911 revolution, 'are essentially an unclean race'; of Asians, only the Japanese (held in higher regard in Europe after defeating Russia in the 1904–5 war) impressed her favourably. Social maturity (and hence the capacity for socialism) inhered in Western Europeans; they would need to exercise an indefinite 'collective guardianship' over the 'non-adult races'; one of the Webbs' main long-term worries was that Europe's 'racial vitality', and hence capacity for proper social organization, would be eroded by the greater fertility of Jews and Slavs (Winter, 1974, pp. 42ff).

Similar sentiments also proliferated among Marxist socialists. Marx, and particularly Engels, were always inclined to judge nations and races, as well as classes and individuals, in terms of their 'reactionary' or 'progressive' character; the behaviour of the Slavs in the 1848 revolutions, for example, showed them to be counter-revolutionary 'racial trash', fit only to be exterminated. Later they became enthusiasts of Darwin's theory of evolution, partly because it offered to provide biological explanations why some human groups and races (such as Germans) were historically more successful and progressive than others (for example Slavs and negroes).

Many German social democrats, particularly after the 'Hottentot election' of January 1907, when their vote was cut back by the government's vigorous pro-colonial campaigning, were inclined to find socialist reasons why colonialism was – or could be – a good thing. The Stuttgart Congress of the Second International in August of that year only narrowly rejected a resolution supporting colonialism as 'an integral element of the universal aim of civilisation pursued by the socialist movement'. Its proposers derided Kautsky's view that it was possible to convey enlightenment to African negroes peacefully; when dealing with 'savages' it was necessary to have weapons in hand. Returning colonies to the native peoples would simply result in 'barbarism': 'The colonies too must go through the stage of capitalism as well and no more there than here can one jump both feet together from barbarism into socialism.' Bernstein made himself the main theoretical spokesman of this trend, and his German supporters urged the case that Germany, the latecomer behind Britain and France, was colonially disadvantaged. (On the colonial debate at the Stuttgart Congress see Riddell, 1984, pp. 3–15.)

It is true that there were also many socialists – including Lenin, who attended the Stuttgart Congress – who took a far more hostile attitude to European colonialism's methods, its avarice and its brutality towards native peoples. But there existed a common underlying view: that the maturing of capitalist relations was an essential precondition of socialism's success. Thus when, as early as 1894, Lenin was arguing against Struve, in orthodox Marxist fashion, that socialism was immediately relevant to Russian conditions, he sought to prove that capitalism was *already* fully developed there; and when, on many later occasions, he bemoaned Russia's partly 'Asiatic', 'semi-barbaric' or 'backward' character, this always implied an admission that – at least in some respects – it might be less than fully suitable for socialism. Lenin saw in Sun Yat-sen's presidency of the Chinese republic evidence that the Asian bourgeoisie was still capable of producing heroic, revolutionary democrats, but the lesson he drew was that 'the East has committed itself to the western path' (Lenin, 1960–78, 18, p. 165).

European socialists' views of the 'backward' nations were entwined with the political and theoretical problems presented by imperialism, and this in turn came to be increasingly dominated by the prospect of war, and the problems of how to prevent it or respond to it. Since a great part of the danger of war arose from the colonial and territorial competition of the powers, socialists tended to divide and redivide into patriots and internationalists, with the latter, at least, stressing the need for social revolution before the fruits of European civilization could be conveyed to the 'backward' countries. This view drew theoretical sustenance from economists' studies of capitalist imperialism (Otto Bauer, Rudolf Hilferding, J. A. Hobson), which showed how industrial and financial capital, far from spreading itself globally, tended to concentrate the ownership and accumulation of wealth in its metropolitan centres. The conclusion – adopted and elaborated in Lenin's *Imperialism: the Highest Stage of Capitalism* (1916) –

was that only socialism in the metropolitan countries could realize the rational development of the world economy.

## RUSSIAN SOCIALISM AND BACKWARDNESS

What, then, was to become of movements and aspirations for socialism outside the most advanced nations? By a concatenation of circumstances this question was explored most thoroughly in Russia – first in theoretical, then in practical terms, and in ways which have an often prophetic relevance to contemporary arguments on modernization, development and under-development. The ideas which later provided the doctrines and influenced the policies of communist movements on the international stage were gestated in the nineteenth- and early twentieth-century debates on the prospects and peculiarities of socialism – especially Marxian socialism – in 'backward' Russia.

Russia, in the late nineteenth century, remained an overwhelmingly rural society, and one in which, moreover, a large fraction of agricultural production went for subsistence, not to market; this economic-social backwardness acted to preserve its political archaism. Modern machine industry was mainly large-scale, and, being concentrated in relatively few locations, had had little impact on much of rural society; foreigners were important in its ownership and control. External influences had produced an educated stratum attuned to cultural and political importations from Western Europe, but by that very fact inclined to look critically on Russian circumstances. The liberal and radical intelligentsia, concentrated in the main cities, were witnesses to desperate and often violent struggles by a young, raw industrial working class, little touched by trade union or socialist traditions. It was clear, moreover, that these new-grown conditions had much to do with official policy, which had done much, by protection, subsidy and credits, to propel industrialization; as a result Russia's industrial growth averaged the comparatively high figure of 5.7 per cent between 1885 and 1913, with a 'spurt' to 8 per cent in the 1890s (Gerschenkron, 1947, p. 149). Russia, it seemed, might well repeat, in an accelerated and more traumatic form, the course of capitalist industrialization on which the nations of Western Europe had preceded her.

But need she, or could she? The traditions of the Russian intelligentsia contained much which disposed thinkers to discern, or urge, a different path. Thus in 1870 the so-called 'legal populist' V. Vorontsov (actually much influenced by Marx) advanced the argument, which was for a time influential in both radical and official circles, that, as one of the countries which were 'latecomers to the avenue of history', Russia would have to take a different route. Competition from the capitalist economies which had already developed prevented Russian private capital from conquering export markets, and restricted its home market. Successful industrialization could not pursue private profits, but must be managed by the state, and Vorontsov – who was followed in this by N. F. Danielson, the translator of *Capital* into Russian – was a *'legal'* populist, in that he proposed this should be done by the Tsarist state. From this followed a part-plebian, part-autocratic conclusion: Russia could show Western workers how to reorganize their social, if not political, circumstances; it was her 'destiny to bring about equality and fraternity, though she is not destined to fight for liberty' (Walicki, 1980, p. 431).

Marx himself doubted whether the historical schemata of *Capital* were applicable to Russia, and thought she might find a different route of development, perhaps one based (as earlier populists had hoped) on her distinctive peasant commune. His view that Russia might be exceptional was shared by the Tsarist censor. In 1871 the authorities allowed the publication of a Russian edition of the first volume of *Capital* – excluding only Marx's portrait – on the grounds that it did not apply to Russia and that, unlike the author's political and historical writings, it was inaccessibly and safely abstruse. (They were not alone in this opinion: Bakunin was originally commissioned to prepare the Russian translation of *Capital*, but became bored and gave up before completing the first chapter.)

However, interest in Marxism in Russia grew rapidly, and by the 1890s, with its 'spurt' of industrial growth, Marxism provided the terminology of both radical and much academic and official discourse in Russia, filling the place taken earlier by economic liberalism in the West. Lenin recalled that 'nearly everyone' became a Marxist, and publishers rejoiced at the extraordinary sale of Marxist literature. In St Petersburg the *Stock Exchange News* opened its columns to the nicer points of Marxist theory, and society *marxisantes* swooned to hear social democratic lecturers expatiate upon the price of grain and capitalism's inexorable inroads into agriculture (Pipes, 1970, pp. 146–9). Marxist ideas became the credo of an educated class in a hurry to catch up.

Marxists of Plekhanov's persuasion firmly believed that *Capital did* apply to Russia, and took a globally orthodox view, arguing – and to that extent advocating – the inevitability of capitalist industrialization. However, even as Marxism applauded the coming to pass of economic necessities, it also had to notice and deplore the fact that, if Russia appeared to be treading the stipulated Western path economically, she showed no signs of doing so politically. There was, at least in terms of historical materialism, a substantial anomaly. Again, they were not the first to sound such a note, even if the anxieties and predictions were different. In the 1870s the 'jacobin' populist, Peter Tkachev, in polemic with Engels, voiced the fear that economic development – and in particular the formation of a property-owning peasantry and a prosperous middle class – was eroding the conditions for revolution in Russia. If the revolutionaries did not make haste they would find themselves cocooned in the detestable, affluent moderation of the West.

## ADVANTAGES OF BACKWARDNESS

This notion of different facets or planes of social development being out of synchronization (whether this provided a 'window of opportunity', as Tkachev saw it, or represented a handicap, as later Marxists tended to regard it) was itself a long-standing theme of Russian social thought. But so also was one of its possible implications: that 'backwardness' in some areas could be a kind of privilege, allowing the conscious negotiation of difficulties that more 'advanced' societies had blundered into and through unthinkingly. This idea had been expressed by Chadaev in the 1830s, and was echoed in Herzen's observation that Russia's unlovable past made a break into an open future all the easier. The thought was widespread in the revolutionary populism of the 1860s and 1870s; Nicolai Chernyshevsky, author of one of Lenin's favourite novels, *What is to be Done?*, caught the sense in an aphorism: 'History is like a grandmother; she is particularly fond of the youngest grandchildren.' Vorontsov made explicit the idea that there could be definite social and economic advantages to learning, from the accumulated historical experience of one's predecessors, what to avoid. Russian Marxism could draw on a broad national current of historical thought: Russia would travel through the landscape of 'progress', but not necessarily at an even pace or on trodden paths.

In fact the sense that lateness could be an advantage, especially for revolutionaries, did enter into the theoretical corpus of Russian Marxism, but sometimes with difficulty, and leaving contradictions unreconciled. The historical process, Plekhanov admonished populism's impatient terrorists of the 1880s, unfolds 'with the unswerving character of astronomical phenomena' (Mendel, 1961, p. 112). He felt, however, the need to accelerate matters, at least theoretically. Capitalist industrialization would be more rapid in Russia than it had been elsewhere, since it could immediately adopt the latest and best techniques; conversely the Russian socialists could profit from the experience of socialism in the West, avoiding some of its trials and errors and preparing the ground for a powerful socialist movement while capitalism was still at an early stage of development. 'Our capitalism', Plekhanov promised in *Our Differences* (1884), 'will fade without having fully flowered'.

During the 1880s and 1890s Russian social democrats-in-embryo, with their stress on historical necessities, looked most intently towards the formation of a sizeable working class, rather than towards the ripening of bourgeois society as a whole; most were agreed on the unnaturally weak and dependent character of the Russian bourgeoisie. But, given the global nature of their doctrine, it was natural that not only their theoretical, but also their political tracks should converge for a time with those – like Struve – who were making their apprenticeship as the radical-liberal spokesmen of national development. The possibility of a short-cut, or a different route, did none the less assert itself in both the ethos and the theories of Russian socialism; it could hardly have generated an effective political movement on the basis of relegating its day to the indefinite future. A long-standing reproach of the workers' circles in Russia against the intelligentsia revolutionaries with whom they uneasily cooperated – repeated in 'economist' criticisms of *Iskra* at the turn of the century – was that by gratuitously stressing political demands the revolutionaries tended to attach the workers' movement to the political 'coat-tails' of the bourgeoisie.

The more radical spokesmen of Russian Marxism in the 1890s, however, stressed – as though to stake out for themselves a role in the nearer future – the feeble, cowardly and unconvincing character of the Russian bourgeoisie. From this it was but a short step to revive a liberating paradox within the Marxist historical scenario – would not the Russian bourgeoisie, like their German cousins in 1849, denounced by Marx for their behaviour in the Frankfurt assembly, flee their own revolution, or at least its full consequences? And would not the Russian workers' movement, on the morrow of the national revolution against despotism, find itself in conflict with bourgeois interests? Thus in 1902 Alexander Martynov and David Ryazanov, then theorists of 'revolutionary economism' (both were later to be Bolsheviks) argued, against the over-orderly perspectives of *Iskra*, for 'revolution *in permanentia*'. Ryazanov added his agreement with Kautsky's suggestion (in the pages of *Iskra*) that Slavs could bring Western Europe 'a new, happy spring': political revolution in Russia would break the ice of reaction in the West, and this in turn would open the way to *social* revolution in Russia (Larsson, 1970, chapter 5).

PERMANENT REVOLUTION

It remained to set out a more systematic international view of 'permanent revolution' to Russia's benefit, and to mesh this not merely into a remote historical panorama, but to nearer prospects for political action. It was Alexander Helphand (Parvus) who – as Trotsky (1975, p. 172) recalled – 'definitely transformed the conquest of power by the proletariat from an astronomical "final" goal to a practical task for our own day.' In a series of articles in *Iskra* in 1904, prompted by the outbreak of the Russo-Japanese war, Parvus urged Mensheviks and Bolsheviks to reunite for imminent battles. World politics was shaped by the economic conflicts among the great industrial states, leading inevitably towards a world war. Caught within these struggles, Russia suffered exceptional internal vulnerabilities, and could become the breaking-point of capitalism's international chains:

The world process of capitalist development brings about a political upheaval in Russia. In turn, this will effect political development in all capitalist countries. The Russian revolution will shake the capitalist world. And the Russian proletariat will assume the role of vanguard of the social revolution. (Knei-Paz, 1979, p. 18)

The vitality of the working class, and the impotence and dependence of the bourgeoisie, meant that revolution in Russia would produce 'a government of working-class democracy'. If the social democrats were willing to seize the nettle they could rule, if not they would degenerate into a sect. Parvus's views were by no means unique; Rosa Luxemburg, for example, was writing in 1905 that the Russian revolution would tend to 'grow over' from the bourgeois to the socialist stage, led by a proletariat that had absorbed the best of Western European Marxism (Weber, 1975, pp. 44–8).

Trotsky, incarcerated following the 1905 revolution, gave this idea a fuller exposition, and historical and sociological premises, as his theory of 'uninterrupted' or 'permanent' revolution. Although the theory was self-evidently an unorthodox departure (and moreover addressed, at this time, only to Russia as a unique exception) none the less Trotsky – fresh from his brief glory as Chairman of the St Petersburg soviet – invested it with powerful tones of historical necessity. He also added an insistent stress on the significance of the state: the peculiarities of Russian society were due to the fact that the Tsarist state had largely shaped social classes from above, and society remained peculiarly dependent on the state.

It is important to notice that the *detail* of the Parvus–Trotsky theory of permanent revolution had no influence on Bolshevik politics; during most of the period after 1905 Lenin had little but abuse for Trotsky's theoretical efforts. And although events in 1917 did much to vindicate Trotsky's views, he diplomatically avoided dwelling on his leader's earlier obtuseness. In fact, however, Bolshevism's political attitudes and practice (if not its theory) did – indeed virtually had to – devise alternatives to the perspective that the revolution against autocracy would be followed by protracted capitalist development. Lenin recoiled from the extremism of Parvus's suggestion of a government representing workers alone, and he himself advanced (in *Two Tactics of Social-Democracy in the Democratic Revolution*, written in the summer of 1905) the awkwardly hybrid formula of 'the revolutionary democratic dictatorship of the workers and peasants', buttressing what he felt, in Marxist terms, to be a dangerous jumping of the gun with the traditional desire of Russian revolutionaries to act in the name of the 'narod'. This formula Trotsky rejected: it would not be possible simply to incorporate the peasants into the workers' revolution; on the contrary the villages would be a standing threat to the socialist or collectivist policies of a workers' government. Only through revolution in the West could proletarian Russia be rescued from collapse.

Almost all shades of Russian Marxism pushed – or were pushed – forward, and as they went they modified orthodoxy in the name of orthodoxy. All retained the industrial working class – stiffened to a greater or lesser extent by its party – at the centre of their revolution's dynamic, but then came the question: how could such a small fraction of the population retain power? Lenin, rather *ad hoc* (but drawing on Kautsky's authority), favoured a coalition of expediency with the peasantry; Trotsky, with larger theoretical dignity, looked to the German revolution. And, as the Second Congress discussion showed, the utility of a strong state, compensating by dictatorship for political and social weakness, was a natural corollary of their theoretical worries. Most thought it a temporary bridge, but the seed of the idea that state action could compensate for historical 'unreadiness' was there, and ready to sprout.

Yet how far, up to 1917, even the most startling departures continued to be thought through within a common mental framework of European Marxism is shown by Felix Dzerzhinsky's casual exchange with his old acquaintance, the Menshevik leader Raphael Abramovitch, as they waited in the queue in the Petrograd Soviet's canteen in August 1917:

'Abramovitch, do you remember Lassalle's speech on the essence of a constitution?'

'Yes, of course.'

'He said that a constitution is determined by the correlation of real forces in a country. How does such a correlation of political and social forces change?'

'Oh, well, through the process of economic and political development, the evolution of new forms of economy, the rise of different social classes, etc., as you know perfectly well yourself.'

'But couldn't this correlation be altered? Say, through the subjection or extermination of some classes of society?' (Abramovitch, 1962, p. 313)

FURTHER READING

Marx and Engels's national and racial views are discussed in Talmon (1981). Carrere d'Encausse and Schram (1969) consider socialism's attitude to colonialism, while Ridell (1984) provides fuller details on the debate at the Second International's Stuttgart congress of 1907. Kemp (1967) and Brewer (1980) include outlines of Marxist theories of imperialism.

The responses of nineteenth-century Russian intellectuals to Russia's 'backwardness' are outlined in Mendel (1961), Venturi (1966) and Walicki (1980). Shanin (1983, 1985) argues that Marx's views on Russia as representing a special case anticipated later conceptions of 'developing societies'. The genesis of the Parvus–Trotsky theory of permanent revolution is discussed in Knei-Paz's (1979) volume on Trotsky, and in the biography of Parvus by Zeman and Scharlau (1965), while Larsson (1970) reviews some of its immediate precursors in Russian and European Marxism.

# 12

# Marxism comes to grips with power

With the Bolsheviks' unexpected success in October 1917, ancient debates were transposed into a new, and continually shifting, context. The question was not whether Marxism could lay hold of political power in such a little-industrialized empire as Russia, but if and how it could retain it, and what sort of society would be the outcome. When the victors divided, they gave theoretical expression and generality to their differences around such questions. Similar issues have arisen for the later generations of communists who have come to power. This chapter looks at some of the ideas which communists have devised in response to these problems: the battle over 'socialism in one country' versus 'permanent revolution'; attempts at the Marxist definition of communist rule; the liberal Bolshevism associated with Bukharin; and Mao's 'Cultural Revolution'.

During the period from Lenin's death, in 1924, to 1927, the upper reaches of the Russian party were convulsed by a series of violent factional struggles over the succession to Lenin. The spirit and tone of the conflicts from which Stalin eventually emerged as sole leader were very different from most later disputes among ruling communists. The leading participants had little inkling of the bloodletting in which their differences would issue, and were moreover the human products not of mute careerism within a monolithic ruling party, but of a triumphant and frequently verbose revolution; both these factors made them less inhibited. Within their disputes were rehearsed some of the central issues in many later communist conflicts and splits.

SOCIALISM IN ONE COUNTRY

Among the factional arguments and antitheses that divided the leading Bolsheviks, the one that eventually became most celebrated is that between the Lenin–Stalin–Bukharin theory that it was possible to build 'socialism in one country', and Trotsky's 'permanent revolution'. Between these two views events established a curious asymmetry. Only half the predictions of the theory of permanent revolution which Trotsky and Parvus had developed in 1905–6 had actually occurred. The Russian revolution had led the way – but it had been followed by no sequel. Yet nor had it collapsed – something for which Trotsky's efforts as military commander-in-chief could claim much credit. The theory was thus left suspended as a set of propositions offering a very poor guide to action. Moreover, it was one by which its author was now somewhat embarrassed, Lenin having polemicized so vigorously against it before the First World War. Until Trotsky was expelled from the party in 1927, the words 'permanent revolution' were mainly uttered by his detractors, who had every interest in recalling his earlier differences with Lenin.

The doctrine of 'socialism in one country' only emerged explicitly after the defeat of revolution in Germany in late 1923 (see chapter 4) and after Lenin's death, in January 1924. At the end of 1924, with the 'triumvirate' at the head of the party (Kamenev, Zinoviev and Stalin) uneasily united against the prestigious figure of Trotsky, Stalin improvised the doctrine upon a passage which Lenin had written in 1915. By this time the notion that socialist construction could and should proceed in just one country had a potentially wide appeal. It was a useful factional weapon and it had the advantage, in its more modest interpretations, of being an almost unexceptional proposition: that socialism could be built in the Soviet Union with only the 'moral support', not the 'state support', of workers and communists in other countries; only later did the argument shift to the more academic and acrimonious issue of whether *full* socialism – an economy of plenty – could ever be constructed in the Soviet Union without socialist revolution in the West. To such an extent did the idea of socialism in one country insinuate itself as unexceptionable that it was not until November 1926 that Trotsky made a public and explicit attack on it.

The assertion that socialism *could* be build in one country carried a message of constructive effort, of self-sufficiency, of inward-turning nationalism, and provided a powerful rallying call for the growing number of practical-minded officials who ran the state and party machinery. For the debate, though it was continuous with earlier arguments among the Russian intelligentsia, was now fought out as a political dispute, before a much larger audience, for whom political and organizational efficacy were far more important.

'Socialism in one country' seemed capable of being put into execution; it could thus claim to have passed Marxism's acid theoretical test, that of practice, and was in a position to reinforce this claim by exercising the state power that was both its theoretical and practical vindication. The state power however, grew with such exercise, and moreover had by the early 1920s come to nourish and protect substantial social inequalities. Official theoretical efforts were circumscribed by the fact that what was developing in their one country bore only a distant relationship to the images of socialism under which the revolution and civil wars had been fought, and the distance was in many respects increasing. The gulf between official definition and actual circumstances gave rise to much theoretical improvisation and in due course to a strategy of general official mendacity.

In the Bolshevik disputes of the 1920s the audience was limited, as in so many subsequent communist debates, by the ground common to all the main factions: defence of the Bolshevik monopoly of power, and of the supremacy of the party leadership. Trotsky and his 'Left Opposition' argued for a better conduct of Comintern, and warned about Soviet 'bureaucracy', both as afflicting the party and state apparatuses, and as an influence on high policy. They claimed to speak in the name of the working class, but in reality they scarcely dared to step beyond the bounds of the Party's leading stratum to gather support. Nor could they, as yesterday's proponents of the militarization of labour and one-man management, have expected much response if they had done so: it was only political repression that prevented a large resurgence of the other left-wing parties in the trade unions and soviets. It was common ground to the disputants not only that the Bolsheviks should retain their monopoly of power, but that this should rest with the full-time officialdom and be concentrated in the top party leaders. The opposition's case, thus, was both hypothetical and tightly circumscribed. They were reduced to arguing, like many subsequent 'reform' communists, that if only *their* party leadership would use other methods, instruments and tempi in the building of (it was for the time being conceded) socialism at home, then the results would be preferable and safer. As far as global strategy was concerned, Stalin was far from having abandoned the Bolsheviks' internationalist principles; he had merely given them a further Russocentric twist. To make socialism in one country fully secure, he told the Fifteenth Party Congress in 1927, 'we must see to it that the current capitalist encirclement be changed to a socialist one; we must strive for the proletariat's winning in at least a few other countries' (Ulam, 1973, p. 269).

Perhaps, since the differences led to so much violence, the similarities were superficial? On one plane they were. Both sides generously larded their case with quotations from Lenin, the plentiful supply being testimony to the portmanteau character of his thought. But on a more directly political level the similarities were substantial, and the differences often ones of degree and timing. Trotsky's main complaint against the party leadership's domestic policy was over its failure to give a strong state initiative in economic planning and industrialization. Featherbedding the peasant and pursuing Bukharin's 'socialism at a snail's pace', the 'left opposition' held, threatened the recrudescence of capitalism. Thus when, from 1928–9, Stalin turned to coercive collectivization of the land and forced-march industrialization, many former oppositionists accepted Stalin's olive branch and switched sides, to help administer what they regarded as their policies, belatedly adopted. One of the ironies of the conflict was that Trotsky and other oppositionists frequently accused Stalin and the Party bureaucracy of conservatism, routinism, the inability to carry out the 'abrupt turns' that had been the hallmark of revolutionary Bolshevism – and were then taken by surprise by each of those very turns. Marxism in power, contemptuous of theoretical niceties, proved itself as a revolutionary force in a series of sudden and violent initiatives, while Marxist theory limped after it reproachfully.

## MARXISM AND SOVIET SOCIETY

What *was* the form of society over whose future they argued? All sides regarded the Soviet Union as a form of, or precursor to, socialism. From the official standpoint its limitations merely indicated its early stage of development, and would be the quicker overcome the more energetically the population supported the regime. The adversaries were agreed in identifying the Soviet Union's character as a 'workers' state' with the Bolshevik Party's tenure of power, and in seeing any threat to that tenure as a threat to the social foundations of the state. Only later did Trotsky settle on his characterization of the Soviet Union as a 'degenerated workers' state', marked by a fundamental bureaucratic deformity which could only be overcome by purging the soviets of 'Stalinists'. And he was five years in exile, before he conceded in 1934, that other 'soviet' – but under no circumstances 'counter-revolutionary' – parties should be allowed political rights. The shared mental framework was not only a matter of theoretical formulations, but powerfully shaped the perceived political choices; the accumulation of peasant wealth was considered a menace to the social order, and it was when Stalin embarked on his fearful 'liquidation of the kulaks' that many of the purged 'left oppositionists' recanted and supported him. The shared framework was that of Marx's historical sequence towards socialism, with argument revolving on the question whether the Soviet Union was travelling along the main track or if it had been displaced to a siding.

Marxist theory has made involved and sometimes scholastic efforts, both in the formulations of opposition communists and in the altering formulae of state constitutions, to come up with a serviceable definition of what Rudolf Bahro (with sensible agnosticism) has called 'actually existing socialism'. Its conceptions offer an object lesson on the hold of theory over practice. The basic requirement imposed by the theoretical inheritance is that existing socialist society must be located within, or at most as on a detour from, the passage from capitalism and the rule of the bourgeoisie, to socialism and the dictatorship of the proletariat. This may be qualified by the official concession that the working class shares political power with the peasantry (and/or sometimes with the democratic bourgeoisie) or that it is held more inclusively by the 'people'. Or it may be joined with the criticism that both political and social structures are marred by bureaucratic deformations, and that these carry within them the risk of a slide back into capitalism – or even with the stronger judgement that this has already occurred, producing 'state capitalism'.

In fact Marx did not insist that all societies must travel the feudalism–capitalism–socialism road. However, Leninists, whether official or oppositional, have seldom moved beyond the categories this sequence provides – as if sensing that to do so would place them outside communism. In 1930–1 Stalin firmly strangled a theoretical discussion – though it was innocuously academic – of concepts of the 'Asiatic mode of production' in Marx's writings. In part he wanted to avoid further examination of the Chinese Communist Party's Comintern-directed débâcle at the hands of Chiang Kai-shek. But there may also have been the fear of reviving the social democrats' unsettling speculations from the early years of the century; Plekhanov, for example, had voiced his fears about the despotic mutations that Russia's 'Asiatic' character might impose on a successful but premature socialist revolution.

Later, at the beginning of the Second World War, Trotsky did contemplate the possibility that what had arisen in the Soviet Union was a form of exploitative society not foreseen by Marx – 'bureaucratic collectivism', in which the ruling class owns property and exercises political power collectively. But he raised the possibility only to reject it, and for reasons that are revealing: if 'bureaucratic collectivism' should prove a reality, he maintained, this would signal that the Soviet bureaucracy had succeeded in developing into a new form of 'collectivist' ruling class, viable on a world scale. And this would imply that the programme of Marxian socialism had proved utopian, at least for a whole further historical epoch. (He might have added, perhaps for ever, since Marx's analysis in *Capital* purported to show that socialism is organically contained within, and necessarily emerges from, capitalism. If what in fact issues from capitalist society is 'bureaucratic collectivism', there is no *Marxist* reason to suppose socialism will ever follow it.) Trotsky's thinking remained shaped by the basic unilinearism within which, as a young man, he developed the idea of permanent revolution. All societies must follow the same essential track, even if some of them succeed in skipping or abbreviating stages. If, therefore, the bureaucratic collectivist 'new class' proves itself viable in the Soviet Union, then it must be so on a world scale. But Trotsky's argument – and before him, those of other 'left' Marxists – also anticipates one element of many postwar lines of socialist thought, which see Marx's smokestack industrial proletariat as a diminishing, and diminishingly active (or, sometimes, 'hegemonic') fraction of society, giving way to increasing numbers of functionaries, mental workers, the 'new middle class', etc. Since the war a number of non-ruling communist parties have made efforts to develop these sorts of bases of support (see chapter 14). However, Trotsky's view made no effort to recruit these strata into a new basis for socialism, but boldly and pessimistically drew the conclusion that, if these groups should prove decisive, socialism would have proved itself an illusion.

Leninists of all persuasions have remained sensitive to the fact that to describe the Soviet Union in any terms other than those of Marx's central route from capitalism through to socialism is to introduce a dangerous and eventually lethal heresy. Thus Ante Ciliga, a Yugoslav communist imprisoned in Stalin's 'isolators' in the 1930s, recalled how some of the oppositionists incarcerated with him maintained that the Soviet Union was a new type of social formation, comparable to 'Kemalist Turkey, fascist Italy, Germany on the march to Hitlerism, and the America of Hoover–Roosevelt', and were politically 'expelled' by their fellow political prisoners for their views (Ciliga, 1979, pp. 280–1). And when Mao came to give a social characterization of what Khrushchev's 'revisionism' had wrought in the Soviet Union, it was as 'social imperialism' and 'social fascism', i.e. further variants of capitalist society.

THE SOCIOLOGY OF POLEMIC AND PURGE

The restricted theoretical framework within which the Bolshevik factions of the 1920s and 1930s assailed each other also entrenched the paradoxical habit – which has endured through virtually all subsequent communist disputes – of classifying the social and political divisions of their socialist society in terms of the classes and divisions of bourgeois society. Indeed, we could put the general paradox more sharply: communist parties' claims to represent working classes are regularly qualified by their discovery of 'bourgeois', 'imperialist', even 'feudal' tendencies in their highest reaches, and under socialism, one of the most intense sites of class struggle turns out to be the party itself.

The opposition critics of bureaucracy in the 1920s spurned the anarchist nomenclature whereby the burgeoning party-state officialdom was a new bourgeoisie, characterized it, more cautiously, as the political expression of the bourgeois economic tendencies allowed to run riot by the NEP, and hinted that it could lead to an overall restoration of private property. When Stalin turned to forced collectivization and state-owned industrialization in the 1930s, Trosky's argument shifted (but still sought to remain consistent with the theory of permanent revolution): the bureaucracy was now the political expression of the *external* pressures of international capitalism, and carried the same dangers of internal restoration. Stalin's critics, of course, all considered themselves as representing the (international) working class.

Stalin, for his part, repaid such accusations within the same sociological framework, and with interest. By 1929 a variety of real and imagined opposition currents within and expelled from the party were being denounced as representatives of bourgeois and kulak tendencies and then, far more directly, were put on trial as the agents of foreign – including fascist – governments. Since the accusations in some cases dated back to 1919, the implication was that capitalism had had its political representatives at the very summits of the party and state machines at least since then. It is easy now to dismiss the accusations of the Moscow trials as fraudulent and even ludicrous; but it is more difficult to explain the large number of Western intellectuals – by no means all of them communists – who freely endorsed them at the time. At least part of the explanation is that the accusations, although they were brought with inadequate *legal* evidence, fitted well into the *social* categories through which it had become conventional to view the Soviet Union's forced march, via industrialization, towards socialism. To see the state organizations of a socialist society as the scene of political warfare between the representatives of the two main classes of bourgeois society was continuous with left-wing criticisms of the mass socialist parties and trade unions of the Western labour movement, whose internal struggles were depicted in these terms.

The more revolutionary socialists were also accustomed to notice that, the more militant and confident grew the rank and file, the more energetic and dangerous became the 'reformists'' attempts at mediation. Such thinking was a foundation-stone of Comintern policy – in either its 'right' or 'left' tactics – towards European labour movements. It was a natural extension of such views for Stalin to promulgate (when he made his turn towards crash industrialization and 'the liquidation of the kulaks as a class') certain crucial supplementary doctrines to the idea of 'socialism in one country' – that the victory of socialism could only be guaranteed by 'catching up and overtaking' the industrial and economic development of the advanced capitalist nations, and that as socialism drew nearer, far from this permitting the state to begin 'withering away', the forces hostile to the working class would intensify their resistance, and that this would require intensified revolutionary efforts on the part of the workers' state.

BUKHARIN

Although the Stalin regime had a clear organizational basis of support in the party machine, in political and intellectual terms its consolidation moved through classical Bolshevik zig-zags, allying in earlier phases with figures and ideas who were to be abandoned and destroyed later on. One of the important casualties of this process was Nicolai Bukharin, Lenin's receptive 'favourite' among the Old Bolshevik intellectuals. He was removed from power in 1929, when Stalin made his 'left turn', and was tried and executed in 1938. Following his fall he became known (among other things) as the 'Soviet Bernstein'; only in 1988 did the Gorbachev leadership annul the criminal findings against him, and allow a cautious reinstatement of his thinking.

Bukharin's ideas, though sometimes mythologized, have kept their substance posthumously as a Bolshevik alternative to Stalinism. Like Trotsky's, his views on Soviet society are anticipated before 1917, mainly in his wartime writings on the 'leviathan state'. 'Bukharinism' allows of even less easy summary than 'Trotskyism'. Partly this is due to Bukharin's vacillating course, from advocate of revolutionary, super-centralized, war communism in 1918–19 to 'rightist' in the 1920s, and partly because he remained in the Soviet Union until his execution, and thus had far less opportunity, after Stalin's triumph, to publish his ideas clearly. (Trotsky, exiled abroad in 1929, wrote prolifically until his assassination in 1940.)

None the less, sufficient elements are clear for 'Bukharinism' to stand in relief as a distinctive approach to Bolshevism's problems in power. There was, in the first place, Bukharin's working through of the implications of Lenin's formula that the Soviet Union was not only a workers', but also a peasants', state. It followed that the state must truly, not just as a matter of expediency, embrace the peasants' interests; the workers' state must, in Bukharin's phrase, learn to 'love' the peasants. More, the relation of countryside to city could be transposed to the international scale (anticipating Mao's notion of 'surrounding the cities from the countryside'): the colonial peasantry, Bukharin argued, constituted a 'world countryside' whose uprisings could also challenge the 'world city' of the metropolitan capitalist states. His strategy was for an international *smychka* (yoke, or alliance) between workers and peasants, complementing the domestic *smychka* of the New Economic Policy.

Defence of the peasant entailed defence of the market. It is ironic that Bukharin became the theorist of the NEP – the period when Soviet bureaucracy grew fastest – by rethinking his earlier enthusiasm for war communism and its economic centralism. The attempt to control the activities of millions of peasants and small producers through a 'Ghenghis Khan plan', he concluded, inevitably led to 'a colossal administrative apparatus', the social costs of which were even heavier than those of the 'anarchy' of petty production. Bukharin also raised, though in purely theoretical terms, a potentially heretical question – whether the working class's reliance on experts and administrators who were socially alien to it to run 'its' state's business might not give rise to 'the embryo of a new ruling class'.

He came to argue that markets and competition should be encouraged between a variety of types of larger enterprises – state-owned, cooperative and private – within which the state sector would successfully strive to demonstrate the advantages of economic planning. It was in this 'extremely original form' that the class struggle within socialism could be allowed to express itself, as coexistence and competition within the framework of a larger cooperation. Both these ideas – of freedom for peasants to produce for the market, and a degree of market 'self-regulation' within socialist economies – have repeatedly resurfaced as nostrums for the ills of communist economies in Russia, Eastern Europe and Asia (see chapter 14).

To his economic 'liberalism' Bukharin added a – circumscribed – preference for literary and intellectual toleration. Though personally an enthusiast of efforts to promote 'proletarian' literature, he advocated support and encouragement for a variety of non-party writers, and, more generally, urged that the party, while it might and should have its own views, should operate a broad policy of non-interference in intellectual matters. Again, such urgings have been heard from post-war communist proponents of economic reforms. Bukharin's essential object, then put forward within an evolutionary NEP-type route to socialism – but often revived by his descendants in other contexts – was for cultural and scientific pluralism, but within the political boundaries of a one-party state.

This limitation belies the image of Bukharinism that is sometimes offered – drawing on his support for the united front in Comintern, his wish for a healing of the 'tragic schism' within European social democracy, and his wholehearted anti-fascism – as the incarnation of democratic socialism within Bolshevism, even the mellowing of the latter into the former. Certainly, there is a detectable penetration of ideas and values from parliamentary social democracy. And Bukharinism also addresses the issues of backwardness and the peasantry. But it remains a specifically *communist* outlook: a response to the problems of a single party and a monopoly of political power which it dare not relinquish. It is the approach most sensitive to the party's dependence on the society it rules, most anxious to avoid traumatic damage and the ossification or silencing of social life, most eager to set itself up as the protector of, and to benefit from, spontaneous developments.

Though the doctrine of socialism in one country became part of the basic ideological armoury of the Soviet Union, and later of Eastern Europe and

China, it did so in senses very different from the theoretical defence of an 'evolutionary' Bolshevism which Bukharin developed after 1923. None the less events have many times produced currents within the leading bodies of ruling parties which (sometimes part-consciously, but usually inexplicitly) have resurrected elements of his approach. They have tended to stand against active moves to extend revolution or political overturn to other countries – one of the central ingredients of the 'Trotskyism' against which it originally took shape. However, the opposition is by no means absolute: Krushchev, in the 1960s, for example, combined elements of liberalization at home (including a reluctant semi-rehabilitation of Bukharin) with an erratically forward policy on Cuba. The appeal of 'Bukharinism' to communist leaders has been that it offers an internal means of overcoming economic stasis and inefficiency; its danger, that economic liberalization requires experiment and intellectual toleration, and this in turn encourages political 'unwinding' – as in Czechoslovakia in 1968, where party demands for reform swiftly led to calls for a plurality of parties.

A corollary of liberalization is decentralization, either in the sense of formal delegation or of the attenuation of actual control over subordinate parts of the administrative machine. It is not a question of scale alone. The functions of lower-level officials, their experience, the extent to which they have developed independent interests and motives, will affect both the central authorities' formal patterns of delegation, and the actual extent to which they relinquish control. Yet all these aspects are in continual change and, taken as a whole, will cause the autonomy of the lower levels to expand, and the actual control wielded by the centre to weaken, unless it takes deliberate steps to reassert it. Bukharinism, in its purer forms, accepts this situation, and merely seeks to regulate it by creating appropriate frameworks of motivation. Yet the problem is a dynamic one, which recurs for all communist regimes (indeed, for all large-scale formal organizations). One of the things that distinguishes Maoism is its active and practical approach – highly ideological, but also *ad hoc* – to regulating and reorienting the machinery of the party itself, and expressed most clearly in the 'mass line' campaigns through which Mao had the CCP execute policy turns or resolve its own internal problems.

MAOISM

One basic starting point of Maoism lies in Stalin's doctrine of building 'socialism in one country', which Mao never rejected, but adapted to China in a number of fundamental ways. As chapter 4 sketched, the most basic of these adaptations was the party's turn to protracted warfare by its peasant-based army. But this entailed a very important difference from the other forms of adaptation to rule that we have discussed in this chapter: in China revolution overlapped for a long time with the possession of rudimentary forms of state power, and Maoism was required to serve as an ideology of territorial and administrative rule many years before it had completed its revolution. Moreover, having learned how to preserve its rule, while reinforcing and extending it with revolutionary initiatives, there was no reason to drop such a hybrid approach when, from 1949, the party controlled the whole of mainland China. There is thus a continuity to the style and methods of Maoism's mass campaigns directed into the party, through their very different periods and purposes – from the 'rectification' movements launched after the party's tumultuous growth in the late 1930s, to the 'Cultural Revolution' of the 1960s. Each includes several, connected, components: a campaign to educate a politically-aroused, but variegated and dispersed, mass of people around a small number of simple ideas and texts; the subordination of intellectual life to political needs; a general sifting or purging to impose renewed political loyalty and obedience; and a drive – often serving to motivate and structure these – against Mao's opponents in the party leadership.

Of course, many of Maoism's campaigns have had goals outside the party – from land redistribution, to the elimination of the house-fly or the sparrow. But they all served also as means whereby Mao or the party leadership could bypass, and to that extent emancipate themselves from and discipline, the party machine below them, entering into a more direct relationship with 'the masses'. Mao was no democrat, certainly, but he did develop a specific mutation of Leninism. It still rejected spontaneity, but sought (as he described it in 1943), to establish 'correct leadership' by going 'from the masses, to the masses'. Leaders were to 'take the ideas of the masses', 'concentrate' them by study into 'systematic ideas', then go back and propagate them until the masses embrace them and test their correctness in action – and then repeat the process 'over and over again, in an endless spiral' (Schram, 1969, pp. 316–17). The emphasis on the 'mass line' continued and did not diminish after state power was secure, and Maoism, more than any previous ruling Marxism, sought to bring mass movements into play outside the party machine, using them as a force to control or galvanize it.

This is one of the things that Maoism's frequent description of its own basis of support as 'the masses' signifies. But the term (and its vagueness) also reflects reserve in face of Marxist orthodoxy, and some of the problems (discussed in the context of Russia in chapter 11) of adapting Marxism to an underdeveloped nation. Chinese conditions, too, impelled Mao and his lieutenants to develop a political practice, and a supporting body of theory, that could carry them to power in an environment that was profoundly 'unready' – and this is perhaps the fundamental circumstance which causes the ideologies of rule and revolution to fuse.

Maoism, like Russian Marxism, often revised orthodoxy inexplicitly. Mao continued to describe his party as 'proletarian' even when it was overwhelmingly made up of peasants. But from the late 1930s he more accurately described the social alliance sustaining it by Stalin's formula of the 'bloc of four classes' (workers, peasants, petty bourgeoisie and national bourgeoisie). Later he defined its form of rule as that of a 'people's democratic dictatorship'. Mao converted the 'four-class alliance', which for Stalin was a temporary device, into a much longer-term strategy for an underdeveloped country with a large peasantry and small working class. The communists stood (as he put it in 1937, distinguishing his view from the Trotskyist theory of permanent revolution) 'for going through all the necessary stages of a democratic republic to arrive at socialism', alliance with the revolutionary bourgeoisie being 'a bridge that has to be crossed on our way to socialism'. The Chinese revolution thus embraced (as he described it in 1940) two distinct stages and sets of tasks: first a bourgeois-democratic revolution (though of a novel, anti-imperialist, type), and later a proletarian-socialist revolution. Moreover, 'the Chinese communist movement as a whole is a complete revolutionary movement embracing the two revolutionary stages' (Schram, 1969, pp. 227–8, 233).

But the implication, even then, was that once the national and democratic revolutions were completed and the Communist Party held power, what would be in place would be a potentially antagonistic coalition of classes. A further protracted phase of conflicts (together with some cooperation) with the bourgeoisie would thus begin. This was, indeed, the general framework within which Mao described his struggles after 1949, culminating in the Cultural Revolution (see chapter 15).

### MARXISM, PERSONALITY CULTS AND PURGES

Before 1917 Marxism was far from preparing for rule with a ready-made body of ideas. It had much to say about the present and future of existing societies, and a good deal about how they should be overthrown, but its view of what would replace them was schematic. Its major variants as an ideology of rule were produced pragmatically rather than reflectively, and generally involved considerable turns and departures with respect to previous orthodoxy. Since communist parties are internally cemented, and order themselves, through ideology, this can raise major problems. When – as with Stalinism and Maoism – the rulers aim to use ideological innovations to reinforce discipline and gear it to large tasks, they face the additional problem of undoing or dissolving previous orthodoxy in order to replace it by their own version. The problem is exacerbated when they rule recently revolutionary parties, with senior colleagues well used to fighting under adverse conditions.

If considered as an ordinary body of ideas new theoretical generalizations are at risk from the ordinary but lethal dangers of criticism. An important function of personality cults has been to raise ideologies of rule above any danger of being examined for heresy. This was a relatively early development with both Stalin (and, posthumously, Lenin) and Mao. Part of the purpose of the 'rectification' movement of 1942–4 was to crush or silence those intellectuals who already detected and criticized a cult around Mao, and by 1945 'Mao Tse-tung thought' had been written into the party constitution. Leszek Kolakowski, in his study of Marxist ideas, has pushed this line of argument further. The function of the Soviet purges of the 1930s, he argues, was actually to *destroy* loyalty to Marxist ideology, as a body of public doctrine, and to show party members 'that they had no ideology or loyalty except to the latest order from on high, and to reduce them, like the rest of society, to a powerless, disintegrated mass' (Kolakowski, 1982, 3, p. 86).

This may be true of the depths of Soviet Stalinism, though the situation in most communist states, most of the time, is less extreme. But it also reminds us that similar effects can be achieved by rather different means. The Cultural Revolution, based on and propelled by a mass youth movement, was very different from Stalin's police purges. But it gave Mao's 'Little Red Book' and his briefest, oracular, pronouncements, much the same reliquary status as the purges gave to Stalin's utterances and his *Short Course*. And it produced a similar condition of the spirit, summed up in the August 1968 editorial that proclaimed: 'we must carry out every one of chairman Mao's instructions . . . even when we do not understand it' (Schram, 1969, p. 447).

Such an outlook is in sharp tension with mundane bureaucratic goals and habits, directed at the 'rational' administration of society and the economy. Communist regimes' dependence on ideology makes them prone to the idolization of leaders and theories. Besides the cults of Stalin and Mao there have been many others, including the not less extravagant ones of Kim Il-Sung and Fidel Castro. In their acute forms they form a vast, uncriticizable (indeed, unmentionable) obstacle, preventing both society and the party from solving or even acknowledging a myriad of prosaic problems. When we discuss the functioning of communist economies and societies (in chapter 14) or the acute crises that can rock them (in chapter 15) it is essential to keep in mind the problems with which their ideologies of rule present them.

FURTHER READING

Shachtman (1962) discusses Trotsky's changing views on bureaucracy in the Soviet state. Cohen (1975) and Haynes (1985) give sympathetic accounts of Bukharin's thinking during his more 'moderate' years. Schram (1969) is a useful guide, organized round extracts, to the development of Mao's thought; Starr (1979) analyses Mao's thought thematically; Wilson (1979) is a biography.

# 13

## Western Marxism

The sight of communist state power has acted as an important inhibitor of communism in other countries. None the less non-ruling communism has continued to thrive, and this chapter considers some of the ideas and methods – ranging from the organizational and tactical to the refinedly theoretical – that underpin the appeal of communism (and more generally of Marxist ideas) in developed nations where it does not hold state power.

The sketch begins with some of Leninism's commonalities with other currents of thought. We have already seen, in chapter 2, that modern communism emerged from wider trends in elitist socialism. But its ambiguous attitudes towards its potential supporters also partake of broader tendencies which gelled in the late nineteenth century. Scientists, intellectuals and artists came to reject, in fields ranging from physics, through painting and literature, to psychology and sociology, notions of a universal rationality based on 'common sense' and perception. Social thought, in particular, became preoccupied with the psychological and cultural, as well as the political consequences, of 'mass society': the emergence of mass urban populations, centred on the industrial working class, giving rise to new forms of collective organization and behaviour, subordinating national politics to their votes or their demands for them, and offering a new large audience, even if passive and fickle, for all kinds of cultural products.

For example, in the 1880s and 1890s psychologists such as Gustav Le Bon and William Trotter developed the theory of crowd behaviour. It was necessary to recognize, they argued, the ways in which the quantitative aggregation of many individuals into a crowd gave rise to a qualitative change in the intellectual and emotional factors animating them. Crowds, though made up of ordinary people, were capable of enthusiasms, cruelties and inconsistencies which the overwhelming majority of individuals composing them, if taken separately, would never have contemplated.

The perception, of course, was nothing new (as Shakespeare reminds us in *Julius Caesar*) but the systematic study of it was. Le Bon drew a central distinction between the unconscious, instinctive and irrational factors which unified a crowd, and predominated in its thinking and behaviour, and the greater rationality shaping individual conduct. Since the leader or leaders of a crowd were not part of it, but rather acted rationally in accordance with their own goals, this offered the possibility of the 'rational' manipulation of mass 'instincts' – a phenomenon which, on the whole, the 'crowd psychologists' feared and regretted. Le Bon, in particular, saw this as taking a particularly dangerous form in modern times, which he traced through from the French revolution into contemporary radical and socialist movements. But his conservatism could not prevent his perceptions being turned to radical purposes. Mussolini, for example, starting in his days as a revolutionary socialist before the war, took Le Bon as his handbook for inflaming the proletarian crowd.

Freud, who revolutionized psychology by taking reason as product, not premise, of civilization and its psychic processes, was much influenced in his social psychology by the stress Le Bon and other 'crowd psychologists' laid on the unconscious. He was concerned, though, with the wider barriers by which society constitutes itself, through and against the population's instinctual drives. Just as he regarded the conscious mind as only a small part of the total psyche, so he saw conscious reason as the attribute of an elite:

It is just as impossible to do without control of the mass by a minority as it is to dispense with coercion in the work of civilization. For masses are lazy and unintelligent; they have no love for instinctual renunciation, and they are not to be convinced by argument of its inevitability; and the individuals composing them support one another in giving free reign to their indiscipline. It is only through the influence of individuals who can set an example and whom masses recognize as their leaders that they can be induced to perform the work and undergo the renunciations on which the existence of civilization depends. All is well if these leaders are persons who possess superior insight into the necessities of life and who have risen to the height of mastering their own instinctual wishes. But there is a danger that in order not to lose their influence they may give way to the mass more than it gives way to them, and it therefore seems necessary that they shall be independent of the mass by having means to power at their disposal. (*The Future of an Illusion*, 1927, in Freud, 1985, 12, p. 186)

When Trotsky – who, while critical of Freud, came to admire him as one of the giants of contemporary thought – offered a justification of the coercion required for war communism it was in similar, if less disdainful, terms. In more prosaic form similar views are commonplace within modern studies of the lesser capacity of the working classes for 'deferred gratification'.

## SUBJECT AND OBJECT

One of the things Leninism is is the crystallization of aspects of modernism in politics – both in its fascination with the interplay and interchange between subject and object, and also in matters of practice and style: its aggressiveness and relish of polemic, its self-confidence and irony in face of reason resting on common sense. The primary distinction of Leninist politics (present also in Marx, but less prominent) is that between the more immediate desires which motivate the majority and the longer-term goals pursued by leaders. This distinction, however, is one it shares with much broader currents of thought. If socialism, the struggle for it and the building of it, are the culminating works of civilization, are these tasks that could properly be entrusted to the proletariat? Like much liberalism (and with attitudes which it shares with much conservatism) Leninism's answer is – a qualified and ambiguous – no: the masses are driven by appetite, but if anything is to be accomplished those that lead them must be guided by something else.

That something is the claim to science. In this respect Leninism emphasizes the limitations of its chosen historical class in a way that gives it common ground with far more conservative opinions, and with the pessimism of cultural critics of industrial society. Political programmes such as ours 'cannot be mastered by hundreds of thousands of backward, semiliterate workers in a year or even a few years,' lamented Axelrod (himself, ironically, a heroic example of the self-educated worker). In fact, Russian social democracy elaborated in quite clear terms, and well before the end of the century, the fact that it expected its political leaders, and those whom they led, to understand the nature and justification of socialism on two quite different bases. Plekhanov codified the matter in 1891 in a distinction between propaganda and agitation that still endures: propaganda consists in explaining many ideas to few people; agitation in explaining few, simple ideas to many (Harding, 1983, pp. 100–7). The former serves to build the party and its lasting support even in quiescent periods; the latter enables the party to set the masses in motion. Lenin's structural definitions of the party, as they emerged in 1900–3, merely gave organizational expression to an educational and cultural dichotomy that was already well recognized.

Leninism defined itself out of, and away from, the class it officially represented in respect of both culture and science, and motivation. The two differences cohere in psychology: a scientific world-view (embodied in organization) is what enables party cadres to pursue difficult or impossible goals in hostile circumstances over long periods. The party embodies rationality, deterred neither by contingent difficulties nor by the ebb and flow of mass opinion. For a cadre to emerge from the mass, therefore, generally requires a psychological change, which includes, but is not limited to, changes of specific doctrine and of motivation.

Leninism thus takes its distance from the Marxian working class through an outlook that denudes the working class of many of the ethical qualities and potentialities that qualified it as Marxism's 'universal' class – i.e. the class to which is entrusted the future of humanity as a whole. One corollary of this is that the Leninist party tends to appropriate such moral-historical claims to itself, upholding them 'on behalf' of the proletariat, whose virtues it treats as, so to speak, hypostasized within itself. Another corollary, which follows naturally from the first, is that communism is ready to look to other and additional social classes and strata for its practical support. How does the Leninist relationship between the political elite and the non- or proto-political majority work out in the context of combinations of diverse classes and groups? The forms are rather various, but it is quite possible to point to some general principles, since politics, like biology, selects for effective strategies – only without the need for a succession of generations.

### DIVERSIFIED POLITICS

First, a diversified Leninism must devise policies for economically and socially very different groups, and must present them effectively and in a differentiated way. Lenin began the tradition – central to the success of many subsequent communist parties – of formulating peasant policy with an eye to what would arouse the peasant – even if the results of it being acted upon on a large scale were (as purists already objected in 1903) to set up an enormous barrier, in the form of a myriad of private peasant plots, to subsequent socialist construction.

Mao's leadership of the Chinese Communist Party (followed, in this respect, by the Vietnamese Communist Party) carried the process of policy differentiation further: starting with the Kiangsi soviets in the late 1920s land policy was finely adjusted from area to area, mainly through the quantities of land taken as defining 'rich', 'middle' and 'poor' peasants. These categories, being used as the basis for land redistribution, were sociological only in form; in substance they were political. Varying them from area to area allowed the communists to build their support on a variety of foundations. In some places it was possible to ameliorate the lot of the poorest and landless, while lessening social tensions and leaving largely intact the traditional dominance and authority of the richer peasants, from whom individuals could be incorporated to support the communists. At the other extreme the hunger of the landless peasants was sometimes met by sharpening village antagonisms, and confiscating all above a certain minimum landholding. In between there were many variants.

Communist peasant policy on the way to power thus created an accumulation of problems, based in the fiercely-held private plots of the peasants and the galaxies of anomalies, resentments and jealousies associated with them. Soviet agriculture remains weak and stagnant today, still traumatized by the violence Stalin had to use to undo the consequences of Lenin's pro-peasant policy in 1917 and during the NEP. And, though Chinese and Vietnamese communism have frequently been gentler towards the peasants, their attempted reforms of agriculture still falter against the legacies of their own earlier policies of revolutionary redistribution.

Gross differentiation of policies was possible in Asian villages in the 1930s and 1940s, with largely illiterate audiences and before the spread of radio. The agitator would often be not only the peasants' only source of political exhortation, but also of news. But in other circumstances it generally proves necessary to separate, blur, and if possible make syntheses between, the different policies being advanced to capture the support of different groups or audiences. The more urban, literate, universal, and politically seasoned and alert is the population, the more important is this second requirement of a diversified Leninist politics. On this front Leninism has advanced very considerably, in both theoretical and practical terms, since Lenin, and its accumulated repertoire now makes its initial efforts look primitive. The first, and most obvious, means for segregating mutually inconsistent policies and bases of support is *time* ('a device', as an admirer of Chairman Mao once pointed out, 'to stop everything happening at once'). Its employment takes two primary strategic forms, zig-zags and reassessments, the distinction between which is subtle but real.

*Zig-zags* consist of changes in the goals put forward by the party, to enable it to capture allies or support denied it by previous policies. These are frequently justified by the assertion that the objective situation has altered so that previous policies, while correct in the past, are not now apposite, and if persisted in would be harmful and reactionary. In extreme cases, however, justification may not be attempted.

*Reassessments*, in contrast, rest on alterations in the ways in which allies or potential allies are assessed. It may be a matter of recognizing that there exist, after all, some common ground with and certain 'honest elements' among, political formations to which the Communist Party was previously hostile. Or it may be a matter of existing allies proving false; variants of the latter are also employed in inner-party purges. In 'salami tactics' reassessments are used in sequence; each 'slice' involves the discovery that a key group or individual, previously trusted, was in fact the agent of a foreign power, a revisionist, a 'capitalist roader', etc. The suddenness, violence and injustice of the assault initially rallies supporters around the target. But this, too, serves its purpose; once the initial victim has been downed, it becomes all the easier to attack those who showed where their true sympathies lay by trying to protect him. Slice by slice the salami is demolished. Laszlo Rajk, speaking to a party audience, defined the tactics of Eastern European communists towards rival political forces after the war as follows:

> Learn from Lenin; if you have five enemies, you should ally yourself with them; arrange to incite four of them against the fifth, then three against the fourth, and so on until you have only one enemy left in the alliance; you can then liquidate him yourselves and kick him out of the alliance. (Nagy, 1948, p. 105)

Normally, of course, methods involving change over time are employed together. Not only are they of limited power taken separately, and require mutual reinforcement, but separation in time attenuates, but does not abolish, the inconsistencies of stance entailed. A battery of shifts, in combination, offer a better chance of generating the confusion, the 'noise' and the realignments and retreats on the part of potential opponents, that can help the strategy as a whole to success. Thus (to take some examples from national politics discussed in other chapters) all of the above tactics are to be found in the Chinese Communist Party's route to power (chapter 5), in Mao's overthrow of the party bureaucracy in the Cultural Revolution (chapter 15), and in the national sequences – leading from broad coalition, through one-party rule to Stalinist purge – which developed in Eastern Europe in 1944/5–52 (chapter 7).

### INDIRECT ACTIVITY

But time – or, at least, enough of it – is not always available. Leninism thus also requires various 'synchronic' methods of projecting differentiated policies simultaneously. In many circumstances the most straightforward approach – addressing different emphases, even different messages, to different audiences – is passably effective; frequently Leninism does not differ fundamentally from many other political parties in having its own special programmes and organs, and putting its case in a particular way, to specific groups – youth, trade unionists, women, racial and national groups, etc. – even if it compasses a wider range and holds the latent contradictions more boldly together. But it has also developed organized but indirect political activity in ways that few other organizations can rival. The 'front' body, or the organization that is to a greater or lesser extent manipulated or steered, while projecting a public image of benign independence, are things that Leninism has made peculiarly its own. The greatest first full flowering of such organizations occurred in the 1930s after Hitler came to power, the lead being given by a political operator of genius, the German communist, Willi Munzenberg.

Front (or heavily influenced) organizations offer large advantages over a party's simply extending activity in its own right. It becomes possible to draw on persons who would not like to be so closely associated with directly communist political activity, either because they are not wholly in sympathy with it or because to do so would be embarrassing or dangerous. Intellectuals, writers, performing artists and so on, jealous of their individualism, can frequently be cajoled onto the platform or notepaper of suitably titled committees, when they would recoil from direct party involvement.

The policies and pressures of such bodies can fairly easily be adjusted so as to assist communist goals in particular areas, while avoiding seriously inconvenient conflicts in others. Thus many organizations which campaign for civil liberties, or peace, in the West include in their membership, besides liberals and libertarians of various hues, a good number of communists and communist sympathizers. Because such bodies naturally take abuses of civil liberties – or militarism – by their domestic authorities, rather than foreign governments, as the main targets of their campaigning, communists can fruitfully channel their energies into them while experiencing minimum friction with the indifferent records of communist states. On the international plane the Soviet Union and its subordinates finance an array of umbrella bodies (of women, students, lawyers, trade unions, peace organizations, etc.; see chapter 9) which serve, in part, to complement communist efforts within national bodies.

Illegality is another obvious case where a front or controlled organization may be able to exist and act where party bodies could not: as, for example, with the National Democratic Front under the Marcos dictatorship in the Philippines. But even where – as with the African National Congress in South Africa – the front organization cannot exert sufficient pressures to become legal, it preserves many of the other advantages.

One of the main types of other organization within which communists or communist supporters work in a systematic way is other, and rival, political parties. The practice, of course, pre-dates Bolshevism, and contemporary communist tactics were already prefigured in the activity of the *Iskra* network within the Russian social democratic movement before 1903. On occasion, the tactic assumes a scope where the communist presence colours the entire character of the host: the organizational and programmatic, and to a certain extent the military, life of the Kuomintang, in the early 1920s was to an important extent shaped by the communist organizations working – though scarcely secretly – within it. In the late 1940s the socialist parties of Eastern Europe proved, in many cases, to have been so thoroughly infiltrated that they – or very substantial fragments which split from them – acquiesced without reserve in the party fusions from above that transformed the communist parties into the sole governing parties (see chapter 7).

The other main use of 'entrism' lies at the other extreme. Where political traditions are such that the Communist Party could attract only slight support in its own right, it becomes highly advantageous to work in and through other parties. The leaders of nationalist parties in the Middle East, for example, have experienced communist factions working within them as an irritant, and sometimes a serious threat, and – as in Egypt, or Iraq – have sometimes taken violent steps against them. British communism has always organized within the Labour Party, sometimes rather boldly, sometimes with greater circumspection. When, in 1955, MI5 succeeded in photographing the British Communist Party's membership records, the 55,000 files proved to contain a large number of covert members in the Labour Party, as well as those in trade unions and government employment (Wright, 1987, pp. 55–6).

Discussion of communism's indirect but deliberate political activity has introduced the categories 'communist supporters' and 'communist sympathizers'. Such people are much more various than simply communist party members minus the formalities of public membership (though that, of course, is one principal type). The range of psychologies and motives involved are important, but we are concerned here with some of the organizational mechanics. For sympathy, though it does not amount to full support, and may be limited to certain issues and be coupled with indifference or hostility on others, none the less provides considerably more purchase if effectively organized. Hence the development, within many organizations in which communism is influential, without exerting direct control, of informal 'left' groupings and caucuses through which the efforts and votes of a spectrum of sympathizers can be brought to bear cohesively. But directing positions within such caucuses, like candidatures for key posts within the host organization itself, are normally filled by people whose actual, if not public, loyalties are those of active, disciplined party members: crypto-communists in the full sense of that term.

### RECONCILING CONTRADICTIONS

Such an extended division of political labour imposes psychological and moral, as well as organizational, stresses, and there is a risk that the 'diversification' of communist politics will be experienced by its cadres as inconstancy and simple duplicity, with consequently corrosive internal effects.

The problem exists, of course, for almost all political parties, but it can be particularly acute for communism, whose efforts to benefit from the maximum political ground are often particularly ambitious, and which relies, more than most, on the activism and consequently the alertness and often the idealism, of its members.

Communism is, however, theoretically equipped to tolerate contradiction. In the first place comes that useful appropriation from Hegel, the dialectic. In the hands of Leninism it has ceased to be merely theoretical, still less a contemplative, device, and has passed into service to explain – and hence to justify – the necessities within the contradictions of policy. Mao's *On Contradiction*, for example, provided millions of activists with a handbook of dialectical arguments and reasons why the zig-zags, and apparently hypocritical revaluations of allies and enemies, of communist political strategy are in fact its most fundamental strength. Suppressing or over-coming 'secondary contradictions' in favour of the 'main contradiction', or concentrating fire upon the 'principal adversary' are given philosophical dignity beyond mere political ploys; in putting incompatible policies suc-cessively into action the activist can understand himself as the instrument of a reason – pure and practical combined – which is coextensive with the universe.

Philosophical arguments in justification or celebration of inconsistency have an essential place. But it is well if communism's stance and vocabulary can also contain strong positive elements serving to synthesize differing policies, rooting them in arguments and values with a general unifying effect. The most obvious of these is nationalism, to which Leninism fre-quently resorts, despite the *general* anti-patriotic and internationalist outlook which it inherited from Marx. (However, this description of Marx must immediately be qualified. While an internationalist in the abstract, and for purposes of pamphlets such as *The Communist Manifesto*, both he and Engels were often ardent germanophiles, and not above hoping for the extermination of other nations or races – such as southern Slavs – which they judged reactionary (Talmon, 1981, pp. 38–48; Rosdolsky, 1987).)

Leninism has developed a whole body of theory in justification of its use of nationalism. Its ever-mobile distinction between oppressed and oppressor nations has given rise to what is almost a meta-theory of class struggle, between as well as within nations. In certain cases communism's inter-twining with nationalism is so fundamental that the party itself becomes caught up in its momentum, and at risk of being its victim. Tito's leadership of the Yugoslav party, for example, based itself heavily upon Serb national-ism – which, in face of German occupation and, later, Soviet denunciation, proved able to set itself at the head of a wider Yugoslav nationalism. Yet, after the war, Yugoslavia's ruling bureaucracies developed within, and in adhesion to, the separate nationalities, with the result that Tito's death opened the way to a gradual 'reconfederalization' of the Yugoslav state (Djilas, 1986).

Other slogans can serve a similar function, but without the danger of taking a party in tow. Communism invokes the doctrine of historical progress (often adjectivally: 'progressive') to explain why different social interests and political intentions should for the time being be grouped behind a common banner.

Similarly 'anti-monopoly' or 'anti-imperialist' alliances exclude, almost by definition, only their targets, who are so few or so distant that the practical effect is often to allow them to act as an umbrella for all-purpose political combination. 'Broad democratic' and similarly titled campaigns aim at the same effect in a more limited way, seeking to establish rights of initiative over a sufficient part of the political spectrum that opponents can be labelled, by suggestion at least, as un- or anti-democratic, or even 'fascist'.

## CULTURE AND HEGEMONY

But a loose command over wide areas of the specifically *political* field is only part of what may be attempted. Politics forms part of, and crystallizes out from, the general culture of a society. Its terms and premises, the yardsticks and horizons against which a people judge politics, emerge from much broader traditions and feelings, which are only in small part political. May not the Leninist party act on this wider terrain, with all the advantages that could bring? Might it not even alter the condition whose necessity Marx reluctantly recognized – that the ruling ideas in society are the ideas of the ruling class – and begin to shift the locus of 'hegemony'? The strategy of achieving a broader *cultural*-political hegemony is particularly associated with the writings of the leading Italian communist incarcerated under fascism, Antonio Gramsci, and, after the war, with the leadership of Palmiro Togliatti and his successors in the Italian Communist Party. But Gramsci's and related ideas have run far wider, stimulating the evolution of many parties' strategies and giving a theoretical framework to practices that had already developed pragmatically. They form a central part of communism's adaptation, in the 'post-industrial' West, to greatly changed social and cultural environments. Moreover, independently of the efforts of organized communism, these environments have provided fertile media for new species of Marxist (and to some degree Leninist) ideas – presenting communist organizations as they had evolved historically with new opportunities, but also dangers.

In the next section, therefore, we briefly examine Gramsci's ideas on 'hegemony' – probably the most successful innovation in Leninism's ideological armoury for the developed West. We then go on to sketch the main social and cultural changes away from 'smokestack' capitalism that communism (and Marxist ideas more generally) have had to adapt to.

## GRAMSCI AND HEGEMONY

The modern concept of hegemony has interesting antecedents. It was Axelrod and Plekhanov, in the late 1890s, who first provided Russian social democrats with their doctrine of 'the hegemony of the proletariat': the Russian working class, although a small minority, would assume the 'leading role' among the forces challenging Tsarism. This perspective is embodied in the manifesto for the abortive First Congress of Russian social democrats in 1898 (Harding, 1983, pp. 223–5). Slightly altered, it underlies Lenin's urgings in *What is to be Done?* that the social democratic party 'must go among all classes of the population' (1960–78, p. 422). But this idea of hegemony retained a fairly narrowly political sense; in its prediction of the working class leading a revolution with wide 'bourgeois' support it resembles later and partly consequent theories of 'permanent revolution'.

Gramsci gave the term a much enlarged meaning. In the notebooks which he composed in Mussolini's prisons in the early 1930s he reworked existing Marxist ideas on the relationship between the economic base of bourgeois society and the institutional and mental superstructure rising from it. At the root of his theoretical project (whose intrinsic subtleties are complicated by the codes he was obliged to employ under prison censorship) lies his 'unpacking' of the Marxist view of the superstructure. Previously, influenced by the older Marx's preoccupation with things economic, Marxist theorists had generally written from a view which held political and intellectual phenomena to be ultimately determined by the economic base, and in that sense derivative. Gramsci, however, brings several crucial distinctions to bear anew.

In the first place he defines the state in a large manner – still as a means of class rule, but including *all* the instruments by which the basic structure of society is maintained. Then, within this realm, he resurrects – but much modifies – Hegel's distinction between *political* society and *civil* society. Political society corresponds to the legal-political state in the narrow sense, with its more-or-less direct instruments of rule. Civil society, on the other, consists for Gramsci of the institutions through which society's opinions, ideas and manners of thought are formed and reproduced. It is, however, a Marxist category and one referring to the superstructure alone: it excludes purely economic institutions and processes, central to Hegel's concept of civil society.

Corresponding to this distinction Gramsci erects a second – between the two fundamental forms of social regulation employed by the ruling class: *domination* and *hegemony*. *Domination* involves the use of coercion, or the ultimate threat of it, to secure compliance; it relies, at bottom, on Engels's 'bodies of armed men'. But there must operate, in addition, forms of 'internal control', through which subordinate groups come to accept and support the prevailing order. To a greater or lesser degree any integrated society must have means for causing the rightness and necessity of existing arrangements – not the details, but the fundamentals – to permeate the thinking of the population, conditioning their theories, values, even (Gramsci was trained as a linguist) their vocabulary. This second means of social control is, in the original sense which Gramsci gives to the term, and then develops: *hegemony*. He sums up his key distinctions in a lapidary formula, 'State in the integral sense = dictatorship + hegemony'.

The insertion of hegemony into the equation revises the Marxist view of existing bourgeois states, but still leaves it as an explanatory proposition. However, from it Gramsci pursues a further argument, with rich practical implications. For hegemony is a phenomenon of many parts and inter-connections. It may be more or less robust – this is most so when it expresses the interests of a rising bourgeois class – or, in its later history, it may begin to decay. Moreover thinking and attitudes are not monolithic, and this is especially so of exploited classes propelled into class struggle. In particular, they are afflicted by 'contradictory consciousness': their prac-tical activity, and their resistance and struggle against prevailing conditions, belie the assent which the 'false consciousness' of their purely mental lives may give to those conditions.

Note how radically (though inexplicitly: one will search him in vain for expressions of disrespect towards the master) Gramsci converted Lenin's view of working-class consciousness as spontaneously bourgeois. In respect of trade unionism and strike struggles, for example, he shifts the emphasis away from the facet which Lenin stressed in his proposals for party organ-ization. What is important is less the *barriers* set to militant energies in strikes by their consciously entertained objectives – accepting capitalist production relations, merely seeking an improved share in distribution – than the *reflex* of this, their actually or potentially corrosive consequences for that general view of the world itself. In Gramsci's view daily life, and in particular the experience of social inequality or conflict, enters into mass consciousness, acting within it as a factor in opposition to the prevailing conservative hegemony.

The looseness and fragility of bourgeois hegemony, and the fact that it must be continually renewed and recomposed through specific institutions, opens a novel and necessary field of struggle for communists (whose party Gramsci terms, in allusion and analogy to Machiavelli, the 'modern prince'). It becomes an essential task – and perhaps the most important arena – to work within bourgeois cultural institutions (understood in a wide sense, but including education systems, the media and press, etc.), to penetrate and disable them, and to substitute, as far as possible, rival ideas and modes of thought. The tactical-ideological objectives (as we may term them) are thus far more eclectic than those of original Leninism. Lenin himself was rather conservative in literature, art, physics, etc., tending to suspect radical departures of unwholesome threats to party doctrine. But much modern Marxism has a far more relaxed attitude: innovation, flux, and even decadence are, taken as a whole, all to the good. (Though it is fair to add that some of Gramsci's own preferences were fairly conservative: for strengthening the minds of his socialist worker-students he favoured Latin grammar exercises.)

By being extended to the cultural front the work of subversion does not necessarily become more genteel. Gramsci develops his enlarged account of political struggle through a simile which is also one of Lenin's favourites – military conflict. He contrasts warfare by the sudden assault of mobile forces against the enemy (the 'war of movement', which corresponds in politics to the abrupt attempt on the state power during a short-lived revolutionary crisis, as in Russia) with the protracted efforts and inconclusive grapplings of trench warfare, that the First World War had made familiar – the 'war of position'. The more mature a particular capitalist society is, the more deep-rooted, complex and resilient will be its hegemonic dominion, and the more important will be the cultural 'war of position' relative to the final insurrectionary assault – if, indeed, the latter proves necessary at all.

Gramsci thus tends to revise Marx at a deeper level: far from the working class becoming more ripe for revolution as capitalism matures (the knell of capitalism was originally to sound through increasing economic polarization) it becomes, on the contrary, better integrated, more deeply embroiled in the hegemonic net. But with the evaporation of economic determinism, new scope for voluntaristic action by communists opens. There is no tendency to cataclysm within the cultural-political 'war of position'; if it is not undermined and substituted the hegemony of the established order will renew itself indefinitely. It is up to the 'modern prince' to develop strategies to undermine it across the board, from the high intelligentsia, through the education system, social administration and the professions, to the media and the yellow press. The outcome will depend on the energy, flexibility, imagination and inventiveness with which the opposed parties contend.

In this struggle the intelligentsia and, more generally, the educated classes are especially important. Lenin identified a necessary role for the intelligentsia in the scientific comprehension of socialism, and in the leadership and theoretical provisioning of the social democratic party. But this need involve only a tiny fraction of them. Gramsci offers them a role as the most important troops on the main fronts, sapping and infiltrating the enemy's defences piecemeal. Moreover, it is a role in which immediate and 'spontaneous' appetites can be aligned with historic goals: the individual hope for advancement of the communist or 'progressive' professional, functionary or journalist allies happily with the grand purpose of extending hegemony. The combination helps account for some of the post-war popularity of Gramsci and Gramsciesque Marxism among the rapidly expanding salaried middle classes in Western Europe, especially those of 'social' education or professions.

How far is the enrichment of communist strategy and its engagement with broader cultural questions an extension, and how far a negation, of more strictly political methods? Will it reconcile communist organizations to pluralist frameworks and habits, their involvement in the complexities of administrative and cultural life atrophying the urge to a monopoly of power? Or does it merely seek to broaden, without relaxing, their centralist grip? To these questions is linked the wider one whether some, at least, of the non-ruling parties in the developed countries with parliamentary regimes will lose their distinctiveness as *communist* parties and be absorbed into the political structure merely as a variety of social democracy. A closely-related development among these parties, their explorations of 'Eurocommunism' (see chapter 10) suggest that their core apparatuses set limits to the extent that their communism will be allowed to 'wither away'. Non-ruling parties face problems analogous to those of ruling parties – between preserving centralized political control, and reaping the advantages of relaxation and decentralization – and no final answer on how they will resolve them is reasonable.

The popularity of Gramsci's ideas since the 1960s is partly an index of the extent to which they have proved useful – but also of their function in providing a theoretical framework and justification for practices that went back far earlier. Martov's first task, in launching the fortunes of *Iskra* in Western Europe in 1901, was a tour of universities to establish its credentials among Russian students. The period of Comintern saw a proliferation of international machinery aimed at exploiting sympathy among opinion-forming groups outside the Soviet Union. And Marxist theory in the West, flowering rather diversely from the 1960s, has produced – in addition to the revival of Gramsci – a number of intellectual currents which take cultural hegemony seriously. These include the 'structuralist' Marxism of one of Gramsci's harshest critics (though also an admirer), Louis Althusser, with his division of state apparatuses into the ideological and the repressive.

CULTURAL AND SOCIAL CHANGES

But it is not only a question of the internal innovation of Marxist theories and political techniques. Changes, in both the technologies of communication and in the cultural composition of the population, have made systematic attention to 'hegemony' more important. The growth of the various mass communications media have two features in common. First, a great *centralization* in production, with extremely sophisticated technical and symbolic means being used by small but highly professional staffs to prepare material for transmission to audiences of tens or even hundreds of millions. Second, and largely as a result of the first, the asymmetry between communicator and audience has enlarged, to the point where it is only by stretching terminology that the relation between the tabloid headline-writer or television producer, and the reader or viewer, can be called 'communication'. Audiences are increasingly passive recipients of a mélange of stimuli, values, facts and fictions, much of it designed principally to manipulate their choice among media.

These changes have greatly affected political processes. To the individual's choice among media channels corresponds an increasingly passive choice among mass parties. For the bulk of the population political thinking and discussion is atomized, and largely reactive to the staged 'debates' between professional politicians on television, the medium which has done most to kill off local political processes in the clubs, public meetings, etc. which were once widespread in industrial societies. One well-placed television journalist may be of more importance than the recruitment of hundreds of rank-and-file workers into party organizations. Under these circumstances the direct promotion of a party's politics is only one, frequently not the most important, and sometimes a counter-productive, area of activity. More important is creating backgrounds and atmospheres in which favoured initiatives or appointments are likely to succeed.

A second area of social change has modified the political environment for communism. This is the growth (and internal differentiation) of the educated strata and of bureaucratic organization. The 'bureaucratization of the world' is not only a matter of the growth of the state, but of numerous other large bureaucracies (para-state, corporate, trade union) reflecting the increasing social weight of occupations having to do with management, supervision, social control and mediation, and human services, relative to physical production. Like the mass media and party-professional politicians, the ubiquitous and intricate machineries of control and representation make a fiction of the notion of sovereignty flowing from a populace of equal, amateur, citizens to a legislature and executive who exercise it on their behalf. Control, supervision, mediation, socialization pervade increasing parts of social life and ramify as mass professions. But the process has one major effect in common with the centralization of the mass media: the typical individual is surrounded by more, and more powerful, complex, and subtle influences, whose nature he or she is less and less able to grasp.

The groups employed in social control and symbolic reproduction and production represent large intermediate audiences, receptive to intellectual penetration in a way that the audiences of the most popular media seldom are. The fact that their training and work entail expertise and social authority predisposes many of them to esteem professionalism and organization above the spontaneous inclinations of the population. Collectively they embody an elaborately differentiated division of intellectual labour in which each individual is dependent on (and consequently requires a simplified acquaintance with) a range of other specialisms. The educated strata now form mass audiences for works of cultural popularization and polemic – audiences which are atomized and passive *vis-à-vis* their sources of intellectual authority and innovation in ways akin to the passivity of the viewer or listener *vis-à-vis* the most popular mass media. They offer similar possibilities for 'leverage' by prominent sources of influence, and are often similarly susceptible to slogans and catch-phrases.

Such conditions help to explain the apparent paradox of communism in many industrialized states with parliamentary democracy: that socialistic ideas and empathy for communism are most concentrated among relatively affluent educated and professional groups – what Lenin was wont to call 'bourgeois intellectuals'. But they find little echo and are viewed with much hostility among the (diminishing) ranks of industrial workers. Communism in the developed market societies has adapted to a deeply altered constituency – perhaps not as profoundly as communism transplanted to peasant societies, but still in a number of basic respects. Its constituency comes to include much greater individualism – only not the individualism of peasant property but the multitude of intangible individualisms of the Western middle classes. Like any serious political force it must also respond to the material, as well as the ideal, appetites of its bases of support. Pressures for material improvement from the traditional working class are mainly expressed through trade union organization and militancy – thus collectively and to a degree homogeneously. But among the middle classes incomes and conditions are influenced far more by individual promotion and preferment. Instead of collective organization and joint action on common demands, spontaneity takes the form of networks of shared opinions, attitudes, contacts and patronage, a crucial ingredient of that quintessentially Gramscian plank of strategy, 'the long march through the institutions'. Communism has adapted to these conditions with particular success, due to its capacity for treating the whole of human experience, from epistemology to appointment procedures, as essentially and properly political.

But, if communism in peasant societies has had to adapt itself to pre-political conditions, the segments of the Western middle classes to which communism mainly orientates itself are hyper-political. It is here that hegemonic strategies' flexibility and their refusal of solidity come into their own, creating areas of welcome for themselves, among expanded, loosened and variegated political and quasi-political structures, in a way that traditional Leninism would never have been able to do. Thus communism has sought to make itself at home, by suitable doctrinal blurrings and organizational insinuations, among some of the most substantial political growths of the 1970s and 1980s – feminism, environmentalism, and black and ethnic politics – towards each of which it had a long previous record of – frequently abusive – hostility. Adaptation has required relatively few abandonments. Althusser, for example, who in the 1970s was a demi-god for many Western Marxists, has been much de-emphasized in communism's intercourse with feminism since he murdered his wife, but Lenin (who was not above patronizing the *Folies Bergère* during the 1905 revolution (Freville, 1968, p. 57)) has been retained almost entirely intact, and on the whole existing doctrines and sages have simply been included within larger pantheons.

Of course, different Leninist organizations differ in the extent to which they have adapted. Generally speaking, the more 'Eurocommunist' parties have adapted better. But if one applies Gramsci's advocacy of work to undermine hegemony to contemporary circumstances then it suggests that the state of advantageous politicization is less well measured by the question: How many cadres has the Communist Party? than by the question: What portion of the politically-engaged population think it good to be 'anti-imperialist' and bad to be 'anti-communist'? – a test by which communism in much of the West is not doing badly. In any case many of the processes sketched can and do develop without connection with any communist or Marxist party – as in the largest capitalist nation, the United States, where Marxism's intellectual influence is large out of proportion to its (minuscule) Communist Party, or any of its even smaller rivals among Leninist political groupings.

## THE IDEOLOGY OF THE EDUCATED?

By the 1890s a small but significant fraction of the 'activists' among Russia's factory proletariat had organized themselves into circles for self-education in – among other topics – Marxism. This development evoked enthusiasm among most intelligentsia revolutionaries, and was the background for Axelrod's original notion of Marxist hegemony (see p. 197 above). But one social democrat, Jan Makhajki, writing at the turn of the century, found in it a comparably momentous but more pessimistic prospect. He concluded that Marxism, contrary to its own central doctrine, was not the world-view of the proletariat, but on the contrary was the ideology of the better educated, those who possessed 'human capital', rather than the physical capital of the traditional bourgeoisie. Through their Marxist ideology, he predicted, the new bourgeoisie of human capital would seek to ride the mass movement of manual workers to power. Once there, Makhaisky maintained, they would wrest back their briefly enjoyed political rights from their former allies, the workers, and expropriate the physical capital of the traditional bourgeoisie. By monopolizing well-paid offices in the state administration they would lay hold of the entirety of the social surplus and become the new – and dictatorial – ruling class.

For Makhaisky, therefore, the minority of workers who were Marxists represented not leaders in the emancipation of their class, but more a fifth column within it, assimilated politically and spiritually to the new bourgeoisie of education. Lenin, while deviating not a whit from Marxism's claim to be the specific and proper outlook of the proletariat, none the less also recognized one of Makhaisky's points: as a body of general ideas Marxism was not something the mass of workers spontaneously found congenial. It would need to be brought into the working-class movement from outside. Plekhanov's distinction between propaganda and agitation, and Lenin's approaches to party organization, followed logically from this view.

Hegemonic Marxism carries this one stage further. It recognizes – tacitly or more explicitly – that Marxist theory is inherently unpalatable to most of the population, and that its leverage over them must be indirect. But Makhaisky's perception of Marxism as an ideology of the intelligentsia retains some truth: society's greatly changed lines of cultural differentiation, and the much altered social proportions defined by them, still leaves Marxism and its various popularizations large audiences. It can offer, as Isaac Deutscher (1970, p. 128) pointed out, a treasured 'mental labour-saving device' for the 'semi-intelligentsia'.

But the image of communism as the ideology of the educated classes is only partly true. It zig-zags in relation to them as it does in relation to other classes, appealing to and using them at some places and times, discarding them at others. Some parts, and in some countries almost the whole, of the educated strata have always been hostile or indifferent to communism. On the whole, non-ruling communism appeals more to the social than the scientific intelligentsia, more to the young than the established, more to those of culturally insecure or excluded groups, more to the aspirant than the reputable.

Leninism's principal internal paradox – which defines its main contours of historical adjustment – lies in this: it began from a doctrine which made it the representative of a definite social class, the industrial proletariat; but at the same time it formed a new departure – in the political methods and organizational machinery it adopted, and in being rather conscious of these as practical means. While principally designed for harnessing the party to the proletariat, its methods and forms of organization proved readily adaptable to other groups. With its multi-purpose equipment, it has evolved as a distinct but elusive form of politics, efficacious because protean. In this it relies on the educated strata less as base than as intermediaries. While nowhere having entirely shed its original self-definition as the true political form of the industrial proletariat it has, both in practice and in areas of its doctrine, gone further than most of its rivals in basing itself on very diverse social groups. And where it holds state power the wheel is turned full circle: politics, dissolving itself, places itself in command of sociology, and party position etches the upper lines of social division and privilege.

But in the states where it does not rule, sophisticated Leninism, in becoming more than a narrow party, also risks becoming less. For (as the example of the United States makes clear) many of the attitudes and habits associated with diffused Marxism have no necessary association with any form of political organization. They can exist just as aspects of a form of life, in which common cause with those who share it with you is a matter of individual inclination, and mutual recognition and assistance, not party discipline. For, while they provide many of its audience and recruits, they also tend to blunt political thrusts, to encumber tactics, and above all to dissolve and tempt away from definite party ties; the larger the penumbra, the slimmer the shadow. Far from the spread of unorganized Marxism bringing nearer Makhaisky's communist dictatorship of the intelligentsia, it has assumed, in reaction against communism in power, a protestant tinge, and raises before much of western communism the spectre of Bernstein's revenge: 'The movement is everything, the final goal nothing.'

FURTHER READING

Kingston-Mann (1983) examines Lenin's peasant policies, prior to the Russian revolution. The essays in Lewis (1974) attack, from a variety of perspectives, the problems of how Asian communist parties have built their peasant and rural support.

Anderson (1976–7) discusses the antecedents of Gramsci's notion of 'hegemony', while Fermia (1981) and Adamson (1983) are good recent examples from the copious literature interpreting Gramsci's political thought. Makhaisky is less well served, but there are interesting articles on him by D'Agostino (1969) and Shatz (1967). The memorable naiveties of fellow travellers and 'political pilgrims' are collected in Caute (1988) and Hollander (1983).

# PART IV

Communist societies

# 14

## Communist societies: their contexts and problems

Most concepts of 'models' of communist societies relate them, explicitly or implicitly, to other forms of society – usually, but not always, developed market societies. A number of these concepts also locate communism (though often implicitly, and sometimes ambiguously) within a general pattern, even an evolutionary sequence, for world society as a whole. In this chapter I make a more modest attempt on this sort of problem, trying to place communism in two respects – first, in relation to other contemporary forms of society, and second, in relation to economic and social changes affecting them all. But to begin with I mention some of the range of ideas in play – ideas to which my account glances aside at various points.

### GENERAL CONCEPTS ABOUT COMMUNISM

Even general concepts vary in the aspects they stress – economic, political or psychological. Thus they may be not at all mutually exclusive. Some of the most telling accounts of communist society have its psychological results, its shaping and splitting of its citizens' mental and moral lives, at their core – from Orwell's dystopias, to descriptions of 'thought reform' in China, such as Bao Ruo-wang's (Bao and Chelminski, 1976), or Alexander Zinoviev's analysis of *The Reality of Communism* (1984) as a system of communally structured egoism. Concentrating on psychological and spiritual life, however, may oversimplify the picture. By bringing the mental and personal into the foreground at the expense of the practical and impersonal, one can exaggerate the extent to which communist regimes have a functional social psychology, underlining the advantages for state control of an 'ideologized' society, but neglecting the economic effects.

Interestingly, critical Marxist theories often do somewhat the same thing, despite having an opposite viewpoint on the relation of base to superstructure. They naturally take the economy as primary, but differ on how communism compares with – and competes with – capitalism. Marxists – both critical and official – are also the most explicit in relating communism to a world-historical sequence. Thus Leninist theories that communist states are 'workers' states' (whether considered healthy or, as in critical versions, politically degenerated) base this contention on their nationalized and planned economies, and it is these they see as giving them the prospect of superseding capitalism. Theories of 'state capitalism' have communism as a yet further mutation of capitalism, an even higher stage than Lenin's 'Imperialism, the highest stage of capitalism'; and they often carry, without stating, the pessimistic implication that state capitalism may have enough life in it to be the successor to market capitalism. An even more heretical and pessimistic mutation of Marxism asserts that communist states are based on a new, collective, form of property, and represent 'bureaucratic collectivism', a post-capitalist social formation which Marx did not foresee but which may or will (depending on the author's temperament) take over the world.

Where most Marxist versions join, though, is in seeing communism's nationalized economy and economic planning as superior to capitalist markets. Conversely, when ruling communist parties come to grips with their economic problems, and begin to experiment with 'capitalist' methods in the attempt to cure them, this generates problems, and sometimes crises, for their official ideologies.

It can be artificial to distinguish political concepts of communism in too clear-cut a way from psychological or economic ones, since the main characteristic of communist polities is the state's unprecedented penetration of other areas of society. The concept of *totalitarianism* develops this central idea, contrasting communist societies (and other forms of totalitarianism, such as fascism) with those in which the actions of the state are limited and regulated under an independent system of law, and in which the explicit competition of interests and ideas is preserved within an institutionalized system of political pluralism. The overall result, outside of the party-state and the structures it controls or permits, is one of psychological and social 'atomization'. The individual finds himself or herself organizationally isolated and psychologically naked *vis-à-vis* the state, which can demand not just external obedience, but active conformity and even inner assent.

The idea of totalitarianism as a model (rather than an ideal type) has come under attack from a number of directions. Critics have pointed out, for example, that if it applies to the Soviet Union under Stalin, it is a much poorer description of other communist states at other times; that communist rule, including apparently monolithic party leaderships, contain a great deal of informal 'pluralism'; that the idea of totalitarianism tends to deny the real support that some communist regimes do enjoy; and that it neglects the fact that communism may incorporate, but cannot eradicate, national cultures, and that these are essential to understanding individual communisms.

Concepts of totalitarianism are primarily political and social-psychological. Related to them is the notion of 'stratocracy' (rule by the military sector), proposed by Castoriadis (1981, 1983) to describe the form of society that has emerged from the maturing and decay of totalitarianism in the Soviet Union. Ideology decomposes, loses its 'delirious' quality, and relinquishes the aspiration to positive control; with it goes the cult of the individual leader, and mass terror and purges. What remains are routine official fictions, and the more 'economical' use of coercion, to silence dissent and secure conformity – but no longer the compulsory enthusiasm which full totalitarianism requires of the population.

The idea of totalitarianism carries a general implication of economic inefficiency. 'Stratocracy' arises from the inefficiency of a centrally planned economy in satisfying the economic demands of society at large. Domination of society by the organizations of coercion then leads to segregation of the controlling, coercive and military apparatuses and substantial economic sectors that serve them, establishing an insulated and privileged archipelago within the larger society. Moreover stratocracy, constituted so that the demands of the coercive segments of the state dominate over other social pressures, is inherently prone to seek external solutions to its problems, in the simplest cases by expansion and conquest. But stratocratic imperialism is rooted in differences of coercive power, not of economic development. Thus Soviet imperialism has extended its rule over nations in Eastern Europe that are, on the whole, *more* economically and culturally developed than itself, and its patterns of dependency and exploitation reflect this. In this regard communist imperialism has less resemblance to modern, capitalist, economic imperialism, than to ancient imperialism, in which a powerful, armed Rome could dominate a more sophisticated but weaker Greece.

ECONOMIC PERFORMANCE

As far as economic comparisons with other types of society are concerned, a considerable period has now elapsed in which communist states have functioned at relatively high levels of industrial development, making it possible to examine the essential dissimilarities and complementarities of communist and market economies. What emerges is a complex and intimate pattern of dependence – comparable in certain respects with that between industrially developed and underdeveloped economies, but with its own distinctive shape.

State economic planning within a Marxist framework, even of the highly centralized, 'command' type developed under Stalin's rule in the 1930s, has demonstrated its *economic* capacity to drive the development of heavy industry and a modern industrial infrastructure. I stress the *economic* advisedly, since communist industrialization in the Soviet Union was achieved only at enormous human and social cost, overshadowing the misery wrought by capitalist industrial revolutions. The trauma has been substantial in other communist societies, including those, like China, which have radically changed economic strategy before being industrially mature.

Moreover, the capacity to industrialize turned on a dependency: state planning was of greatest economic effect where it was a question of mobilizing resources for large enterprises and projects which employed already known – and in some cases imported – technology and know-how. The advantages of state planning were thus not only partial, but also relative, depending (as Vorontsov, in the 1880s, already recognized; see chapter 11) on the state which was to realize them being a 'late-developer'. They did not imply that, even from a narrowly economic point of view, one could visualize an alternative historical route for the *pioneers* of industrialization – say, a hypothetical planned alternative to the *ad hoc* inventiveness of eighteenth- and nineteenth-century capitalism in Britain. (Though the development experience of *some* market societies which industrialized later, and under the pressure of more advanced competitors, such as Germany, do suggest advantages to state involvement.)

Marxists, too, sometimes depict communism's capacity to industrialize as its general (and, perhaps, mitigating) ground; as Royden Harrison puts it: 'Marxism has become the ideology of the industrial revolution of the twentieth century where that revolution is accomplished on the basis of the international transfer of an already achieved technology and under the conditions of imperialism' (Harrison, 1983). But to this generalization we immediately think of exceptions; just in the period since the Second World War – Taiwan, South Korea, Singapore, Hong Kong, several Mediterranean countries, and, incipiently, such states as Brazil, Argentina and Mexico. Evidently communist central planning is a possible route of industrialization for 'late-comers', but by no means the only one. This raises one of the questions of this chapter: What circumstances make it likely that a nation will take a communist route? Implicit in this is a further question: How far should we think in terms of defined routes over a settled terrain at all?

## CATCHING UP AND OVERTAKING

Even if state planning helps in coming from behind, this leaves the question of what happens when much of the 'catching up' is completed. Communism's official doctrine – accepted by many of its dissident currents – has always been that planned economy would then overtake its market competitors. The Bavarian social democrat George von Vollmar, in an essay entitled *The Isolated Socialist State*, published in 1879, first drew attention to the fact that it was unlikely that socialism would conquer simultaneously in all major nations. Vollmar explored the implications of its succeeding in just one country (he expected this would be Germany) while capitalism persisted elsewhere. This raised the problem of protecting an 'isolated socialist state', and to this Vollmar projected a twin solution: military vigilance, coupled with appeals to the labour movements in the remaining capitalist countries to restrain their governments from military aggression. But, provided the peace could be kept, there would then, Vollmar argued, ensue a period of vigorous economic competition, in which the socialist nation would surpass the others and go on to demonstrate its superiority more and more clearly; the effect on other nations would be to strengthen the forces within them which were working for socialism, and weaken those in favour of conserving capitalism, and thus open up the possibility of peaceful transitions to socialism on their part.

Vollmar's scenario has proved extremely prescient of certain schools of communist *ideology*, but less so of its economic reality. Even where communist economies have achieved much in the way of 'catching up', overtaking and travelling ahead has thus far proved beyond them. There have been bold predictions of this sort – such as Krushchev's 1957 forecast that the Soviet Union would exceed the United States' output of major industrial and consumer goods in fifteen years, or Mao and Liu Shao-chi's claim shortly afterwards, at the beginning of their emulative 'Great Leap Forward', that China would overtake British industrial production in the same period (McFarquhar, 1974, vol. 1, p. 17). But the economic drives which these claims announced could not be sustained.

If we compare communist with market economies on the basis of patterns of trade, rather than standards of living or output per head, the result is still very asymmetric. Trade between the OECD and the Soviet Union and the European Comecon states accounts for the majority of communist countries' foreign trade. Within that, manufactures, and especially capital equipment, form a much larger proportion of most communist states' imports than their exports. The only exception is East Germany, whose imports and exports very roughly reflect each other in terms of their composition by broad categories. At the other end of the spectrum is the Soviet Union, accounting for about half of trade with the West. Its imports are dominated by manufactures, about half of which are capital equipment, and foodstuffs (a fluctuating category, dependent on Soviet grain harvests); exports, however, are dominated by oil and other raw materials. Moreover accounts in terms of broad product categories do not capture the full asymmetry, since a crucial part of communist imports of capital goods from the West is formed of technologically sophisticated equipment, while few of the manufactures they export come into this category.

INNOVATION AND DEPENDENCY

At root the economic problems of communist states turn on the fact that economic mechanisms form part of, and are deeply conditioned by, wider organizational structures and social processes. While 'command' central planning – which has fundamental effects not just on economic activities, but on psychological and political ones – can be a powerful means for assimilating and applying certain ranges of *existing* technologies, it is less successful at innovation. The metaphor by which economic competition among the advanced states is sometimes pictured as a running-race is very misleading. It is not simply a question of who can cover a certain distance along an existing track fastest, even when allowance is made for the psychological and 'aerodynamic' advantages of 'travelling in the slipstream' of the leaders. For the leaders in the economic 'race' are those who are *building* the track along which they will travel and others follow. The 'track', in the sense of technical and economic innovation, far from being laid down and neatly swept in advance, is being explored, surveyed, blasted and built as the race proceeds – and much of the burden, together with the advantages, of doing this necessarily falls to those at the front.

Not, of course, that communist regimes, even in their most 'Stalinist' phases, are incapable of innovation, but they achieve it only with greater effort, and have greater difficulties in applying it practically, than pluralist societies. Where they are able to import or imitate external innovation free of much of its development costs they do so. Most communist states have avoided becoming signatories of the major international patent and copyright agreements, recognizing that the advantages to them of appropriating others' developments outweigh what they might expect to gain. An important part of their economic dealings with Western companies is aimed at acquiring advanced technology – by direct purchases (sometimes with a view to copying the equipment in their own products), even by 'turnkey' contracts for the supply of whole plants, or in joint ventures in which technology and 'know-how' are provided by the Western partner. Enlarging the flow of technology has been an importive motive in China's opening up of concession zones in coastal areas since 1979, in which Western private companies are given incentives to establish operations.

Conversely, in areas where technical leadership is crucial, but the possibilities for imitation are circumscribed by secrecy – as, for example, in the Soviet Union's efforts in advanced military technology – the communist economy finds it necessary to segregate and organize personnel and resources in a manner which approximates to a 'dual economy'. In the 1970s, while the Soviet Union was laying the basis for its pioneering of long-distance space travel, consumer shortages were such that the population wasted time standing in queues equivalent to the full-time employment of fifteen million workers (Smith, 1976, p. 87). Even the consumer spin-offs of military production do not easily percolate through to the civilian economy; Soviet officers use high-quality, Soviet-made refrigerators, coffee-machines, etc. which are unavailable to civilian purchasers. But – as the concept of 'stratocracy' emphasizes – the protection of privileged sectors from constraints takes place only at the cost of civilian consumption being satisfied with the 'leavings', both in terms of personnel and materials.

The asymmetry between communist and market industrially developed societies is also reflected in the resources devoted to foreign intelligence and information-gathering. Many of the large numbers of intelligence officers attached to communist embassies in Western countries spend their time on routine sifting and analysis of unprotected or published technical and commercial information, and on filling out background to it. Of their espionage activities that come to light, a high proportion are directed at scientific or technical knowledge. For Western intelligence services a bigger emphasis goes on the discovery of political intentions and concrete military plans and dispositions; their agents are more rarely caught spying on communist science. Communist states depend on the flow of innovation from advanced industrialized societies, and the inability of Western states to limit it greatly without stifling its source. Where Western authorities *do* try to control information the attempt is often cosmetic rather than substantial. The US government, for example, prohibits the searching of certain *public* computer databases over the telephone lines from the Soviet Union or Eastern Europe.

Communist societies' integration with the world economy is expressed only in part through trade, including the physical transfer of technologies; it also involves a wider cultural 'parasitism'. This problem is one which Marxism did not foresee and, in power, has been slow to recognize. In the early years of the century (as we saw in chapter 11) Russian Marxists debated the special political and social arrangements, and the external help, that would be necessary for a socialist regime in their country to 'catch up' industrially and escape from its dependence on the more advanced economies. In the economic arguments between Bolshevik factions in the 1920s the basic shape of the dependence – essentially as a pattern of lacks of what other societies had – was a common premise; the issue was by what combination of internal and external policies it should be overcome. It did not occur to them that the instruments they used to overcome their backwardness might give rise to novel disadvantages *vis-à-vis* market-based societies.

This was an issue that economic planners began to confront, and not more than implicitly, only in the 1960s. Yet relationships have evolved as part of an overall pattern of dependence in which the major communist nations buy, borrow or take techniques from more open societies, while retaining a state form adapted for the regimentation or coercion of their populations.

### IDEOLOGY AND SCIENCE

There remain, of course, important tensions between these two functions, of which the main one is that between ideology and science. Creative assimilation, never mind innovation, in science and technology requires some freedom from political obligations and inhibitions, whereas communist parties' efforts to maintain generalized control push in the opposite direction. The results have sometimes been traumatic. After the imprisonment of the geneticist Vavilov in 1940, Soviet biology became the stamping ground of Stalin's favourite, Lysenko. After the war it was espionage which came to the rescue of Soviet nuclear weapons development, Soviet physics having been set back not only by the purges but by Stalin's declaration that the theory of relativity was a 'petty bourgeois idealism'. Chinese intellectual life has been similarly scorched; during the Cultural Revolution scientists of all disciplines were hounded unless they placed Mao's *Little Red Book* at the centre of their efforts.

The worst of these phases occur with the extreme concentration of power in one man, with the scope this gives for his arbitrarinesses to be universalized. Such experiences have led most party leaders to favour a sustained truce between technology and natural science, and politics. Scientists are permitted to work and publish without reference to politics, and the internal debates and cultures of the domestic sciences are encouraged to align – and to some extent become integrated – with those of the international academic cultures of their disciplines. However, a line of demarcation is drawn, within the necessarily fuzzy zone dividing the natural from the human sciences: beyond it obeisances to Marxism-Leninism become more requisite. (Yet even in the most sensitive areas – empirical sociology, for example – the needs of policy-makers for accurate information and the 'spontaneous' impetuses of scholarship mean that areas of objectivity may be found. Thus Western academic studies of economic conditions and inequality in the Soviet Union, such as Yanowitch (1977) and McAuley (1979), have been able to exploit a great number of inconspicuous but published sources.)

The truce in intellectual life is not underwritten by any theoretical self-limitation on the part of official Marxism. The Party retains, in principle, the right to intervene if it judges it necessary; and it is wise to do so, since there is no knowing when, and from what quarter, intellectual controversy may begin to unwind towards political dissent. Moreover segregation can, as Bukovsky describes, produce some areas of relative advantage:

. . . science is the common escape of intellectuals who want to keep their integrity – science and mathematics. These disciplines are extremely difficult to politicise. They provide a safe haven for those who want to use their minds to some purpose and evade the corruptions of the system. That is why there are so many scientists in the USSR and why theoretical physics, for example, is so highly developed. (Bukovsky, 1987a, p. 7)

Other, more practical reasons for the relative appeal of theoretical science and mathematics lie in communist economies' difficulties in translating even their own scientific advances into new products. Technologists who innovate are frequently frustrated by the fact that enterprise managers generally have little incentive to manufacture new products. And experimental scientists often have great difficulty in finding satisfactory equipment, or purchasing it abroad.

Despite ups and downs, communist rulers have learned to manage the frontier between cultural-scientific life on the one hand, and the ideologization of the system on the other, with increasing sophistication. The key lies in gradations of attitudes and functions within the intellectual strata. As early as 1953 Czeslaw Milosz's *The Captive Mind* (1980) sketched some of the interlocking character-types – with their different adaptations of personality – through which communism managed to confine and employ even the Polish intelligentsia: the realigned Catholic moralist, the nihilist poet turned corruscating journalist, the deft and cynical cultural administrator. What matters is their combination. Individuals must be found niches in which they can live and work; most of them will recognize and accept the invisible walls, and what they produce can be carried away and put to use by others. The low-key integration of the bulk of the educated middle classes into the system is sometimes the despair of democratically-minded intellectuals. In Hungary's mature and undemanding communism, Haraszti observes, a 'professionalist ethos' has replaced ideology. Conversely, even the creative intelligentsia have adapted; the artist and the censor 'diligently and cheerfully cultivate the gardens of art together' (Haraszti, 1988, pp. 7, 142).

The system works, but it creaks abominably. Consider the following contrast. Those who administer large organizations in the West habitually complain of the poor flow of information within them. They thus readily adopt technical innovations which can speed the flows: hence their by now universal, casual use of photocopiers (which have become in turn the butt of new complaints about important information being drowned by the proliferation of paper). Soviet organizations use photocopiers, too – though rather fewer. Yet employees who require photocopying have very restricted access to them – they are generally kept in locked rooms, to be used only under supervision. The purpose is not economy, it is to prevent the circulation of unapproved material: unauthorized use of a photocopier is a criminal offence! The KGB even tries to monitor the 'authorized use' of photocopiers in the Moscow offices of American companies.

To physical restrictions of this sort are added the stereotyping and confusion imposed on all but the most informal acts of communication by the requirement to observe official conventions – a requirement enforced by censorship. Most communist states have general censorship, employing a small army of officials whose daily, prosaic, task it is to prevent society considering its chief problems, or alternative solutions to them. Critics of the notion of totalitarianism may be right when they protest that it is impossible to eradicate differences of views and values, and that a measure of pluralism inevitably asserts itself. But freedom to organize around opinions or interests and to attempt to put them into effect is largely restricted to factions and clans within the party apparatus; outside that it faces a most hostile climate.

In retrospect, therefore, Lenin and Stalin's arguments on the economic vulnerability of the Soviet state and the need for a fortified 'socialism in one country', and Stalin's gloss that the state will not begin to wither away with the approach to socialism, but must be reinforced, have a sort of substance. However, the state is required not so much to prevent the capitalist market from invading the socialist economy while it is catching up, as to attach socialism advantageously into the international market economy, while protecting it from the damaging politicization which society tends to nurture.

### ECONOMIC DISCIPLINE

The relationship between industrialized centrally planned and market societies is not, of course, only that of a one-way dependency. In relatively labour-intensive production central planning enjoys some substantial advantages, of which the most important is its greater powers of labour discipline. While their membership is very large, the 'trade unions' of communist states are subordinate to the party, its 'transmission belt', as Lenin expressed it. Their independence of management is normally limited to very secondary matters, individual grievances, etc.; management therefore have much of the freedom which capitalist managers may enjoy, in the absence of unions, on such matters as safety standards. And, while forms of 'collective bargaining' may be simulated, there are no independent labour movement bodies to exert pressure on wage levels. While party leaders frequently promise that steps will be taken to improve the consumption standards of workers, it does not occur to them to suggest that trade union militancy should play any part in this.

The different conditions of labour in East and West can attract Western firms to explore forms of 'investment' in centrally planned economies – something that has been attempted since Lenin sought to attract concessionaires to exploit Soviet raw materials in the 1920s. This frequently takes the form of Western companies or consortia constructing – and often to some extent operating – plants or projects in the East, usually in exchange for a share in the output. But a frequent limitation to such arrangements is that Western firms are normally not eager to take their share of profits in the domestic currency, of which they can make little commercial use; such foreign plants, therefore, are generally conditional on a proportion of the output being marketed for hard currencies, to be shared by the investors.

Centrally planned economies are also able to use forced labour under conditions that workers in the developed West would not tolerate. Thus the Soviet Union, for example, built the pipeline supplying gas from Siberia to Russia and Western Europe using large numbers of workers under extremely arduous conditions – in contrast to the Alaskan pipeline, where skilled and highly-paid construction workers were supported at very high cost. It was estimated in the 1970s that 2–3 per cent of the Soviet labour force were prisoners (though this was still a much lower proportion than in the 1930s and 1940s). Almost all were engaged in forced labour, including women with small children, and disabled people. The very large majority of them were imprisoned for criminal, rather than political, offences (though the disproportionately high number of certain resistive nationalities, such as Ukrainians, and faiths, such as Baptists, among them, suggests a quasi-political component to many of their offences). The scale of their contribution to the labour force, and the fact that they are central to certain sectors – timber extraction, and mining, for example, where the authorities have the greatest difficulty persuading people to work in the remote regions of the Soviet Union – mean that they are incorporated in the economic plans, and that the police and criminal law systems have the function not merely of repressing crime, but of contributing to the labour supply. In the Soviet Union's economic plans for 1941, when the camps' population was swollen by the purges and the conquest of eastern Poland and the Baltic states, no less than 18 per cent of total capital investment was in projects administered by the NKVD, two-thirds of that in lumber-cutting and much of the rest in gold mining – an NKVD monopoly. Today, the consumer goods sold in the West include a number produced in labour camps (as were many of the trinkets distributed to visitors at the Moscow Olympics). In China, too, the prison and forced labour systems are built into economic planning.

Forced labour on such a scale, of course, also has a psychological effect throughout society. It is one of the coercive measures available to centrally planned economies as they attempt to exert control over the labouring population. Most communist states have vigorous provisions against 'vagrancy', and draconian punishments for economic crime. In the Soviet Union capital punishment remains in widespread use for crimes against state property. China is one of the very few states in the world still to carry out public executions, and most of those selected to be done to death have been convicted of economic crimes. Like the many other abuses of human rights in China, these attract astonishingly little censure from the West's politicians and press.

In part the use of direct coercion represents the attempt to compensate for the lack of the threat of unemployment which in the West still acts to reinforce discipline over labour. Most centrally planned economies, in most periods, suffer over- (i.e. dual and moonlighting) employment rather than structural unemployment. Labour is, of course, still wasted, but *within* the production process rather than outside it. The difference is also reflected in the relatively inefficient pattern of incentives that planned economies present to the individual worker, and the need for direction, backed by and merging into coercion, in the effort to supplement them.

### COERCION AND TERROR

Coercion in this more 'routine' sense may merge into and be reinforced by the state's use of terror on a wide scale. By 'terror' I mean generalized arrests, maltreatment or killings not actually based on individual wrongdoings – though campaigns of terror vary in the extent to which they allege such wrongdoings and operate through a simulacrum of law. The principal targets may be whole social groups (as in drives against private property in land), they may (especially in periods of turmoil or when a new regime is trying to stabilize itself) be parts of the population suspected of hostility to it, or they may be sections of the communist party itself – or a phase of terror may fuse these types. In addition to direct victims, a much greater number often suffer hardship or death as a result of economic and social disruption. Thus what was probably the most intense communist terror campaign to date, the rule of Pol Pot's Khmer Rouge over Kampuchea from 1975 to 1979, started immediately after their conquest of the country with the forced removal of the whole population (about 2.5 million people, or one third of the total population) from the capital, Phnom Pen – which in itself caused immense hardship. It then systematically executed officials of the previous regime, and later moved on to a general extermination of the professional and middle classes. Terror was also applied within the party apparatus, concentrated among officials who had been involved in its earlier collaboration with the Vietnamese communists.

The Kampuchean terror was the most intense because it fell upon such a small country. A recent, careful, estimate (Vickery, 1984, p. 187) is that about 750,000 died, about 2–300,000 being executed, most of the rest dying from starvation or disease. But in a country of about 7–8 million this was about one person in ten of the population. Other terror campaigns have taken many more victims. Mao himself admitted that about 800,000 'counter-revolutionaries' were killed in the early 1950s (the period of the main land redistribution) but the true figure must have been much higher (MacFarquhar, 1960, pp. 270ff). Much larger numbers died as a result of Stalin's 'liquidation of the kulaks' in 1929–32, and in the party purge and general terror of 1934–9. In the Ukraine over a quarter of the rural population died as a result of the drive against the 'kulaks' and consequent famine (Conquest, 1986, p. 306). During 1988 items in the Soviet press revised sharply upwards the numbers estimated to have died under Stalin's rule – to an astonishing 50 million, *excluding* war deaths.

One important function of many terror campaigns is stabilization. In this respect the Kampuchean terror over-reached itself, and undoubtedly made the regime vulnerable to the Vietnamese invasion of 1979. But even terror campaigns aimed at securing the regime often direct their violence within the communist party, or at rival currents: in the first period of terror in Afghanistan, in 1978–9, when the Parcham faction of the party fell victim; in the Angolan purge against the supporters of Nito Alves in 1977; in Ethiopia, where Mengistu's military-cum-Leninist junta found that its first steps, if it was to build up a secure regime, involved extinguishing potentially rival Marxist currents, particularly the Ethiopian People's Revolutionary Party, the main target of the 'red terror' of 1976–9; and in the People's Republic of the Congo, where Marien Ngouabi almost destroyed his tiny ruling party with a series of purges in 1972, and then again (after denouncing the entire party membership) in 1975–6.

The initial Soviet terror, under Lenin, was not directed within the party. But it was, emphatically, a weapon of stabilization, directed at rival political currents, at economic expropriation, and at 'reactionary' social classes. Only later did Stalin use the security services on a large scale against party members. There seems, very frequently, a need for a communist party to make violent internal adaptations after reaching power, as well as to secure its external position by violence. In the Soviet Union the two phases were somewhat separated, reflecting the different political tradition of Bolshevism, its inclusion of radically different currents, before and during the revolution. But one, at least, of the processes at work in the great Soviet purge was something it had in common with many later purges: the party's 'cleansing' itself of some of the divers outlooks, human types and habits of work which had proved serviceable to it on its route to power, but were now an encumbrance. Communism's eclectic character on the way to power is, paradoxically, one reason for the violence with which it often pursues internal homogeneity once it has come to rule. It is not unique in this. Hitler found it necessary, eighteen months after coming to power, to carry out a sudden bloodletting in which the main targets were Ernst Röhm and other leaders of the SA, the plebian troopers of Nazism. Stalin was profoundly impressed by Hitler's 'night of the long knives' (30 June 1934) and a few weeks later, after the assassination of Kirov, began to direct his own, much larger, terror into the ruling party.

The harsh relationships of communist states to their subjects, particularly their use of coercion and terror, have significant political effects in the industrially developed market societies, most of which have a pluralist-parliamentary political order; they help to legitimate the West's flawed and bureaucratized, but resilient, liberalism. While in its early years the Soviet Union was rather successful in projecting itself as a beacon of radicalism and even freedom, that has long faded, and its appeal now (though not less widespread) is rather different. China's international image has evolved similarly. Communism in power has become one of the dominant experiences of the twentieth century, doing much to strengthen 'consensual' political parties and practices in the West. The effect has been to encourage a reluctant toleration of social inequities and political malpractices at home, in the belief that the available alternatives are worse. This effect is well-recognized among politicians. Even among the most conservative of them it is common to discover that their standard denunciations of communist society and politics, and expressions of sympathy for the populations who suffer them, are often accompanied by a more discreet acceptance of a long-term mutual adaptation of Western and communist political orders, and an unmistakeable empathy for their communist opposite numbers when their positions are threatened by popular unrest. It is certainly not the case that the further one moves to the right across the conventional geometry of the political spectrum, the less the empathy for communist states.

The best indicators of ordinary attitudes and expectations are perhaps to be found in patterns of migration. There is a small but persistent flow – growing in moments of crisis to a flood – of emigrants and absconders from almost all communist states, for a mixture of motives: racial or religious pressures (Jews from the Soviet Union, or Chinese from Vietnam, for example); political dissidence; the reuniting of families; and economic hardship or ambition. But the numbers relocating permanently in the opposite direction are negligible. Far more American Poles are transported to Poland after death, to be buried, than return to settle in their homeland. The economic motive, in particular, is absent: from the point of view of the individual citizen economic statistics are only a very partial measure of the success or otherwise of the centrally planned economies at 'catching up' the advanced market economies. In day-to-day life the poor quality of consumer goods, and the everlasting round of queueing and waiting, not only for high-quality goods, but even for the most basic items of consumption, depress real standards of living even for those on higher money incomes. A life of comfort can be had, but not with roubles or zlotys alone: it requires influence (usually to be had by seniority in the apparatus) and/or resort to the black market.

### COMMUNISM AND 'POST-INDUSTRIALISM'

Thus far we have discussed the relative efforts and successes of the two forms of society as though – if not exactly racing along a track – they were none the less travelling through the same, settled, landscape. But this – a premise of much discussion of 'catching up' – is itself very misleading. By the 1980s the Soviet Union had exceeded the United States in per capita production of steel. In the 1930s, and even the 1940s or 1950s, this would have been considered a momentous event. Targets for steel production stood at the centre of the Soviet Union and other communist states' plans in the period of their most intensive drives to industrialize. Yet in the 1980s, when the event occurred, it went almost unremarked. At the same time Romania suffered from the most severe economic crisis in Eastern Europe, largely because it had incurred massive foreign debts to build a steel industry for whose products it could not find outlets.

What the silence illustrated was the speed with which new technologies and other economic sectors than heavy industry had become of critical importance for industrialized economies. By the 1960s most forms of steel suffered from surplus capacity on the world market, and by the 1970s it had become a major export of nations like South Korea which had industrialized since the Second World War. The burgeoning manufacturing sector of the developed market economies was electronics, but the proportion of their labour forces employed on manufacturing as a whole was falling, with an increasing number employed in non-manual and service jobs, many of them requiring higher education and sophisticated technical skills. Within this, the 'knowledge sector' generated the new techniques that were exploited to yield increasing manufacturing outputs, at falling relative cost, and with falling labour-output ratios. While the Soviet Union and most other communist states were passing through the great shifts of population from countryside to town, from agriculture into industry, that were traditionally associated with industrialization (the exceptions were East Germany and Czechoslovakia, already industrially developed before the Second World War), the most technically advanced market economies were becoming (in one of the phrases which became popular) 'post-industrial' societies. The economic route to be travelled, that is to say, was changing underfoot.

How far are communist societies able to reap 'advantages of backwardness' in relation to 'post-industrial' developments? Their problems in doing so and the demands and strains it places upon them are rather different from those of much industrialization. The combined consequence of continuing 'technical' advance (in the broad sense – that is, to include new methods of organization, planning, communication, etc.) and uneven development as between nations is not merely that latecomers need not follow in all the footsteps of the leaders, being able to use the most advanced techniques right away, but that they are in many respects *compelled* to skip intermediate stages.

Yet it is easiest to transplant techniques into a less developed society when they are such as can be understood and controlled by a relatively thin stratum of technical experts and administrators, using large numbers of less skilled workers who can be fairly directly managed (and whose consumption levels can be contained). But as sectors using a larger proportion of highly educated labour, services rather than industry, and the process of innovation itself, begin to occupy centre stage, the advantages of backwardness shift and to some extent dissolve. Post-industrial development contains a number of elements of which direct imitation or adoption is more difficult. An increasing proportion of the labour force is employed in knowledge occupations: creating, maintaining and updating knowledge (all of which require direct social investment in specialist and higher education) and transmitting it to further generations. Many of these occupations are in uneasy friction with too interventionist or rigid a political order.

This problem is episodically but increasingly recognized within ruling communist parties. We have mentioned Bukharin's views, and the forms of 'truce' between Marxism and natural science. In 1957, in the aftermath of the Soviet Communist Party's Twentieth Congress, Mao launched the first of several campaigns by the Chinese Communist Party in power to 'let a hundred flowers bloom'. Many of these, however, began to flower as political questions, the blooms being then nipped in the bud. Janos Kadar's regime in Hungary rather successfully sought to operate a low profile in cultural and intellectual matters (as well as running the Eastern European economy in which market decentralization went furthest, producing a small 'economic miracle' in comparison with its Eastern European neighbours). Politically dissident currents have existed there since the 1970s, tolerated far more than in Brezhnev's Soviet Union or most of the rest of Eastern Europe; Kadar took as his regime's motto, 'He who is not against us is for us.' The balancing act of running a domestically 'liberalized' communist society also depends, even now, on the traumatic effects of the suppression of the Hungarian revolution, and on that small nation's memory of what happened when they allowed Nagy's 'new course' to evolve out of control, and were left helpless in face of Soviet military force.

In Czechoslovakia the problem of reconciling the emergent centrality of science to society with communist rule became the subject of explicit – and remarkably candid and open-minded – discussion among party leaders during the 'Prague spring' of 1968. For example, a party-sponsored commission on science policy headed by Radovan Richta (Richta, 1969) sailed very near the wind of Marxist heresy. It treated science itself not just as *a*, but as *the* principal force of production, displacing the working class and by implication querying the labour theory of value and Marx's economic arguments as a whole. The larger premises of the Richta report's argument simply broadened the heresy: overturning Marxism-Leninism's 'sociologism', it took the autonomous development of technique, rather than the changing of social relations, as the basis of historical progress. With this went concern for the creative intelligentsia, especially scientists, the source of this rising force of production, and sympathetic discussion of their need for liberal, fructifying conditions if they are to be fully productive – a group of arguments which, again, flew in the face of orthodoxy (and echoed Western sociologists' discussions of 'post-industrialism' and of an educated and expert 'new class' as the coming bearer of historical initiative).

The Richta report was buried after the Soviet invasion in 1968 (though its chief author was soon reconciled to the Husak regime, and resumed a senior position within it). But the dilemmas it addressed have continued to grow. Gorbachev's new economic programme for the Soviet Communist Party, in 1985, put great stress on advanced industries, such as computers and electronics, and promised that, across the board, higher productivity would be achieved by increased automation, and that manual work would be phased out – though it also repeated the conventional promise to promote *more* workers to leadership functions.

Increasing technological complexity and organizational flexibility are not the only problems. The increase of services relative to manufactures raises, in the absence of competitive markets, enlarged problems of standards and of appropriate provision. The tasks of 'monitoring' output inevitably get dispersed, away from the quality-control units of large manufacturing enterprises, towards large numbers of points of use. Knowledge of, and therefore effective control over, outputs, shifts downwards and fragments, and becomes, as it does so, less amenable to overall direction by a central plan.

Where the user is single – or a complex of organizations which can make some approximation to being the sole 'client' – then, provided costs are not taken as close restrictions, the quality even of technically complex products can be sustained at adequate levels. This is the case, to take the main example, with production of much military equipment. But the costs for civilian society are large: both the direct absorption of resources by a sector not subject to normal cost constraints, and the effects on civilian morale of the gap, the sense of living (as the Soviet quip has it) in an 'Upper Volta with Rockets'. One symptom of the degradation of consumer production is the generalized hunger for Western goods, even where they are not significantly superior. In this the Soviet Union also exhibits its 'backwardness' as an imperialist power: nationalist and chauvinist Russian attitudes towards the Eastern European nations are coupled with widespread demand for consumer imports from Hungary, East Germany and Czechoslovakia. Another symptom of economic decay is the fact that, in many periods, the aggregate quantity and quality of supply to consumers is insufficient to absorb personal money incomes. In the Soviet Union, for example, the increase in savings deposits during 1985 was more than double the increase in total retail sales. Such a situation represents a landmine of latent inflation threatening attempts to introduce 'market' reforms.

The effects on consumers' attitudes and morale are only part of much larger problems. Large and inherited social differences, though officially concealed, are part of the daily experiences of every citizen of a communist state. Through education systems which are, in practice, markedly socially discriminatory, they are transmitted onwards to future generations. Social rank is strongly correlated with bureaucratic seniority. The higher salaries of senior officials are only one part of their privileges: more importantly, rank gives non-market access to goods and services not available through the general channels, and opens the door to the use and exchange of 'influence' or 'clout', merging, at connected edges, into corruption and the black market. The almost ubiquitous use of bribes and other inducements – all technically illegal, but seldom prosecuted until they reach large proportions – reflects inadequate supply and bureaucratic allocation in the economy.

### INCENTIVES AND ECONOMIC REFORM

Individual enrichment outside the apparatuses does, of course, occur. But the general problem lies in the great difficulty of centrally planned economies – in face of scarce resources and, consequently, individual interests within the struggle over distribution – in gearing individual efforts to social production. The black and grey markets, with official policy continually fluctuating in the extent to which it tolerates them, are one symptom of the problem but only a very partial solution to it. It is one thing to ease the food shortage by allowing peasants to come to city markets with produce grown on their individual plots, to encourage cooperatives of spare-time cooks, shoe repairers, etc., or to allow teachers to 'moonlight' giving private lessons to schoolchildren to prepare them for university entrance; it is another – though an extension of the first – to wink at syndicates of 'rouble millionaires' flying Georgian oranges to sell in wintertime Moscow, at factory officials purchasing parts and supplies on grey markets, or at private contractors building cottages for the successful (with its incentive to theft of state property). But it is a different, and more significant, step to permit private enterprise to operate on a large scale – to provide air transport or personal computers, for example.

So far communism's main efforts at gearing the personal to the social within the economy have taken the form of liberalizing markets and allowing enterprises to accumulate surpluses and distribute part of these as bonuses. On the whole they have stopped short of legitimizing substantial property in the means of production, and enterprises and individuals thus cannot reap the full advantages that a free-market sector would offer for generating and assimilating innovation. But there are signs that some economic reforms may go a good deal further.

The two countries which have moved furthest, with economic reform, away from 'Stalinist' central planning are Hungary and China. In both cases the reforms got under way in the aftermath of massive state and political violence – the suppression of the 1956 revolution in Hungary, and the Cultural Revolution in China. The effect of these experiences was to leave most people fearful of further political upheaval, and thus to make it easier for the regime to experiment with economic reform without risk to the political order.

In both cases the reforms began, and established their first successes, by passing agriculture back to peasant initiative. In Hungary the collective farm system collapsed during the 1956 revolution, with many peasants resuming individual cultivation. The government did not try to restore the old collectives. Instead it applied pressure on them to combine into cooperatives, offering them, however, a measure of genuine internal self-government, much improved prices for their crops, and an end to compulsory deliveries to the state. The result – enduring through the vicissitudes of Hungary's industrial and financial reforms – has been a relatively healthy agriculture, the basis of sizeable exports of processed foods (including food exports for hard currency to the Soviet Union).

In China Deng Xiaoping's rehabilitation and return to power (in 1977–8), coupled with near-famine conditions in parts of the countryside, allowed the rural communes to disintegrate. Once the national authorities allowed the 'family responsibility system' (in all its many local guises) to spread, it rapidly took over; by 1984 98 per cent of peasants had switched to individual cultivation. Under the 'responsibility system' peasant families contract to farm an individual plot in return for a set quantity of crop delivery, or money rent-cum-tax, to the state. Anything the family produces above this, it is free to sell for whatever it can get; in effect, the state procurement agencies purchase in partly open markets. The initial effect was rapid increases in agricultural output, which rose over 50 per cent between 1978 and 1984. When, from 1987, the state allowed contracted plots to be leased, there were soon reports of large farms being worked by hired labour. As in Hungary, inequality increased sharply, and prices of foodstuffs to city-dwellers have risen. Moreover social investment on the land (drainage, irrigation, reafforestation, etc.) has sharply declined, and even existing works are often not being properly maintained.

These agricultural reforms have been successful in increasing output, but on very different bases. Kadar succeeded with large-scale, relatively mechanized, cooperatives, while Deng fell back on the cohesion, effort and ingenuity of the Chinese peasant family. Neither of them, therefore, necessarily represent blueprints to solve the problems of other communist states, with different family and social relations, different histories, and different climatic conditions. In the Soviet Union, for example, the lack of rational incentives to the peasant has bedevilled agriculture since Stalin's forced collectivization. Even today, transport and storage facilities are so poor, and the organization of labour at harvest-times so chaotic, that 20 per cent of Soviet crops get left to rot. By holding down basic food prices, the state creates further irrationalities. While queues, shortages and rationing are endemic, especially in provincial cities, peasants find that it pays them to sell grain to the state, and buy back its subsidized bread to feed to their livestock, or even to buy meat from the state butchers to feed to fur-bearing animals.

China's industrial and financial reforms (and, over a longer period, and with reverses, those in Hungary) have not yet been as far-reaching as the changes in the Chinese countryside, but they have still been profound. At bottom, however, they have simply pushed much further with the types of reform attempted by Krushchev in the early 1960s. Then, Soviet reforming economists sought to free enterprises from the grip of Stalinist central planning, in which economic ministries in Moscow tried to regulate, with 'material balances', the *physical* inputs and outputs, and flows between, individual plants all over the Soviet Union.

The core of virtually all reform plans is the effort to give individual enterprises freedom to choose in aspects of their operations (inputs purchased, quantity and nature of outputs, prices, customers, sources of investment funds, labour employed, wages paid) together with incentives which will cause them to operate in a more rational and efficient way. The incentives generally centre on some form of operating surplus or profit, which enterprises (or managers) are free to use for new investment, bonuses or employee welfare. At its maximum, widening enterprise freedom would amount to restoring fully open markets – between enterprises, with workers, suppliers and customers, in labour, capital and materials. But even the boldest of reform plans stops short of this, and all of them run into the entrenched, covert resistance of established economic bureaucracies, who fear their powers and privileges being eroded. In many cases there is also opposition from workers in state enterprises. For them, economic reform often means accelerated work tempos, while any extra pay is offset by price increases. When the Czechoslovak reform programme began to be introduced in 1968, for example, Novotny and other 'old guard' party leaders managed to gather some support among factory workers against Dubček on such a basis.

The Hungarian New Economic Mechanism, first launched in 1968, was virtually halted by resistance within the party between 1973 and 1978. When relaunched, it then produced inflation which outstripped many money incomes, and in 1982 led to a serious foreign exchange crisis (exacerbated by Soviet and Libyan withdrawals of their deposits from the Hungarian state bank). However, after an unprecedentedly open debate, the main lines of reform continued. Hungary has greatly relaxed central planners' control over prices, outputs and supplies, reducing both the powers and staff of the planning ministries. It has encouraged cooperatives, and allowed small-scale private businesses in many sectors, has legalized much 'moonlighting' private work by allowing cooperatives for part-time work, has allowed large enterprises to trade abroad directly, has decentralized credit banking, and has introduced formal bankruptcy procedures for unprofitable enterprises. Perhaps most radically, it has allowed enterprises to issue fixed-interest bonds and has allowed the central bank to make a market in them, in which individuals can buy and sell – though the amount of capital involved is only a tiny fraction of total savings.

China has gone even further in reintroducing capital markets. As of 1987 there were 'stock exchanges' in Shanghai and Beijing, at which securities issued by hundreds of state enterprises were traded. Private trade was licensed, and 18 million people were in it by 1985 – though many of these were richer peasants regularly trading in their own produce. Private businesses were permitted in a number of sectors, theoretically limited to seven non-family employees, but with the limit being widely exceeded. In some large cities private businessmen's associations developed, partly to protect themselves against the exactions of bureaucrats. Similar, in some ways, are the voluntary associations which have been formed by managers of state enterprises in the larger industrial centres to lobby for their interests. Price controls, though, remain more rigid than in Hungary, and enterprises are not free to trade abroad. For interchange with world markets, and the inflow of sophisticated technology from abroad, China still relies on state-controlled trading enterprises, and on special arrangements, such as the coastal concession zones where foreign companies are encouraged to establish themselves (but where ordinary Chinese are not allowed to travel).

However, the process of 'privatization' in industry and the countryside is far from ended; in 1987 party general secretary Zhao Ziyang stated that by 1990 only 30 per cent of the economy would be controlled by the state. The reforms as a whole are explained and justified within the theory of 'initial stage socialism' – the idea that China has never passed through a capitalist stage of development, but has jumped directly from feudalism into socialism. It thus never properly absorbed some of capitalism's most useful institutions, and must now deliberately introduce market pressures, profit and loss, individual enrichment, etc. if it is to modernize. Since the full modernization programme is projected to last 75 years, the innovations of the 1980s are not being proposed as temporary adjustments.

Another important element of Chinese industrial reform under Deng was a major shift from heavy to light industry. This was necessary in motivating the agricultural reform – without consumer goods to buy, peasants would not market their crops. But downgrading heavy industry meant that military spending could not be sustained. China thus became the first communist power in modern times to make a substantial, un-negotiated reduction in military spending and manpower. That Deng could achieve this relatively easily in face of the military establishment speaks against using notions like 'stratocracy' to describe contemporary Chinese society. His ability to do so turned on the hostility which much of the *party* bureaucracy felt to the army following its support for Mao in the Cultural Revolution. Reportedly, Deng persuaded the military to accept a reduction in manpower with the promise that, before long, economic reform would allow the armed forces to be re-equipped with more sophisticated weaponry and equipment – that is, that the shift of resources out of heavy industry would allow faster technological development and innovation.

The economic reform programme started in the Soviet Union since Mikhail Gorbachev came to power has so far been less sweeping than those in Hungary or China. Part-time private enterprise is encouraged in selected fields, mainly services, through family businesses and small cooperatives. Collective farms and state farms can sell anything they produce above their 'targets' at higher prices. The industrial reforms have in part repeated earlier moves, in that central economic ministries have been grouped into 'super-ministries', and their powers and some of their staffs reduced, in the hope that the central planners will concentrate on genuinely strategic issues, and reduce their day-to-day involvement in enterprise management. But managers' powers are being significantly increased, including their right to retain surpluses for the enterprise, and to choose among suppliers and customers. Forms of joint venture between Soviet and Western enterprises have been made legal. A number of large organizations can now trade abroad and retain some of the hard currency they earn. A new, and it is hoped independent, quality inspectorate oversees the output of many plants, and must be satisfied before bonus payments are made. And to stimulate innovation, research and technical agencies linked to individual ministries and plants are being encouraged to combine.

It is part of the shift to 'post-industrialism' that the innovation process itself becomes increasingly central, absorbing a rising proportion of the total social effort. Innovation, rather than depreciation, becomes the major factor determining many product lifetimes; in technologically fast-moving sectors of market economies the difference between large profits and losses may turn on a few months or even weeks in bringing out a product. The structural conservatism of centrally planned economies in relation to innovation becomes, hence, a disadvantage of rising, rather than falling, significance, and this is now an important issue for economic strategists in the Soviet Union and most other communist states.

Not all the disadvantages, however, are on one side. Innovation centres on advances in knowledge and its application, and much knowledge is, or approximates to being, a free good – the main reason why communist economies avoid entering international agreements on intellectual property. Nor are their political cultures in all respects inimical to innovation; many large Western corporations, including some which are undisputed technical leaders, operate rather rigid and bureaucratized organizations, and make considerable psychological demands for irrational 'company loyalty' on individuals. The ethos maintained within IBM, for example, is such that it has for long successfully prevented any form of trade union organization developing (as well as manipulating prices to exclude competitors from its markets). True, corporations tend to put their research and development efforts where advances can be relatively directly exploited, and if possible kept from their competitors, and seek to draw on academic research for results of more general applicability, but the division between commercial and academic research has become very blurred, and in neither area are the motives of those directly engaged in research linked in a very immediate way to prospects for practical exploitation.

The economic disadvantages we have discussed are such from the standpoint of governments, interested in effectiveness and efficiency in pursuit of their goals. They are, of course, offset by certain advantages. At the level of macroeconomic control planned economies are free of the instabilities produced by the movements of capital markets. Monetary and fiscal policies are more derivative of the 'physical' targets of the plan than distinct instruments of policy – although the extent to which this is so varies substantially, depending on the scale of market adjustment permitted. Inflation and unemployment do not pose the immediate political threats that they do in the West. Communist governments are, sometimes, forced out of office, but not by elections, and while they cannot be indifferent to the reactions of their subjects, they are free of the neurotic sensitivity to public opinion which afflicts Western politicians at constitutionally prescribed intervals and they can, to that extent, act with a longer time-horizon.

## THE EVOLUTION OF DEVELOPMENT

How may we sum up our list of interconnected advantages and disadvantages – first in relation to economic development? We must try to gauge them against a rather broad variety of situations for national societies – situations both in historical time, and, within that, in the relative development of, and relations between, different societies. They range from the position of a little-industrialized country at a time when the world economy was unevenly passing through its mature, electricity-based, phase of industrialization (that of Russia in the first decades of this century); through the predicaments faced by unindustrialized countries now, when the most dynamic sectors of the world economy are 'post-industrial', and when most raw materials, and an increasing number of manufactures, face slack world markets; to the position of largely industrialized communist economies seeking 'post-industrial' development (approximately, the situation of the Soviet Union and much of Eastern Europe today).

Communism's economic record to date does allow a broad assessment across these varied situations. Centralized state planning under a communist party represents *one* feasible route of industrialization, based largely on already achieved technologies. It is not the only route and, other things being equal, it tends to be the more difficult the later in the world's process of economic development it is attempted (though other factors, such as the ability of national cultures to adapt to modernization, may profoundly affect the results). As far as the transition beyond industrialization is concerned, to join with or surpass the leading sectors of the world economy, communism is now making visible and strenuous efforts, but with rather little success.

In assessing communism's economic problems and possibilities it is essential to keep in mind the historical (that is, moving, interconnected, conscious and non-repeatable) course of the world economy. Categorizing countries by social system and economic level can obscure this – as in the simplistic terminology of a first, second and third world, or in notions of development that imply that followers traverse the same ground as leaders.

## COMMUNIST ELITES

However, communism's past and prospects are in no way reducible to economics. Economic factors alone might suggest that its heyday lay in the past: communism was a feasible resolution of dilemmas of industrial under-development; but as the relative weight of industrial activity in the economy and society peaked and then declined, communism's 'window of oppor-tunity' began to close. In fact, however, communist rule continues to spread, and has scarcely anywhere been removed once it has established its power reasonably securely. Choices among political orders are not made on economic grounds alone – nor by societies as a whole. In particular (as Lenin recognized) the choice to seek or preserve a communist political order is one made by a rather small, highly conscious and self-conscious, elite – repeated and reinforced by the decisions of individuals as the elite assembles itself in processes of political recruitment and training. And what may recommend itself to such an elite may overlap little with the preferences of other parts of society.

Communism's future thus turns on the capacities of such elites to ger-minate, grow and survive. Elites (like all other parts of society) will be attracted or repelled by many conditions that are not directly economic – and they may well tolerate or welcome economic conditions that are a disadvantage for society as a whole. Economic inequality is a positive advantage if you happen to be one of the privileged. Chronic shortages and bureaucratic channels of distribution not only institutionalize and conceal inequality, they provide innumerable, molecular, means of social control and opportunities for patronage. The Leninist party – in its various national adaptations – may be grasped as an unrivalled means of cohesive political action, and may explode in size when it offers social advancement and economic privilege. Leninist ideology, too, is mutable. Some may find it irksome or oppressive, but it can be made available in many versions and dilutions, and can provide all-purpose theoretical justifications for political actions.

The Marxist historian Edward Thompson, in his study of *The Making of the English Working Class* (1972), assaulted the notion of class as a purely economic category, formed by passive processes of social settlement. Class is an active process; a national working class, Thompson insisted, is one that has formed itself through conscious processes: political development, self-education, religion, journalism. His insight is even more true of the self-formation (and recompositions) of *representatives* of working classes, communist parties. But one difference is that, unlike a national proletariat, there is nothing economically necessitated about the development of a national communist elite. The English and other working classes would have been formed anyway, by industrialization; what their activity did was to shape their character and traditions.

A communist movement, however, must make and preserve itself 'by its own bootstraps'. Modern economic and social conditions – together with the international traffic in political ideas – may cause communism's seeds to

settle widely. But survival and success is another matter. For this communism must also adapt – first of all to the national conditions in which it
finds itself. This is clear as much from its failures as its successes. Trotskyism, defined in the 1920s in opposition to the ruling coalition in the Soviet
Union, represented the codified failure of national adaptation, the loss, in
effect, of Leninism's protean character.

Leninism proper, starting with its Russian original, is more pragmatically
and profoundly national. Before the First World War Lenin had a fundamentally different attitude to Russian social democracy – where he would
pursue and exploit the minutest differences – than to foreign socialist
parties, where he took a more live-and-let-live attitude. The 'internationalism' by which he separated himself from much of European socialism in
1914 was adapted to taking advantage of conditions in Russia, and became,
quite shortly after 1917, subordinate to the national interests of the Soviet
Union. But adaptation is more than a simply political matter; frequently
ruling Leninism absorbs a great deal from the entire culture into which it is
transplanted – as with Chinese communism. Even where there is a more
superficial adaptation to nationalism, it can produce startling results. The
Ceausescu regime in Romania, for example, has set out to establish its
continuity with figures from the country's remote past, such as Vlad the
Impaler (1431–76), the original of Bram Stoker's Dracula, now reappraised
as a progressive prince.

In explaining why Leninism has succeeded where Marxism did not predict
– in less developed countries – national adaptability, and the ability to
exploit nationalism, are at least as important as its being an ideology of
industrialization. The two are, in any case, closely connected. In an unevenly
developed world resistance concentrates in the disadvantaged nations, but it
can most effectively be organized by those who take a long-term and
combative stance towards international inequality. Leninism can be particularly effective at linking utopian yearnings to its sense of 'progress' where
masses of people contrast their own misery and humiliation with the afflu-
ence and arrogance of distant nations who were lucky enough to grab a
head start.


RULING PARTIES


The self-making of communist elites continues when they come to rule.
Indeed, especially with parties, such as most of those in Eastern Europe,
which were relatively suddenly installed in power by external support, the
process virtually begins anew at that point. It is then that the main shift
from being a political elite to being a social and economic one occurs
(though the generalization must be qualified: a number of Western, non-
ruling, communist parties are already concentrated in higher social strata).

Moreover, while the membership of a ruling party may be, very approximately, concentric with broader or narrower definitions of a social elite, the *scale* of membership, as a proportion of the population, varies enormously. It ranges from ratios of the order of 1 in 10 of the population for the Soviet Union and Eastern Europe, to 1 in 250 (Congo, Angola) and even estimated 'densities' as low as 1 in 10,000 (Kampuchea) or 1 in 20,000 (Ethiopia and Benin). On the whole the less economically developed states have lower membership ratios (the main exception to this being North Korea, with the highest of all, 1 in 6) (Holmes, 1986, p. 142).

This broad correlation is what one might expect. The weight of party membership in society principally reflects two intertwined processes: extension and consolidation of the party-state's administrative grip, and processes of social incorporation, drawing on traditionally higher-status or influential groups. Thus the average educational level of party members is always much higher than the surrounding average, and managers and white-collar workers are heavily over-represented in comparison with manual workers and peasants. In less developed societies the rural population forms a larger fraction of the total, and continues in more traditional forms of life, less susceptible to modern ideas or affected by measures of state administration. The scale of party membership reflects the fact that it seeks to monopolize state functions, or at least exert control over them, and one of the important factors affecting it is the extent and maturity of urbanization. Moreover statistics on the social composition of parties often understate the extent to which they are dominated by educated and white-collar groups, since applicants for party membership and posts frequently find it an advantage to describe themselves as 'workers' or 'peasants'. All ruling communist parties are also predominantly male organizations, especially in their higher reaches (Jancar, 1978, pp. 88–118).

A ruling party's policy on the numbers and types of people it draws into membership is closely bound up with its attempt to provide itself with forms of legitimacy, by incorporation and by co-opting some potential sources of dissent or opposition. Thus, for example, the high membership figures as a proportion of the population in some Eastern European states, such as Romania (15 per cent of the population, or about one adult in five) or Czechoslovakia (10 per cent of the population) do not necessarily indicate greater legitimacy of their regimes. Rather the contrary: party channels serve as conduits of privilege and preferment in an effort to attenuate the regime's relative *un*popularity – in the case of Czechoslovakia, especially, the sense of a foreign-imposed government, and in Romania economic breakdown and hardship for the population.

The problem of 'legitimacy' is not only a matter of trying to forestall major crises which may endanger the regime (which frequently take party leaders by surprise, in any case), but of 'lubricating' the day-to-day local, often informal, minutiae of administration. Another component of this is the system of local government which, although controlled by the party overall, can in many countries be the scene of lively disagreements on particular issues. Since there are many areas of state administration and decision-making (construction plans, for example) which virtually *must* be delegated down to local level to work sensibly, giving some effective power to local representative bodies is useful in several respects. It offers a convenient way of operating national policies while reducing frictions with local sensibilities, it provides easy-to-control outlets for impulses to political life, and it can serve as a 'nursery' for apparatchiks.

Yet the party membership as a whole (except perhaps in some of the very smallest ruling parties) is not a power-wielding group – ruling parties are deeply differentiated internally. (We have already discussed this central point in chapter 12, in connection with Trotsky and Mao's critiques of bureaucracy; neither of them took the party overall as their target.) The most important distinction is between the party membership as a whole, and the much smaller *apparatus*: the party's full-time officials, employed by it and making their careers within it. It is they who organize the party's (partly indirect) control over state administration. For example, out of a total Soviet party membership of 18 million, or about 1 in 15 of the population, the party apparatus is estimated at something between 100,000 and 200,000 persons. This much narrower elite controls – through an elaborate system of dossiers and nominations, the *nomenklatura* – appointments to all important posts. Similar systems operate in other communist states.

It is within this rather highly privileged elite that rival factions and clans form, organize and subdivide, and what political pluralism can be said to exist consists largely of their competition and conflicts. But the apparatus as a whole defends its 'oligopoly' over politics with a sophisticated and flexible system. A patient strategy of large-scale 'co-option', from within the population into the party's ground-level organizations is an important component of this. It forms part of the means which most ruling communist elites have evolved to preserve and renew themselves, and is complemented by others – for example, the use of loose criteria of political conformity in selection for higher education, and hence in recruitment to the educated and controlling strata.

None the less, despite the resilience and experience of their elites, communist societies are prone to fundamental crises, generated (as we shall see in the next chapter) by both internal and external pressures. On the other hand, they have also learned a good deal about how to avoid and, if necessary, survive them.

Possible points of entry into the large literatures on *theories* of communist states and societies are Bellis (1979) or Westoby (1983). Schapiro (1972) illuminates the concept of 'totalitarianism'; Castoriadis (1983) explains his notion of 'stratocracy'.

Ellman's textbook (second edition, 1988) on centrally planned economies has been revised to take account of recent developments. As far as the Soviet Union is concerned, Goldman (1987) highlights the problems facing Gorbachev's economic reformers; Simis (1982), a former Soviet lawyer, analyses corruption and the black market, and their interpenetration with officialdom; and Graham (1987) discusses the relations between science and dialectical materialism. Bell (1974) sets out the notion of 'post-industrialism'.

Holmes (1986) includes a summary overview of coercion and terror in communist states. Of particular studies Conquest's books on Stalin's 'liquidation of the kulaks' (1986) and great purges (1973) are outstanding and moving works. For a recent critique of Western literature on Stalin's purges see Getty (1985). Among writings on elites and privileges in communist societies Lasswell and Lerner (1965) analyse the social backgrounds of communist (and other revolutionary) leaderships; Wiles (1974) compares income distribution between East and West, while Matthews (1978) and McAuley (1979) examine economic inequality in the Soviet Union. Vozlensky (1984) examines the Soviet *nomenklatura* system, and Burns (1987) its Chinese equivalent. Toranska (1987) consists of devastatingly candid interviews, first published in the Polish underground press, with elderly survivors from the very senior ruling communists of the 1950s (including Jakub Berman, Edward Ochab, and Hilary Minc's widow).

Holmes (1981 and 1986) are useful general works on ruling communism. Szajkowski (1981) has edited a three-volume reference work *Marxist Governments: a World Survey*, whose essays on sixteen ruling communist parties are written to a helpful common format. Szajkowski is also the general editor of a 36-volume series on *Marxist Regimes* (being published by Frances Pinter, London, during 1985–90); when complete, this will include a cumulative index volume. The Hoover Institution Press (Stanford, CA) is in progress of publishing a series of monographs, under the general editorship of Richard F. Staar, on the histories of the world's ruling communist parties. Hammond (1975) is a collection of country-studies on the techniques of communist takeovers.

# 15

## Crises of communist states

A communist regime, especially a mature one, is, in Disco's phrase, an impressive example of a 'smart' bureaucracy; that is, one which:

not only pursues the formalized and rule-bound deployment of centralized authority in the tradition of its Weberian ancestors but also senses, theoretically comprehends, plans and selectively reconstructs its particular environment. While doing so it pays particular attention to the effects of its own interventions, utilizing each instance as a learning experience in which to sharpen and streamline future policy. (Disco, 1987, p. 51)

### REFORM AND ITS DANGERS

This is true of areas ranging from ruling parties' strategies for recruitment and self-renewal to their international action. An area where the learning process is especially important is in a party's attempting to 'selectively reconstruct' its economic and social environment, while holding in check the political dangers this raises. As we described in the last chapter, the efforts at economic reform on which Gorbachev has embarked (like its precursors in Eastern Europe and the Soviet Union) need to be complemented by decentralization and relaxations of control over intellectual and social life – measures which can amount to, and be seen as, the first cautious steps of political reform.

Thus the twin programme of *glasnost* (openness) and *perestroika* (restructuring) in the Soviet Union has involved highly significant changes relative to the Brezhnev period. The press has been encouraged to carry much less fettered discussion of party policies and of certain historical questions, particularly from the Stalin period. While orthodoxy continues to be reaffirmed on most matters, major judicial 'rehabilitations', such as those of Bukharin and the 'right opposition' to Stalin, serve as legitimizing signals for the new policies. The press has also been given, in some areas, a free hand to criticize corrupt or intransigent officials – part of a general drive to reform or neutralize bureaucratic fiefdoms by removing some gags on protest against them. The regime has undertaken a concerted effort at reconciliation with the critical or disaffected intelligentsia. Among many motives, Gorbachev wants their support against bureaucratic resistance to his policies, and hopes for a more active and productive interchange with international intellectual life.

Lay associations, for social or cultural purposes, are encouraged. Some have begun to have a real effect; ecological groups, for example, have defeated industrial plans which would have further polluted Lake Baikal. Elections with a plurality of genuine candidates have been introduced for various types of office, principally in enterprise management, local government, and local 'trade union' organizations. These were not 'free' elections in the Western sense since there was no relaxation of the prohibition on political association outside the Communist Party. Indeed the core of Gorbachev's programme of political reform – and its central contradiction – consists in the effort to introduce real competition and a plurality of points of view *within* the party, while preventing any movements from forming that could rival the party. Despite the empathy between them Gorbachev's reforms of the party are in a certain sense the opposite of the 'Eurocommunists'', the difference arising from their quite different environments. Most 'Eurocommunist' leaders have sought to adapt the policies and image of their party to a surrounding political pluralism, while dissolving far less of the advantages they derive from the internal regime. The Soviet reformers, on the other hand, seek to develop forms of democracy (such as competing candidates and secret ballots) *within* the party, and generate greater flexibility and debate in it. By doing so they hope to obviate the problems caused by the general suppression of politics, while heading off political development outside the party and in challenge to it.

The Soviet leadership's caution stems from the forces which – as experience tells them – reforms can release. So far, the main challenges have come from nationalist dissatisfactions within the Soviet Union, the most important being Kazakh resistance to Russian appointments and policies, which triggered riots in Alma Ata in 1986, hostility between Azerbaijanis and Armenians which provoked very large demonstrations in Armenia in 1988, and growing pressures for independence in the Baltic States. But, in promoting elements of political reform within their own frontiers, the Soviet leadership reinforce the pressures for such changes in Eastern Europe – where their ability to graduate and control developments is far less. Inhabiting the dominant state of an informal 'federation', they run the additional danger that their reforms, imitated abroad, may run ahead of what they intend, increasing by example the pressures upon them, or even that reform in Eastern Europe may simply run out of control, producing a major challenge to communist party rule.

Gorbachev's changes are, indeed, being reflected in the Soviet bloc states of Eastern Europe. The initial effect has been strongest in Hungary. There, a trade union association of scientific workers has been allowed to organize as a rival to the official union, and a faction within the party leadership apparently floated the idea (in the run-up to the May 1988 Party congress, at which Kadar was replaced as party leader by Grosz) that the 'leading role' of the party should be reinterpreted, away from meaning a political monopoly, towards the curious – but looser – sense of providing a 'service' for society. But even the more radical reformers are acutely sensitive to the dangers inherent in such ideas. Imre Poszgay, one of those who was promoted to the Hungarian Politburo by the 1988 congress, explained their dilemma rather clearly:

The reason why political reform has always been a very delicate question is that people tend to think in terms of a party system; they conceive of reforms in terms of a liberal democracy. But this approach has two disadvantages. It frightens those people who at present defend the existing political system. And it gives illusions to radical groups. There is one strategic point that you cannot overlook here in this society. Both the internal political situation and our international ties require that any process of change should be based on stability. The level of integration that society has achieved so far should be viewed as a basic precondition and not as something to be destroyed. ... The political reform cannot have another starting point: otherwise it might unleash all sorts of uncontrollable processes. (Kaldor, 1988, p. 21)

I do not attempt, in this chapter, to crystal-ball gaze on future possibilities in Eastern Europe and the Soviet Union. However, by studying past crises of communist party rule (and the attempts at self-reform from which some of them stemmed) we may gain a clearer picture of the reefs through which Gorbachev is trying to negotiate a passage.

### EXTERNAL AND INTERNAL CRISES

As an initial simplification we may distinguish two sources of communist crisis: crises caused by opposition or activity external to the ruling party, by which the legitimacy of communist rule is challenged and its stability threatened, and internal crises of the party. But they are not really distinct types: each may flow into the other, and all past crises exhibit a fascinating interplay between internal and external developments.

The Czechoslovak crisis of 1967–8 started as an internal party matter. It began with the attempts by 'reform' economists to revitalize the economy. But differences in the party leadership became serious and irreconcilable, and produced a relaxation of the regime in which the long-suppressed liberal and social-democratic traditions of Czech politics began to reassert themselves, both within and outside the party. Although the 'Prague spring' unrolled entirely without violence, it soon affected the party to the point that it was unable to reassert its political monopoly on its own, and communist rule was resecured only by the Soviet invasion.

Though the 1956 crises in Poland and Hungary were different in detail and outcome, what they had in common with the Czech crisis were threats to the party from internal disarray. Party leaderships in Eastern Europe were weakened and unsettled by 'de-Stalinization'; this in turn encouraged popular movements of opposition and rebellion, to which divided party leaders reacted with the uncertainty born of weakness; and external pressures then precipitated an 'internal revolution' in the Hungarian and, to a lesser extent, the Polish party.

Mao's 'Cultural Revolution' involved, during its peak, in 1966–8, a crisis of comparable scope, and it also had internal origins. However, they were dissimilar from Eastern European attempts at reform. In late 1965 Mao began an attempt to recapture, purge and galvanize the party bureaucracy, and oust his opponents within the national leadership. But he soon found it necessary to resort to a mass movement, the Red Guards, to attack party officialdom, and their violence generated widespread resistance, particularly in the industrial cities. As a result the authority of the Communist Party centre collapsed in most of China by early 1967.

However, upheaval in a party need not endanger it. One of the greatest of all internal party crises, Stalin's purges of 1936–9, elicited no external opposition remotely capable of challenging either the party or its leader. Nor do crises that threaten the party's rule necessarily divide it. The strike wave in Petrograd in February 1921, and the revolt of the Kronstadt soviet, were fuelled by the same pressures that gave rise to Kollontai's 'Workers' Opposition' within the Bolshevik party – extreme shortage, the visibility of political privilege, and the Bolshevik dictatorship over the unions and left-wing parties. But the party united. The Workers' Opposition, who could have considered themselves vindicated by the revolt against the party, anticipated many later 'reform' communists and protested their loyalty. Their delegates to the Tenth Congress took the lead in urging on Tukhachevsky's assault troops against Kronstadt, and the crisis merely reinforced Lenin's case that political control both inside and outside the party should be tightened.

In Poland in 1980 the formation of Solidarity in the August strikes produced much eddying, but no fundamental division over principles, within the Communist Party. As Solidarity grew into a mass, national movement it in any case attracted all significant opposition and even reforming currents into itself, with the result that the party was left impotent either to project a reforming image in order to regain control, or to effect a crackdown. As a result General Jaruzelski's coup in 1981 had to be organized through the army and under the legal form of a 'state of emergency' – outside and in a sense against the party machine which it later, cautiously, escorted back into power.

These examples (and we could have added a number of others, increasing the variety) remind us that no simple set of models will embrace the crises of communist states. We may provisionally agree with Lenin in defining a revolutionary situation as one in which the existing order is no longer able to rule in the old way. We should further qualify the definition by specifying an inability due mainly to internal causes (i.e. excluding overthrow in war) and one not limited to and resolved within the upper ruling circles (excluding merely leadership coups). It is clear, however, that the incidence of revolutionary crises in communist states is considerably higher than in industrialized 'capitalist' states. Most large-scale movements of industrial workers against the state nowadays occur in the communist world.

An overview yields one further, and more clear-cut, generalization. All popular movements aiming at the overthrow of established communist regimes have – at least so far – failed. There exists not one case in which a consolidated communist state has been removed by internal forces. While communism can generate widespread and bitter hostilities, and lethally deep divisions among its ruling elites, the instabilities and crises thus produced are not fatal for the regime – though they frequently lead to changes of personnel at the head of party and state. Whence come these powers of recuperation?

Communism's powers of recovery rest, paradoxically, in the same conditions that give rise to its abrupt crises. Its successes in stabilizing itself and surviving (frequently while reorganizing its upper leadership) turn on the great extent to which it reinforces the state and concentrates power within it, and the corresponding straitjacket this imposes upon society. But it is these same conditions which make the party-state allergic and vulnerable to major shifts of its relationships with the rest of society. Moreover, because these conditions require the party-state, with rare exceptions, to prohibit substantial organizations forming which are beyond its control, there exist no natural channels down which opposition currents can flow and negotiations with them be conducted. When such currents *do* succeed in taking organizational form, the organizations that result are frequently new-grown in a sudden upsurge, with only primitive differentiation between leaders and led, and rudimentary internal machinery. Often enough, an opposition movement is essentially a vigorous epidemic of similarly named local bodies, their leaders catapulted into their roles by passion and accident, not protracted political experience. Such bodies are not easy partners for communism to negotiate a national crisis with – even if it were disposed to seek a lasting compromise. The lack of conventionally political characteristics also makes them exceptionally vulnerable to the centralized, secret action by which the state protects itself, and makes it difficult for them to respond in kind. Communism, by its monopoly of the state, creates both the conditions that rock it and those that rescue it. Because it seeks to depoliticize society as a whole, what rises up to threaten it (a century after Marx purged the First International of the Bakuninists) has something in common with anarchy; and, conversely, a frequent cry of communism in crisis is that ancient alarm-call of embattled establishments: 'Après moi le déluge!'

## KRONSTADT

Of course, such generalizations immediately need qualifying. But the variations across time and country bring out the general rule. The Kronstadt resistance of 1921, for example, is such a partial exception. In this case, opposition to the Bolshevik monopoly of power gathered *within* part of the existing institutions of the state, the soviet of the Kronstadt naval base, and it was able to lay hands on and briefly defend itself with the established machinery of administration. It therefore proved more difficult for the regime to crush than the more amorphous strike movement in nearby Petrograd that preceded and partly overlapped with it. This exceptional occurrence – a segment of the communist state passing into the hands of the anti-communists – reflected two atypical circumstances:

First, enforcement of the political monopoly of the Bolshevik party leadership was still incomplete (as, indeed, was its doctrine: it was only at the Tenth Party Congress, in session during and under the pressure of the Kronstadt events, that Lenin secured his ban on factions *within* the party). But it had progressed far enough that the communists were able to stop the opposition in Kronstadt spreading or eliciting support elsewhere.

Second, the soviets themselves were the product of a spontaneous revolutionary movement just four years earlier, in February 1917. The Bolsheviks played a significant but still secondary part in the February revolution, whose result was briefly to make Russia (in Lenin's phrase) 'the freest country in the world', and the soviets' structures still reflected something of this. This was peculiarly so in Kronstadt, whose sailors and workers prided themselves on having created an exemplary form of direct, egalitarian democracy, and who sent their delegates as missionaries to soviets in many other parts of Russia in the summer and autumn of 1917, explaining the principles on which they operated. Thus even as late as March 1921 it was possible for the Kronstadt soviet, always suspicious of parties, and now driven by starvation and terror, almost to shrug off Bolshevik rule and resurrect its ultra-democratic but effective tradition of local government. But Kronstadt was quite exceptional; in all other areas soviet democracy had been far more thoroughly crushed, and the Kronstadters were to be bitterly disappointed at the fading of the Petrograd strikes and the failure of other areas to support them. In later anti-communist uprisings no such pre-existing democratic bodies were to hand; they had to be built in the moment of the crisis, and were, consequently, often less well prepared for defending themselves.

Conversely, after the suppression of Kronstadt Lenin and his colleagues embarked on a further tightening of their control over local soviet organizations, and under Stalin's constitution of 1936 even the formal vestiges of the soviets' original character as mass assemblies of workplace representatives were eliminated. True, Russian communism has never abandoned its semantic link with the bodies created in the 1905 and 1917 revolutions, but of subsequent communist regimes only Yugoslavia has followed suit (the Chinese communists dissolved their soviets in 1937 in order to realize the anti-Japanese united front with the Kuomintang). Most communist states have opted for legislatures of a rather conservative formal design, based on European parliamentary traditions. The nearest relatives of the soviets of 1917 in communist states have been bodies set up by their revolutionary opponents: the 'workers' council' movement in Hungary in 1956–7, for example.

The suppression of the Kronstadt revolt served as a prototype for later communist strategies in dealing with opposition in a number of respects. The Bolsheviks' counter-offensive sought to capitalize on the *general* political conditions which they had (or hoped they had) created, identifying opposition to the regime with political and social 'reaction'. Thus Trotsky, Bukharin and Radek inaugurated a long tradition in attributing Kronstadt's reassertion of independence to White generals and French intriguers. To this Bolshevik propaganda added a (quite untrue) 'social' condemnation of the rebels, claiming that the ultra-revolutionary sailors and soldiers of the original Kronstadt garrison, 'sword of the revolution', had been dispersed and killed in the civil war, and their places had been taken with raw peasant lads and 'accidental elements'. It was the latter who had revolted against Soviet power, and had, consequently, to be suppressed, claimed Trotsky and the government press (Getzler, 1983, p. 257).

RETREATS AND MANOEUVRES

Branding opposition as the work of malign or foreign agents is not always possible. Sometimes it is necessary to negotiate, or appear to negotiate, or even temporarily to give way – accepting, therefore, that opposition at least reflects legitimate grievances, and perhaps even suggesting that the party might cohabit with it. However, such a position is not, in the long term, consistent with a communist monopoly of power. Thus the two stances are often – if contradictorily – combined, the essential purpose being to split the opposition.

This occurs even when extreme violence is being used. After the second Soviet attack on Budapest, in November 1956, it took almost two weeks of bitter fighting before their armoured forces controlled most of the city. Yet Krushchev and Kadar continued to combine concessions, even the promise of negotiations on basic institutions, with their 'war on reactionaries'. Kadar and the Soviet commanders recognized the authority of the 'Central Workers' Council' that led the strike movement, to the point of issuing special passes allowing the members of the Council to travel about freely after the curfew, and even to carry weapons. Kadar's premature attempt to arrest the members of the Council in December was answered by a 48-hour general strike, 'the like of which has never before been seen in the history of the Hungarian workers' movement', as even the Communist Party press described it. Repression could be stepped up only gradually. In November Hungarians were liable for the death penalty for carrying arms; in December, for striking; by January, for distributing leaflets. It was only as late as November 1957 that the government felt it safe to cancel its earlier recognition of the workers' councils by formally dissolving them – although in reality they had ceased to function months before. The combination of political stances shifted in line with repression, but implausibly and often incongruously. As the slogan on the wall of one of Budapest's largest factories wryly put it: 'The forty thousand aristocrats and fascists of the Czepel works strike on!' (Lasky, 1957, p. 233). Or, as Kadar explained to the National Assembly in May 1957, 'If the wish of the masses does not coincide with progress, then one must lead the masses in another direction' (Lomax, 1976, p. 196).

Often a more practical ploy within a general strategy aiming to drain support away from opposition movements is to accompany political repression with economic concessions. This is exactly what Lenin – acting on his low estimation of workers' 'economism' – did in launching the New Economic Policy after the Kronstadt revolt. Thus one of the main demands of the Kronstadters – that peasants be allowed to bring grain and other foods to sell freely in the towns – was largely conceded even as those who had raised it were being shot or shipped to labour camps. That general strategy has been many times repeated in Eastern Europe and in dealing with outbreaks of resistance in the post-war Soviet Union. Resources can almost always be found to raise living standards in the short term, and if the active oppositionists can be isolated or repressed, economic concessions can be withdrawn or eroded in the longer term. Whatever undertakings may be given at the time, the greater cohesion and longer time-horizon of the party-state, together with a capacity for political manoeuvre that a mass movement cannot match, can give it a decisive advantage in 'retreating in order to

advance'. However, it *is* possible for the repeated use of economic concessions to backfire on the regime – as they did in Poland in the 1976 and 1980
strikes – encouraging workers to threaten the authorities with potentially
political challenges in order to win economic improvements.

## INTERNATIONALISM

Often, communism's chief advantage is its capacity to act internationally,
while the movements that oppose it remain limited within national boundaries. This allows it – as it has several times done in post-war Eastern
Europe – to use or threaten to use overwhelming military force. Krushchev's
resolution of the linked crises in Poland and Hungary in 1956 turned on
precisely this advantage. The uprising in Poznan in June, and the looser
strike movement which followed it, generated a profound crisis of the
Polish party leadership, exacerbated during September–October by the
spread of workers' councils. By the middle of October Gomulka, trading on
his reputation as a victim of Stalinism, had been restored as party leader.
He retained his position by threatening, in effect, to resist with the Polish
armed forces should Krushchev apply military pressure, and Krushchev,
who then flew to Warsaw along with most of the Soviet Politburo, retreated
and endorsed Gomulka.

But there was a condition. Gomulka undertook to restore the Polish
domestic situation as far as possible to normal, and in particular he was to
give Krushchev a free hand in Hungary by preventing any coalescing of the
Polish and Hungarian movements. In this he was successful. Poland
seethed at the second Soviet intervention in Hungary, but did not threaten
to become a 'second front', and Krushchev could lean on Gomulka as he
sent in his forces to destroy Nagy. The Polish party leadership's main efforts
during the Hungarian crisis aimed at restraining 'rabble-rousing' and 'anti-
soviet agitation' in the interests of 'Polish *raison d'état*' (Dziewanowski,
1976, pp. 282–3). The communist leaders employed the same threat in the
1957 elections, in which they made the concession of allowing more than
one candidate for a number of seats: 'Deletion of our party's candidates',
Gomulka warned, 'is synonymous with obliterating Poland from the map
of Europe' (Staar, 1982, p. 158). Communist leaderships in the Soviet bloc
were severely fractured in 1956, but when the chips were down they
managed to act within a common strategy. This included Tito, who was
closely identified with the various 'reform' currents set in motion by the
Twentieth CPSU Congress in the other Eastern European leaderships,
including Nagy in Hungary. None the less he acceded to Krushchev's pleas
and supported Soviet action in Hungary, and shortly afterwards handed

over Nagy and his supporters (who sought asylum in the Yugoslav embassy in Budapest) to the KGB and eventual execution.

Even more important in Eastern Europe than Leninism's ability to cooperate across large differences, and join in dividing and overcoming its enemies, has been the sheer military weight of the Soviet Union. In times of crisis the communist party-state shows itself to be far more than a national state, being able to deal with its own society by calling upon 'bodies of armed men' (as Engels characterized the essence of state power) from beyond its own borders. Internationalism gives state power a decisive advantage, and the outcome of every major crisis in Eastern Europe since the war has been determined by Soviet military force or the threat of it. Soviet tanks quelled the East German strikes of June 1953. In 1956 they crushed the Hungarian revolution, while Gomulka held the Poles who would have supported it at bay with the threat that, if they did not restrain themselves, the same would happen in Poland. When the Dubček leadership found itself adrift in the 'Prague spring' of 1968, and the Soviet leadership sent in the armies of the other Warsaw Pact states, Gomulka's Poland contributed 50,000 troops to the invasion force, the largest contingent after the Red Army. The Czech party initially served as the main channel of protest, but also as the main advocate of restraint, and in due course provided the personnel of a new collaborationism.

In Poland, it is true, foreign troops have not been used against internal resistance since 1947 (though the Defence Minister in charge of the Polish armed forces from 1949 to 1956, the years of Gomulka's disgrace, was a Soviet marshal – Konstantin Rossokovski, the hero of Stalingrad, but also the commander who kept Soviet forces halted on the Vistula during the Warsaw rising). To Poland, one-sixth of whose population died as the result of Nazi and Soviet invasions, the threat of external force has been a potent one in all the post-war crises – not only the 1956 crisis, but the student demonstrations in March 1968 (an echo of the Czechoslovak movement); the strikes of December–January 1969–70, which evicted Gomulka; those of June 1976, which forced Gierek to withdraw his food price rises; the escalating strike movement of July–August 1980, provoked by further increases in food prices, which culminated in the formation of Solidarity and the fall of Gierek; and Jaruzelski's coup of December 1981, in which the Polish military command succeeded in taking the population by surprise, and rescued an isolated and paralysed party.

## WESTERN ATTITUDES

All the outbreaks of opposition to communist rule in Europe have been undercut by one other international factor, though it is facilitative rather than active. The governments, and most of the political leaders, of all the Western Powers have consistently adopted a hands-off stance, accepting the political relations imposed by the Soviet Union under the Yalta agreements, limiting themselves in the main to rhetorical protest at Soviet or Soviet-backed repression and accepting – for all their protests – Eastern European governments as legitimate. The one serious attempt by Western governments to topple an Eastern European communist regime was that mounted by Britain and the United States against Enver Hoxha in Albania in 1950–2. But it was based on slender internal support (it contemplated the restoration of the exiled King Zog), and relied heavily on parachuting forces in from outside; it was therefore quite easily destroyed when it came to be supervised by the British intelligence officer Kim Philby, then one of the Soviet Union's most valued agents.

Where large-scale opposition or resistance movements against communism have developed, the attitude of Western governments, since the war, has been at best lukewarm, at worst hostile. In the closing stages of the war Soviet forces were struggling to contain nationalist partisans in subsidiary wars in the Ukraine, Byelorussia and the Baltic states, and a two-year armed struggle was beginning in Poland. The Western Allies carefully refrained from suggesting that the principles for which the war had ostensibly been waged might apply to these struggles. More, they acquiesced in Stalin's mass transportations of peoples (motivated in part by his wish to eliminate internal resistance) and even assisted by handing over large numbers of people to the Soviet and Yugoslav forces. One result was to swell greatly the population of the Soviet Union's labour camps, and to introduce into them many rebellious new prisoners, including a large number with military experience. Before Stalin's death there were major revolts in Kolyma in the Siberian Far East in 1946 and in Vorkuta in 1948. In 1950, when Western forces were thrusting into North Korea, the Soviet authorities made preparations to liquidate as many prisoners in the Kolyma complex as possible, if they attempted to rebel and join up with Western forces; at about the same time there was a further rising in Vorkuta. With eight million or more people held in slave-labour camps, the danger of coordinated rebellion was one of Stalin's nightmares, but the camps were always treated by the Western Powers as a Soviet 'internal' problem.

Much the same attitudes have been applied to the struggles in Eastern Europe since Stalin's death. In June 1953 strikes began among building workers in the Soviet sector of Berlin, with goals which started as economic but which quickly extended to the call for free elections, and snowballed into a general strike movement throughout Eastern Germany. The occupation authorities in West Berlin joined the West German social democrats in calling for 'restraint', prevented strike leaders from broadcasting over the Western radio services, and sealed the boundary to prevent West Berliners who wished to support the strike from crossing into the eastern sector. In the October 1956 crisis Eisenhower sent private assurances to Moscow (through Tito) that NATO would not intervene against Soviet military action in Hungary; the Anglo-French-Israeli invasion of Egypt then completed Krushchev's freedom of action in Budapest. Johnson sent similar assurances to Brezhnev in August 1968: that he would respect the Yalta–Potsdam division of Europe into spheres of influence; and after the invasion of Czechoslovakia Western governments readily acceded to Dubček's request (agreed under duress while he was a captive in Moscow) that the UN drop the matter. Moreover, in none of the post-war crises of Soviet intervention in Eastern Europe did the Western Powers make any significant use of advance intelligence information to warn against, and try to abort, Soviet intentions.

THE EROSION OF COMMUNIST COHESION

As well as the advantages of a greater array of military force, communism's international coercive action can also reduce the danger of troops becoming infected by the movements they are required to repress; using foreign soldiers helps establish distance and allows greater discipline and brutality. Even Soviet soldiers, however, are not immune to revolution: those used in the first Soviet intervention in Hungary in October 1956 had been stationed in the country some time, and there were many cases of disobedience and fraternization, with a few even changing sides and fighting with the rebels. These forces were withdrawn, and the second Soviet intervention used fresh troops from outside Hungary, some from the Soviet Asian republics, who were told they were being sent to counter a US invasion. Moreover, the commanders of the second intervention took the precaution of first bombarding Budapest with artillery and tank fire.

Fraternization by troops is just one form of a more general problem for ruling communism: that of political pressures working within the party-state machine, dissolving its discipline and unravelling its unity. This, too, is often an international process; we see it at work very clearly if we look in a little more detail at the political evolution of the 1953–6 crises in Eastern Europe and the Soviet Union.

The national party leaderships, so recently tempered and disciplined by the purges and trials of 1948–53, were thrown into flux in 1953–6 by the divisions in the Soviet party following Stalin's death. One element of the situation was Soviet leaders seeking to consolidate their own bases of support by intervening in Eastern European parties. But more generally, uncertainty and weakness encouraged political relaxation and effervescence in the satellite state, both within and outside the communist parties. Consequently divisions in Eastern Europe were not neat reflections of those among their Soviet patrons; they principally reflected domestic pressures. In any case, in so far as the divisions among the Soviet leaders turned on differences over policy, that meant policy in a global context.

When Stalin died in March 1953, he was initially replaced not by his expected successor, Malenkov, alone but – after brief skirmishing – by a loose and divided triumvirate: Malenkov as the leading figure within the state and government apparatuses; Krushchev, whose zone of patronage rested mainly in party organizations; and Beria, head of the security apparatuses. After Stalin's death Beria merged and briefly controlled the Ministry of Internal Affairs, the MVD (by this time a vast economic ministry controlling the forced labour industries and most of Siberia) and the more specifically repressive functions of the Ministry for State Security (MGB).* But Krushchev persuaded the other leaders that Beria was far too dangerous to them all. With the aid of the army he was arrested in June, and secretly tried and shot in December. However, Krushchev did not achieve clear primacy until some time later, when Malenkov was removed in February 1955.

The East German rising in June 1953 was the most important, but by no means the only, outbreak triggered by Stalin's death. Early in June there were strikes in over 100 Czechoslovak factories, mainly against currency reform, which abolished rationing of basic goods and raised their prices, as well as devaluing personal savings; troops had to be sent from Prague to

---

* A long series of changing titles has covered similar functions. The first Soviet internal security force was the Cheka (All-Russian Extraordinary Commission for Combating Counter-revolution and Sabotage), formed in December 1917, and headed by Dzerzhinsky. In 1922 the Cheka was replaced by the GPU (State Political Directorate), a division of the NKVD (People's Commissariat of Internal Affairs). With the federation of the Soviet republics to form the USSR in 1923 the GPU became the OGPU (Unified State Political Directorate) and was detached from the NKVD. When Dzerzhinsky died in 1926 he was succeeded as head of the OGPU by V. R. Menzhinsky. When Menzhinsky died, in 1934, Stalin converted the OGPU into the GUGB (Chief Directorate for State Security) and reabsorbed it into the NKVD, appointing Menzhinsky's deputy, G. G. Yagoda, to head the latter. Yagoda was shot in 1936 and was replaced by N. I. Yezhov. Yezhov was shot in 1938 and replaced by L. P. Beria.

As a result of collectivization and the purges, the NKVD came to administer a large economic sector, mainly of forced labour. In 1941, therefore, the GUGB was again transformed into an independent agency, the NKGB (People's Commissariat for State Security) under Beria's protégé, V. N. Merkulov, while Beria continued to head the NKVD. In 1946 both organizations became ministries – the NKGB became the MGB (Ministry for State Security), headed by Merkulov, and the NKVD became the MVD (Ministry for Internal Affairs), headed by S. N. Kruglov – and Beria joined the Politburo. After Stalin's death, in 1953, Beria succeeded in merging the MGB and MVD under his own control, but was arrested with the aid of the army. A further reorganization then created, in 1954, the present KGB (Committee for State Security), responsible for internal security, frontiers, and most overseas intelligence work – though it continued to share the last area with the military intelligence organization, the GRU (Chief Intelligence Directorate), originally formed from a division of the Cheka in 1920. The MGB's powers to try and sentence were transferred to the courts. In 1973 Yuri Andropov, head of the KGB, became a full member of the Politburo, and in 1982 he succeeded Brezhnev as party leader.

disperse a demonstration of over 20,000 workers from the Skoda complex at Pilsen. At about the same time there were strikes in Romania, and 20,000 steel workers in Budapest struck for wage increases, gaining a partial victory; there were similar struggles in eastern Hungary and peasant demonstrations in the great plains. In late July the movement touched the Soviet Union itself, when a mass strike broke out in the camps of the Vorkuta mining complex in Siberia. On 1 August 120 strike leaders were shot, yet the strike continued. Though it was finally broken by force, the Malenkov–Krushchev leadership began releasing prisoners from the camps, thereby heightening the conditions of 'thaw' and criticism in the cities.

In Hungary the Soviet leaders were already intervening. In late June 1953 (that is, following the German strikes, and at the time Beria was arrested) they clipped the authority of Rakosi, Hungary's 'little Stalin'. Though he kept control of the party organization he was replaced as prime minister by Imre Nagy, a demotee of the 1949 purges. The economic aspects of Nagy's 'new course' – increases in consumption and real wages, a shorter working week, more scope for private farming and small businesses – were a clear bid for greater popular acceptability and were also carried out in milder forms elsewhere: Romania, Bulgaria, Czechoslovakia, Poland, East Germany and areas of the Soviet Union. But the lifting of political repression was particularly dramatic in Hungary; it brought the release of about 100,000 prisoners, whose accounts did much to fuel demands for a settlement with those who had organized the purges. Nagy's first period in office was a short one; he was removed early in 1955 as a result of the ending of the Soviet 'new course' and Krushchev's ousting of Malenkov; but he had opened Pandora's box.

In Germany, however, the divisions in the Soviet leadership had quite different results. There is some evidence that Beria formed part of a current in the Soviet leadership that favoured negotiations with the West for German reunification, with a guarantee of military neutrality as a *quid pro quo*. Such a move would have demolished Ulbricht's ruling apparatus in East Germany; reports speak of SED officials expecting at that time to have to return into opposition. This, plus the knowledge that he was dealing with a divided leadership in Moscow, may be the explanation for Ulbricht's action in early June (surprising, on the face of it) in refusing Soviet suggestions that he should slow 'forced industrialization', improve living standards, and allow greater scope for private businesses. In any event, the rising of 17 June put an end to experimentation, forcing the Soviet leaders to rescue and re-establish Ulbricht, and give their backing to his crackdown on opposition; they arrested Beria shortly afterwards. However, those who arrested him flew a kite for an even more extensive deal – free all-German elections, and the withdrawal of all foreign troops from both Germany and Poland – in February 1955, immediately before Malenkov's dismissal.

If this sketch of the German events is essentially accurate, it provides a striking example of the difficulty of analysing communist 'liberalization' initiatives. Beria's record was, to say the least, not that of a 'liberal'; he was, under Stalin, the executor of some of the largest enslavements and exterminations in human history. Similarly, later Soviet leaders who have launched reforms, such as Krushchev and Gorbachev, have placed themselves in a position to do so only by lengthy and skilful conformity with the evils which they later, from the top, attacked.

None the less, in 1953–6, opposition currents and moods did reach deep into some ruling parties. The strikes and demonstrations in East Germany, for example, involved large numbers of party members (as well as a few demonstrators who sang 'Deutschland, Deutschland über alles'). Afterwards, Ulbricht was forced to organize a major membership purge in which over a third of those removed had been Communist Party members *before* Hitler came to power in 1933. In Hungary, Nagy's first period in office left a foment which the restored Rakosi was unable to still. Nagy had filled many senior state and party posts with people who had been sent to labour camps in the purges, and even after he and his faction were removed, vigorous oppositional discussion continued within the party, especially the 'Petofi circles' of the communist youth organization in Budapest. Later, as details of Krushchev's admissions about Stalin filtered out in the spring of 1956 they encouraged and accelerated similar developments in other countries. In Czechoslovakia, for example, the Congress of the Writers' Union in April 1956 became a platform for demands for reform, and the lower reaches of the legal non-communist parties (subordinated to the Communist Party in the National Front since 1948) began to revive; in May the communist leadership formally restricted the permitted number of members of the other parties (Kaplan, 1986, p. 46).

## REFORM COMMUNISM

In 1953–6, in most of Eastern Europe, politics forced its way *into* the party; the same was broadly true of the Czechoslovak 'thaw' of 1967–8. No national organizations were able to form which rivalled the party. Political life developed within the increasingly fictitious framework of a single, united party; communist parties came therefore, to include organized currents that in freer conditions would have formed natural parts of social democratic, liberal or nationalist parties, as well as currents who were essentially loyal to the communist monopoly of power, but who favoured a reforming stance as a means of heading off or co-opting external opposition, keeping it within a loosened communist dominion. The proposals and rhetoric of the two types were often closely similar, and there was much overlap between them. They are, therefore, not easily distinguishable – even in the motives of participants. Imre Nagy formed a government with a majority of non-communists (Smallholders and social democrats), and announced Hungary's withdrawal from the Warsaw Pact, at the end of October 1956. None the less he was contemplating a mass round-up of 'anti-soviet' elements a few days later, on the eve of the second Soviet intervention and in a vain attempt to forestall it. But later, in Russian captivity, he refused to debase himself by the 'self-criticism' which could have saved his life, and was hanged in 1958.

The interpenetration of 'reform' communism with democratic currents is often an ingredient in the former's rescue of the regime in times of crisis. Yet, together, they express the central dilemma of a ruling communist party in trying to depoliticize society and keep it depoliticized: the more successful it is in preventing the articulation of demands outside itself, the greater the pressure which it builds up for conflicting interests to crystallize *within* the party, with their consequent threats to the organization's cohesion and the leaders' control. Of course, this heuristic 'trade-off' could only operate in a neat manner if other things were equal, which they never are. In particular, the internal conditions and the history of each party strongly influence its will and ability to restrict discussion and politics beyond its boundaries. Moreover, the forces for and against relaxation are never so simple as, for example, the balance between 'technicians' and economic functionaries (conventionally thought to favour relaxation) and those responsible for ideology and organization (conventionally thought to view it with suspicion). Personal experience and ethical dispositions, as well as practical functions, become active factors. The 'reform' communisms of 1953–6 were fundamentally conditioned by the experience of the purges *within* the party, preferring for their leaders men – like Nagy and Gomulka – who had suffered in Stalin's last years, discovering their martyrs and precedents among those he executed, and recoiling from the use of force to resolve political disputes. Under such leaders, a party may well draw much of any sudden release of political energy into itself.

When, however, another movement or organization appears as a serious alternative to the communist party, it tends to drain political interest and ferment towards itself, and away from the party. Such was the case with Poland's Solidarity in 1980. Originating in the strikes in the Baltic ports, Solidarity rapidly formed itself into a national organization, growing to 3.5 million members in its first month of existence. In deference to Poland's 'geopolitical' situation the Solidarity leadership took, in the main, the position that it was a trade union and a social, but not a political organization, and refrained from themselves questioning the 'leading role' of the Communist Party or Poland's 'friendship' with the Soviet Union. They limited themselves to the demand that the authorities negotiate with Solidarity on domestic matters, and that independent organizations be allowed to exist and supervise the settlements reached. This last demand reflected their accumulated sense of betrayal at the hands of 'reforming' communist leaders; by 1980 in Poland, no one seriously looked to another Gomulka or Dubček. But, whatever the Solidarity leaders' formal self-denial of politics, the very existence of such an organization brought about a massive revival of popular political discussion, within and around it.

The effect of political relaxation on the party was consequently quite different. The Polish party was deeply fissured, but they were the fissures of paralysis. The democratization of party structures and elections, which by the spring of 1981 was causing such official alarm from the Soviet and Czech leaderships, was perceived as less important in Poland itself, mainly because it had become clear how little genuine support the party had. When an opinion poll in the autumn of 1980 asked Poles what party they would vote for in free elections, just 3 per cent gave the Communist Party; and when a further poll in June 1981 asked what institution they most trusted, the Church came first, Solidarity second, and the army a surprising third, while the party came fifteenth, lower than the police (Garton Ash, 1985, p. 175). No party 'reform' current could make great headway under such conditions; the mould had been broken. Party factions competed over their ability to manouevre *vis-à-vis* Solidarity, but none was able to reduce or subordinate it. Consequently the re-establishment of the party's monopoly of power required an army coup, outside the main party-state machinery.

Even when it is accomplished within national boundaries, the restoration of communist rule, like its unwinding, is often an international development in the sense that it turns on specific international conditions. The ease of Jaruzelski's coup, for example, turned on there being a regime in the Soviet Union that most Poles believed would, *in extremis*, be prepared to commit force to securing communist rule in Poland. Of the Brezhnev leadership, even in his last years, this remained true. But Gorbachev's reform programme has opened up a quite different situation, one in which communist leaders in Eastern Europe, faced with popular movements of opposition, will have a far less plausible spectre of Soviet force with which to ward off danger; after all, all Gorbachev's interventions in Eastern European communist parties have been directed at shifting them in a more reform-minded direction.

What is equally important is that the potential instability this introduces can easily feed back. A communist regime in crisis in Eastern Europe, requiring Soviet military force to stay in power, would face Gorbachev with an acute dilemma: to use troops in Eastern Europe but torpedo his domestic reform efforts, or not to do so and risk the collapse of Soviet dominion over Eastern Europe. Either way, his own position would be extremely vulnerable. Intervention in Eastern Europe would require a wider and far more conservative coalition within the party and military apparatuses, a coalition of which Gorbachev would be, at best, a political prisoner. Refusal to intervene, apart from its 'domino' effect, could create the conditions for a successful coalition, possibly through a military coup, against him, restoring communist control abroad and a further variant of communist Bonapartism at home, the army rescuing the party from its self-created impasse.

The dilemma reminds us how artificial it can be to think in terms of sovereign nation-states. The communist regimes of Eastern Europe remain in power only as a result of Soviet protection; in that sense the Soviet Union and Eastern Europe form a combined complex of state power. In the past, the existence of independent states in Eastern Europe has allowed the communist parties which Stalin placed in power in the 1940s to adjust better to the changing pressures of their own national circumstances. But when Soviet communism, forty years later, attempts its own major process of adjustment, its 'delegation' of state power proves to have formed, at its periphery, inflexibilities and potential sites of crisis for the whole system. (Moreover, Eastern Europe is not the only potential source of dangerous 'feedback'. The immediate impact of political examples – unlike economic ones – means that pressures for political reform in China and the Soviet bloc can even reinforce each other.)

Yet the dilemma is fundamental, since the pressures towards reform lie not in political choices but in basic developments of the world economy. Gorbachev's domestic programme rests on a delicate equilibrium: shaking up many of the habits and interests of established state and party bureaucracies, reducing, stepwise, dangerous concentrations of power, trying to invest the apparatus with greater sensitivity, flexibility and popularity, while still preserving its monopoly of rule and its essential self-confidence. Such changes cannot be produced by central directives. The attempt to achieve them undermines bureaucratic bases of power, and generates a need for independent popularity; Gorbachev's travels and speeches within the Soviet Union have made him seem, sometimes, like a Western politician seeking election. That he was forced in 1987 to dismiss one of his closest supporters in the Politburo, Boris Yeltsin, merely for criticizing the opponents of reform too energetically (and, moreover, to dismiss him in the old manner, complete with humiliating self-criticism) was an index of how precarious Gorbachev felt his position within the party apparatus to be.

Under certain circumstances communist leaders *have* stepped outside the party to mobilize support against the apparatus – Mao in his Cultural Revolution, for example. But for Gorbachev, like Dubček and other apparatus-bred 'reform' communists, this is very unlikely. They emerge from invisible clan warfare in the upper reaches of the party, not from revolutionary or war leadership. The policies they speak for prevent them developing a Stalin-style personality cult; and, for similar reasons, they are not likely to be able to turn to the armed forces to overcome domestic opposition.

When major forces independent of the ruling party manage to form, or the party itself evolves in such a way that its ability to maintain its political monopoly begins to unravel, then communism can no longer continue to rule in its 'normal' way, and it is accurate to speak of a revolutionary or pre-revolutionary crisis. However, not all fundamental crises fit these types. Ruling communist parties are also subject to violent convulsions which do not mainly reflect pressures from society, but have more internal causes. In their 'pure' form these occur simply as purges: the leader's or leading faction's destruction of competitors, actual or potential, real or imagined. With purges, as with reform movements, the party's continuity with the wider society tends to carry the process beyond its boundaries. Stalin's purges of the late 1930s, and those of 'Tito-Trotskyites' in Eastern Europe from 1948, were all principally directed at alleged enemies within the party, but they cast long shadows beyond it. One important function this served was to give the party a measure of self-protection; by also traumatizing society at large it ran less risk of being threatened from outside during its violent self-reconstruction. Purges, however, like reform movements, may also overflow the limits of the party in a different sense, if the authors of the purge take the dangerous step of summoning up external forces to push through their drive within the party. The greatest of such hybrid crises was Mao's 'Great Proletarian Cultural Revolution'.

The Cultural Revolution resembled Stalin's purges in that it involved an attack upon a generation of revolutionary leaders now settled in bureaucratic power, and also in that it changed the substance of political life by much less than its claims would imply. Its closer antecedents, however, lay in the Chinese Communist Party's previous movements of mass mobilization since it took power in 1949, some of which involved the Party's deliberately unleashing popular energies beyond anything seen up to that time in Eastern Europe or the Soviet Union. The 'hundred flowers' movement in 1956, for example, followed close upon (and was in part an attempt to compensate for) the four-year 'campaign for the remoulding of intellectuals'. But it took on a vigorous momentum of its own and in 1957 had to be corrected in turn, in the mass repression of the 'anti-rightist campaign', in which about 400,000 people were punished.

There was another major difference from Stalin's purges. The Cultural Revolution was propelled by the efforts of a displaced revolutionary leader to regain overall command. In the early 1960s Mao continued to be publicly venerated, but was actually rather isolated in the upper reaches of the party. His economic 'Great Leap Forward' (a campaign aiming at break-neck industrialization through small-scale plants in the countryside) over-reached itself and collapsed in 1959–60. (It was, in fact, a social catastrophe; later demographic data showed that it caused upwards of sixteen million deaths.) Mao's highly personal method, with its bold thrusts, opaque compromises and violent internal shake-ups – essential parts of the party's route to power – were intolerable to an administrative hierarchy fifteen years removed from revolution. Mao was acceptable as a figurehead but not as a peacetime leader; by 1965 he felt himself, as his revealing phrase had it, 'alone with the masses'. The Cultural Revolution was Mao's response to this situation – an assault, in which he was supported by a relatively tiny faction of senior figures, on the established party apparatus, principally full-time officials. It was not an attack on the party at large, but rather drew rank-and-file members into its campaigns. Yet, being aimed at the actual apparatus of power, it came near to destroying the party as a functioning machine.

The international situation was important. Foreign policy and strategic problems gripped the party and People's Liberation Army leaders in early 1965, during the suspension of Sino-Soviet polemics that followed the over-throw of Krushchev in October 1964, and under the pressure of US bombing of North Vietnam from February 1965. It was brought to a head when Brezhnev and Kosygin proposed Soviet air bases in south China to support the Vietnamese. Should China (as Lo Jui-ching, the People's Liberation Army chief of staff, argued) realign towards Moscow and Hanoi against Washington, resuming a partly subordinate place under the Soviet nuclear umbrella? Or should she keep her distance from Moscow, consequently seeking at least a tacit agreement with the Johnson administration to limit the Vietnam war, and rely for defence on 'people's war', using her vast reserves of manpower (by the methods popularized by Mao's lieutenant, Defence Minister Lin Piao, in 'Long live the victory of people's war!'). By November 1965, following the coup in Indonesia the previous month, which destroyed the Indonesian Communist Party, and left Communist China more isolated than at any time before, the Lin–Mao line had won out, Lo Jui-ching had disappeared from view, and a tacit *modus vivendi* existed with Washington. The Cultural Revolution thus had cautious international premises.

To begin with Mao employed classical 'salami' tactics, taking his blade first to Wu Han, the playwright and deputy mayor of Peking. From there it moved to his supporters among the Peking literati, and thence to the Peking party machine, under Peng Chen. At the May 1966 Politburo meeting, with Liu Shao-chi absent and Chou En-lai and Deng Xiaoping supporting him, Mao obtained a complete purge of Peng and his Peking supporters, and a party 'circular' warned against 'those representatives of the bourgeoisie who have sneaked into the Communist Party', who 'wave red flags to oppose the red flag', and against their 'bourgeois slogan' that 'everybody is equal before the truth'. The effect was to expose the bigger figures of the party machine who, by abandoning Peng, had exposed themselves. But for this forces outside the party were needed, and these Mao found among the students – especially those from peasant families who, brought up in countryside schools, and often selected for higher education by political rather than educational criteria, found academic work most difficult. Students formed the core constituents of the early Red Guards detachments.

The Red Guard movement which spread through much of China during the second half of 1966, 'criticizing' and assaulting 'capitalist roaders', was fuelled by free rail transport for 'Red Guards', and the suspension of schooling; their victims included numerous unpopular teachers. In fact the local movements were extremely heterogeneous, all claiming adherence to 'the thought of Chairman Mao', but often manipulated by local influential figures. Moreover they generated a large backlash in many areas, frequently where party officials, their local organization threatened with disintegration, made common cause with workers, who felt their economic conditions threatened; Red Guards often denounced wage requests as the work of the 'class enemy'.

But Mao and his group retained, and exploited to the full, two additional advantages. First, none of his victims (like so many of Stalin's) ever felt able to attack him directly; nearly all the polemics were conducted between rival 'true' exponents of Mao Tse-tung thought. Secondly Mao retained, as many of the party and state organizations disintegrated, command over both the army and Kang Sheng's security services.

The general strike in Shanghai in January 1967 formed a climax. It was after the Maoists (Red Guards stiffened by army and Security Service units) had broken the strike that public 'struggle', in mass kangaroo courts, was joined against the most senior 'capitalist roaders', such as Liu Shao-chi. Another huge confrontation developed at Wuhan, a large industrial conurbation on the inland Yangtze, in the summer of 1967. The local garrison rebelled, and, defying Chou's direct instructions, supported the industrial workers against the Red Guards. It took Lin Piao, with a vast military force, a fortnight to subdue the city. In the following weeks heavy fighting was also reported in Canton, hundreds of buildings were razed in Chengtu, and in Szechwan province rival Red Guards fought with tanks and artillery, all in the name of Mao.

The process was running out of control, and the 'Great Helmsman' leaned further on the army to effect a reaction. The 'leftists' of the Cultural Revolution Group (with the exception of Chiang Ching) were themselves purged in late August 1967, and the People's Liberation Army was set to 'helping' students return to their studies. Where some Maoists finally turned against their idol they were violently put down, as in Canton and in a four-month war in Kwangsi, in which 50,000 were reported killed. There were public executions of 'anarchists', 'hoodlums' and 'Kuomintang agents' – the Maoists of the first hour. Conversely, the drive to restore central state power brought a systematic rehabilitation of party officials, who were now said to be '95 per cent of them ... good or comparatively good'.

Officially, the Cultural Revolution lasted for ten more years. (Hua Guo-feng declared it completed in 1977, after Mao's death and the arrest of the 'Gang of Four'.) But the main crisis subsided during 1968. In the course of it Mao and his shifting faction had turned the party upside down, while keeping urban Chinese society in turmoil with an unprecedented combination of violence, bombast and confusion. It is more difficult, however, to say what Mao's grouping expressed as against the main, more settled, body of the party bureaucracy. One factor was independence of the Soviet Union. This had been a constant of Mao's career since 1927. The Cultural Revolution began with the defeat of those in the party leadership who hoped for some reconciliation following Krushchev's departure; as it developed it subjected vast numbers of people to the accusation of being a supporter of 'Soviet imperialism'; and later it nailed some of its own early leaders (most prominently Lin Piao) to the same cross. Moreover, for all its sanguinary rhetoric, it proved to lead quite easily into the US–Chinese rapprochement being negotiated by Chou En-lai and Kissinger in 1971–2.

Domestic pressures were even more important. The Cultural Revolution released a large, pent-up hostility to the rigidities and privileges of communist rule. It served, thus, as an unprecedented engine for settling scores and for individual mobility – particularly for students, but for other sections of the urban population as well. The extreme case was Wang Hung-wen, a Shanghai textile foreman who 'rose like a helicopter' to become number three in the Politburo and later one of the Gang of Four. Yet, like Stalin's purges, the Cultural Revolution liquidated bureaucrats, but not bureaucracy. In fact the reconstruction of the state apparatus after 1968 left intact the same hierarchy of thirty grades of state officialdom that had been laid down in 1956.

But Mao and his 'Great Proletarian Cultural Revolution' were perhaps also backward-looking in a more profound sense. There was a fairly consistent thread to Mao's policies once in power, one continuous with peasant revolution and 'surrounding the cities from the countryside': a suspicion, even hostility, towards urbanization and the growth of a large, settled industrial working class. Mao's 'Great Leap Forward' foundered in 1959, principally on its efforts to make the countryside industrially self-sufficient, with steel-furnaces in rural backyards, but still in 1963 Po I-po (then head of economic planning, and later a prominent figure of the Cultural Revolution) was declaring that China's urban population should be *reduced* by 20 million to 110 million. And one of the bitterest sources of workers' resentment against Maoism during the Cultural Revolution was the Mao-inspired system of 'contract' workers, aimed at cutting labour costs. Peasants were sent by their communes to work in the cities, but on lower pay and with no welfare or trade union benefits, the workers they replaced being 'assigned' to the remote countryside.

By the 1960s China's officialdom were, in their majority, rooted in and content with a conventional pattern of urban industrialization. But it is as though Mao's faction – like some of the Russian socialists mentioned in chapter 11 – preserved the suspicions and cautions of the peasants who had carried them into the cities, and sought, by reviving their experience of revolution, to carve a path to modernization which would be less dominated by the precedents of bureaucracy and the city. They, too, hastened to catch up, their Cultural Revolution being a traumatic attempt to reconstruct their vehicle even as they rode upon it. Yet, the trauma notwithstanding, the same bureaucracy recomposed itself once the turmoil died down.

### RULING AND NON-RULING PARTIES

This chapter started with Disco's conception of communist states as 'smart' bureaucracies, consciously attempting to reconstruct both their social environments and themselves. It is possible for serious – if limited – reforming and even anti-bureaucractic movements to develop within the party-state. But, although it was aimed against the party bureaucracy as a whole, the Cultural Revolution was a rather exceptional case, which broke out when (and partly because) the conditions for it were already vanishing – a party's revolutionary past, forged in a traditional society, reasserting itself against its modernizing present. In this it was unlike ruling communism's attempts at modernizing reform and self-reform, which rest in more general and lasting conditions.

But there is another, conservative, side to 'smartness'. By concentrating on moments of crisis and periods of uncertain change, one can overlook the cumulative effects of time in helping a regime to stabilize itself. Over decades it is able gradually to select appropriate occupants, not just for key positions, but for a very much larger number of more minor, modestly privileged, roles. Equally important, it is able to refine and 'automate' its selective mechanisms, and integrate them into other institutions – education, local government and party organizations, etc. It can create a mattress of prosaic but very real support for itself, which did not exist before it took power. The 'appropriateness' of those selected for preferment is certainly a matter of personality-type and political disposition (as well as 'technical' competence, etc.), but it need not imply mechanical or active conformity. Rather, a mature communist regime will seek to draw much nonconformity within it, if possible as constructive criticism; as Kadar expressed it, a sole ruling party must make special efforts to serve also as an opposition. Claims to legitimacy can turn upon such elasticity.

In the Introduction I set out the general conception of communism as highly malleable, even protean. This characteristic persists when a non-ruling party comes to rule, and underlies the distinctive character of communist states. But while, in coming to rule, a party gains numerous possibilities it lacked before, it may be that it also begins to lose some capacities. In particular, by becoming the party of order and the main road to privilege, it comes to attach its members to it with more egocentric, atomized motivations. Most of the time this has many advantages, and forms one of its main means of adaptation. But when the position of a ruling party is put seriously in question – when, that is to say, it needs to act to some extent as a non-ruling party – it may be quite unable to adapt back. In the extreme case its discipline and structure may disintegrate; in the 1956 revolution the Hungarian party simply collapsed as a force for maintaining communism. In other cases, too, a ruling party can reach such a point of paralysis that only an external force can organize the restoration of communist rule – as in the Cultural Revolution, or in Poland in 1981.

There are not, so far, any instances in which a 'mature' ruling party has been removed, and forced to revert to being a non-ruling party. But these partial examples suggest that communism's protean character may – in this respect – be limited. When a party comes to rule, however 'smart' the bureaucracy which it forms, it sets irreversible processes in train. Beyond a certain point it cannot necessarily reassume the characteristics that brought it to power.

COMMUNISM'S INTERNAL ALTERNATIVE

I should like to end by mentioning what seem to me some significant and hopeful pointers which emerge from the study of communist rule and its crises. Even though the organizations that are thrown up by opposition to communism are hastily built and usually short-lived, the spirit of criticism and resistance is much more lasting, accumulating its experience into an alternative set of traditions. These traditions are ones from which not only the citizens of communist states, but those of western parliamentary democracies, can learn.

One important ingredient arises in reaction against the impersonality and moral imperviousness of the state, especially marked under communism. It involves the ancient problem of relations between the individual's sense of moral responsibility, and the proper scale and functioning of groups and communities. Aristotle (1908, p. 267) was emphatic that the good state should have a maximum size of population, since 'if the citizens of a state are to judge and to distribute offices according to merit, then they must know each other's characters'. Yet politics includes numerous devices, of which communist party organization is one of the most effective, for insulating officials from their fellow citizens' ethical judgement. Aristotle's thought recurs rather strikingly in the reflections of a member of the Kronstadt Revolutionary Committee, after fleeing to exile in 1921: what Russia needed was 'Soviets in every district, where people know one another and know whom they do and do not wish to elect. Local Soviets will prevent that manipulation of elections which the Bolsheviks have been so good at' (Getzler, 1983, p. 236).

Aristotle's ideal state, however, was posited on economic self-sufficiency. With peasant and handicraft production it might have been possible to have a large enough population for a viable economy, while retaining a measure of ethical community. But modern states must oversee telecommunications, air travel, foreign trade, the production of electricity and pharmaceuticals. If the scale, and therefore the character, of organizations is a matter of function, then the communist state may be just an extreme expression of a world-wide tendency.

The Czech critic of communism, Vaclav Havel, also criticizes Western politicians who think that communism is 'some kind of painful ulcer in the world's stomach, and that all that is required is a surgical operation to put things right'. In his view:

Soviet totalitarianism is an extreme manifestation – a strange, cruel and dangerous species – of a deep-seated problem which equally finds expression in advanced Western society. These systems have in common something that the Czech philosopher Vaclav Belohradsky calls 'the eschatology of the impersonal', that is, a trend towards impersonal power and rule by mega-machines or colossi that escape human control. (Havel, 1987, p. 81)

Superficially, this view might be slotted into the long tradition of theories of 'bureaucratization of the world', 'managerial revolution', etc., with their predictions of convergence between communist and Western systems. But this would be to miss the fact that under communism the serious social critic is unable to be academic, and is more-or-less forced to adopt an active rather than theoretical attitude. Havel's own stance is far from prostrating itself before historical inevitabilities. His 'anti-politics' proposes that people's conscience can be made a determining factor. To those who regard his urging that individuals should 'assert the truth' as preachiness, he points out that, even on such a small scale as the Czech Charter 77 group, communist regimes certainly do not take individual conscience and veracity lightly, but recognize and try to forestall their catalytic effects.

It is easier to observe one's conscience within social groupings who also respect it. In Poland, Solidarity generated widespread discussion of social organization and its relation to individuals' attitudes and responsibilities. In their efforts to preserve their legal space Solidarity's national leadership strove, during 1980–1, to adhere to their definition of themselves as a social, not political, movement, with the right to negotiate with the party-state, and supervise the agreements reached, but not to displace the existing political powers. But in parallel (and encouraged by proposed government legislation) there grew up a widespread movement for 'self-government' of enterprises, linking up, from the spring of 1981, into nationwide 'Network' movements. These, somewhat to the alarm of Solidarity leaders busy in national political negotiations, became the sites of blueprints and vigorous debates on how the process of production, and social life more generally, could and should be managed, locally and nationally. The common core was that as far as possible sovereignty should be shifted down, to the self-governing 'social enterprise', where ordinary members could mostly know their representatives, and administration be on a more communal scale. But how should the enterprises coordinate and exchange their production? And what of distribution, consumers' associations, control over the decaying structures of local government? Far more was involved than organizational redesign; the new thinking relied on changes in the very bonds and feelings that make up social solidarity. The reshaping of the future went hand-in-hand with criticism of the present, abstract blueprints transmuting, in the hope of obtaining peaceful reform and avoiding bloodshed, into pragmatic but hopeful compromises.

The top-down reform movements promoted by Gorbachev in the Soviet Union and – especially – Hungary have produced a further mushrooming of independent initiatives. Party reformers regard such developments with deep ambivalence: on the one hand, they can help them build their own position within the party (as happened with the removal of Kadar in 1988), but on the other, they erode the party's overall position. Party leaders are placed in the curious position of seeking to draw strength from movements that the official press is denouncing as illegal and Western-inspired.

In the short term Solidarity was set back by military rule. Yet, meeting armed force with non-violent resistance, it emerged in moral victory, and continued as a decentralized flux of voluntary but resilient bonds and social activity (and as an example and experiment with an influence well beyond Poland's borders). The problems Solidarity sought to solve are endemic to all industrialized communist states, and underlie both their attempts at self-reform and their crises; 'the sociology of surprise', as Adam Michnik (1985) reflected from prison, 'is hidden in the nature of the Leading System'.

His warning also applies to much Western comment, which tends to see communism's problems, and possible solutions, simply through the prism of comparisons with a superior democratic order. Yet party-political pluralism and generalized civil rights do not prevent the growth and self-interest of state bureaucracies. The burdens they represent, and the need to reduce them, have become one of the main planks of neo-conservatism within Western governments in the 1980s. Neo-conservatism's solutions, however, centre on the extension of the market and individualized choice; they have little to say on the problems of *collective* control of public (or private) bureaucracies. Consequently such reforms leave the established loci of power within large organizations largely unaffected, and frequently contain or deflect expenditure only at the cost of deteriorating services for those who depend on them.

Liberal criticisms of communism's economic performance – both from within and from the West – share similar limitations. Concentrating on market disciplines and the extension of economic private property rights, their core arguments are relatively independent of politics – which explains why they arise in similar forms in East and West, and why both envisage retaining much of existing large economic and state organizations, only streamlined and disciplined by market and market-type pressures. Yet – as Solidarity showed – it is very far from certain that a movement which was successful in dismantling the ruling party's monopoly of power in a communist state would wish – or be able – to limit itself to extending market pressures over existing organizations, or to embark on 'privatizing' large-scale economic assets. On the contrary, it is communist rulers who have rediscovered the advantages of large-scale capitalist property and the stock exchange. And it is an interesting if ironic fact that Western politicians of neo-conservative persuasions are usually flattered, rather than alarmed, when totalitarian leaders bent on economic reform hold them up as models.

Criticism of communist states which compares them abstractly with the West often fails to give proper weight to their different histories, including the popular experience of communism. It can to that extent be utopian. The communist experience is not an accident or mistake from which societies can withdraw, and resume an alternative route of development. Exit from communism requires societies to reassess, reaffirm and reorganize themselves *vis-à-vis* the state. And from societies who attempt this even others, which avoid a communist phase, have much to learn.

FURTHER READING

The Kronstadt events are described in Avrich (1974) and Getzler (1983). Brant (1955) and Baring (1972) deal with the June 1953 uprising in East Germany. Skyrop (1957) and Lewis (1959) describe the 1956 events in Poland. Lasky (1957), Zinner (1962) and Lomax (1976) are accounts of the October 1956 revolution in Hungary. The central book on the 1968 Czechosovak crisis is Skilling (1976); see also Kusin (1972 and 1978). Birchall (1974) is an overview of struggles against that state in Eastern Europe up to and including the Czech crisis. Garton Ash (1985) describes the formation and suppression of Solidarity in Poland in 1980–1. Dawisha (1988) examines the potentially dangerous feedback between reforms in the Soviet Union and in Eastern Europe.

Dittmer (1987) carries the story of Chinese communism from 1949 to 1972, while Domes (1973) provides a sketch of Communist Party leadership politics from 1949 to 1972. MacFarquhar (1974–) traces in detail the decade up to 1965. On the Cultural Revolution itself see Robinson (1971), Dittmer (1974) and Leys (1977); Tang Tsou (1986) analyses some of its repercussions in China's subsequent history.

# Chronology

This chronology concentrates on political events; it goes into somewhat greater detail on matters covered in the text. All dates are given according to the Western calendar.

**1870**
Lenin born.

**1879**
Stalin born.

**1885**
Plekhanov, *Our Differences.*

**1890**
Ho Chi Minh born.

**1893**
Mao Tse-tung born.

**1898**
First (Minsk) Congress of Russian Social Democratic and Labour Party (RSDLP).

**1900**
*Iskra* begins publication.

**1902**
Lenin, *What is to be Done?*

**1903**
*July–August* Second Congress of RSDLP (Brussels and London) splits into Bolshevik and Menshevik factions.

**1904**
*February* Japanese navy attacks Russian fleet at Port Arthur; start of Russo-Japanese War.
*February Iskra* publishes Parvus's articles on permanent revolution.

**1905**

*22 January* ('Bloody Sunday'): massacre of demonstrators in St Petersburg begins revolutionary struggles in Russia.

*October* General strike in Russia. St Petersburg workers form 'Soviet'.

*3 December* Trotsky and other leaders of St Petersburg soviet arrested.

*7–19 December* Bolsheviks prominent in Moscow insurrection; heavy fighting.

**1906**

*April–May* Stockholm Congress of RSDLP: Bolsheviks and Mensheviks recombine.
Trotsky, *Results and Prospects.*

**1907**

Stuttgart Congress of Second International: debates on colonialism, and war.

**1909**

Lenin, *Materialism and Empiriocriticism.*

**1911**

Revolution in China; republic proclaimed.

**1914**

*August* Germany declares war on Russia.

**1915**

*September* Zimmerwald conference; Lenin organizes international 'Zimmerwald left' grouping.

**1916**

Lenin, *Imperialism, the Highest Stage of Capitalism.*

**1917**

*March* Strikes in Petrograd lead to revolution; Tsar Nicholas II abdicates; formation of Soviets.

*March* All-Russian Congress of Bolsheviks.

*April* Lenin travels through Germany and Sweden to Petrograd.

*June* First All-Russian Congress of Soviets.

*July* Bolsheviks lead large demonstrations against Provisional Government. Government accuses Bolsheviks of receiving German money; Bolshevik leaders arrested or go into hiding.

*August–September* Lenin writes *State and Revolution.*

*8 September* Russian commander-in-chief Kornilov leads unsuccessful revolt.

*25 September* Lenin demands that Bolshevik central committee prepare insurrection.

*23 October* Bolshevik central committee accepts Lenin's policy of armed insurrection.

*25 October* Bolsheviks form Military Revolutionary Committee of Petrograd Soviet.

*7 November* Bolshevik coup, led by Trotsky through Military Revolutionary Committee, overthrows Provisional Government.

*7–8 November* Second All-Russian Congress of Soviets assumes power.

*5 December* Russo-German armistice signed at Brest-Litovsk.

*7 December* Formation of Cheka.

*21 December* Brest-Litovsk peace negotiations begin.

**1918**

*18 January* Constituent Assembly meets; Socialist Revolutionaries in the majority; dispersed by Bolshevik troops.

*March* Soviet–German peace treaty signed at Brest-Litovsk; anti-Bolshevik forces begin to mobilize.

*October–January 1919* Revolution in Germany.

*4 November* Communist Party of German Austria formed in Vienna.

*9 November* Kaiser Wilhelm II abdicates.

*24 November* Hungarian Communist Party formed in Budapest.

*15 December* Polish Communist Party formed in Warsaw.

*29 December* German Communist Party (KPD – Spartacists) formed.

**1919**

*5–11 January* Rising by Spartacists in Berlin.

*15 January* Rosa Luxemburg and Karl Liebknecht arrested and murdered.

*2–6 March* First Congress of Third (Communist) International.

*22 March* Soviet republic declared in Hungary.

*4 April–1 May* Soviet in Munich.

*25 May* Bulgarian Communist Party formed.

*1 August* Hungarian Soviet republic collapses; Admiral Horthy's dictatorship.

**1920**

*13–15 March* Military ('Kapp') *putsch* in Germany; social democratic government restored by general strike.

*April* Pilsudski leads Polish offensive into Ukraine.

*19 July–7 August* Second Congress of Comintern: adopts Bordiga and Lenin's twenty-one conditions for affiliation; debates national and colonial policies.

*1 August* Communist Party of Great Britain formed.

*14–16 August* Polish forces repel Red Armies outside Warsaw.

*1 September* Communist organization formed in the United States.

*1–7 September* Baku Congress of Toilers of the East.

*10 September* Turkish Communist Party formed at Baku.

*September* Factory occupations in Milan.

*30 December* Tours Congress of French Socialist Party; the majority converts the organization into the French Communist Party.

**1921**

*15 January* Italian Socialist Party (affiliated to Comintern) splits at Livorno Congress; Italian Communist Party formed.

*28 January* Mustafa Subhi and other leaders of the Turkish Communist Party murdered at Trebizond.

*9 February* Peace treaty of Riga between Soviet state and Poland.

*24 February* Strike wave begins in Petrograd.

*26 February* Soviet-Persian treaty.

*28 February* Soviet-Afghan treaty.

*2 March* Kronstadt Soviet rejects Bolshevik control.

*8–16 March* Tenth Congress of Russian Communist Party (Bolsheviks): bans inner party factions; adopts New Economic Policy; delegates volunteer for assault forces against Kronstadt.

*16 March* Anglo-Soviet trade (and political) agreement.

*17 March–* KPD attempts insurrection ('March Action').

*18 March* Kronstadt soviet falls to Bolshevik troops.

*14 May* Czechoslovak Communist Party formed.

*May (–October 1921)* Kuchik's separatist 'Gilan republic' formed in northern Iran; initially has Soviet support.

*May* Rival communist organizations in United States fuse on the Comintern's instructions to form Communist Party of America.

*22 June–12 July* Third Comintern Congress: urges policy 'to the masses'.

*July* Chinese Communist Party formed.

*12 October* German Independent Socialist Party (USPD) splits at Halle congress; majority joins KPD.

*30 October* Fusion of national communist organizations to form Communist Party of Czechoslovakia.

*18 December* Comintern Executive declares 'united front' policy.

*21 December* Soviet–Turkish friendship treaty.

**1922**

*January* Moscow Congress of Toilers of the Far East.

*16 April* German–Soviet treaty at Rapallo.

*26 May* Lenin suffers stroke.

*15 July* Japanese Communist Party formed.

*24 September* USPD and SPD reunite in Germany.

*28 October* Mussolini organizes 'March on Rome', forms government.

**1923**

*11 January* French troops occupy the Ruhr.

*23 January* Joffe and Sun Yat-sen agree Soviet–Kuomintang alliance, Soviet aid for Kuomintang.

*February* Arrests of communist and socialist leaders in Italy.

*June* Stamboulsky government in Bulgaria removed by military coup; Bulgarian CP driven underground.

*6 August* Streseman replaces Cuno as German Chancellor; begins policies to halt inflation, appease France.

*23 August* Soviet Politburo plans communist insurrection in Germany.

*10 October* KPD ministers enter SPD governments in Saxony (and Thuringia, 16 October).

*23 October* Aborted KPD rising; heavy fighting in Hamburg, suppressed by 25 October.

*8–9 November* Hitler's *putsch* in Bavaria fails.

**1924**

*January* Comintern Executive discusses German failure, reorganizes KPD leadership.

*21 January* Lenin dies.

*July–* Bolshevization of Comintern parties.
*December* Stalin advances notion of 'socialism in one country'.

**1925**
*12 March* Death of Sun Yat-sen; Chiang Kai-shek becomes leader of Kuomintang.
*March–April* Fourteenth Russian Party Conference agrees Stalin's formulation on 'socialism in one country' without opposition.
*December* Fourteenth Russian Party Congress: Stalin defeats Zinoviev.

**1926**
*20 March* Chiang Kai-shek's 'coup' to contain Chinese communists.
*April* Formation of Soviet Joint Opposition (Zinoviev, Kamenev and Trotsky).
*4–12 May* General strike in Britain.
*12 May* Pilsudski's coup in Poland, initially supported by the Communist Party.
*July* Comintern instructs Chinese communists to remain in Kuomintang ('united front from within').
*25 October* Zinoviev removed as head of Comintern; replaced by Bukharin.
*26 October–3 November* Fifteenth Party Conference unanimously condemns Trotsky and Zinoviev.
*November (–January 1927)* Communist rising in Dutch East Indies.

**1927**
*January–February* Mao Tse-tung writes his *Report on an Investigation of the Peasant Movement in Hunan.*
*12 April* Chiang Kai-shek's forces enter Shanghai, begin massacre of communists.
*July* Chinese communists break with Wuhan Kuomintang government.
*August–December* Chinese Communist Party launches unsuccessful uprisings.
*15 November* Trotsky and Zinoviev expelled from Soviet party.
*December* Fifteenth Soviet Party Congress announces first five-year plan.
Fidel Castro born.

**1928**
*January* Stalin demands grain requisitions from 'kulaks'.
*17 July–1 September* Sixth Comintern Congress: policy of 'class against class'.

**1929**
*31 January* Trotsky expelled from USSR.
*July* Comintern Executive: Bukharin removed; social democrats declared to be 'social fascists'.
*October* Collapse of US stock markets.
*November* Bukharin and his supporters expelled from Russian Politburo.

**1930**
*August* Chinese communist forces under Chu Teh and Mao Tse-tung form a Soviet regime in Kiangsi province.

**1931**
*August* KPD supports Nazis against SPD in Prussian 'Red referendum'.

**1932**
*January* Second Soviet five-year plan begins.

*July* Large gains for Nazis in Reichstag elections.

**1933**

*30 January* Hitler appointed German Chancellor.
*27 February* Reichstag fire.

**1934**

*February* Riots in France following Stavisky scandal; under pressure from rank-and-file communists Thorez allows joint demonstrations with socialists.
*30 June* 'Night of the long knives': Hitler purges senior Nazis.
*27 July* Unity of action pact between communists and socialists in France.
*October* Faced by sixth Kuomintang 'encirclement campaign' Chinese communist forces evacuate Kiangsi soviet areas, beginning the Long March.
*October–November* Revolt of Asturian mineworkers crushed by General Franco.
*1 December* Kirov assassinated; OGPU begins purge in Russian Communist Party.

**1935**

*January* Zinoviev convicted of treason.
*25 July–20 August* Seventh Comintern Congress: Dimitrov sets out 'popular front' policy.
*September–October* Chinese communist forces, including Mao Tse-tung, form base in Shensi province, northwest China.

**1936**

*16 February* Popular Front wins majority in Spanish elections.
*3 May* Popular Front wins majority in French elections.
*May–June* Strikes and factory occupations in France; Communist Party urges compromise to preserve the Popular Front.
*13 July* Spanish Communist Party declares full support for Popular Front government.
*18 July* Franco leads army revolt against Spanish government; civil war begins.
*August* Second trial, and executions, of Zinoviev and Kamenev.
*25 November* Germany and Japan sign Anti-Comintern Pact (Italy joins November 1937).
*5 December* New Soviet Constitution.
*December* Sian Incident: Chiang Kai-shek captured by pro-communist forces, then released by Chou En-lai.

**1937**

*January* Radek and others tried in Moscow.
*January* Chinese Communist Party establishes headquarters at Yenan.
*May–June* Spanish communists crush anarchists and radical socialists in Barcelona.
*July* Sino-Japanese war begins. Communists' Second United Front with Kuomintang.
*August* Soviet-Chinese non-aggression pact.

**1938**

*11 March* German troops enter Austria: *Anschluss.*
*March* Trial and execution of Bukharin and 'bloc of Rights and Trotskyites'.
*September* Munich conference: Britain and France agree to Hitler's dismemberment of Czechoslovakia.

*November* International Brigades withdraw from Spain.

**1939**

*5–6 March* Germany occupies Czechoslovakia.

*March* Collapse of Spanish republic.

*28 March* Germany denounces her 1934 non-aggression pact with Poland.

*4 May* Molotov replaces Litvinov as Soviet Foreign Minister.

*23 August* Molotov and Ribentropp sign Soviet-German non-aggression pact.

*1 September* Germany invades Poland.

*3 September* Britain and France declare war on Germany.

*17–30 September* Soviet Union occupies eastern Poland.

*October* Soviet Union signs mutual assistance treaties with Baltic states.

*30 November* Soviet Union invades Finland.

**1940**

*12 March* Finland cedes territory in peace treaty with Soviet Union.

*9 April* Germany invades Denmark and Norway.

*April* (circa) Soviet authorities murder Polish prisoners at Katyn and elsewhere.

*10 May* Germany invades Low Countries.

*14 June* German forces enter Paris.

*17–23 June* Soviet Union occupies Baltic states.

*July* Soviet Union annexes Romanian territories of Bessarabia and Bukovina.

*21 August* Trotsky murdered in Mexico.

**1941**

*5 April* Soviet Union signs treaty of friendship and non-aggression with Yugoslav government.

*6 April* Germany invades Yugoslavia.

*13 April* Soviet Union signs non-aggression pact with Japan.

*9 May* Soviet Union withdraws recognition from Yugoslav government-in-exile.

*22 June* Germany attacks Soviet Union.

*12 July* Anglo-Soviet mutual assistance treaty.

*11 August* Britain and Soviet Union occupy Iran.

*September* German forces approach Leningrad.

*November* German forces approach Moscow.

*7 December* Japan attacks Pearl Harbor, Philippines, Hong Kong, Malaya.

**1942**

*2 January* Allied Powers pledge no separate peace.

*11 January* Japan attacks Dutch East Indies.

*8 February* Japan captures Rangoon.

*15 February* Japan captures Singapore.

*February* (*–1944*) Mao Tse-tung and Liu Shao-chi extend 'rectification' movement to purge of lower-level party organizations.

*13 September* German seige of Stalingrad begins.

**1943**

*31 January* Surrender of German forces surrounded at Stalingrad.

*April–May* Uprising of Warsaw ghetto.

*22 May* Comintern dissolved.

*July* German offensive near Kursk defeated; large Soviet counter-advance.

*10 July* Allied landings in Sicily.

*26 July* Mussolini overthrown.

*8 September* Allied forces land at Salerno.

*25 September* Soviet forces retake Smolensk.

*18–30 October* Moscow conference of Allied foreign ministers.

*6 November* Soviet forces retake Kiev.

*28 November–1 December* Teheran conference (Stalin, Roosevelt and Churchill).

## 1944

*March* Togliatti returns from Soviet Union to lead Italian Communist Party.

*26 July* Soviet Union recognizes Gomulka's 'Lublin committee' as authority for Poland.

*1 August–3 October* Warsaw rising by main Polish resistance force, the 'Home Army'.

*23 August* Romanian communists, allied with King Michael, lead insurrection against Antonescu regime.

*9 September* Communist-led Fatherland Front comes to power in Bulgarian rising.

*October* Tito's partisans and Soviet forces enter Belgrade.

*November* Communist partisans complete their control of Albania.

*December* Fighting between British troops and communist-led Greek partisans in Athens.

## 1945

*17 January* Soviet forces enter Warsaw.

*4–11 February* Yalta conference (Stalin, Roosevelt, Churchill).

*13 February* Budapest falls to Soviet forces.

*6 March* Vyshinsky forces Romanian King to appoint pro-Soviet prime minister Groza.

*4 April* Eduard Beneš forms National Front government in liberated Czechoslovak territory.

*12 April* Roosevelt dies; succeeded by Vice-President Truman.

*25 April* Socialist Karl Renner made Chancellor of provisional Austrian government.

*28 April* Mussolini captured and executed by communist partisans.

*30 April* Hitler commits suicide in Berlin.

*2 May* Soviet forces enter Berlin.

*May–June* Chinese Communist Party Congress; writes 'Mao Tse-tung Thought' into party statutes, passes 'resolution on some questions of party history'.

*5 June* Germany divided into four occupation zones.

*17 July–2 August* Potsdam conference (Stalin, Truman, Churchill, Attlee).

*6 August* US explodes atomic bomb over Hiroshima.

*14 August* Japan surrenders.

*17 August* Sukarno proclaims Indonesian independence at Jakarta.

*September–October* Mao–Chiang Kai-shek talks.

*2 September* Ho Chi Minh declares a Democratic Republic of Vietnam in Hanoi.

*13 September* British troops enter Saigon.

*4 November* Smallholders' Party wins Hungarian elections, forms coalition.

*18 November* Communists win Bulgarian elections.

*25 November* People's Party wins Austrian elections.

*December* Moscow Foreign Ministers' Conference establishes four-power trusteeship over Korea.

**1946**

*January* Truce in civil war between Chinese communists and Kuomintang (collapses in November).

*21 April* Forced merger of Social Democratic Party with communists in Soviet zone of Germany.

*26 May* Communists win 114 out of 300 seats in Czechoslovak parliamentary elections.

*October* Greek civil war recommences.

*December* French bombard Hanoi; Vietnamese communists retreat to countryside.

**1947**

*10 March* Moscow conference of Allied foreign ministers: fails to agree on German question.

*12 March* Truman announces policy of aid to states threatened by communism.

*4 May* French communists excluded from government.

*27 May* Italian communists excluded from government.

*31 May* Ferenc Nagy, Smallholder prime minister of Hungary, forced to resign.

*5 June* US announces Marshall Aid (European economic recovery programme).

*September* Formation of Communist Information Bureau (Cominform).

**1948**

*January* Bulgarian party leader Dimitrov proposes Balkan federation.

*25 February* Communist takeover in Czechoslovakia.

*February* Social democrats fused with communists in Romania.

*February* Withdrawal of Soviet support for Greek communists.

*12 June* Social democrats fused with communists in Hungary.

*24 June* (*–September 1949*) Soviet Union blockades surface transport to Berlin; airlift by Western Powers.

*28 June* Yugoslav party expelled from Cominform.

*31 August* Zhdanov dies; Malenkov subsequently purges Voznesensky and other associates of Zhdanov.

*September* Gomulka removed from Polish party leadership.

*September* Indonesian communists form rival government to Sukarno's nationalist republic.

*September* (*–early 1949*) Indian government suppresses widespread communist-led peasant 'soviets' in Hyderabad.

*November–December* Chinese communist armies inflict major defeats on Kuomintang.

**1949**

*18 January* Formation of Comecon.

*September* Trial and execution of Rajk and others in Hungary.

*1 October* Mao proclaims People's Republic of China in Peking.

*November* Kostov repudiates his 'confession' in Bulgarian show trial; convicted and executed.

**1950**

*June* Chinese leadership approves land redistribution law, launches 'ideological remoulding' (1950–2 is the period of most violence in the agrarian revolution and establishing communist control).

*25 June* North Korean forces attack into South Korea, advance rapidly southwards.

*27 June* United Nations votes to support South Korea.

*15 September* United Nations forces (United States troops under General MacArthur's command) land at Inchon, west coast of Korea.

*20 October* United Nations forces take Pyongyang.

*27–31 October* Chinese offensive in Korea stops United Nations forces' advance northwards.

*October* Chinese forces enter Tibet (occupied during 1951).

**1951**

*15 March* United Nations forces take Seoul.

*11 April* President Truman removes General MacArthur from command in Korea for risking war with China.

*April* Kadar and other leading Hungarian communists arrested.

*July* Armistice negotiations begin in Korea.

**1952**

*4 November* General Eisenhower elected United States President (2–5 December tours Korean front).

*November–December* Trial and execution of Slansky and others in Czechoslovakia.

**1953**

*5 March* Stalin dies.

*April* Jagan's People's Progressive Party wins British Guiana elections.

*17 June* Strike and rising in East Germany.

*c.25 June* Beria arrested (shot in December).

*June–July* Strikes and demonstrations in Eastern Europe and Soviet labour camps.

*27 June* Armistice signed in Korea.

*5 July* Imre Nagy replaces Rakosi as Hungarian prime minister, launches 'New Course'.

*26 July* Fidel Castro leads unsuccessful assault on Moncada barracks.

*12 September* Krushchev becomes First Secretary of Soviet party.

**1954**

*26 April–21 July* Geneva conference on Korea and Indochina.

*7 May* Surrender of French garrison besieged by Vietminh at Dien Bien Phu.

*June* US-backed invasion topples communist-supported Arbenz government in Guatemala.

*20 July* Geneva agreement partitions Indochina.

Communist-led Huk movement heavily defeated by Philippine government forces. Communist party (PKP), decimated, reverts to parliamentary struggle.

**1955**

*8 February* Malenkov removed from Soviet leadership.

*March–April* Hungarian 'New Course' reversed; Nagy removed from state and party positions.

*15 May* Treaty between Soviet Union and Western Allies established Austria as an independent but neutral state.

*26 May* Khrushchev and Bulganin visit Yugoslavia.

*December* Nagy expelled from Hungarian Communist Party.

**1956**

*14–25 February* Twentieth Congress of Soviet Communist Party; Krushchev's 'secret speech' denounces Stalin.

*17 April* Cominform dissolved.

*2 June* Tito visits Moscow.

*4 June* Krushchev's 'secret speech' published in the West.

*mid-June* Togliatti urges 'polycentrism' for the international communist movement.

*28–29 June* Strike and demonstrations suppressed by troops in Poznan; 53 dead.

*June* Strikes in Hungary.

*26 July* Nasser seizes Suez canal.

*6 October* Large demonstrations in Budapest for reburial of Rajk.

*Early October onwards* Formation of Workers' Councils in Poland.

*17 October* Gomulka resumes Polish party leadership, reorganizes Politburo.

*19–20 October* Krushchev leads surprise Soviet delegation to Warsaw threatening military action against Poland; Krushchev backs down when Gomulka leadership threatens to resist with Polish armed forces.

*23 October* Revolution in Budapest.

*24 October* Nagy becomes Hungarian prime minister.

*29 October* Soviet forces withdraw from Budapest.

*29 October* Israeli troops invade Sinai.

*30 October* Nagy forms coalition cabinet with non-communist parties.

*30 October* Britain and France bomb Egypt.

*1 November* Nagy announces Hungary's withdrawal from Warsaw Pact.

*4 November* Soviet forces attack Budapest; heavy fighting throughout Hungary.

*14 November* Central Workers' Council formed in Budapest.

*15 November Granma* sails for Cuba carrying Castro and armed supporters of the 26 July Movement.

**1957**

*27 February* Mao Tse-tung's speech 'On the Correct Handling of Contradictions among the People' urges 'letting a hundred flowers bloom and a hundred schools of thought contend'.

*5 April* Communist-led coalition takes office in Kerala, south India.

*May* Major reorganization of Soviet economic planning.

*June* Chinese Communist Party launches 'anti-rightist' campaign to counteract 'hundred flowers' movement.

*29 June* Soviet 'anti-party group' (Molotov, Malenkov, Kaganovich) ousted.

*4 October* Soviet rocket places Sputnik 1 in earth orbit.

**1958**

*March* Castro declares all-out war on Batista regime.

*May (–Autumn 1960)* Chinese leadership launch Great Leap Forward.
*17 June* Imre Nagy executed.
*31 July* Krushchev visits Peking.
*August–September* Communist China bombards Kuomintang forces on Quemoy and Matsu islands; Soviet Union gives only qualified support.
*December* Mao retires as head of Chinese government; replaced by Liu Shao-chi.

**1959**
*1 January* Castro's 26 July movement advances on Havana; President Batista flees Cuba.
*March* Rising against Chinese communist occupation of Tibet suppressed; Dalai Lama flees to India.
*August* Lushan plenum of Chinese Communist Party central committee. Defence Minister Peng Teh-huai criticizes Mao; purged and replaced by Lin Piao.
*September* Krushchev visits Peking.

**1960**
*January* Santiago Carrillo becomes leader of Spanish Communist Party.
*April* Chinese press attacks Tito's (and implicitly Krushchev's) 'peaceful coexistence'.
*1 May* US U-2 reconnaissance aeroplane shot down over Sverdlovsk (leads to cancellation of planned Krushchev–Eisenhower summit).
*June* Krushchev circulates criticism of Chinese at Romanian party congress.
*July–August* Soviet technicians withdrawn from China.
*September* Hoxha defeats pro-Soviet faction in Albanian party, begins explicit criticism of Krushchev.
*19 October* US trade embargo, in retaliation against Cuban nationalizations of US-owned properties.
*November* Moscow meeting of 81 communist parties; Russians and Chinese clash on 'peaceful roads' to socialism.

**1961**
*17–19 April* US-backed anti-Castro forces defeated in Bay of Pigs landings.
*August* East Germany builds Berlin Wall.
*October* Twenty-second CPSU Congress; Krushchev attacks Albanian leadership.
Carlos Fonseca and Tomas Borge form Nicaraguan Sandinista National Liberation Front (FSLN), and begin guerrilla war.

**1962**
*March* Castro expels Annibal Escalante and other leading communists from his 'Integrated Revolutionary Organization'.
*20 October–20 November* Sino-Indian border war.
*22 October* Kennedy demands withdrawal of Soviet missiles from Cuba, imposes naval 'quarantine'.
*28 October* Krushchev announces withdrawal of missiles from Cuba.

**1963**
*July* Soviet Union signs nuclear non-proliferation treaty with US and Britain, excluding China from nuclear weapons technology.
*July onwards* Sino-Soviet dispute becomes fully explicit.

*13–15 August* Demonstrations in Congo-Brazzaville topple President Youlou; army takes power under Massamba-Debat, who proclaims the Congo's adherence to Marxism.

*1 November* US-supported army coup in South Vietnam; President Diem assassinated.

*22 November* President Kennedy assassinated; succeeded by Vice-President Johnson.

**1964**

*15 October* Krushchev removed as leader of Soviet Communist Party; replaced by Brezhnev.

*November* Sino-Indonesian treaty.

**1965**

*February* US Air Force begins bombing North Vietnam.

*1 October* Coup and counter-coup in Indonesia; massacre of communists begins.

*October* Mao attacks playwright Wu Han, begins attacks on Peking party leaders.

*October* New Cuban Communist Party formed, under control of Castro and his supporters.

**1966**

*May* Chinese Politburo purges Mao's opponent, Peng Chen, head of Peking party organization.

*July* First Red Guard detachments formed in Peking.

*August–November* Red Guard rallies in Peking; violence spreads through China.

*September* Japanese Communist Party expels Maoists.

**1967**

*January* Red Guards suppress general strike in Shanghai.

*March 1967* Purge and 'struggle' against Liu Shao-chi, Teng Hsiao-ping and other leading Chinese communists.

*July* Lin Piao leads army in recapture of Wuhan.

*September (–Summer 1968)* Army restores order in China; rehabilitation of party officials.

*5–10 June* Arab-Israeli war.

*June (–March 1968)* 'Anti-Zionist' campaign in Poland.

*June* Conference of Czechoslovak Writers' Union criticizes party leader Novotny.

*October* Student demonstrations in Czechoslovakia.

*27 November* Yemeni National Liberation Front declares People's Republic of South Yemen.

**1968**

*5 January* Dubček replaces Novotny as Czechoslovak party leader.

*February* 'Tet' offensive in South Vietnam.

*March* Student demonstrations in Poland repressed.

*1 May* Jose Maria Sison and supporters announce Politburo of new Communist Party of Philippines.

*May–June* Student demonstrations and general strike in France.

*20–21 August* Warsaw Pact forces invade Czechoslovakia.

**1969**
*May* Communists enter Nimeiri's government in Sudan.
*21 October* General Siad Barre leads army coup in Somalia.

**1970**
*September* Allende, with communist support, elected President in Chile.
*October* Barre regime in Somalia declares adherence to Marxism.
*December (–January 1971)* Strikes in Poland against food price rises; workers killed in Gdansk.

**1971**
*February* Gierek replaces Gomulka as Polish party leader.
*July* Nimeiri defeats attempted communist coup in Sudan, executes leading communists.

**1972**
*February* Mao–Nixon talks in Peking.
*26 October* Kerekou leads army coup in Benin.

**1973**
*27 January* Paris agreements lead to withdrawal of US troops from South Vietnam.
*8 February* United States resumes bombing of Kampuchea.
*11 September* US-backed military coup in Chile overthrows Allende government and installs military junta under General Pinochet.

**1974**
*25 April* Radical officers' Armed Forces Movement overthrows Caetano dictatorship in Portugal.
*9 August* Nixon resigns following Watergate scandal.
*12 September* Emperor Haile Selassie deposed following protracted unrest in Ethiopia; Derg (military committee) assumes power.
*November* President Kerekou, military ruler of Benin, announces principles of Beninois socialism.

**1975**
*17 April* Khmer Rouge capture Phnom Penh and begin evacuation of the city.
*30 April* North Vietnamese and Vietcong forces enter Saigon.
*August* Pathet Lao take control of Laos.
*11 November* MPLA, in control of Luanda, proclaims independent People's Republic of Angola as Portugal surrenders sovereignty.
*21 November* General Franco, Spanish dictator, dies.

**1976**
*January* Demonstrations in Peking following death of Chou En-lai.
*February* MPLA, assisted by Cuban troops, controls most of Angola.
*February* Hua Guofeng becomes prime minister of China.
*April* Socialist gains in Portuguese elections.
*May* Military regime in Benin creates People's Revolutionary Party.
*June* Strikes in Poland force government to withdraw food price rises.
*June* East Berlin conference of 67 communist parties.

*July* Portuguese communists removed from government.

*July* Police interference against Spanish Communist Party ended.

*September* Formation of Workers' Defence Committee (KOR) in Poland.

*September* Mao Tse-tung dies; Hua Guofeng establishes his position as leader of Chinese party and arrests 'Gang of Four', including Mao's widow, Chiang Ching (tried November 1980).

*November* Kampuchean leadership begin purges of opponents.

## 1977

*3 February* Mengistu shoots other members of Ethiopian Derg, assumes sole power.

*3–7 February* Third Congress of Frelimo (the ruling organization of independent Mozambique) transforms itself into a Leninist vanguard party.

*May* Vietnamese–Kampuchean border fighting.

*July* Teng Hsiao-ping (Deng Xiaoping) reinstated to the Central Committee of the Chinese party.

*July* Somali offensive against Ethiopia captures Ogaden (repelled, with Soviet and Cuban aid, in March 1978).

## 1978

*April* Afghan communists, supported by army, seize power.

*July* China breaks its alliance with Albania.

*23–25 August* Eden Pastora leads armed FSLN occupation of Nicaragua's National Palace.

*November–December* Deng Xiaoping and his followers consolidate their position in the leadership of the Chinese party.

*December (–January 1979)* Vietnamese forces invade Kampuchea.

## 1979

*7 January* Pro-Vietnamese regime established in Phnom Penh.

*February–March* Chinese forces invade Northern Vietnam.

*13 March* New Jewel Movement overthrows Gairy regime in Grenada.

*June–July* Insurrections and Sandinista-led civil war overwhelm Nicaraguan dictator; 17 July Somoza flees Nicaragua.

*December* Soviet forces occupy Afghanistan; communist leader Noor Taraki killed and replaced by Babrak Karmal.

## 1980

*July (–August)* Strikes in Poland against food price rises.

*14 August* Strike and occupation at Lenin shipyards in Gdansk; occupations spread.

*31 August* Gdansk accords; Polish government recognizes occupation committees.

*6 September* Kania replaces Gierek as Polish party leader.

*7 September* Zhao Ziyang replaces Hua Guofeng as Chinese Prime Minister.

*October* Communist Party of the Philippines (CPP) and Philippine Communist Party (PKP) merge their trade union organizations.

## 1981

*14–18 July* Extraordinary Congress of Polish Communist Party.

*18 September* General Jaruzelski replaces Kania as Polish party leader.

*October* Hu Yaobang replaces Hua Guofeng as Chinese party leader.

*14 December* Jaruzelski declares 'state of war' in Poland; arrest of Solidarity leaders.

**1982**

*November* Carrillo resigns leadership of Spanish Communist Party following electoral failure.

*10 November* Brezhnev dies; succeeded by Andropov as head of CPSU.

**1983**

*October* Murder of Bishop in internal coup of Grenada's New Jewel Movement; invasion of Grenada by United States and Caribbean allies.

*November* British Communist Party Congress splits over support for Soviet Union and control of party's newspaper, *Morning Star*.

**1984**

*February* Andropov dies; succeeded by Chernenko as CPSU general secretary.

*May–June* 'Eurocommunist' leaders of British Communist Party purge their critics.

**1985**

*March* Chernenko dies; succeeded by Gorbachev as CPSU general secretary.

**1986**

*January* Civil war between communist leaders in South Yemen.

*February* Marcos regime in the Philippines ousted following Corazon Aquino's victory in presidential elections.

*December* Riots in Alma Ata, Soviet Kazakhstan.

**1987**

*November* Gorbachev demotes his Politburo supporter, Yeltsin, head of the Moscow party, for being too aggressive in pursuit of reform. (Yeltsin removed from Politburo, February 1988.)

*December* Jakes replaces Husak as Czechoslovak party leader.

INF treaty.

**1988**

*February–* Ethnic conflicts in Armenia and Azerbaijan.

*February–March* Demonstrations in Estonia, Latvia and Lithuania against 1939 Molotov–Ribentropp pact.

*March* Soviet Supreme Court annuls Bukharin's conviction.

*1 April* Young Democrats Alliance formed in Hungary.

*April* French communist vote falls to 6.7 per cent in presidential elections.

*April–May* Polish strikers demand pay rises and legalization of Solidarity.

*14 May* Independent scientific workers' trade union formed in Hungary.

*22 May* Grosz elected by Hungarian party congress to replace Kadar as leader.

*June* Soviet Supreme Court annuls convictions of Zinoviev, Kamenev and Radek.

*July* Soviet Party Conference endorses Gorbachev reform programme.

# Selected glossary of names

Individuals appear under the name by which they are most commonly known. Some entries contain the titles of works written by the individual; the dates given for these are those when they were written or first published. Items mentioned in brackets at the *end* of entries are biographies, autobiographies, memoirs, or other works containing substantial biographical information; full references are given in the list of *Works Cited* (pp. 303–19).

**Aidit, Dipa Nusantara** (1923–65) Son of a forestry worker, became the leader of the Indonesian Communist Party (PKI) in 1951. Supported China in the Sino-Soviet split, and encouraged Sukarno's rapprochement with China, taking a ministerial post in 1962. Killed following the 1965 coup in Indonesia.

**Allende, Salvador** (1908–73) Socialist President of Chile, elected with communist support, from 1970 to 1973, when he was overthrown and killed in a military coup. (Davis, 1985)

**Akimov, Vladimir** (1872–1921) Russian Populist, subsequently a social democratic activist in the 1890s. Sole spokesman for the 'economist' critics of *Iskra* at the 1903 Congress of the RSDLP. Returned to Russia in 1905, but withdrew from practical politics, writing on the history of the social democratic and cooperative movements. (Frankel, 1969)

**Althusser, Louis** (1918–) French communist philospher, author of *For Marx* and *Reading Capital*, which contrast the mature and 'scientific' Marx of *Capital* to his 'humanist' youth.

**Andropov, Yuri** (1914–84) Russian communist leader. A full-time party official before the Second World War, he then organized guerrilla activity against the German forces. Joined the Moscow Central Committee apparatus in 1951 and became ambassador to Hungary in 1953. Because of his able work during the revolution of 1956, given responsibility for diplomatic affairs in the Moscow Central Committee offices, and made a Central Committee member in 1961. Promoted to head the KGB in 1967 and made a full Politburo member in 1973. Succeeding Brezhnev as general secretary in November 1982, he launched a campaign against corruption and inefficiency, but was in poor health until his death. (Medvedev, 1983)

**Antonescu, Ion** (1882–1946) Pro-German dictator in Romania, 1940–4.

**Ataturk, Mustafa Kemal** (1881–1938) Turkish officer and revolutionary, head of the nationalist government, 1920–38.

**Axelrod, Pavel** (1850–1928) Populist organizer in southern Russia in the 1870s. Joined with Plekhanov in forming the Marxist Emancipation of Labour Group in exile in 1883. An editor of *Iskra* 1900–3, he became a leading Menshevik after the 1903 Congress of the RSDLP. A participant in the Zimmerwald conference during the First World War, he opposed the Bolshevik seizure of power in October 1917, and subsequently emigrated. (Ascher, 1972)

**Bakunin, Mikhail** (1814–76) Anarchist thinker and revolutionary leader, opponent of Marx in the First International. (Mendel, 1981)

**Batista, Fulgencio** (1901–73) Cuban soldier and politician, dictator following a military coup in 1952, until ousted by Castro's 26 July Movement in 1958.

**Beneš, Edward** (1884–1948) President of Czechoslovakia from 1935 until resigning over the Munich agreement (1938). Led the Czechoslovak government-in-exile during the Second World War, re-elected President in 1946, but resigned following the communist takeover in February 1948.

**Beria, Lavrenty** (1899–1953) Head of the Soviet political police under Stalin from 1938 to 1953. Arrested and shot by Stalin's successors.

**Berlinguer, Enrico** (1922–84) Leader of the Italian Communist Party. Joined the party in 1943 and became a member of the Executive by 1948. Assistant secretary in 1972, and secretary general from 1972 (succeeding Luigi Longo) until his death. Strongly identified with 'Eurocommunism', the strategy of an 'historic compromise' with the Christian Democratic Party, and a stance of critical independence towards the Soviet Union.

**Bernstein, Edward** (1850–1932) German socialist politician and theoretician, and Engels's literary executor. Developed a 'revisionist' critique of orthodox Marxism, summed up in his *Evolutionary Socialism*. During the First World War he took a pacifist position and joined the German Independent Socialist Party (USPD). In 1918 he rejoined the Social Democratic Party (SPD), and was a Reichstag deputy from 1920 to 1928.

**Blum, Léon** (1872–1950) French Socialist Party leader, prime minister in the Popular Front government of 1936–7.

**Bogdanov, Alexander** (1873–1928) Physician and writer, who joined the Bolshevik leadership in 1904, and was one of its most prominent figures in the 1905 revolution. Leader of a Bolshevik majority opposed to participation in the Duma in 1907, he was attacked and isolated by Lenin and in 1911 left the RSDLP altogether and concentrated on cultural and scientific work. After 1917 he became a prominent figure in the Proletkult movement, attempting to create a distinctive proletarian aesthetic. (Williams, 1986)

**Bordiga, Amadeo** (1889–1970) Italian socialist and communist leader, with an anti-parliamentary outlook. Prominent at the Second Congress of the Comintern

(1920) he reinforced Lenin's 'twenty-one conditions' for parties to affiliate to the Comintern. First leader of the Italian Communist Party after the Livorno split of 1921, he was placed in a minority as the Comintern shifted to a 'united front' line, isolated by Togliatti at the Lyons Congress of the Italian party in 1926, and later the same year arrested by the fascist police. He was expelled by the Italian party in 1930, but after the Second World War developed a small movement in Italy, centred on Naples. (Craver, 1974)

**Borodin, Mikhail Markovich** (1884–1951) Member successively of the Russian Jewish Bund, the Bolsheviks (from 1903) and the Socialist Party of America. Comintern advisor with the Kuomintang 1923–7. Arrested in the Soviet Union in 1949 and died in a prison camp. (Jacobs, 1981)

**Brandler, Heinrich** (1881–67) Leader of the German Communist Party (KPD). Sent to Moscow as a KPD representative in 1921, and made political secretary of the KPD in August 1922. Blamed for the KPD's defeat in October 1923, and removed from party posts; expelled from the party in 1929 as a supporter of Bukharin. Led independent socialist groupings in the 1930s and after the Second World War.

**Brezhnev, Leonid Ilyich** (1906–82) Joined the Soviet Communist Party in 1931, becoming a party official in 1938. Made his career during the war in the Ukraine under Krushchev's patronage. Joined the Central Committee and its secretariat in 1952, and the Politburo in 1957. Head of state 1957–64. Moved in July 1964 to become Krushchev's deputy in the party secretariat, whence he participated in the manoeuvres to remove Krushchev. Secretary general (replacing Krushchev) from October 1964, from 1969 he emerged as principal figure of the 'collective' leadership until his death.

**Browder, Earl Russell** (1881–1973) Trade unionist and member of the Socialist Party in the United States, he supported the Bolsheviks from 1917 and served as a Comintern officer during the 1920s. Head of the Communist Party of the United States from 1930 to 1945, he was denounced by Moscow in 1945 for having dissolved the Party during the Second World War, and subsequently expelled.

**Brusilov, Alexei** (1853–1926) Russian general, commander of Tsarist armies during the First World War. Joined the Red Army, acting as staff officer during the 1920 Soviet–Polish war.

**Bukharin, Nikolai** (1888–1938) Bolshevik leader and theoretician. Joined the Bolsheviks in 1906. In emigration from 1911, he returned to Russia in 1917. Opposed peace with Germany in 1918. Editor of *Pravda* from 1919. Head of the Comintern 1925–8, he was removed from power and expelled from the party by Stalin in 1929, but later recanted and was readmitted to secondary offices. Tried and shot for treason in 1938. (Cohen, 1975)

**Bukovsky, Vladimir** (1941–) Soviet biologist, writer and dissident, imprisoned for his views from 1963, and released to the West (in exchange for the imprisoned Chilean communist, Luis Corvalan) in 1976. (Bukovsky, 1987)

**Bulganin, Nikolai** (1895–1975) Soviet Premier under Krushchev, 1955–8, demoted thereafter for association with the 'anti-party group'.

**Cachin, Marcel** (1869–1958) Member of Guesde's French *Workers' Party*, of the Socialist Party from 1905, parliamentary deputy from 1914, and leader of the French Communist Party from its formation in 1920. Remained a communist parliamentary representative (interrupted by the Second World War) until his death, being a supporter of the Soviet leadership throughout.

**Carrillo, Santiago** (1915–) Leader of the Spanish Communist Party from 1960 to 1982, and a prominent exponent of 'Eurocommunism'. Prominent since 1985 in the Communist Party of Spain, Marxist-Revolutionary. Works include *Eurocommunism and the State* (1977).

**Castro, Fidel** (1926–) Leader of the 26 July Movement which overthrew Batista in 1959; subsequently prime minister of Cuba. (Halperin, 1981; Szulc, 1986)

**Ceausescu, Nicolae** (1928–) Romanian communist from 1936, holder of government positions after the war, and secretary general of the Romanian Communist Party since 1965.

**Ch'en Tu-hsiu** (1879–1942) Chinese academic and founder (with Li Ta-chao) of the Chinese Communist Party in 1921. He led the party until its defeat by Chiang Kai-shek in 1927, but then resigned and subsequently became a sympathizer of Trotsky. (Feigon, 1983)

**Chernenko, Konstantin** (1911–85) Child of a Siberian peasant family, he began his party career as a propaganda and agitation official in Krasnoyark in 1929, serving also in the border forces during the 1930s. Trained in the Central Committee Higher School 1943–5, he became a protégé of Brezhnev, and in 1956 was promoted to head the Central Committee propaganda department. A full member of the Central Committee from 1971 and of the Politburo from 1978, he was thought likely to succeed Brezhnev when the latter died in 1982. The general secretary's post, however, went to Andropov. Chernenko took over when Andropov died two years later.

**Chiang Kai-shek** (1887–1975) Chinese officer, trained in Japan, and a supporter of Sun Yat-sen in the 1911 revolution. Visited Moscow in 1923 to study military methods, and organized the Kuomintang's Whampoa Military Academy. Following Sun's death in 1925 he opposed the communists within the Kuomintang, launching a violent offensive against them in 1927. By 1928 he had consolidated his position as military dictator over much of China. Driven from the mainland in 1949, he remained President of the Republic of China on the island of Taiwan until his death.

**Chicherin, George** (1872–1936) Russian diplomat until 1904. Joined RSDLP during 1905 revolution, and Bolsheviks in 1918. People's Commissar (Minister) for Foreign Affairs from 1918 to 1930. Responsible for the preparations for the First Congress of the Comintern, 1919.

**Chou En-lai** (1898–1976) Chinese communist leader and close associate of Mao Tse-tung. A founding member to the Chinese communist organization in France in 1921, he returned to China to take charge of political instruction at the Kuomintang's Whampoa Military Academy. A member of the Chinese Communist Party's Politburo from 1928 onwards, he was prime minister of communist China from 1949, being particularly active in foreign relations. (Wilson, 1984)

**Chu Teh** (1886–1976) Supporter of Sun Yat-sen who participated in the 1911 Chinese revolution. Joined the Chinese communist group in Berlin in 1922, returning to China shortly before Chiang Kai-shek's attack on the communists in 1927. Led the Nangchang uprising, and from 1931 onwards was commander of the communist armies. After the communist victory in 1949 he remained commander-in-chief until 1954, afterwards holding ceremonial posts.

**Crispien, Arthur** (1875–1946) SPD politician who joined the Independent Socialist Party (USPD) at its foundation in 1917 and was co-president from 1919. Part of the USPD delegation to the Second Congress of Comintern in 1920, he opposed the USPD's acceptance of the 'twenty-one conditions' and fusion with the Communist Party, and subsequently participated in the reunification with the SPD.

**Cyrankiewicz, Josef** (1910–) Secretary of the Polish Socialist Party from 1935, he was active in the resistance near Cracow, but was arrested and imprisoned in Auschwitz. Leader of the Socialist Party from 1945, he collaborated with the communists as architect of the communist-socialist merger in 1948, and was prime minister 1947–52 and 1954–72.

**Danielson, Nikolai Frantsevich** (1844–1918) Russian economist who translated and published Marx's *Capital* in Russia (1872–1896).

**Deng Xiaoping** (1904–) Joined the Chinese communist organization in France, where he was a student 1920–4. From 1929 served as a political officer with the communist armies. Held economic and military ministries after 1949, was associated with Liu Shao-chi in the party leadership, and was ousted from all his posts and disgraced during the Cultural Revolution. Reinstated in 1977, he became the dominant figure of the party leadership from 1979.

**Dimitrov, Georgi** (1882–1949) Bulgarian social democrat and leading founder member of the Bulgarian Communist Party. Tried by the Nazi regime for the Reichstag fire in 1933, but acquitted. Secretary general of the Comintern from 1935 to 1943, and post-war leader of communist Bulgaria until his death.

**Djilas, Milovan** (1911–) Yugoslav communist leader until 1953; thereafter a dissident and critic of communist bureaucracy. Works include *The New Class* (1957).

**Dubček, Alexander** (1921–) Czechoslovak communist leader. Born in Slovakia, but brought up in the Soviet Union. Active in the resistance in Slovakia during the Second World War, he became a Communist Party official in 1949, underwent political training in Moscow 1955–8, and was then promoted rapidly, joining the Praesidium in 1963. Became First Secretary of the party in March 1968 when the leadership adopted the reforming Action Programme, but was removed from the leadership and successively demoted following the Soviet invasion of Czechoslovakia in August 1968.

**Duclos, Jacques** (1896–1975) Member of the Central Committee of the French Communist Party from 1926 and of its Politbureau from 1931, he was also a communist parliamentary deputy as well as being active in the Comintern. A leader of the communist resistance during the war, he resumed his parliamentary career afterwards and was the Communist Party's presidential candidate in 1969. In 1947 he was the French communist representative at the founding meeting of the Cominform.

**Dzerzhinsky, Felix Edmundovich** (1877–1926) Polish Bolshevik, member of the Bolshevik Central Committee, head of the Cheka from its formation in December 1917, and holder of several other government positions in the Soviet state. (Leggett, 1981)

**Eberlein, Hugo** (1887–1944) Member of German Communist Party Central Committee, KPD delegate to the First Congress of the Comintern and prominent in the Comintern until removed from leading posts in 1928. Fled to Soviet Union after Hitler came to power in 1933, appointed member of the Comintern's Control Commission in 1935, but arrested during purges in 1937 and died in prison.

**Engels, Friedrich** (1820–95) Close friend, supporter and intellectual collaborator of Marx, co-author with him of *The German Ideology* (1846) and the *Communist Manifesto* (1848). Lived in exile, mainly in England, following the German revolution of 1848–9. His own works include *The Condition of the Working Class in England* (1845), *Origin of the Family, Private Property and the State* (1884). After Marx's death in 1883 Engels completed volumes 2 and 3 of *Capital*. (McLellan, 1978)

**Fischer, Ruth** (1895–1961) Austrian socialist and founding member of the Austrian Communist Party in 1918. Moved to Germany and joined KPD in 1919, becoming a leader of its more revolutionary wing. Member of the Comintern Executive 1924–6, and leader of the KPD during 1925–6, but opposed Stalin and expelled from the KPD in 1926; briefly supported Trotsky after 1933.

**Fraina, Louis** (1894–1953) First leader of the Communist Party in the United States; broke with the Comintern in 1922.

**Frossard, Louis-Oscar** (1889–1946) First leader of the French Communist Party. In conflict with the Comintern leadership from 1921, he resigned in 1923. Thereafter pursued a parliamentary career in the Socialist Party. Minister in governments during the 1930s and in Pétain's government in 1940.

**Furubotn, Peder** (1890–1968) Leader of the section of the Norwegian Workers' Party that joined the Comintern in 1919. He became leader of the Communist Party after the majority of the Workers' Party broke with the Comintern in 1923. A Comintern official in Moscow during the 1930s, he returned to Norway in 1937 and organized communist resistance during the war. Leader of the Norwegian Communist Party again from 1945, he was expelled as a Titoite-Trotskyist in 1949, but formed a small communist organization which continued to express confidence in the Soviet Union and Stalin.

**Gierek, Edward** (1913–) Polish communist, recruited by the French Communist Party in the 1930s and active in the wartime resistance in Belgium. Returned to Poland in 1948, became a member of the Central Committee in 1954 and of the Politburo in 1959, coming to control the party machine in Silesia. In 1971, following food riots in the coastal cities, he succeeded Gomulka as party leader, but in September 1980, after the emergence of Solidarity, he was replaced by Kania.

**Gomulka, Wladyslaw** (1905–82) Polish communist who became leader of the clandestine Polish Workers Party in occupied Poland in 1943 (the former Polish Communist Party was dissolved by Stalin in 1938). During 1945–7 he was the minister in control of the territories annexed from Germany, but in 1948 he was dismissed, accused of 'nationalist deviations', and kept in detention from 1951 to 1955. Restored to party membership in 1956, he became party leader in the 1956 crisis, introducing a policy of liberalization and reform. Replaced as party leader by Gierek following the strikes against food price rises in December 1970–January 1971, and thereafter lived in retirement. (Bethell, 1972)

**Gorbachev, Mikhail** (1931–) General secretary of the CPSU. Son of a peasant family in the Stavropol region, he joined the CPSU in 1952, receiving higher education in law, and later agriculture. First secretary of the Stavropol region party organization from 1970; joined the Central Committee in 1971. As a protégé of Andropov, head of the KGB, joined the Politburo in 1980. Made general secretary on Chernenko's death in 1985. Launched initial campaigns against alcoholism, inefficiency and corruption; subsequently responsible for policies of *perestroika* (restructuring), *glasnost* (openness), and withdrawal of Soviet troops from Afghanistan. (Schmidt-Hauer, 1986)

**Gottwald, Klement** (1896–1953) Leader of the Czechoslovak Communist Party from 1929. In the Soviet Union during the war, he became prime minister in the communist takeover of February 1948, and president from June 1948.

**Gramsci, Antonio** (1891–1937) Italian communist leader and intellectual. Born in Sardinia, he moved to Turin as a student and there, in 1919, formed the Ordine Nuovo group within the Italian Socialist Party. A founding member and leading figure of the Italian Communist Party, he held Comintern positions abroad from 1922 to 1924, returning to Italy to become leader of the Communist Party. Arrested by the fascist authorities in 1926, he spent the rest of his life in prison, where, in the *Prison Notebooks*, he developed original Marxist theories on hegemony and the state. (Cammett, 1967; Clark, 1977; Joll, 1978)

**Guesde, Jules** (1845–1922) French revolutionary socialist leader, who fought in the Paris Commune (1871). Founder in 1880 (with Paul Lafargue, 1842–1911) of the Workers' Party.

**Guevara, Ernesto ('Che')** (1928–67) Argentinian revolutionary, supporter of Castro's 26 July Movement. Following the Cuban revolution, advocated revolutionary guerrilla war in Latin America, and in 1966–7 led a small armed movement in the Bolivian countryside, where he was killed. (Hodges, 1977)

**Hilferding, Rudolf** (1877–1941) German social democratic leader and Marxist economist, author of *Finance Capital* (1910). Member of the German Independent Socialist Party (USPD) during the war, rejoined the SPD and served as Finance Minister under Stresemann (1923) and Mueller (1928–9). In exile after 1933, he was killed by the Gestapo in Paris.

**Ho Chi Minh** (1890–1969) Vietnamese communist leader. Trained as a Comintern agent in Moscow, 1923–5, he was also active in China. Led the Indochinese Communist Party from its foundation in 1930, and in September 1945 became president of the Democratic People's Republic of Vietnam. (Lacouture, 1968)

**Honecker, Erich** (1912–) East German communist leader. Joined the German Communist Party in 1929 and imprisoned by the Nazis 1933–45. Became a member of the Politburo in 1958, and succeeded Ulbricht as party leader in 1971.

**Horthy, Admiral Nicholas** (1868–1957) Authoritarian ruler of Hungary from the defeat of the revolution of 1919 until 1945.

**Hoxha, Enver** (1908–85) Albanian who joined the French Communist Party when in France as a student, returning to Albania in 1936. Founder of the Albanian Communist Party in 1941, he was a leader of the wartime partisan struggle, and (with Tito's help) became leader of the party from 1943. Following Stalin's breach with Yugoslavia in 1948 he purged and executed suspected Titoite rivals in the party leadership. Sided with the Chinese leadership against Krushchev following the latter's reconciliation with Tito and denunciation of Stalin.

**Hua Guofeng** (1912–) Member of the Chinese Politburo from 1973 and subsequently Minister for Internal Security. Became Prime Minister on Chou En-lai's death in February 1976, and in October, after Mao's death, he established his position as leading figure in the regime by arresting the 'Gang of Four'. Displaced following the return to power of Deng Xiaoping in 1978–9, yielding the premiership to Zhao Ziyang in 1980 and the leadership of the party to Hu Yaobang in 1981.

**Husak, Gustav** (1913–) Czechoslovak communist, jailed for 'bourgeois deviations', 1954–60. Part of Dubček's leadership in 1968, he sided with the Soviet leadership after the August invasion, becoming party leader in 1969. Replaced by Jakes in 1987.

**Hyndman, Henry M.** (1842–1921) British businessman and popularizer of Marx, founder in 1881 (with William Morris, 1834–96) of the Social Democratic Federation, and subsequently leader of the British Socialist Party.

**Jaruzelski, Wojciech** (1923–) Polish officer and party leader. In the Soviet Union after the German–Soviet occupation of Poland, he joined the Soviet-organized Polish army in 1943, fought against the anti-communist partisans in the civil war of 1945–7, and joined the Communist Party in 1947. Chief political commissar of the army in 1960, Defence Minister from 1968, Politburo member from 1971. Prime minister from February 1981, succeeding Kania as party leader in October. Declared 'state of war' in December, arresting main Solidarity leaders, and in 1982 declared Solidarity dissolved.

**Jiang Quing** (1913–) Actress who became Mao Tse-tung's third wife in 1939. Played a prominent part in the Cultural Revolution, but arrested in 1976 following Mao's death. Placed on public trial with the others of the 'Gang of Four' in 1980, receiving a suspended death sentence. (Terrill, 1984)

**Joffe, Adolf** (1883–1927) Russian social democrat, close associate of Trotsky, who joined the Bolshevik party with him in 1917. Leading figure in Brest-Litovsk negotiations, ambassador in Berlin during 1918, Soviet representative in Japan and China 1922–3. Supporter of Trotsky in the inner-party struggles; committed suicide.

**Jogiches, Leo** (1867–1919) Leader of Polish social democracy, later active in the German movement; companion of Rosa Luxemburg. Organizer of Spartacist League during the First World War and briefly leader of the German Communist Party after the murders of Luxemburg and Liebknecht in 1919. Himself murdered in March 1919.

**Kabakchiev, Khristo** (1878–1940) Bulgarian 'narrow' socialist who became a founder-member of the Bulgarian Communist Party in 1919. A Comintern official from 1920, he attended the Halle Congress at which the German Independent Socialist Party split (1920), intervened for the Comintern at the Livorno Congress (and split) of the Italian Socialist Party in 1921, and became leader of the Bulgarian Communist Party in January 1923. Arrested in the 1923 coup, he was released from jail in 1926, and lived thereafter in the Soviet Union. Briefly imprisoned in 1937, he died of natural causes.

**Kadar, Janos** (1912–) Member of the Hungarian Communist Party from 1931, active in the wartime resistance. In 1948 he replaced Laszlo Rajk as minister of internal security after the latter was purged, but was himself imprisoned during 1951–4, being released under Imre Nagy. Sided with Nagy in 1956, but switched sides before the second Soviet intervention in November, and succeeded Nagy as party leader and prime minister. His initial repressions were followed, from 1961, by economic and political relaxation. Ousted by Grosz at the 1988 party congress.

**Kamenev, Lev** (1883–1936) Russian social democrat from 1901, Bolshevik from 1903, and brother-in-law of Trotsky. With his associate Zinoviev opposed Lenin's policy of a party coup in the autumn of 1917. A 'triumvirate' of Kamenev, Zinoviev and Stalin held the party leadership after Lenin's death in 1924, but Kamenev and Zinoviev lost power by 1925. Arrested in 1934 and tried and executed in 1936.

**Kang Sheng** (1899–1975) Chinese communist leader and close associate of Mao. Organized an internal security organization in the Kiangsi soviets. Joined the Politburo in 1945. Prominent in Mao's support during the Great Leap Forward (1958–60) and the Cultural Revolution.

**Kapp, Wolfgang** (1858–1922) Founder of nationalist Fatherland Party in Germany; leader of an attempted military *putsch* in 1920.

**Kautsky, Karl** (1854–1938) Czech socialist, protégé of Engels, active in the German Social Democratic Party (SPD) as a leader and writer. Favoured a reformist and pacifist approach, but opposed Bernstein's 'revisionism', as well as supporting the Mensheviks against the Bolsheviks. Took a pacifist position during the First World War, and was later a critic of the Bolsheviks' terror in power. Joined the Independent Socialist Party (USPD) in 1917; rejoined the SPD in 1922. (Salvadori, 1979)

**Kerensky, Alexander** (1881–1970) Russian social revolutionary (and son of Lenin's headmaster). A leader of the Petrograd Soviet formed in the February 1917 revolution, he joined the Provisional Government and became prime minister in July. Lived in exile from 1918.

**Kim Il-Sung** (1912–) Joined the Korean communist organization (then part of the Chinese Communist Party) in 1931 and participated in the war against Japan. Fought with Soviet forces on the European front during the Second World War and returned to northern Korea with the Soviet occupation forces in 1945. United the existing Korean communist organizations into the Korean Workers' Party under his leadership, a position he has retained ever since. The subject of a considerable personality cult.

**Kirov, Sergei** (1886–1934) Soviet leader, head of the Leningrad party organization (in succession to Zinoviev) from 1925 and member of the Politburo from 1930. His assassination (probably on Stalin's orders) triggered the terror against party members in the 1930s. (Biggart, 1972)

**Kollontai, Alexandra** (1872–1952) Russian feminist, social democrat and (from 1915) Bolshevik. A leader of the Workers' Opposition current within the party, 1920–1, she served in the Soviet diplomatic service from 1923. (Porter, 1980)

**Kostov, Traicho** (1897–1949) Joined the Bulgarian Communist Party in 1920, active in the wartime resistance, and became vice-premier in 1945. In 1949 he was tried for treason, found guilty (though he repudiated his forced confession) and executed. (Horner, 1979)

**Kosygin, Alexei** (1904–80) Member of the CPSU Central Committee from 1939 and the Politburo from 1948. An economic administrator, he was part of the grouping that removed Krushchev in 1964, whereupon he became prime minister.

**Krupskaya, Nadezhda** (1869–1939) Russian revolutionary and teacher and (from 1898) Lenin's wife and close collaborator. After the 1917 revolution played an independent part in organizing education, but had little power in the party leadership.

**Krushchev, Nikita Sergevich** (1894–1971) Joined the Bolsheviks in 1918 and became a member of the Politburo in 1939. Emerged as party leader following Stalin's death in 1953, and made a 'secret speech' denouncing Stalin at the Twentieth CPSU Congress. Architect of economic reform measures and of 'peaceful coexistence' in great power relations, and a key figure in the Sino-Soviet schism, he was removed by a coalition against him in the party leadership, and lived afterwards in retirement. (Khrushchev, 1977; Medvedev, 1982)

**Kun, Bela** (1886–1939) Organized communist groups among prisoners of war in Russia in 1917–18, founded the Hungarian Communist Party in 1918, and led the Hungarian Soviet Republic of 1919. After its collapse he returned to Soviet Russia and became a member of the Praesidium of the Comintern in 1921. He encouraged the 'March action' (1921) by the German Communist Party, and was censured by Lenin, but resumed a significant role in the Comintern from 1924 to 1935, adhering closely to the line of the Soviet leadership. Arrested in the Soviet Union in 1937 and executed in 1939.

**Largo Caballero, Francisco** (1869–1946) Spanish Socialist Party leader, Prime Minister in the Republican government 1936–7.

**Larsen, Axel** (1897–1972) Founding member of the Danish Communist Party in 1921 and its leader from 1932. An organizer of the communist resistance from 1941, he was arrested in 1942, but survived Sachsenhausen concentration camp and resumed the leadership of the Communist Party after the war. Expelled from the party in 1958, he formed, with his followers, the People's Socialist Party, which soon grew to be much stronger than the remaining communist organization.

**Laufenberg, Heinrich** (1872–1932) German revolutionary socialist, leader of Hamburg workers' councils in 1918–19, founding member of German Communist Party (KPD), leader of expelled group which formed German Communist Workers' Party (KAPD) in 1919.

**Lenin, Vladimir Ilyich** (1870–1924) Revolutionary propagandist and defender of orthodox Marxism in the 1890s, exiled to Siberia 1897–1900. Co-founder of *Iskra* (*The Spark*) in 1900 and leader of the Bolshevik faction of the Russian Social Democratic Labour Party after its split at its 1903 Congress. Participant in the 1905 revolution but otherwise lived in exile in Europe until 1917. From the outbreak of the First World War in 1914 proposed a policy of 'revolutionary defeatism'. Returned to Russia with German assistance in April 1917, and after the Bolshevik takeover in November became head of the Soviet government. Seriously ill from 1922, he died in January 1924; Peter the Great's capital (Petrograd) was renamed Leningrad in his honour. His many works include *The Development of Capitalism in Russia* (1899), *What is to be Done?* (1902), *Materialism and Empiriocriticism* (1908), *Imperialism: the Highest Stage of Capitalism* (1916), *State and Revolution* (1917), and *Left-Wing Communism; an Infantile Disorder* (1920). (Service, 1985–; Shub, 1966; Ulam, 1978; Harding, 1983; Valentinov, 1968)

**Levi, Paul** (1883–1930) German socialist lawyer who defended Rosa Luxemburg, he was an associate of Liebknecht and Luxemburg in the leadership of the Spartacus League during the First World War, and collaborator with Lenin in Switzerland. Founding member of the German Communist Party (KPD), and party leader from 1919, after the murders of Liebknecht, Luxemburg and Jogiches. Expelled from the KPD in April 1921, after publicly opposing the 'March action'. Joined USPD and SPD, becoming a leader of the 'left'. Committed suicide.

**Li Ta-chao** (1888–1927) Peking academic and early leader of the Chinese Communist Party. A member of the Kuomintang from 1922 and of its Executive Committee from 1924, he led the Chinese delegation to the Fifth Congress of Comintern in 1924. Arrested in conjunction with the police raid on the Soviet legation in Peking in April 1927, he was executed shortly afterwards.

**Liebknecht, Karl** (1871–1919) German revolutionary socialist leader and parliamentarian, son of Wilhelm Liebknecht (1826–1900). Opposed to Germany's part in the First World War, he formed the Spartacus League in 1915 and was imprisoned until the end of the war. A founding leader (with Rosa Luxemburg) of the German Communist Party in December 1918, he was (with Luxemburg) murdered by *Freikorps* soldiers following the rising in Berlin in January 1919. (Trotnow, 1984)

**Lin Piao** (1910–71) Member of the Chinese Communist Party from 1925 and a military leader after 1927. Worked for the Comintern in Moscow from 1937 until returning to Yenan in 1942. Commander of the Chinese forces in the Korean war (1950–3) and a member of the Politburo from 1955. A close associate of Mao, he played a prominent role in the Cultural Revolution and was nominated as Mao's successor, but died in September 1971 in an aeroplane crash, apparently after his conspiracy to remove Mao was aborted.

**Litvinov, Maxim** (1876–1951) Founder member of the RSDLP in 1898, Bolshevik from 1903, and, after 1917, a senior Soviet diplomat. Foreign Minister 1930–9 he was (being both Jewish and associated with the policy of 'collective security') removed when the negotiations for the 1939 Nazi-Soviet pact began.

**Liu Shao-chi** (1898–1974) Founder member of the Chinese Communist Party in 1921, joining the Central Committee in 1927 and the Politburo in 1931. A writer and theoretician, he was also important in the party's urban work as a labour organizer in Shanghai and Canton. Succeeded Mao as President of the People's Republic of China in 1959. Denounced as 'China's Krushchev' during the Cultural Revolution, and expelled from the party in 1969.

**Longo, Luigi** (1900–1981) Joined the Italian Socialist Party in 1920 and supported the communist minority in the split at Livorno in 1921. Arrested and imprisoned in 1923–4, he left Italy in 1924 and was thereafter active in the Italian Communist Party in exile and the Comintern. A senior political officer of the International Brigades during the Spanish Civil War, he was subsequently interned in France then handed over to the Fascist authorities in Italy. Released after the fall of Mussolini in 1943, he became a leader of the communist resistance in the north in the latter stages of the war. In 1947 he was the main Italian communist representative to the founding conference of the Cominform. In 1960 he became deputy leader of the Italian party, and succeeded to the leadership on Togliatti's death in 1964. He relinquished the position in 1972.

**Longuet, Jean** (1876–1938) French socialist deputy, grandson of Karl Marx, and leader of the pacifist faction within the SFIO that held the majority at the close of the war. Attacked by the Comintern as part of the strategy of splitting the SFIO and forming the French Communist Party at the Tours Congress (1920).

**Luxemburg, Rosa** (1870–1919) Polish revolutionary socialist leader and theoretician, member of the German social democratic party from 1898, and of the International Bureau of the Second International, 1904–14. Opponent of German participation in the First World War, she (with Karl Liebknecht) organized the Spartacus League in 1915, but was imprisoned for opposition to the war. A founding leader of the German Communist Party in December 1918, she was (with Liebknecht) murdered by *Freikorps* soldiers following the rising in Berlin in January 1919. Her works include *The Accumulation of Capital* (1913). (Nettl, 1966)

**Lysenko, Trofim** (1898–1976) Soviet biologist, patronized by Stalin in the 1930s, who dominated Soviet genetics and agrobiology until the 1950s. Associated with the theory that characteristics acquired during an organism's lifetime can be inherited by its offspring.

**Machajski, Jan Waclav** (1867–1926) Polish revolutionary socialist and writer, critical of the intelligentsia's dominance in socialist movements, who developed the theory that the intelligentsia, equipped with 'intellectual capital', is a new exploiting class and that Marxism is an ideological expression of its interests. His main work is *The Intellectual Worker* (1898). (D'Agostino, 1969)

**Malenkov, Georgi** (1902–79) Joined the Bolsheviks in 1920, becoming a member of the Central Committee in 1939 and of the Politburo in 1946. Briefly prime minister and party leader in 1953, after Stalin's death, he was then demoted by Krushchev, and removed from power as part of the 'anti-party group' in 1957.

**Mao Tse-tung** (1893–1976) Introduced to Marxism by Ch'en Tu-hsiu in 1919, he was a founding member of the Chinese Communist Party in 1921. As a Kuomintang peasant organizer he developed his opinion (in *Report on an Investigation of the Peasant Movement in Hunan*, 1927) that peasants would form the majority in the Chinese revolution. After the communists' defeats in 1927 he played a major part in establishing their soviet bases in Kiangsi in the early 1930s. He secured the leadership of the party in 1934, during the Long March, and led the party during its subsequent wars against Japan and the Kuomintang. The object of a substantial personality cult from 1945, he proclaimed the People's Republic of China in 1949 and became its President. The major initiatives of the ruling party particularly associated with him are the 'hundred flowers' movement (1957), the 'Great Leap Forward' (1958–60) and the Cultural Revolution. Senile in his last years, he did not appear in public after 1971. His numerous works are mainly short pieces, written or spoken for particular occasions, but also including poetry and calligraphy. Short anthologies of his 'thoughts', such as the *Little Red Book*, were published in hundreds of millions of copies. (Ch'en, 1967; Schram, 1969a; Wilson, 1979)

**Marchais, Georges** (1920–) Leader of the French Communist Party. Joined the party in 1947, its Political Bureau in 1959, and became secretary general in 1974. Loosely associated with 'Eurocommunism' until the French party's support for the Soviet invasion of Afghanistan in 1980.

**Maring, Hendricus (Sneevliet)** (1883–1942) Dutch socialist and founding member of the Indonesian Communist Party in Java in 1920. As Comintern representative in China, 1921–3, he played a major part in forming the Chinese Communist Party and in encouraging the Chinese communists to cooperate with the Kuomintang; however he broke with the Comintern in 1927. A supporter of Trotsky, 1929–38, he subsequently headed an independent Dutch grouping which led Amsterdam dockers in the only strike against Jewish deportations in occupied Europe. Arrested by the Gestapo and shot. (Bing, 1971)

**Martov, Yuri** (1873–1923) Russian social democrat, close friend of Lenin and co-founder with him of *Iskra* in 1900. At the 1903 Congress of the RSDLP he opposed Lenin and subsequently became a leading Menshevik. Opposed to militarism in the First World War, he was a critical defender of the Bolshevik regime during the civil war. Emigrated to Germany in 1920, where he established the Menshevik journal *Socialist Courier*, well-informed on Soviet affairs. Works include a history of Russian social democracy. (Getzler, 1967)

**Martynov, Alexander** (1865–1935) A Russian social democratic activist in the 1890s, and an 'economist' critic of *Iskra*. Supported the Mensheviks after the 1903

Congress of the RSDLP, being associated with Martov. Joined the Communist Party in 1923, became a Comintern employee and supported Stalin's policies in the 1930s.

**Marx, Karl** (1818–83) Student at the universities of Berlin and Jena, then editor of the *Rheinische Zeitung*, 1842–3. Moved to Paris, where he became the friend of Friedrich Engels. Collaborated with Engels in writing *The Holy Family* (1845) and *The German Ideology* (1846), and in preparing the programme of the Communist League, published in 1848 as *The Communist Manifesto*. Returned to Germany during the 1848–9 revolution, where he published the revolutionary *Neue Rheinische Zeitung*. Exiled from 1849, he lived in London, where he began his study of capitalist political economy, publishing *A Contribution to the Critique of Political Economy* (1859) and *Capital* (only the first volume of which was published in his lifetime, in 1867). Helped found, in 1864, the International Working Men's Association (the First International), in which he subsequently clashed with Bakunin and his supporters; in 1876 Marx dissolved the organization. (Nicolaievsky and Maenchen-Helfen, 1976; Berlin, 1978)

**Mihajlovich, Draza** (1893–1946) Yugoslav general and commander of the Serbian Chetnik forces who fought Croatians and Tito's communists, as well as the occupation troops, in Yugoslavia during the Second World War. Captured, tried and shot by the communist regime in 1946.

**Molotov, Viacheslav Mikhailovich** (1890–1988) Founding editor of the Bolsheviks' *Pravda* in 1912. An early supporter of Stalin, becoming a member of the Politburo in 1926, he was Soviet prime minister 1930–41 and foreign minister 1939–49 and 1953–6, negotiating the Nazi–Soviet pact (1939) and participating in the Teheran (1943), Yalta (1945) and Potsdam (1945) conferences. Removed by Krushchev in 1957 as part of the 'anti-party group', he was appointed Soviet ambassador in Mongolia (1957–61).

**Munzenberg, Willi** (1880–1940) German socialist, supporter of 'Zimmerwald left', founding member of the KPD, and secretary of Communist Youth International. Architect of communist front organizations, particularly during the Popular Front period. Became critical of Stalin and expelled from the KPD in 1938. Murdered in France during the German advance in 1940.

**Mussolini, Benito** (1883–1945) Italian revolutionary socialist, editor of Socialist Party newspaper *Avanti!*, 1912–14. From 1914 supported Italian entry into the First World War; founded fascist movement in 1919; head of Italian government from 1922 and dictator 1926–43. Ousted and imprisoned in 1943, but rescued by German forces and installed as puppet ruler in northern Italy. Executed by communist partisans in 1945. (Mack Smith, 1983)

**Nagy, Imre** (1896–1958) An underground communist organizer in Hungary during the 1920s, he worked in the Soviet Union as an agronomist from 1930 to 1944. Returning to Hungary as part of the party leadership, he held ministerial posts overseeing land reform, then internal security. Prime minister in 1953 under the 'new course' of the post-Stalin Soviet leadership, he was dismissed from all positions in 1955. His reforms, though, made him the most popular communist leader of 1956.

He resumed the premiership on 24 October and led the government during the revolution forming a coalition with non-communist parties, and withdrawing Hungary from the Warsaw Pact. After the second Soviet intervention he sought refuge in the Yugoslav embassy, but was handed over to the Soviet authorities, imprisoned, and hanged in 1958. Writings include *On Communism* (1956).

**Novotny, Antonin** (1904–75) Founding member of the Czechoslovak Communist Party, he spent most of the Second World War in a German concentration camp. Became a central committee member in 1945, then party leader from 1953 to 1968, when he was displaced by Dubček.

**Parvus, Alexander Israel** (1867–1924) Russian social democrat, also active in the German socialist movement. In 1904 he advanced the notion of the Russian working class as vanguard of international revolution, taken up and developed by Trotsky. A successful businessman, he helped organize Lenin's return through Germany to Russia in 1917, and acted as intermediary in the German government's provision of funds to the Bolsheviks during 1917. (Zeman and Scharlau, 1965)

**Pauker, Ana** (1893–1960) A member of the Romanian Communist Party from its foundation in 1921 and of its Central Committee from 1922. Active on behalf of the Comintern until arrested by the Romanian authorities in 1935, she was released to Moscow in an exchange of prisoners in 1940. A signatory of the act dissolving the Comintern in 1943, she was a leading figure in rebuilding the Romanian Communist Party after Romania switched to support the Soviet Union in 1944. Foreign Minister from 1947, she was purged and placed under house arrest in 1952.

**Pilsudski, Josef** (1867–1935) Founder of the Polish Socialist Party in 1892. Leading figure of the Polish republic from 1919, he retired in 1923, but returned to power in a coup in 1926 and ruled Poland until his death.

**Plekhanov, George Valentinovich** (1856–1918) A Populist until 1883, he then became, as an émigré in Western Europe and founder of the Emancipation of Labour Group, the theoretical 'father' of Russian Marxism. Joining forces with Lenin to oppose 'revisionism' among Russian social democrats, he was an editor of *Iskra* (*The Spark*) and supported Lenin at the RSDLP's Second Congress in 1903, but thereafter broke with the Bolsheviks and inclined to the Mensheviks. A supporter of Russia in the First World War, he returned there after the February 1917 revolution, but played no significant political role. His works include *Socialism and the Political Struggle* (1883), *Our Differences* (1884), *The Development of the Monist View of History* (1895) and *The Role of the Individual in History* (1898). (Baron, 1963)

**Pol Pot** (1928–) Cambodian communist leader, student in Paris 1949–52, part of a group of Kampuchean Marxists affiliated to the French Communist Party. Joined communist guerrilla movement in Kampuchea on his return in 1952, joining the Politburo of the Kampuchean Communist Party in 1960 and becoming leader in 1963. After the overthrow of the Lon Nol government in 1975, he became prime minister (from April 1976), presiding over purges and massacres of both party cadres and the population. Overthrown by Vietnamese invasion in 1979, and retreated, in the leadership of the Khmer Rouge, to occupy border areas with Thailand. Retired as head of the Khmer Rouge in 1985, retaining an advisory position.

**Quelch, Tom** (1886–1954) Member of the Social Democratic Federation and the British Socialist Party who took a pacifist position during the First World War and urged affiliation to Comintern in 1919. Attended the Second Congress of Comintern in 1920, where he was the only Briton elected to the Executive Committee. Subsequently worked as an official of the building workers' trade union.

**Radek, Karl** (1885–1939) Active in the Polish, Russian and German revolutionary movements before the First World War, and a member of the 'Zimmerwald left' bureau, he joined the Bolshevik party from abroad in 1917, and helped form the German Communist Party in 1918. A fluent journalist, he was the Comintern's senior specialist on Germany until 1923, he was eclipsed by the German party's defeat in October of that year. Associated with Trotsky, he was expelled from the Russian party in 1927, but readmitted in 1930 after writing an apologia to Stalin. He was arrested and tried in 1937, and died in a labour camp. (Tuck, 1988)

**Rajk, Laszlo** (1909–49) Hungarian communist, fought in the International Brigades during the Spanish civil war and active in the underground movement in Hungary during the Second World War. Minister of the Interior 1946–8, then Foreign Minister, he was arrested in 1949, tried for treason and executed. Rehabilitated in 1956, the reburial of his remains in September 1956 became a mass demonstration, leading into the national revolution in October.

**Rakosi, Matyas** (1892–1971) Founding member of the Hungarian Communist Party, he was a minister in Bela Kun's soviet republic during 1919, and after it was overthrown, a Comintern agent in Europe. Arrested and jailed in Hungary in 1925, the Soviet government obtained his release in 1940, in exchange for Hungarian flags of the 1848 revolution. In the Soviet Union during the Second World War, he became leader of the Hungarian party when Soviet troops entered the country in 1944. His authority was reduced by the Soviet leaders in 1953, and in July 1956 they removed him as party secretary. In the revolution of October 1956 he fled to the Soviet Union, and in 1962 he was expelled from the Hungarian Communist Party for his abuses under Stalin, but remained in the Soviet Union and died there.

**Reed, John** (1887–1920) Radical American journalist, in Petrograd during 1917, who wrote a vivid account of the Bolsheviks' coming to power, *Ten Days That Shook the World*. Helped form the American Communist Labour Party in 1919 and attended the Second Congress of the Comintern in 1920, but died of typhus in Moscow. (Rosenstone, 1982)

**Renner, Karl** (1870–1951) Austrian socialist politician, supporter of the 'revisionist' current, and patriot during the First World War. Chancellor 1919–20 and President 1931–3, and again Chancellor of the restored Austria 1945–50.

**Riazanov, David** (1870–1938) Russian social democrat and intellectual; expert on Marx. Joined the Bolsheviks in July 1917 and in 1921 became director of the Marx-Engels Institute. Expelled from the party in 1931 and died during the purges in 1938.

**Roy, Manabendra Nath** (1893–1954) Indian nationalist, born in Bengal, who travelled widely during the First World War in quest of weapons to fight British rule. Prominent at the Second Congress of the Comintern in 1920, where he opposed Lenin's openness to collaboration with 'bourgeois nationalists' in colonial countries.

Helped organize an Indian communist movement, mainly from exile, and active for the Comintern in Mexico and China. Expelled from the Comintern as a supporter of Brandler in 1929. Resumed activity as a nationalist, within Congress, but expelled in 1940 for supporting the British (as anti-fascist) in the war. From 1946 wrote as a theorist and leader of a political humanist movement. (Roy, 1964; Roy, 1987; Haithcox, 1971)

**Serrati, Giacinto** (1874–1926) Militant Italian Socialist leader, supporter of the 'Zimmerwald left', and editor of *Avanti!* during the First World War. He attended the Second Congress of the Comintern in 1920 and was elected to its Praesidium. However at the Livorno Congress of the Italian Socialist Party (1921), he led the largest, 'centre' faction, who refused to support the expulsion of the 'right', led by Turati, or the split away by the Italian Communist Party. Attended the Fourth Congress of the Comintern and led the remerger of the left wing of the Socialist Party into the Communist Party in 1924, becoming a member of the Central Committee.

**Shliapnikov, Alexander** (1884–1937) A metalworker, he was member of the Russian Social Democratic Labour Party from 1901 and of its Bolshevik faction from 1903. Acting head of the Bolshevik organization in Russia from 1914 to 1917, he became commissar of labour in the first Soviet government. From 1920 he led the Workers' Opposition current. He was removed from all leading positions in the party in 1924 and died in the purges in 1937.

**Sik, Ota** (1919–) Prominent economist in Czechoslovakia in the 1960s, advocate of the 1967–8 proposals to combine market forces with central planning. Emigrated following the Soviet invasion of 1968.

**Slansky, Rudolf** (1901–52) Jewish Czechoslovak communist, member of the Politburo from 1929 and secretary general from 1945. Arrested in 1951 and accused of Titoism, Trotskyism and Zionism, he was executed in 1952 after a trial with a marked anti-semitic tenor.

**Stalin, Joseph Vissarionovich** (1879–1953) Georgian seminary student, expelled for revolutionary activities in 1899. A social democrat, he sided with Lenin after 1903 and became a principal figure of the Bolsheviks' illegal organization in the Caucasus. During 1912 he was editor of the Bolsheviks' newspaper *Pravda*. He returned to Petrograd from one of his several periods of Siberian exile in March 1917, but played a secondary part in the October overturn. However, in charge of party organization from 1922, he overcame competitors (Trotsky, Zinoviev and Kamenev, Bukharin) in a series of manoeuvres and alliances, and by 1929 was in undisputed control. Identified with the theory of 'socialism in one country', he was responsible for the 'liquidation of the kulaks', the drive to industrialization, and the purges and terror of the 1930s, for Soviet expansionism and the transformation of Eastern Europe, and for several post-war purges. He was the object of a considerable personality cult, and was buried in Lenin's mausoleum in Moscow. However in 1961 Krushchev had his remains reburied with those of lesser Soviet leaders in the wall of the Kremlin. His works include *Marxism and the National and Colonial Question* (1913), *Problems of Leninism* (1924) and *On Marxism and Linguistics* (1949). (Ulam, 1973; Deutscher, 1970; Tucker, 1973)

**Stambolisky, Alexander** (1879–1923) Bulgarian Agrarian leader, head of a reforming government from 1919 until being overthrown and assassinated in a military coup in 1923.

**Stoecker, Walter** (1891–1939) A leader of the pro-communist faction of the German Independent Socialist Party (USPD) from 1918, he joined the Communist Party after the USPD's split in 1920, and became a member of the Comintern secretariat from 1922. A communist deputy from 1920, he was chairman of the communist group in the Reichstag from 1924 to 1931. Arrested on the night of the Reichstag fire (27 February 1933) he was sent to Buchenwald concentration camp, where he remained until he died.

**Struve, Peter** (1870–1944) Russian intellectual and politician. He wrote the manifesto for the RSDLP's first congress in 1898, but moved towards liberalism after 1901. An opponent of the Bolshevik seizure of power, he supported the anti-Bolshevik forces in the civil war, and subsequently lived in exile. (Pipes, 1970–74)

**Subhi, Mustafa** (1883–1921) Turkish radical nationalist, and member of socialist grouping from 1910. Formed communist organization among Turkish prisoners of war in Russia in 1918, founded the Turkish Communist Party at Baku in 1920, but murdered, with the rest of its leadership, when he returned to Turkey in 1921. (Harris, 1967)

**Sun Yat-sen (Sun Ixian)** (1866–1925) President of the Chinese republic after the 1911 revolution, founder of the Kuomintang in 1912, head of Kuomintang government in Canton from 1923.

**Suslov, Mikhail** (1902–82) Joined the Bolshevik Party in 1921, supported Stalin, and was brought on to the Central Committee in 1941. After Stalin's death he continued to be treated as a senior authority on ideological matters, and joined the Politburo in 1966.

**Tasca, Angelo** (1892–1960) Italian radical socialist, associated with Mussolini before the First World War, later with the *Ordine Nuovo* group in Turin, then a founding leader of the Italian Communist Party, and a principal organizer of its underground work in 1924–6. Elected to the Praesidium of the Comintern, he came to support Bukharin, and was expelled from the Italian party by Togliatti in 1929. A writer on foreign policy for the French Socialist Party during the 1930s, he acted as a propagandist for the Vichy regime in the early part of the war, but later joined a Belgian resistance group. Under the pseudonym A. Rossi he wrote on the development of Italian fascism, and on communist policy during the Second World War. (De Grand, 1987)

**Thalheimer, August** (1884–1932) Founding member of the German Spartacus League and leader of the KPD; expelled in 1929 and (with Brandler) led an independent communist grouping.

**Thorez, Maurice** (1900–64) French communist leader. A supporter of Stalin from 1925, he became party leader in 1930. He spent the war years in the Soviet Union, but returned to France in 1944 and held ministerial offices under De Gaulle and Ramadier. A loyal supporter of Stalin, he accommodated to 'de-Stalinization' after 1956 and led the party until his death.

**Tito, Josip Broz** (1892–1980) Yugoslav communist leader. As a prisoner of war in Siberia in 1917 he participated in the Russian revolution, then joined the Yugoslav Communist Party, becoming active in Comintern work in Europe and leader of the Yugoslav party in 1939. From 1941 he led the communist partisan movement, establishing a provisional government in 1943, and eliminating internal opposition after the war. Stalin expelled Yugoslavia from the Cominform and excoriated 'Titoism' from 1948, but in 1955 the Soviet leadership under Krushchev took steps to heal the breach. (Auty, 1974; Djilas, 1981)

**Togliatti, Palmiro** (1893–1964) A founding member of the Italian Communist Party and its secretary general from 1927. Member of the Executive Committee of the Comintern from 1925, and a Comintern agent in Spain during the civil war. In the Soviet Union during the war, he returned to Italy in 1944 to lead the party, which rapidly grew into the largest in Western Europe. Became a prominent voice of 'de-Stalinization' and 'polycentrism' after 1956 and is sometimes considered a prophet of 'Eurocommunism'. None the less after his death the Soviet leadership named a large automobile plant built by Fiat after him – at 'Togliattigrad' on the Volga.

**Trotsky, Leon** (1879–1940) A writer for *Iskra* during 1902–3, he opposed Lenin at the 1903 Congress of the RSDLP. Developed Parvus's theory of 'permanent revolution'. Chairman of the St Petersburg Soviet during the 1905 revolution. Led small intermediate faction of the RSDLP 1904–17, mainly from exile. In May 1917 he returned to Petrograd, joined the Bolsheviks, and was the main organizer of their seizure of power. Chief negotiator at Brest-Litovsk (1917–18), he then commanded the Red Armies during the civil war (1918–20), and subsequently took an active part in economic policy and in the affairs of Comintern. Becoming a critic of Soviet bureaucracy, he moved into opposition after Lenin's death in 1924, but was outmanoeuvred by Stalin and expelled from the party in 1927. Exiled in 1929, he lived in Turkey, France, Norway and Mexico, writing prolifically in criticism of Stalin and his policies. Tried in his absence for treason by the Soviet authorities in 1938, he was sentenced to death; in the same year he and his supporters formed a Fourth International, uniting small parties in various countries. In 1940 he was assassinated in Mexico on Stalin's orders. His works include *Our Political Tasks* (1904), *Results and Prospects* (1906), *My Life* (1930), *History of the Russian Revolution* (1931–3) and *The Revolution Betrayed* (1936). (Deutscher, 1979, 1979a, 1979b; Howe, 1978; Knei-Paz, 1979)

**Tukhachevsky, Mikhail** (1897–1937) Russian officer who joined the Bolsheviks in 1918 and became one of the most successful commanders of Trotsky's Red Armies during the civil war and the 1920 war with Poland, and an advocate of spreading revolution by force of arms. Remained a very senior military figure until 1937, when, as part of Stalin's purge among senior officers, he was secretly tried and shot for collaboration with Germany.

**Turati, Filippo** (1857–1932) Reformist socialist, founder of the Italian Socialist Party in 1892.

**Ulbricht, Walter** (1893–1973) Founding member of the German Communist Party, trained in the Soviet Union, and a Reichstag deputy from 1928 until Hitler came to power in 1933. Then a Comintern agent abroad, active in Spain during the civil war. In the Soviet Union during the war, he returned in 1945 to lead the German party in the Soviet occupation zone. Organizer of the forced fusion with the social democrats in 1946, he became prime minister when the Soviet zone became the German Democratic Republic in 1949 and formal leader of the fused party from 1950. Retired from the party leadership in 1971 but remained head of state until his death. (Stern, 1965)

**Unszlicht, Josef** (1879–1938) Polish socialist, joined the Bolshevik Party after the February 1917 revolution, deputy head of the Cheka 1921–23. Part of the team selected by the Bolshevik leadership to direct the German Communist Party's (KPD) insurrection in 1923, he was to have been responsible for the suppression of counter-revolutionaries following a KPD victory. Held various senior military and civilian offices in the Soviet state, until he was arrested in 1937, being executed in 1938. (Leggett, 1981, pp. 271–3).

**Vyshinsky, Andrei** (1883–1955) A Menshevik before the Russian revolution, who joined the Russian Communist Party in 1920 and became a protégé of Stalin. A state prosecutor in political trials during the 1920s, he became Procurator of the Soviet Union in 1935 and acted as prosecutor in the main Moscow show trials of 1936, 1937 and 1938. Deputy Foreign Minister 1940–9, Foreign Minister 1949–53, and again Deputy Foreign Minister from 1953 until his death. Active in the political transformation of Eastern Europe.

**Webb, Sidney** (1859–1947) and **Beatrice** (1858–1943) Moderate English socialists, founders of the Fabian Society (1884) and the London School of Economics (1895). Under the influence of George Bernard Shaw they became sympathetic visitors to the Soviet Union in the 1930s and wrote a large and appreciative study, *Soviet Communism: A New Civilization* (1935).

**Yagoda, Genrikh** (1891–1938) Bolshevik from 1907 who made his career in the Cheka after 1917 and in 1934 became head of the NKVD. He was responsible for a great expansion of the forced labour system and for organizing the first treason trials, but was removed by Stalin in 1936 for insufficient ruthlessness (being replaced by Yezhov), arrested in 1937 and tried with Bukharin and executed in 1938.

**Yezhov, Nikolai** (1894–1939) Joined the Bolsheviks in 1917, became a protégé of Stalin, joined the Central Committee in 1934, and in 1936 replaced Yagoda as head of the NKVD, where he directed the most intense period of terror. Succeeded by Beria in 1938, he apparently met his death the following year.

**Zasulich, Vera** (1851–1919) Russian Populist who assassinated a senior Tsarist prison official in 1878 but was acquitted after a sensational trial. Became an associate of Plekhanov in exile, served on the editorial board of *Iskra* (*The Spark*) 1900–3, and took the Menshevik side in the 1903 split of Russian Social Democracy. (Bergman, 1983)

**Zetkin, Klara** (1857–?1933) Associate of Rosa Luxemburg and a leading figure in the German Social Democratic Party and the Second International before the First

World War, being particularly active in their work among women. Joined the German Communist Party's Central Committee and the Executive of the Comintern in 1921.

**Zhdanov, Andrei Alexandrovich** (1896–1948) A Bolshevik from 1915, he became head of the Leningrad party organization on the assassination of Kirov in 1934, and a member of the Politburo in 1939. After the war he became the leading proponent of 'socialist realism' in art and culture, and was closely involved in the formation of the Cominform. After his death a major purge of his associates took place. (Hahn, 1982)

**Zinoviev, Gregory** (1883–1936) Joined the RSDLP in 1901 and was a close associate of Lenin from the 1903 split onwards, a member of the 'Zimmerwald left' bureau during the First World War, returning to Russia with Lenin in April 1917. With Kamenev, he opposed Lenin's plans for a party seizure of power in the autumn of 1917, but remained on the party leadership. First Chairman of the Comintern (1919–26) and leader of the Leningrad party organization, he was part of the ruling 'triumvirate' (Zinoviev, Kamenev and Stalin) after Lenin's death in 1924. Joining forces with Trotsky he was expelled from the party in 1927, but recanted, was readmitted, and again expelled in 1932. Sentenced to imprisonment in 1935, he was tried for treason and shot in 1936.

# Works cited

Abel, Elie (1969) *The Missiles of October: the story of the Cuban missile crisis*, MacGibbon and Kee, London.

Abramovitch, Raphael R. (1962) *The Soviet Revolution, 1917–39*, George Allen and Unwin, London.

Adamson, Walter L. (1983) *Hegemony and Revolution: a study of Antonio Gramsci's political and cultural theory*, University of California Press, Berkeley CA.

Adereth, M. (1984) *The French Communist Party: a critical history (1920–1984): from Comintern to 'the colours of France'*, Manchester University Press, Manchester.

Adler, Alan (ed.) (1983) *Theses, Resolutions and Manifestos of the First Four Congresses of the Third International*, Pluto Press, London.

Akimov, Vladimir (1969) *Vladimir Akimov on the Dilemmas of Russian Marxism: two texts in translation*, Cambridge University Press, Cambridge.

Alba, Victor (1983) *The Communist Party in Spain*, Transaction Books, Brunswick NJ.

Anderson, Perry (1976–7) 'The antinomies of Antonio Gramsci', *New Left Review*, 100.

Angress, Werner T. (1963) *Stillborn Revolution: the Communist bid for power in Germany, 1921–23*, Princeton University Press, Princeton, New Jersey.

Aristotle (1908) *Politics*, tr. Jowett, Clarendon Press, Oxford.

Ascher, A. (1966–7) 'Russian Marxism and the German Revolution, 1917–1920', in *Archiv für Sozialgeschichte*, VI/VII, pp. 428–9.

Ascher, Abraham (1972) *Pavel Axelrod and the Development of Menshevism*, Harvard University Press, Cambridge MA.

Auty, Phyllis (1974) *Tito*, Penguin, Harmondsworth.

Avrich, Paul (1974) *Kronstadt 1921*, Norton, New York.

Badgley, John (1974) 'Burmese Communist schisms', in Lewis (1974), pp. 151–68.

Bajanov, Boris (1930) *Avec Staline dans le Kremlin*, Éditions de France, Paris.

Baku Congress (1977) *Congress of the Peoples of the East (Baku, September 1920): Stenographic Report*, New Park, London.

Banac, Ivo (ed.) (1983) *The Effects of World War I: the class war after the Great War: the rise of Communist Parties in East Central Europe, 1918–1921*, Brooklyn College Press, New York.

Bao Ruo-wang (Jean Pasqualini) and Rudolph Chelminski (1976) *Prisoner of Mao*, Penguin, Harmondsworth.

Baring, Arnulf (1972) *Uprising in East Germany: June 17th 1953*, Cornell University Press, Ithaca, NY.

Baron, Samuel (1963) *Plekhanov, the Father of Russian Marxism*, Stanford University Press, Stanford CA.

Batatu, Hanna (1978) *The Old Social Classes and the Revolutionary Movements of Iraq*, Princeton University Press, Princeton NJ.

Beckman, George M. and Okubo Genji (1969) *The Japanese Communist Party, 1922–1945*, Stanford University Press, Stanford CA.

Bell, Daniel (1974) *The Coming of Post-Industrial Society*, Heinemann, London.

Bell, John D. (1986) *The Bulgarian Communist Party from Blagoev to Zhivkov*, Hoover Institution Press, Stanford CA.

Bellis, Paul (1979) *Marxism and the USSR: the theory of proletarian dictatorship and the Marxist analysis of Soviet society*, Macmillan, London.

Benton, Gregor (1975) 'The Yenan "literary opposition" ', *New Left Review*, 92, July–August.

Bergman, Jay (1983) *Vera Zasulich: a biography*, Stanford University Press, Stanford CA.

Berlin, Isaiah (1978) *Karl Marx: his life and environment*, 4th edition, Oxford University Press, Oxford.

Besançon, Alain (1981) *The Intellectual Origins of Leninism*, Basil Blackwell, Oxford.

Bethell, Nicolas (1972) *Gomulka*, Penguin, Harmondsworth.

Betts, Reginald Robert (ed.) (1950) *Central and Southeast Europe 1945–1948*, Royal Institute of International Affairs, London.

Bianco, Lucien (1971) *Origins of the Chinese Revolution, 1915–1949*, Oxford University Press, London.

BICO (British and Irish Communist Organization) (1975) *The Cult of the Individual*, BICO, Belfast.

Biggart, John (1972) 'Kirov before the revolution', *Soviet Studies*, 23, 3, pp. 345–72.

Bing, Dov (1971) 'Sneevliet and the early years of the CCP', *China Quarterly*, 48, pp. 677–97.

Birchall, Ian Harry (1974) *Workers against the Monolith*, Pluto Press, London.

Blit, L. (1965) *The Eastern Pretender: Boleslaw Piasecki, his Life and Times*, Hutchinson, London.

Bloomfield, Jon (1979) *Passive Revolution: politics and the Czechoslovak working class, 1945–1948*, Allison and Busby, London.

Booth, John A. (1985) *The End and the Beginning: the Nicaraguan revolution*, Westview Press, Boulder CO.

Bramsted, E. J. (1965) *Goebbels and National Socialist Propaganda 1925–45*, Cresset Press, London.

Brandt, Conrad, Benjamin Schwartz and John K. Fairbank (1973) *A Documentary History of Chinese Communism*, Atheneum, New York.

Brant, Stephan (pseud., Klaus Harpprecht) (1955) *The East German Rising, 17th June 1953*, Thames and Hudson, London.

Braunthal, Julius (1980) *History of the International: Volume 3, 1943–1968*, Victor Gollancz, London.

Brewer, Anthony (1980) *Marxist Theories of Imperialism: a critical survey*, Routledge and Kegan Paul, London.

Brown, Archie and George Schopflin (1979) 'The challenge to Soviet Leadership: effects in Eastern Europe', in Filo della Torre, Mortimer and Story (1979).

Brown, MacAlister and Joseph J. Zasloff (1986) *Apprentice Revolutionaries: the Communist movement in Laos, 1930–1985*, Hoover Institution Press, Stanford CA.

Brzezinski, Zbigniew Kazimierz (1967) *The Soviet Bloc: unity and conflict*, 2nd edition, Harvard University Press, Cambridge MA.

Bukovsky, Vladimir (1987) *To Choose Freedom*, Hoover Institution, Stanford.

Bukovsky, Vladimir (1987a) (interviewed by George Urban), 'Hope and despair in the Soviet system', *Encounter*, 69.

Burns, John P. (1987) 'China's *Nomenklatura* system', *Problems of Communism*, 36, 5 (September–October), pp. 36–51.

Callaghan, John (1988) 'The British road to Eurocommunism', in Waller and Fennema (1988), pp. 224–43.

Cammett, John McKay (1967) *Antonio Gramsci and the Origins of Italian Communism*, Stanford University Press, Stanford.

Carr, Edward Hallett (1969) *The Interregnum 1923–1924*, Penguin, Harmondsworth.

Carr, Edward Hallett (1977) *The Bolshevik Revolution, 1917–23*, 3 vols, Penguin, Harmondsworth.

Carrere d'Encausse, Hélène (1987) *The Soviet Union and Soviet Europe*, Holmes and Meier, London.

Carrere d'Encausse, Hélène and Stuart R. Schram (eds) (1969) *Marxism and Asia*, Allen Lane, London.

Castoriadis, Cornelius (1981) *Devant la Guerre*, Fayard, Paris.

Castoriadis, Cornelius (1983) 'The destinies of totalitarianism', *Salmagundi* (Saratoga Springs), pp. 107–22.

Caute, David (1988) *The Fellow Travellers: intellectual friends of communism*, revised and updated edition, Yale University Press, New Haven CT.

Ch'en, Jerome (1967) *Mao and the Chinese Revolution*, Oxford University Press, London.

Chesneaux, Jean (1968) *The Chinese Labour Movement, 1919–1927*, Stanford University Press, Stanford CA.

Ciliga, Ante (1979) *The Russian Enigma*, Ink Links, London.

Clark, Martin (1977) *Antonio Gramsci and the Revolution that Failed*, Yale University Press, New Haven CT.

Claudin, Fernando (1975) *The Communist Movement – From Comintern to Cominform*, Penguin, Harmondsworth.

Cohen, Stephen F. (1975) *Bukharin and the Bolshevik Revolution: a political biography, 1888–1938*, Vintage Books, New York.

Communist International (1977) *Second Congress of the Communist International: Minutes*, 2 vols, New Park, London.

Conquest, Robert (1973) *The Great Terror: Stalin's purges of the thirties*, revised edition, Macmillan, London.

Conquest, Robert (1986) *The Harvest of Sorrow: Soviet collectivization and the terror-famine*, Hutchinson, London.

Craver, Earlene (1974) 'The rediscovery of Amadeo Bordiga', Survey, 20, 2/3, pp. 160–75.

D'Agostino, Anthony (1969) 'Intelligentsia socialism and the "workers' revolution": the views of J. W. Machajski', *International Review of Social History*, XIV, 1.

D'Agostino, Anthony (1988) *Soviet Succession Struggles: Kremlinology and the Russian question from Lenin to Gorbachev*, Allen and Unwin, Boston MA.

Davies, Norman (1972) *White Eagle, Red Star: the Polish–Soviet war, 1919–20*, Macdonald, London.

Davies, Norman (1977) 'Poland', in MacAuley (1977).

Davies, Norman (1986) *God's Playground: a history of Poland*, 2 vols, Oxford University Press.

Davis, Nathaniel (1985) *The Last Two Years of Salvador Allende*, Cornell University Press, Ithaca NY.

Dawisha, Karen (1988) *Eastern Europe, Gorbachev and Reform*, Cambridge University Press, Cambridge.

Debo, Richard K. (1979) *Revolution and Survival: the foreign policy of Soviet Russia 1918–19*, Liverpool University Press, Liverpool.

Decalo, Samuel (1985) 'Socio-economic constraints on radical action in the People's Republic of Congo', *Journal of Communist Studies*, vol. 1, 3–4 (September–December) (special issue on military Marxist regimes in Africa, edited by J. Markakis and Michael Waller), pp. 39–57.

de Flers, René (1984) 'Socialism in one family', *Survey*, 28, 4 (123), pp. 165–74.

De Grand, Alexander J. (1987) *In Stalin's Shadow. Angelo Tasca and the Left in Italy and France, 1910–1945*, Northern Illinois University Press, Dekalb IL.

Degras, Jane (ed.) (1956–65) *The Communist International, 1919–1943: Documents*, 3 vols, Oxford University Press, London.

Deutscher, Isaac (1970) *Stalin: a political biography*, Penguin, Harmondsworth.

Deutscher, Isaac (1979) *The Prophet Armed: Trotsky, 1879–1921*, Oxford University Press, Oxford.

Deutscher, Isaac (1979a) *The Prophet Unarmed: Trotsky, 1921–1929*, Oxford University Press, Oxford.

Deutscher, Isaac (1979b) *The Prophet Outcast: Trotsky, 1929–1940*, Oxford University Press, Oxford.

Dewar, Hugo (1976) *Communist Politics in Britain: the CPGB from its origins to the Second World War*, Pluto Press, London.

de Weydenthal, Jan B. (1978) *The Communists of Poland: an historical outline*, HIP, Stanford CA.

Disco, Cornelis (1987) 'Intellectuals in advanced capitalism: capital, closure and the new-class thesis', in Ron Eyerman, Lennart G. Svensson and Thomas Soderqvist (eds) *Intellectuals, Universities and the State in Western Modern Societies*, University of California Press, Berkeley, pp. 50–77.

Dittmer, Lowell (1974) *Liu Shao-chi and the Chinese Cultural Revolution: the politics of mass criticism*, University of California Press, Berkeley CA.

Dittmer, Lowell (1987) *China's Continuous Revolution: the post-liberation epoch, 1949–81*, University of California Press, Berkeley CA.

Djilas, Alexsa (1986) 'Creeping confederalisation in Yugoslavia', *Labour and Trades Union Press Service*, XI, 2, March.

Djilas, Milovan (1969) *Conversations with Stalin*, Penguin, Harmondsworth.

Djilas, Milovan (1977) *Wartime*, Martin Secker and Warburg, London.

Djilas, Milovan (1981) *Tito: the story from inside*, Weidenfeld and Nicolson, London.

Domes, Jürgen (1973) *The Internal Politics of China 1949–1972*, Hurst, London.

Dominguez, Jorge (1978) *Cuba: order and revolution*, Harvard University Press, Cambridge MA.

Drachkovitch, Milorad M. and Branko Lazitch (eds) (1966) *The Comintern: Historical Highlights. Essays, recollections, documents*. Pall Mall Press, London.

Draper, Theodore (1966) *The Roots of American Communism*, Viking Press, New York.

Druhe, David N. (1959) *Soviet Russia and Indian Communism, 1917–47* (with Epilogue to 1959), Bookman Associates, New York.

Dunn, David (1984) 'A good Fabian fallen among the Stalinists', *Survey*, 28, 4 (123), pp. 15–37.

Dziewanowski, Marian K. (1976) *The Communist Party of Poland: an outline of history*, Harvard University Press, Cambridge MA.

Ellman, Michael (1988, forthcoming) *Socialist Planning*, revised edition, Cambridge University Press, Cambridge.

Enzenberger, Hans Magnus (1976) *Raids and Reconstructions*, Pluto Press, London.

Eudes, Dominique (1972) *The Kapetanios: Partisans and Civil War in Greece, 1943–1949*, New Left Books, London.

Eudin, Xenia J. and Robert C. North (1957) *Soviet Russia and the East, 1920–1927: a documentary survey*, Stanford University Press, Stanford CA.

Feigon, Lee (1983) *Chen Duxiu, the Founder of the Chinese Communist Party*, Princeton University Press, Princeton NJ.

Fejto, Ferenc (1973) *Chine–URSS: de l'alliance au conflit 1950–72*, Seuil, Paris.

Fejto, Ferenc (François) (1974) *History of the People's Democracies: Eastern Europe since Stalin*, Penguin, Harmondsworth.

Fermia, Joseph V. (1981) *Gramsci's Political Thought*, Oxford University Press, Oxford.

Feuer, Lewis S. (1975) *Ideology and the Ideologists*, Basil Blackwell, Oxford.

Filo della Torre, P., E. Mortimer and J. Story (eds) (1979) *Eurocommunism: myth or reality?*, Penguin, Harmondsworth.

Fowkes, Ben (1984) *Communism in Germany under the Weimar Republic*, Macmillan, London.

Frankel, Jonathan (1969) *Introduction: the polarization of Russian Marxism (1883–1903)*, in Akimov (1969), pp. 3–98.

Frankel, Jonathan (1981) *Prophecy and Politics*, Cambridge University Press, London.

Freud, Sigmund (1985) *Civilisation, Society and Religion*, Penguin, Harmondsworth.

Freville, Jean (1968) *Lenine à Paris*, Éditions Sociales, Paris.

Galindez Suarez, Jesus (1973) *The Era of Trujillo, Dominican Dictator*, University of Arizona Press, Tucson AR.

Garton Ash, Timothy (1985) *The Polish Revolution: Solidarity*, Coronet Books, London.

Gerschenkron, A. (1947) 'The rate of growth of industrial production in Russia since 1885', *Journal of Economic History*, VII–S.

Getty, J. Arch (1985) *Origins of the Great Purges: the Soviet Communist Party reconsidered, 1933–1938*, Cambridge University Press, Cambridge.

Getzler, Israel (1967) *Martov: a political biography of a Russian social democrat*, Cambridge University Press, Cambridge.

Getzler, Israel (1983) *Kronstadt 1917–1921: the fate of a soviet democracy*, Cambridge University Press, Cambridge.

Gittings, John (ed.) (1964) *The Sino-Soviet Dispute, 1956–1963*, Royal Institute of International Affairs, London.

Gittings, John (1968) *Survey of the Sino-Soviet Dispute: a commentary and extracts from the recent polemics, 1963–1967*, Royal Institute of International Affairs, London.

Gluckstein, Ygael (1952) *Stalin's Satellites in Europe*, George Allen and Unwin, London.

Goldenberg, Boris (1970) 'The rise and fall of a party: the Cuban Communist Party (1925–1959)', *Problems of Communism*, 29, 4 (July–August).

Goldman, Marshall (1987) *Gorbachev's Challenge*, W. W. Norton, New York.

Graham, Helen and Paul Preston (eds) (1987) *The Popular Front in Europe*, Macmillan, Basingstoke.

Graham, Loren R. (1987) *Science, Philosophy, and Human Behaviour in the Soviet Union*, Columbia University Press, New York.

Griffith, William Edgar (ed.) (1964) *The Sino-Soviet Rift*, George Allen and Unwin, London.

Guillermaz, Jacques (1972) *A History of the Chinese Communist Party, 1921–1949*, Methuen, London.

Hahn, Werner G. (1982) *Postwar Soviet politics: the fall of Zhdanov and the defeat of moderation, 1946–53*, Cornell University Press, Ithaca NY.

Haithcox, J. P. (1971) *Communism and Nationalism in India: M. N. Roy and Comintern policy 1920–39*, Oxford University Press, London and Bombay.

Halliday, Fred (1980) 'Revolution in Iran: was it possible in 1921?', *Khamsin*, 7, pp. 53–64.

Halperin, Maurice (1981) *The Taming of Fidel Castro*, University of California Press, Berkeley CA.

Hammer, Ellen Joy (1966) *The Struggle for Indochina, 1940–1945*, 2nd edition, Stanford University Press, Stanford CA.

Hammond, T. T. (ed.) (1975) *The Anatomy of Communist Takeovers*, Yale University Press, New Haven CT.

Haraszti, Miklos (1988) *The Velvet Prison: artists under state socialism*, I. B. Tauris, London.

Harding, Neil (1983) *Lenin's Political Thought*, Macmillan, London.

Harding, Neil (ed.) (1983a) *Marxism in Russia: Key Documents, 1879-1906*, Cambridge University Press, Cambridge.

Harris, George S. (1967) *The Origins of Communism in Turkey*, Hoover Institution Press, Stanford.

Harrison, James Pinckney (1972) *The Long March to Power: a history of the Chinese Communist Party, 1921-72*, Macmillan, London.

Harrison, Royden (1983) 'British Labour, Marxism and the Soviet Union', summary of paper to Society for the Study of Labour History, in *Bulletin of the Society for the Study of Labour History*, 47, pp. 10-11.

Harrison, Royden (1987) 'Sidney and Beatrice Webb', in Levy (1987), pp. 35-89.

Havel, Vaclav (1987) 'Doing without utopias: an interview with Vaclav Havel', *Times Literary Supplement*, 23 January.

Haynes, Michael (1985) *Nikolai Bukharin and the Transition from Capitalism to Socialism*, Croom Helm, London.

Heller, Michael and Aleksandr Nekrich (1982) *Utopia in Power*, Hutchinson, London.

Hodges, Donald C. (1977) *The Legacy of Che Guevara: a documentary study*, Thames and Hudson, London.

Hodges, Donald C. (1986) *Intellectual Foundations of the Nicaraguan Revolution*, University of Texas Press, Austin, Tex.

Hollander, Paul (1983) *Political Pilgrims*, Harper Colophon Books, London.

Holmes, Leslie (ed.) (1981) *The Withering Away of the State? Party and state under Communism*, Sage, London.

Holmes, Leslie (1986) *Politics in the Communist World*, Oxford University Press, London.

Horner, John E. (1979) 'Traicho Kostov: Stalinist orthodoxy in Bulgaria', *Survey*, 24, 3, pp. 135-42.

Howe, Irving (1978) *Trotsky*, Harvester, Hassocks.

Howe, Irving and Lewis A. Coser (1958) *The American Communist Party: a critical history, 1919-1957*, Beacon Press, Boston MA.

Huynh Kim Khanh (1982) *Vietnamese Communism, 1925-45*, Cornell University Press, Ithaca NY.

Isaacs, Harold (1961) *The Tragedy of the Chinese Revolution*, 2nd revised edition, Stanford University Press, Stanford CA.

Jacobs, Dan N. (1981) *Borodin: Stalin's man in China*, Harvard University Press, Cambridge MA.

Jancar, Barbara Wolfe (1978) *Women under Communism*, Johns Hopkins University Press, Baltimore MD.

Johnson, Chalmers Ashby (1963) *Peasant Nationalism and Communist Power*, Oxford University Press, London.

Joll, James (1978) *Antonio Gramsci*, Penguin, Harmondsworth.

Jones, Howard Palfrey (1971) *Indonesia: the possible dream*, Harcourt Brace Jovanovich, New York.

Kaldor, Mary (1988) 'Poszgay - Hungary's man of the hour' (interview), *New Statesman*, 27 May, pp. 21-2.

Kaplan, Karel (1986) *The Overcoming of the Regime Crisis after Stalin's Death in*

*Czechoslovakia, Poland and Hungary*, Study no. 11 of Research Project on Crises in Soviet-type systems, Vienna.

Kaplan, Karel (1987) *The Short March: the communist take-over in Czechoslovakia, 1945–48*, Hurst, London.

Keep, J. L. H. (1963) *The Rise of Social Democracy in Russia*, Oxford University Press, London.

Kemp, Tom (1967) *Theories of Imperialism*, Dobson, London.

Kendall, Walter (1969) *The Revolutionary Movement in Britain, 1900–21: the origins of British communism*, Weidenfeld and Nicolson, London.

Kerkvliet, Benedict (1977) *The Huk Rebellion: a study of peasant revolt in the Philippines*, University of California Press, Berkeley CA.

Khrushchev, Nikita S. (1971) *Khrushchev Remembers*, Sphere, London.

Kiernan, Ben (1985) *How Pol Pot Came to Power: a history of communism in Kampuchea 1930–1975*, Verso, London.

Kiernan, Victor G. (1974) *Marxism and Imperialism*, Edward Arnold, London.

Kindersley, Richard (ed.) (1982) *In Search of Eurocommunism*, Macmillan, London.

King, Robert R. (1980) *A History of the Romanian Communist Party*, Hoover Institution Press, Stanford CA.

Kingston-Mann, Esther (1983) *Lenin and the Problem of Marxist Peasant Revolution*, Oxford University Press, London.

Kitrinos, Robert W. (1984) 'International Department of the CPSU', *Problems of Communism*, 33, 5 (September–October).

Knei-Paz, Baruch (1979) *The Social and Political Thought of Leon Trotsky*, Oxford University Press, London.

Kolakowski, Leszek (1982) *Main Currents of Marxism: its origins, growth and dissolution*, Oxford University Press, Oxford.

Korn, David A. (1986) *Ethiopia, the United States and the Soviet Union*, Croom Helm, London.

Kostiner, Joseph (1984) *The Struggle for South Yemen*, St Martin's Press, New York.

Kousoulas, D. F. G. (1976) *Revolution and Defeat: the story of the Greek Communist Party*, Oxford University Press, London.

Kovrig, Bennett (1979) *Communism in Hungary: from Kun to Kadar*, Hoover Institution Press, Stanford CA.

Kriegel, Annie (1972) *The French Communists: profile of a people*, University of Chicago Press, Chicago IL.

Krupskaya, Nadezhda K. (1975) *Reminiscences of Lenin*, International Publishers, New York.

Kusin, Vladimir V. (1972) *Political Groupings in the Czechoslovak Reform Movement*, Macmillan, London.

Kusin, Vladimir V. (1978) *From Dubcek to Charter 77: a study of 'normalisation' in Czechoslovakia, 1968–1978*, Q Press, Edinburgh.

Lacouture, Jean (1968) *Ho Chi Minh*, Allen Lane, London.

Laitan, David D. and Said S. Samatar (1987) *Somalia: a nation in search of a state*, Westview Press, Boulder CO.

Langer, P. (1972) *Communism in Japan: a case of political naturalization*, Hoover Institution Press, Stanford CA.

Larsson, Reidar (1970) *Theories of Revolution: from Marx to the first Russian revolution*, Almqvist and Wiksell, Stockholm.

Lasky, Melvin J. (ed.) (1957) *The Hungarian Revolution*, Secker and Warburg, London.

Lasswell, Harold D. and Daniel Lerner (eds) (1965) *World Revolutionary Elites*, MIT Press, Cambridge MA.

Lazitch, Branko and Milorad M. Drachkovitch (1972) *Lenin and the Comintern*, 2 vols, Hoover Institution Press, Stanford CA.

Lee, Chong-sik (1978) *The Korean Workers' Party: a short history*, Hoover Institution Press, Stanford CA.

Leggett, George (1981) *The Cheka: Lenin's political police*, Oxford University Press, Oxford.

Leighton, Marian (1985) 'A balance sheet of Sandinista rule in Nicaragua', *Survey*, 29, 3 (126), Autumn, pp. 73–111.

Leonhard, Wolfgang (1979) *Child of the Revolution*, Ink Links, London.

Lenin, Vladimir Ilich (1960–78) *Collected Works*, 45 vols plus index vols, Lawrence and Wishart, London, and Foreign Languages Publishing House, Moscow.

Levy, Carl (ed.) (1987) *Socialism and the Intelligentsia, 1880–1914*, London, Methuen.

Lewis, Flora (1959) *The Polish Volcano*, Secker and Warburg, London.

Lewis, John Wilson (1966) *Leadership in Communist China*, Cornell University Press, Ithaca NY.

Lewis, John Wilson (ed.) (1974) *Peasant Rebellion and Communist Revolution in Asia*, Stanford University Press, Stanford CA.

Leys, Simon (1977) *The Chairman's New Clothes: Mao and the Cultural Revolution*, Allison and Busby, London.

Lomax, Bill (1976) *Hungary 1956*, Allison and Busby, London.

Lotveit, Trygve (1979) *Chinese Communism 1931–34: experience in civil government*, 2nd edition, Curzon, London.

McAuley, Alistair (1979) *Economic Welfare in the Soviet Union*, George Allen and Unwin, London.

McBriar, A. M. (1966) *Fabian Socialism and English Politics, 1884–1918*, Cambridge University Press, Cambridge.

McCauley, Martin (ed.) (1977) *Communist Power in Europe 1944–49*, Macmillan, London.

McCauley, Martin (1977a) 'East Germany', in McCauley (1977).

McCauley, Martin (1979) *Marxism-Leninism in the German Democratic Republic: the Socialist Unity Party (SED)*, Macmillan, London.

MacFarquhar, Roderick (ed.) (1960) *The Hundred Flowers*, Atlantic Books, London.

MacFarquhar, Roderick (1974–) *The Origins of the Cultural Revolution*, 3 vols, of which two (1974, 1983) published, Oxford University Press, London.

McInnes, Neil (1975) *The Communist Parties of Western Europe*, Oxford University Press, London.

Mack Smith, D. (1983) *Mussolini*, Paladin, London.

MacKerras, Colin and N. Knight (eds) (1985) *Marxism and Asia*, Croom Helm, London.

McLellan, David (1978) *Friedrich Engels*, Penguin, Harmondsworth.

Macleod, Alex (1984) 'Portrait of a model ally: the Portuguese Communist Party and the international communist movement, 1968–1983', *Studies in Comparative Communism*, 17, 1, pp. 31–52.

McVey, Ruth Thomas (1965) *The Rise of Indonesian Communism*, Cornell University Press, Ithaca NY.

Mastny, Vojtech (1979) *Russia's Road to the Cold War*, Columbia University Press, New York.

Matthews, Mervyn (1978) *Privilege in the Soviet Union*, Allen Lane, London.

Mawdsley, Evan (1987) *The Russian Civil War*, George Allen and Unwin, London.

Medvedev, Roy (1982) *Khrushchev*, Basil Blackwell, Oxford.

Medvedev, Zhores (1983) *Andropov*, Basil Blackwell, Oxford.

Mendel, Arthur P. (1961) *Dilemmas of Progress in Tsarist Russia: legal Marxism and legal populism*, Harvard University Press, Cambridge MA.

Mendel, Arthur P. (1981) *Michael Bakunin*, Praegar, New York NY.

Michnik, Adam (1985) 'Letter from the Gdansk Prison', *New York Review of Books*, 18 July, pp. 42–8.

Middlemas, Keith (1980) *Power and the Party*, André Deutsch, London.

Milosz, Czeslaw (1980) *The Captive Mind*, Penguin, Harmondsworth.

Mintz, Jeanne S. (1960) 'Marxism in Indonesia', in Trager (1960).

Mitchell, Alex (1984) *Behind the Crisis in British Stalinism*, New Park, London.

Molnar, Milos (1978) *A Short History of the Hungarian Communist Party*, Westview Press, Boulder CO.

Mortimer, Edward (1984) *The Rise of the French Communist Party, 1920–1947*, Faber, London.

Mortimer, Rex Alfred (1974) *Indonesian Communism under Sukarno: ideology and politics, 1959–1965*, Cornell University Press, Ithaca NY.

Mujal-Leon, Eusebio (1983) *Communism and Political Change in Spain*, Indiana University Press, Bloomington.

Mujal-Leon, Eusebio (1986) 'Decline and fall of Spanish Communism', *Problems of Communism*, 35, 2 (March–April), pp. 1–27.

Nagy, Ferenc (1948) *The Struggle behind the Iron Curtain*, Macmillan, New York.

Narkiewicz, Olga A. (1981) *Marxism and the Reality of Power, 1919–1980*, Croom Helm, London.

Narkiewicz, Olga A. (1987) *Eurocommunism 1968–1986: a select bibliography*, Mansell, London.

Nettl, J. P. (1966) *Rosa Luxemburg*, 2 vols, Oxford University Press, London.

Nguyen, Van Cahn (1983) *Vietnam under Communism, 1975–82*, Hoover Institution Press, Stanford CA.

Nicolaievsky, Boris and Otto Maenchen-Helfen (1976) *Karl Marx*, Penguin, Harmondsworth.

Nixon, Richard (1979) *The Memoirs of Richard Nixon*, Arrow Books, London.

North, Robert and Xenia Eudin (1963) *M. N. Roy's Mission to China*, Berkeley CA.

Nossiter, T.J. (1982) *Communism in Kerala: a study in political adaptation*, Hurst, London.

Oren, Nissan (1971) *Bulgarian Communism: the road to power, 1934–44*, Columbia University Press, NY.

Oren, Nissan (1973) *Revolution Administered: agrarianism and communism in Bulgaria*, Johns Hopkins University Press, Baltimore MD.

Ottaway, David and Marina (1978) *Ethiopia – Empire in Revolution*, Africana, New York NY.

Overstreet, Gene Donald and Marshall Windmiller (1959) *Communism in India*, University of California Press, Berkeley CA.

Pelling, Henry M. (1958) *The British Communist Party: a historical profile*, Adam and Charles Black, London.

Pepper, Suzanne (1978) *Civil War in China: the political struggle, 1945–9*, University of California Press, Berkeley CA.

Pike, Douglas (1978) *History of Vietnamese Communism: 1925–1976*, Hoover Institution Press, Stanford CA.

Pipes, Richard (1963) *Social Democracy and the St Petersburg Labour Movement, 1885–1907*, Harvard University Press, Cambridge.

Pipes, Richard (1970) *Struve, Liberal on the Left, 1870–1905*, Harvard University Press, Cambridge MA.

Pipes, Richard (1980) *Struve, Liberal on the Right, 1905–1944*, Harvard University Press, Cambridge MA.

Pipes, Richard (1974) *The Formation of the Soviet Union: Communism and Nationalism, 1917–1923*, revised edition, Atheneum, New York.

Porter, Cathy (1980) *Alexandra Kollontai: a biography*, Virago, London.

Porter, Gareth (1987) 'Philippine Communism after Marcos', *Problems of Communism*, 36, 5 (September–October), pp. 14–35.

Prifti, Peter R. (1978) *Socialist Albania since 1944*, MIT Press, Cambridge MA.

Radek, Karl (1923) 'Schlageter, "The Wanderer into the Void" (A Speech delivered by Karl Radek at the session of the Enlarged Executive of the Comintern on 20 June 1923)', *Inprecorr*, III, no. 47, pp. 460–1.

Randle, Robert F. (1969) *Geneva 1954: the settlement of the Indo-Chinese war*, Princeton University Press, Princeton NJ.

Reale, Eugenio (1966) 'The Founding of the Cominform', in Drachkovitch and Lazitch (1966), pp. 253–68.

Reynolds, Jaime (1978) 'Communists, socialists and workers: Poland 1944–48', *Soviet Studies*, XXX, 4 (October).

Richta, Radovan et al. (1969) *Science at the Crossroads*, International Arts and Sciences Press, White Plains NY.

Riddell, John (ed.) (1984) *Lenin's Struggle for a Revolutionary International. Documents: 1907–1916: The Preparatory Years*, Pathfinder, New York.

Riddell, John (ed.) (1986) *The German Revolution and the Debate on Soviet Power: Documents, 1918–1919: Preparing the Founding Congress*, Pathfinder, New York.

Riddell, John (ed.) (1987) *Founding the Communist International: Proceedings and Documents of the First Congress, March 1919*, Pathfinder, New York.

Rieber, Alfred J. (1962) *Stalin and the French Communist Party, 1941–1947*, Columbia University Press, New York.

Robinson, Thomas W. (ed.) (1971) *The Cultural Revolution in China*, University of California Press, Berkeley CA.

Rosdolsky, Roman (1987) *Engels and the 'Nonhistoric' Peoples: the national question in the revolution of 1848*, special issue of *Critique*, 18–19, Critique Books, Glasgow.

Rosenberg, David A. (1984) 'Communism in the Philippines', *Problems of Communism*, 33, 5 (September–October), pp. 24–46.

Rosenberger, Leif (1985) 'Philippine Communism and the Soviet Union', *Survey*, 29, 1 (124) (Spring), pp. 113–45.

Rosenstone, Robert A. (1982) *Romantic Revolutionary: a biography of John Reed*, Penguin, Harmondsworth.

Roy, M. N. (1964) *M. N. Roy's Memoirs*, Allied Publishers, Bombay.

Roy, M. N. (1987) *Selected Works: Volume 1, 1917–23*, Oxford University Press, New Delhi.

RSDLP (Russian Social-Democratic Labour Party) (1977) *The Bolsheviks and the October Revolution: Minutes of the Central Committee of the Russian Social-Democratic Labour Party (Bolsheviks), August 1917–February 1918*, Pluto Press, London.

RSDLP (Russian Social-Democratic Labour Party) (1978) *1903: Second Ordinary Congress of the RSDLP: complete text of the minutes*, New Park, London.

Sachs, I. Milton (1960) 'Marxism in Vietnam', in Trager (1960).

Salvadori, Massimo (1979) *Karl Kautsky and the Socialist Revolution 1880–1938*, New Left Books, London.

Samuel, Raphael (1985–6) 'The lost world of British Communism', *New Left Review*, 154 (November–December 1985) and 156 (March–April 1986).

Sandford, Gregory W. (1983) *From Hitler to Ulbricht: the Communist reconstruction of East Germany, 1945–46*, Princeton University Press, Princeton NJ.

Sassoon, Donald (1981) *The Strategy of the Italian Communist Party from the Resistance to the Historic Compromise*, Frances Pinter, London.

Sawer, Marion (1975) 'Plekhanov on Russian history: a Marxist approach to historical pluralism', *Science and Society*, 35, 3, pp. 292–319.

Scalapino, Robert A. (1967) *The Japanese Communist Movement, 1920–1966*, University of California Press, Berkeley CA.

Scalapino, Robert A. and Chong-sik Lee (1972) *Communism in Korea*, 2 vols, University of California Press, Berkeley CA.

Schapiro, Leonard (1972) *Totalitarianism*, Macmillan, London.

Schapiro, Leonard (1978) *The Communist Party of the Soviet Union*, Methuen, London.

Schmidt-Hauer, Christian (1986) *Gorbachev: the path to power*, I. B. Tauris, London.

Schorske, Carl E. (1983) *German Social Democracy, 1905–1917: the development of the great schism*, Harvard University Press, Cambridge MA.

Schram, Stuart R. (1969) *The Political Thought of Mao Tse-tung*, Penguin, Harmondsworth.

Schram, Stuart R. (1969a) *Mao Tse-tung*, Penguin, Harmondsworth.

Schwartz, Benjamin (1958) *Chinese Communism and the Rise of Mao*, Harvard University Press, Cambridge MA.

Selden, Mark (1971) *The Yenan Way in Revolutionary China*, Harvard University Press, Cambridge MA.

Selznick, Philip (1952) *The Organizational Weapon: a study of Bolshevik strategy and tactics*, McGraw-Hill, New York.

Semprun, Jorge (1980) *Communism in Spain in the Franco Era: the autobiography of Federico Sanchez*, Harvester, Brighton.

Service, Robert (1979) *The Bolshevik Party in Revolution 1917–1923*, Macmillan, London.

Service, Robert (1985) *Lenin: a political life*, vol. 1, Macmillan, Basingstoke.

Seton-Watson, Hugh (1956) *The East European Revolution*, 3rd edition, Methuen, London.

Shachtman, Max (1962) *The Bureaucratic Revolution*, The Donald Press, New York.

Shanin, Teodor (ed.) (1983) *Late Marx and the Russian Road*, Routledge and Kegan Paul, London. Use near beginning of ch. 11.

Shanin, Teodor (1985) *Russia as a 'Developing Society'*, Macmillan, Basingstoke.

Sharma, T. R. (1984) *Communism in India: the politics of fragmentation*, Sterling, New Dehli.

Shatz, Marshall (1967) 'The "conspiracy" of the intellectuals', *Survey*, 62 (January).

Shaw, George Bernard (1897) 'The illusions of socialism', in *Forecasts of the Coming Century*, ed. E. Carpenter, Manchester, 1897.

Shub, David (1966) *Lenin*, Penguin, Harmondsworth.

Simis, Konstantin M. (1982) *USSR: the corrupt society: the secret world of Soviet capitalism*, Simon and Schuster, New York.

Simmons, Robert (1975) *The Strained Alliance: Peking, Pyongyang, Moscow and the politics of the Korean war*, The Free Press, New York.

Skilling, Harold Gordon (1976) *Czechoslovakia's Interrupted Revolution*, Princeton University Press, Princeton NJ.

Skyrop, Konrad (1957) *Spring in October: the Polish revolution of 1957*, Weidenfeld and Nicolson, London.

Slusser, Robert M. (1987) *Stalin in October: the man who missed the revolution*, Johns Hopkins University Press, Baltimore MD.

Smith, Hedrick (1976) *The Russians*, Sphere Books, London.

Smith, R. B. (1983) *An International History of the Vietnam War*, Macmillan, London.

Souvarine, Boris (1939) *Stalin. A critical survey of Bolshevism*, Secker and Warburg, London.

Spaulding, Wallace (1987) 'Shifts in CPSU International Department', *Problems of Communism*, 35, 4 (July–August), pp. 80–6.

Spriano, Paolo (1967) *Storia del Partito communista italiano: da Bordiga a Gramsci*, Einaudi, Turin.

Staar, Richard F. (1975) *Poland 1944–1962: the sovietization of a captive people*, Greenwood Press, Westport CN.

Staar, R. F. (1982) *Communist Regimes in Eastern Europe*, 4th edition, Hoover Institution Press, Stanford CA.

Starr, John Bryan (1979) *Continuing the Revolution: the political thought of Mao*, Princeton University Press, Princeton NJ.

Steele, Jonathan (ed.) (1974) *Eastern Europe Since Stalin*, David and Charles, Newton Abbot.

Stephan, John Jason (1978) *The Russian Fascists: tragedy and farce in exile 1925–1945*, Hamish Hamilton, London.

Stone, Isidor Feinstein (1969) *The Hidden History of the Korean War*, revised edition, Monthly Review Press, New York.

Stuart-Fox, Martin (1986) *Laos: Politics, economics and society*, Frances Pinter, London.

Suda, Zdenek (1980) *Zealots and Rebels: a history of the Communist Party of Czechoslovakia*, Hoover Institution Press, Stanford CA.

Sukhanov, N. N. (1984) *The Russian Revolution, 1917*, edited and abridged by J. Carmichael, Princeton University Press, Princeton NJ.

Szajkowski, Bogdan (ed.) (1981) *Marxist Governments: a world survey*, 3 vols, Macmillan, London.

Szulc, Tad (1986) *Fidel: a critical portrait*, William Morrow, New York NY.

Talmon, Jacob Lieb (1981) *The Myth of the Nation and the Vision of Revolution*, Secker and Warburg, London.

Tang Tsou (1986) *The Cultural Revolution and post-Mao Reforms: a historical perspective*, University of Chicago Press, Chicago IL.

Terrill, Ross (1984) *The White-boned Demon: a biography of Madame Mao Zedong*, Heinemann, London.

Thomas, Hugh (1971) *Cuba or The Pursuit of Freedom*, Eyre and Spottiswoode, London.

Thomas, Hugh (1986) *Armed Truce: the beginning of the Cold War, 1945–6*, Hamish Hamilton, London.

Thompson, Edward P. (1972) *The Making of the English Working Class*, Penguin, Harmondsworth.

Thomson, J. S. (1960) 'Marxism in Burma', in Trager (ed.) (1960).

Thorndike, Tony (1985) *Grenada: politics, economics and society*, Pinter, London.

Tiersky, Ronald (1974) *French Communism 1920–1972*, Columbia University Press, New York.

Toranska, Teresa (1987) *Oni: Stalin's Polish Puppets*, Collins Harvill, London.

Trager, Frank Newton (ed.) (1960) *Marxism in South East Asia: a study of four countries*, Stanford University Press, Stanford CA.

Trotnow, Helmut (1984) *Karl Liebknecht (1871–1919): a political biography*, Archon, Hamden CN.

Trotsky, Leon (1962) *The Stalin School of Falsification*, Pioneer Publishers, New York.

Trotsky, Leon (1966) *Problems of the Chinese Revolution*, Pathfinder Press, New York.

Trotsky, Leon (1964–71) *The Trotsky Papers*, ed. Meijer, 2 vols, Mouton, The Hague.

Trotsky, Leon (1973) *The First Five Years of the Communist International*, 2 vols, New Park, London.

Trotsky, Leon (1975) *My Life: an attempt at an autobiography*, Penguin, Harmondsworth.

Trotsky, Leon (1979–81) *How the Revolution Armed: military writings and speeches, 1918–1923*, 5 vols, New Park, London.

Trotsky, Leon (n.d. [1980]) *Our Political Tasks*, New Park, London.

Tuck, Jim (1988) *Engine of Mischief: an analytical biography of Karl Radek*, Greenwood Press, New York.

Tucker, Robert C. (1973) *Stalin as Revolutionary, 1879–1929*, Norton, New York.

Turley, William S. (1986) *The Second Indochina War: a short political and military history, 1954–1975*, Gower, London.

Turner, Robert F. (1975) *Vietnamese Communism: its origins and development*, Hoover Institution Press, Stanford CA.

Ulam, Adam Bruno (1952) *Titoism and the Cominform*, Harvard University Press, Cambridge MA.

Ulam, Adam Bruno (1973) *Stalin: the man and his era*, Allen Lane, London.

Ulam, Adam B. (1974) *Expansion and Coexistence; Soviet foreign policy 1917–1973*, Praeger Publishers, New York.

Ulam, Adam B. (1978) *Lenin and the Bolsheviks*, Fontana, London.

Ullman, Richard (1961–73) *Anglo-Soviet Relations, 1917–21*, 3 vols, Princeton University Press, Princeton NJ.

Urban, George R. (ed.) (1979) *Communist Reformation: nationalism, internationalism and change in the world communist movement*, Temple Smith, London. Ten RFE talks.

Urban, Joan Barth (1986) *Moscow and the Italian Communist Party: from Togliatti to Berlinguer*, I. B. Tauris, London.

Valenta, Jiri and Virginia (1984) 'Leninism in Grenada', *Problems of Communism*, 33, 4 (July–August), pp. 1–23.

Valentinov, Nikolay (pseud., N. V. Volsky) (1968) *Encounters with Lenin*, Oxford University Press, London.

Van der Kroef, Justus Maria (1965) *The Communist Party of Indonesia: its history, programme and tactics*, University of British Columbia, Vancouver BC.

Van der Kroef, Justus Maria (1980) *Communism in Southeast Asia*, University of California Press, Berkeley CA.

Venturi, Franco (1966) *Roots of Revolution: a history of the populist and socialist movements in nineteenth century Russia*, Grosset and Dunlap, New York.

Vickery, M. (1984) *Cambodia: 1975–1982*, South End Press, Boston MA.

Vidali, Vittorio (1984) *Diary of the Twentieth Congress of the Communist Party of the Soviet Union*, Journeyman Press, London.

Vozlensky, Michael (1984) *Nomenklatura: anatomy of the Soviet ruling class*, Bodley Head, London.

Vucinich, Wayne S. (ed.) (1983) *At the Brink of War and Peace: the Tito–Stalin split in a historic perspective*, Brooklyn College Press, New York.

Walicki, Andrzej (1980) *A History of Russian Thought from the Enlightenment to Marxism*, Oxford University Press, Oxford.

Waller, Michael (1981) *Democratic Centralism: an historical commentary*, Manchester University Press, Manchester.

Waller, Michael and Meindert Fennema (1988) *Communist Parties in Western Europe*, Basil Blackwell, Oxford.

318 *Works cited*

Warburg, Gabriel (1978) *Islam, Nationalism and Communism in a Traditional Society*, Cass, London.

Weber, Nicholas S. (1975) 'Parvus, Luxemburg and Kautsky on the 1905 Russian revolution: the relationship with Trotsky', *Australian Journal of Politics and History*, 21, 3, pp. 39–53.

Wesson, R. G. (ed.) (1982) *Communism in Central America and the Caribbean*, Hoover Institution Press, Stanford CA.

Westoby, Adam (1981) *Communism since World War 2*, Harvester, Brighton.

Westoby, Adam and Robin Blick (1982) 'Early Soviet designs on Poland', *Survey*, 26, 4 (117) (Autumn), pp. 110–26.

Westoby, Adam (1983) 'Conceptions of communist states', in David Held et al. (eds) (1983) *States and Societies*, Martin Robertson, Oxford, pp. 219–42.

Wiarda, Howard J. (1968) *Dictatorship and Development: the methods of control in Trujillo's Dominican Republic*, University of Florida Press, Gainesville FA.

Wilbur, C. Martin and Julie Lien-ying Howe (eds) (1956) *Documents on Communism, Nationalism, and Soviet Advisers in China, 1918–1927: Papers seized in the 1927 Peking raid*, Columbia University Press, New York.

Wildman, Allan K. (1967) *The Making of a Workers' Revolution: Russian social democracy, 1891–1903*, University of Chicago Press, Chicago.

Wiles, Peter J. D. (1974) *Distribution of Income: East and West*, North-Holland, Amsterdam.

Williams, Robert Chadwell (1986) *The Other Bolsheviks: Lenin and his critics, 1904–1914*, Indiana University Press, Bloomington IN.

Wilson, Dick (1971) *The Long March 1935: the epic of Chinese communism's survival*, Hamilton, London.

Wilson, Dick (1979) *Mao, the People's Emperor*, Hutchinson, London.

Wilson, Dick (1984) *Chou: the story of Zhou Enlai, 1898–1976*, Hutchinson, London.

Wilson, Duncan (1980) *Tito's Yugoslavia*, Cambridge University Press, Cambridge.

Winter, J. M. W. (1974) *Socialism and the Challenge of War; ideas and politics in Britain, 1912–18*, Routledge and Kegan Paul, London.

Wittfogel, Karl A. (1964) *Oriental Despotism: a comparative study of total power*, revised edition, Yale University Press, New Haven CT.

Wohl, Robert (1966) *French Communism in the Making, 1914–1924*, Stanford University Press, Stanford CA.

Wolfe, Bertram D. (1981) *Revolution and Reality: essays on the origin and fate of the Soviet system*, University of North Carolina Press, Chapel Hill NC.

Woodhouse, C.M. (1948) *Apple of Discord: a survey of Greek politics in their international setting*, Hutchinson, London.

Wright, Peter (1987) *Spycatcher*, Viking, New York.

Yanowitch, Murray (1977) *Social and Economic Inequality in the Soviet Union*, Martin Robertson, London.

Zabih, Sepehr (1966) *The Communist Movement in Iran*, University of California Press, Berkeley CA.

Zeman, Z. A. B. and W. B. Scharlau (1965) *The Merchant of Revolution: the life of Alexander Israel Helphand (Parvus), 1867–1924*, Oxford University Press, London.

Zinner, Paul Ernest (1962) *Revolution in Hungary*, Columbia University Press, New York.

Zinner, Paul Ernest (1963) *Communist Strategy and Tactics in Czechoslovakia 1918–1948*, Pall Mall Press, London.

Zinoviev, Alexander (1984) *The Reality of Communism*, Gollancz, London.

Zinoviev, G. E. (1973) *History of the Bolshevik Party*, New Park, London. (Translated from the 1923 Russian edition.)

# Index

*Index compiled by Meg Davies*